THE LITERARY POLITICIANS

MITCHELL S. ROSS

The Literary Politicians

Doubleday & Company, Inc., Garden City, New York
1978

Library of Congress Cataloging in Publication Data

Ross, Mitchell S
The literary politicians.

Includes bibliographical references.
1. Intellectuals—United States—Political activity.
I. Title.
HT690.U6R67   320′.092′2
ISBN 0-385-13077-5
Library of Congress Catalog Card Number 76-52222

The following material is used with permission:

Up from Liberalism, by William F. Buckley, Jr. Copyright © 1959, 1968 by William F. Buckley, Jr. Published by Arlington House, New Rochelle, New York. All rights reserved.

McCarthy and His Enemies, by William F. Buckley, Jr. Copyright © 1970 by Arlington House, New Rochelle, New York. All rights reserved.

United Nations Journal, by William F. Buckley, Jr. Reprinted by permission of G. P. Putnam's Sons. Copyright © 1974 by William F. Buckley, Jr.

Four Reforms, by William F. Buckley, Jr. Reprinted by permission of G. P. Putnam's Sons. Copyright © 1973 by William F. Buckley, Jr.

Inveighing We Will Go, by William F. Buckley, Jr. Reprinted by permission of G. P. Putnam's Sons. Copyright © 1970, 1971, 1972 by William F. Buckley, Jr.

Cruising Speed, by William F. Buckley, Jr. Reprinted by permission of G. P. Putnam's Sons. Copyright © 1971 by William F. Buckley, Jr.

The Governor Listeth, by William F. Buckley, Jr. Reprinted by permission of G. P. Putnam's Sons. Copyright © 1967, 1968, 1969, 1970 by William F. Buckley, Jr.

The Unmaking of a Mayor, by William F. Buckley, Jr. Reprinted with permission of author. Published by Viking Press, New York.

"Playboy Interview with William F. Buckley." Copyright © 1970 by Playboy. Originally appeared in *Playboy.*

"The Historian and History," by Arthur M. Schlesinger, Jr. Excerpted with permission from *Foreign Affairs,* April 1963. Copyright © 1963 by Council on Foreign Relations.

This book is dedicated with love and gratitude to my parents, Aaron and Raquel Ross, to my living grandparents, Nathan and Freda Moss, and to my late grandparents, Harry and Ethel Rosenfeld.

Acknowledgments

I owe a special debt to Sue Kriszenfeld, who typed several chapters and encouraged this project from its earliest stages. John Schrock, William Kellie, Robert Longe, Andrew Ross, Douglas Ross, and Karen Ross contributed in various ways to make composition easier. I thank them all.

Contents

THE LITERARY POLITICIANS

Introduction: Of Literary Politicians

Never was a refrain so dominant and so dreary in the history of National Letters than the "whither, America?" which has darkened our own. From the earliest days of the Republic, when Charles Brockden Brown was the reigning genius and the star of Washington Irving was in the ascendant, this *cri di coeur* has been heard from every generation. Somber Puritans joined wheezy poets in choruses hymning the manifest destiny of the New World. The mumbling of Emerson was succeeded by the caterwauling of Whitman, which in turn gave way to the anxious threnodies of Van Wyck Brooks. Public men, too, from stone-faced Washington forward, have missed no opportunity to instruct their countrymen in the mission God laid out for them. Most recently, we have survived a Bicentennial celebration in which each self-interested party in the land projected its own appetites as symbolic of the national will. This was adorned by a presidential election campaign in which the candidates dueled over the question of who was best qualified to represent the national virtue. The eventual winner captivated the populace with his lurid promise to inaugurate a government as full of love as the American people. It is expected that an exhibition featuring "A Tribute to Narcissism" will be mounted at the Smithsonian Institution.

Like any other people, we have a certain love of pomp. Unlike those nations which maintain a monarch or some other ceremonial head of state, we lack a figure in whom to invest this love. Our solution is to create a political language as pompous as any ever devised by man. Our campaigns dwell on themes like "prestige," "honor," "freedom," "dignity," and "justice" which are entirely without meaning to the politicians who use them, but which strike deeply in the hearts of their listeners. It is very likely that people do not believe what their politicians tell them, just as it is likely that they did not believe the tales of Hell told them by their grandmothers and Sunday school teachers; but they would be deeply disappointed if these things were not said. There is no figure in America so disreputable as the irreverent politician. He is quickly set upon by the press as a frivolous fellow, and is, if lovable, written off as a "quixotic" campaigner, or, if unlovable, denounced as an egotist.

In contrast, a politician who is trying to get into office by blasting the establishment is described as a "crusader," often one who is running "against the bosses" or "against the machine," and frequently as someone reaching out to the public by raising "moral issues." He is normally required to provide some evidence of his patriotism if he is a man of the Left, and often accomplishes this by citing the spirit of the Founding Fathers, whom he admires as a rebellious bunch. If he is a man of the Right he will be asked to prove that he is not an "extremist." Usually this will be managed by quoting the same Founding Fathers, who are now seen to be a flinty pack of individualistic conservatives. All politicians, if they get very far, must be prepared to offer a tearful recitation of their love of country.

Our political rituals have bewildered foreigners for two centuries. There is nothing comparable in the nations which have come to democracy more recently. Imagine the leader of the Gauls moving his audience to a swoon as he exhorted it toward "the French dream." Consider the Federal Chancellor extolling "the German way of life," and your ears perk to hear the first strains of the Horst Wessel song. Picture the Prime Minister of Her Majesty's government praising the "British genius," and listen to the peals of laughter that rebound from the audience.

I do not contend that these nations are without empty rhetoric. They are, after all, democracies. France shares with the United States a situation where the head of government and head of state are one, and indeed that nation was led for more than a decade by an aging general whose sales pitch was "glory." But in none of these countries is patriotic bombast so integral and necessary to the acquisition of office. Our political discourse, if barely literate, is anything but literary. Should two professors oppose each other for an American Senate seat, the campaign is more likely than ever to adopt a vulgar tone. This is because it is essential to present oneself as a "friend of the common man," and there is no simpler way to do this than to twit your opponent for his "highbrow arrogance" or "ivory tower perspective" and allow matters to degenerate from there. Often, there is a strenuous effort made to stress humble origins, where they exist. This is the fastest way to illustrate commonness, and make the patriotic pitch more believable. In case the candidate is not of humble origins, he will present television commercials of himself wearing a loosened tie and rolled-up sleeves. This is his way of showing that, even if not a "common man," the candidate is a "man of the people," as opposed to being a "stuffed shirt." The removal of the suit jacket, presumably, is to permit the viewer to see for himself that the candidate's shirt is not stuffed.

Our tradition of rhetoric is so feeble that it has proved necessary for another tradition to develop, one in which only the rare and exceptional politician participates. I refer to the distinctive hybrids of our day, the literary politicians: those who have chosen to practice politics by writing books.

If "whither, America?" is the theme of our political and literary rhetoric, literary politicians are hardly an exclusive American property. One thinks of Erasmus, Edmund Burke, Voltaire and the other philosophes of the French Enlightenment. All met the most important qualification of literature, which is the enhancement of our perception of life. All were primarily engaged in politics. Among the classic authors, Cicero, Seneca, Thucydides, and Tacitus rank with Catullus, Virgil, Homer, and Petronius. Dante gained fame as a politician, suffered the humiliation of the loser, and stoked the fire of his masterpiece by casting his enemies into Hell. The memoirs of leaders from Caesar to Churchill have held their place on the literary honor roll.

But the American Republic presents a peculiar set of circumstances. It is a country where the artist has never been a respectable figure, and where, conversely, the first qualification of a successful politician has been respectability. Most artists have accepted their assigned role, and pursued Bohemianism with singular devotion. Politicians offer themselves to the public as paragons of those qualities presumably held dear by their countrymen. In addition to those features already cited, I add that of being a "good family man." This is perhaps the least desirable image for a conscientious Bohemian to project.

Because the United States is more or less a classless society, in which men of mean birth and little visible intelligence can become President, much energy is expended on imagery. Our literary politicians, like their more practical counterparts, hide behind a variety of titles. Several have risen from the ancient "whither, America?" school and are moralists at heart. They are led to rhapsodize over the national destiny upon hearing a State of the Union address, studying a table of economic statistics, or biting into the first ear of corn from an Iowa harvest. Some are historians, firmly committed to their art but determined that it have some bearing on current modes of thought. Others practice as journalists, and presume to comment on the passing scene. There are those who emerge from the world of traditional literary art—novelists, poets, critics—and prefer classification among the creators of beautiful letters. Finally, there remain those who have shattered the occupational shield and committed a book, meaning they are retired politicians, defeated politicians, or politicians who are disguised as academicians.

The literary politician has emerged as a notable type in our times because politics in America has assumed a heightened importance since the Second World War. Circumstances—most notably, wars—have borne heavily on people's minds. Intellectuals are subject to the same alarms as everyone else. They respond to them with more refined sensitivities than ordinary politicians, however, and their refinement is what captivates their audiences. They come forward with their verses, novels, essays, and histories, and transport the literate citizen into the subterranean world lying beneath the televised news reports and the headlines of the daily paper.

Every literary politician is marked by a sense of urgency about the political situation of the United States and the world. It is his ability to describe society in political terms that sets him off from

other writers. Not for him the pious exhortations of the church-
man, though he is not necessarily innocent of self-righteousness.
Not for him the wheeling and dealing of the cloakroom, though
he is not always above swallowing some cherished idea in order to
attain a practical result. If he clothes himself in an ideology, he
learns to dress seasonably. His writings both mark and redirect the
shifting political winds. The work of a literary politician joins personal experience to political occurrence; it is likely to be full of
surprises. His task is that act of public education so often wrongly
listed among the duties of the professional politician. The purpose
of the professional politician is to gain and maintain office; the
purpose of the literary politician is to explain the people to the
people. This makes him one of the most powerful unanointed
officials of the Republic.

II

"Whither, America?" is rephrased and asked in every generation
because it cannot be answered and so keeps the industry of literary politicians thriving. They come mocking, jeering, exhorting,
and instructing us anew, and we listen to them because the professional politicians are lost in platitudes. When we find a writer,
usually a news analyst, who begs political candidates to "elevate"
the tone of their debates, we may be certain that the writer is a
minor literary politician. He knows that he is asking for something that cannot possibly be granted, and so can reassure himself
that his own voice is essential to the clarification of great matters.

A minor literary politician is likely to be a newspaper columnist
or a college professor in the social sciences. He is minor because
either he is insufficiently original, like most columnists, or he is so
original that ordinary readers find him incomprehensible, like
most professors. His influence is thus sharply restricted.

The limitation, however, is not determined by his position, but
by his ability. Indeed, three of the literary politicians surveyed in
this volume have had distinguished careers as college professors,
and a fourth has been a newspaper columnist. In an earlier generation, Walter Lippmann was not only a first-rate columnist, but
one of the very greatest literary politicians in the history of the
United States. Even the maintenance of strong religious views

does not bar membership in this elect fraternity. The theologian Reinhold Niebuhr was a great literary politician, and the Deacon Carter, once removed from the demeaning chores of office, might prove worthy of an effort sound enough to propel him from his meager standing in our final chapter.

What, then, marks this corps of major literary politicians? In three words: variety, fecundity, and influence. Several people were dropped from consideration because they did not meet one or another of these qualifications. I am here engaging a phenomenon, not digging for buried treasure. Only in the final chapter, in examining a peculiar genre, do I lower the standard of fecundity. Also, I am concerned with the literary politicians of a certain generation, born in the second and third decades of this century (I slide back a couple years for Galbraith) and formed by the experiences of the Great Depression and the Second World War. Finally, I did not wish to spend time on authors I find uninteresting. This eliminated quite a few possibilities, most of them warhorses of the left.

What remains is seven men brought before a searchlight, a handful more seen in momentary relief. All descend from the line of Henry Adams, John Calhoun, and Thomas Paine. This means they must play by the aesthetic rules of democracy, waging long and sometimes unsuccessful battle against vulgarity. All have managed to transcend their labels—diplomat/political scientist, economist, historian, polemical journalist, novelist, poet. All etch their images on the mind of America in our time. I begin with the labels and the images and retreat to the places of origin. Galbraith remains the oversized Canadian looking down a long nose at all the American pygmies. Schlesinger, the son of a first-rate historian, is never without the sense of history at his side and the stamp of Harvard morality at his fingertips. Buckley is the scion of a rich Catholic family which thought its Church, and by extension itself, superior in Protestant America. Mailer is the urban Jew who learned how to hustle and get ahead on the sidewalks of New York. Lowell stands as the latest in the line of a family which feels the national destiny in its bones. Vidal was bred in the national capital, the grandson of a senator in whose library he prowled as a boy. Kissinger retains the mental trappings of a lad raised in German schools as a member of an Orthodox Jewish family, forced to flee and then negotiate his way to the top of American society. The rest consecrated their honor to the service of the Republic, and lost themselves in dreams of glory.

I grant myself the job of telling what these men have been about. Buckley, Schlesinger, and Galbraith are the characteristic literary politicians; if there are more obvious candidates for inclusion in a volume of this sort, I would like to know of them. The learned journals may bring forth the names of several wise professors who have enlightened the lives of their subscribers; the reader may drop the name of someone whose harangues he has regularly enjoyed through the years; the pressure groups will recall their beloved prophets. I remind them all of my criteria.

Rather than lose myself in the tangle of minor-league hortatory, I have chosen, in the second and third sections, to play two sets of variations on our theme. Mailer, Lowell, and Vidal are more political literati than literary politicians. In either case, the motivation for their labor derives from a jangling of the political nerve. As imaginative writers, they are among the products peculiar to this age. There is a tradition behind them, but not a strong one. The proletarian writers of the thirties held the stage for no more than a day. Dos Passos alone stood out from the Lost Generation as one of the breed. Dreiser in old age became a politician after he had ceased to write novels, and he was so silly as a politician that he barely counts. It has been the critics who have held ground in politics among the literary crowd. In this century Edmund Wilson was the greatest of these. But, more than anything else, Mailer, Lowell, and Vidal indicate yet another merger of our literary tradition with that of old Europe, particularly France, where literary politicians are as common as *vin ordinaire*.

The third and briefest section deals with the politicians who have fulfilled literary aspirations. As he does in so many other respects, Kissinger stands apart here; he approaches the stature of genuine literary politicians, and his forthcoming memoirs could elevate him to full title. The other statesmen, however, expose a clear inferiority as literary politicians, and I feel obliged to catalogue them as "subliterary." Their supporters need not feel too gloomy, however, as they are reminded that the American Republic has produced few statesmen who were also literary politicians, and even their position is in doubt. John F. Kennedy does not qualify with his grade-school history, *Profiles in Courage*; Woodrow Wilson and Theodore Roosevelt can build slight cases with their respective theses; Jefferson left little beyond the Declaration of Independence and his farmer's notebook; and Lincoln was but an occasional poet. All have their advocates. Even so, it should be remembered that the finest memoir by an American President is the work of one Ulysses S. Grant, who was also one of the very worst chief magistrates in history. One must satisfy oneself with the likes of Albert Beveridge, late distinguished senator from Indiana and biographer of Chief Justice Marshall; or Oliver Wendell Holmes, late justice of the Supreme Court, if one seeks men of affairs who could handle a pen. Churchills and Clemenceaus we have not.

III

The search for style is the search for the man. It is a tenet of pedagogy in the arts, faithfully repeated in theory and ignored in critical practice, that unclear writing reflects unclear thinking. I can think of many eminent thinkers whose reputations would be immediately and ruthlessly devalued were this belief actually applied to critical analysis. But it is not. Philosophers, economists, sociologists, political scientists, historians, and literary critics all expand the lists of jargon in their various trades, and retreat to contemplate the mysteries they have created. Style among these writers is a dimly perceived instrument, not the key to the ideas and personality of an author. Muggy prose is less disreputable in our own time than in any previous era of the American Republic. Despite all disavowals, it appears that our thinkers are held in thrall by a handful of dead German philosophers. More people are writing less well on a greater variety of subjects than ever before.

Literary critics are more to be blamed than any other group. They should be the leaders of analytical style, and more appreciative than their counterparts of the fact that criticism is an art. Instead, they content themselves with a narrow definition of literature which includes only prose fiction, verse, drama, and certain kinds of essays, particularly those on literary subjects. By permitting itself to deal only in those subjects, criticism has become self-conscious, lifeless, and itself infested with code words. Where are the great humane studies and vivid polemics of yesteryear?

This critical lapse is one of the latest, and certainly the least noticed, consequence of the receding interest in classical studies. The student of the classics, confronted with Plato, Cicero, and Thucydides, could not possibly adopt the narrow view of literature which is prevalent in our own day. It is not necessary to restore the primacy of classical studies in order to redress the balance. Gore Vidal has written of the contrast between what he terms the "Public Novel" and the "University Novel": one is written to be read and the other is written to be taught. So, on a larger scale, we may recognize the public as well as the private interest, the urbane literary politician as well as the star-gazing, slum-dwelling poet.

It is to be hoped that intimacy with esoteric phenomena, the mark of reputability among the critics of our day, will become a less desirable goal among the critics of the future. Wrote J. E. Spingarn, more than half a century ago, "Poets do not really write epics, pastorals, lyrics, however much they may be deceived by these false abstractions; they express *themselves, and this expression is their only form.* There are not, therefore, only three or ten or a hundred literary kinds; there are as many kinds as there are individual poets." Substitute writer for poet, and novels, histories, and political polemics for epics, pastorals, and lyrics, and you will understand my intention. "Let the reader consider," begged the great Taine, "a few of the great creations of the intelligence in India, Scandinavia, Persia, Rome, Greece, and he will see that, throughout, art is a kind of philosophy made sensible, religion a poem taken for true, philosophy an art and a religion dried up, and reduced to simple ideas."

Once the critic has accepted the interchangeability of forms, he will find himself prepared to give serious consideration to a writer's style. This will present a contrast to the contemporary critic, whose appreciation of style is warped by the provinciality of his interest. A man who appoints himself an expert on existential fiction is unlikely to understand the particular excellence of a Macaulay or even a Dickens: to do so would require him to acquaint himself with an entirely new frame of reference, the last thing to be expected of a committed specialist. But the generalist must scan the horizon. He may sacrifice depth in favor of breadth, but the depth of the specialist penetrates only so far as his limited tools can guide him, and never to the source of the literary impulse itself.

There is no mystery to critical understanding; one takes one's openings where one finds them, and crawls inside. It would be helpful if criticism were less solemn, less moralistic, more tolerant of a wider range of expression, and, above all, less concerned with establishing Great Truths. Do I prescribe critical anarchism? I do, with the caveat that the true critic is a natural aristocrat. So it is the critic's job to assess, and often to explode, the Great Truths of others; he cannot afford to offer his own in competition. He must desist from separating style and substance, from supporting either the provincial or the eccentric solely on the grounds that they are "quaint" or "avant-garde," and from endorsing the generally established as if it were already ultimately adjudged and beyond the pale of his discretion. He must take his chances and accept the fact that sometimes he will be wrong; he must create a style for himself in assessing the styles of others, and trust that the free play of his mind can be brought into harmony with the surrounding atmosphere—and, if not, cherish the thought that he may be sounding a fresh theme and not merely a discordant noise.

IV

Thus armed, we enter the fray. My own biases become clear soon enough, and I leave them to the revelation of the text. Politically, I am not a very interesting fellow, resembling as I do the ancient Greeks, who thought that wisdom lay somewhere in the middle of an argument. I grouchily insist on my status as an Independent voter, and give no quarter to the blathering politicians who can make life such a strain for the civilized minority. Accordingly, I feel warmly toward all literary politicians, even those I disapprove of. It seems to me that they lighten the air each time they set their words to wings. Imagine our public life without them: congressmen hurtling insults at each other; senators invoking the guidance of the ages as they fill their pork barrels; Presidents rattling sabers and ranting about the national security; journalists filing daily reports in which such things are noted. In the work of the literary politicians is the promise of another dimension, one to which literate folk can aspire in their dizzier moments.

PART ONE

———◆———

The history of partisan literature is as long and proud and forgotten as any. Its artifacts survive, to remind us of those days when politicians addressed each other as gentlemen and rolling periods separated scholars from stevedores. To write and speak gracefully were legitimate aspirations of public men. Guizot imposed his *History of France* upon the polity of the nation. Michelet did likewise, in memory of the Revolution. Thiers punched, and Taine countered. Anatole France stood back and mocked them all. Across the channel, the drama was played out by Macaulay and Carlyle, Coleridge and Mill. All of these men wrote books intended to start people marching.

If their history has been forgotten, and all have been safely categorized by college professors as "historians," "essayists," or "philosophers," their tradition is not dead. Philosophy remains an instrument of politically minded men. Once, in England, a man was identified as a "Tory essayist" or a "Whig historian" and there was no complaint. Today it is less fashionable to attach one's literary reputation to an ideology, but it is not surprising that the three finest literary politicians in postwar America have denied fashion and openly proclaimed their preferences.

The practice of the literary politician is to adapt ideology to the surrounding environment. In America this means that, unless one wishes to become known as an extremist and thereby exclude oneself from effective power, one chooses the side of liberalism or conservatism. There are several shades to each side, but these remain the basic classifications, superseding the Democratic and Republican parties in significance. Identification of one side is made by noting its denunciations of the other. Liberals, ever fond of asserting their station on the side of Progress, and the idea of Progress on the side of the angels, are given to citations of the "conventional wisdom," "reactionary ideologues," and "Neanderthal thinking" of the other side. This tactic serves to create the image of the liberal-as-underdog, heroically introducing fresh thoughts in a Republic controlled by smug and self-interested men. Meanwhile, the conservatives employ the same sort of rhetoric, substituting "liberal establishment" and "facile moralists" when the moment of opprobrium arrives. The conservatives, of course, like to see themselves defending all the good things in life against the uprising of the mobocracy, led by its scribes.

The position of the underdog is cherished on both sides of the aisle, because it is the surest way to secure public sympathy in America. It is evident that neither the liberals nor the conservatives could be fully accurate in their charges. Indeed, we shall see how the two camps are similar in their use of varied premises. Henry Kissinger, whom I read as a conservative but of a peculiar stripe, sounds more European than American. He also has certain ends in mind, which is why I examine him in the third part of this book. William Buckley, on the other hand, is undeniably a native literary politician and a conservative. We find him blasting the liberal devotion to "democracy" in one decade and laying down articles of "conservative democracy" in the next. Philosophical pronouncement is rarely without a certain irony. Walter Lippmann proclaimed a "public philosophy" of natural law which inclined toward pessimism and conservatism, and urged Lyndon Johnson to get on with the creation of the Great Society. Arthur Schlesinger, Jr., writes, only slightly in jest, "As an historian, and therefore a conservative . . ." And Galbraith is fond of pointing to his proposed reforms and indicating that these give proof of his conservative instincts. I am reminded of the old Abbott and Costello routine, "Who's on First?", in which two baseball men argue ceaselessly over the identity of the baserunners ("Who's on first? What's on second? I don't know who's on third!") because they cannot distinguish questions and statements from the names of the players.

What, then, has marked off liberalism from conservatism in the post-World War II years? There is no single idea, nor any clear set of ideas, which has prevailed as liberal doctrine in the past three decades; likewise with conservatism, which has often settled for opposing whatever the liberals propose. Once upon a time a liberal was someone who believed fervently in the righteousness of powerful Presidents and big labor unions; who thought that the spread of Communism must be met at every corner, and that our mission was to bring democracy to all the peoples of the earth; who assumed that all serious economic troubles had vanished, or at least could be handled in the manner of the New Deal, and who looked forward to feeding the hungry of the world with the surpluses of affluence. No liberal accepts all of these propositions today, and a great many liberals accept none of them. This is not because liberalism is dead, but because it represents more a manner of thought than a philosophy. So, too, with conservatism: philosophy is a combination of rationalized bias and circumstance.

Overtly, the liberal would seem to think in more secular terms than the conservative. When seeking to uplift humanity, the liberal looks more to the government, the conservative to God, or at least to Principle. There is a righteous air to the cries of both schools, but the conservative is more apt to sanctify the familiar and the liberal speak on behalf of the unknown future. There are, obviously, the shadings: we are likely to view the extreme conservative as more than just reactionary—as a mystic; we are likely to see the extreme liberal as more than radical—as a utopian. Of course, both liberals and conservatives claim the support of justice and freedom, particularly when God seems an inconvenient patron in an agnostic age.

Conservatism, proclaiming the wonders of order and tradition, has its innings now and then. Buckley is the most provocative man in America, and he scores regularly. But, for the most part, postwar America has preferred change, movement, progress, and the pains and delights of secularism. Despite all the disappointments of American liberalism, there remains a solidity and centrality in its affirmations and criticisms throughout three decades. If they have not always had their way (and have not always agreed among themselves) on the major, specific issues, the liberals have had the comfort of knowing they moved astride the

main currents of the times. This gave them the leisure to recon-
struct the past, and project the future, with minimal reliance on
stern doctrines and theological certitudes. It allowed Galbraith to
write that "it is possible that our greatest danger, in these days of
massive introspection, is from our terrible solemnity"; and Schlesinger to note, "Freedom is inseparable from struggle; it is a process, not a conclusion. And freedom, as Brandeis said, is the great
developer; it is both the means employed and the end attained.
This, I believe, states the essence of the Politics of Hope—this
and the understanding that the struggle itself offers not only a
better life for others but a measure of fulfillment, even of pleasure, for oneself." Thus liberalism in its way signifies satisfaction
with a way of life.

Each of these men is a moralist, cast in an individual mold:
Buckley a Catholic romantic, waging a campaign for an aesthetic
standard of life; Schlesinger, history personified with a Harvard accent, holding to his guarded optimism, seeking to improve man
but preparing to be disappointed; and Galbraith a Scotsman, stub-
bornly righteous, maintaining definite views on the condition of
man and adorning them with a humor which permits him to
join Buckley's symposium on social aesthetics. The traditional labels are useful as we start our survey of these careers, but they decline in importance as we begin to penetrate each man's peculiarities.

William F. Buckley, Jr.

Fashionable intellectual circles now dismiss liberalism as naive, rit-
ualistic, sentimental, shallow. With a whoop and a roar, a number of conservative prophets have materialized out of the wilder-
ness, exhuming conservatism, revisiting it, revitalizing it, preaching
it—Russell Kirk, saber in hand, a cavalier on a black horse; Peter
Viereck, rearing high on a charger while he fires his six-shooter
vigorously in all directions; Clinton Rossiter, cool and business-
like, driving an unassuming Ford; all with dozens of disciples
deploying behind them, and many more well-wishers cheering
them on from the sidelines.[1]

ARTHUR SCHLESINGER, JR.,
"The Politics of Nostalgia,"
1955

Where in this fancy array stood the man who would overshadow
them all within a decade? Nowhere to be seen, apparently; certainly not in the vanguard of the New Conservatism, at least so
far as one of its foremost adversaries was concerned. At thirty,
William F. Buckley, Jr., was a veteran of the U. S. Army and the
CIA, a graduate of Yale University, and the author of two books,
one of them castigating his beloved alma mater for its indifference
and occasional hostility toward Christianity and free enterprise, the

[1] Arthur M. Schlesinger, Jr., *The Politics of Hope*, Boston: Houghton Mifflin
Co., 1962, p. 72.

other supplying an enthusiastic defense of the work of Senator
Joseph McCarthy of Wisconsin—"around which," he wrote,
"men of good will and stern morality can close ranks." Those who
knew nothing of young Buckley personally, and chose to regard
him on the basis of his writings, need not have thought him much
more than a cranky right-wing extremist. His prose had not yet
achieved its distinction. His thought was rigid and uninspiring.
His manner of speech, which brought the qualities of a well-tuned
cello to public discourse, was not widely know.

Yet, within a year, he would scrape together enough funds from
the family fortune and a few friendly investors to start a new journal of conservative opinion, proclaiming it the rival of the liberals'
New Republic. Six years after that, he would augment his work
on the journal, *National Review*, by entering the column-writing
business; his name was now flashed before the eyes of most literate
Americans. In 1965 he would capture the support of more than
one of every ten New York City voters in a campaign to become
mayor, and the following year he would begin hosting his own television program, on which he scratched and cooed at the great
and humble in the worlds of politics and ideas. Finally, in 1970,
his brother James would profit from William's fame and earn
election to the U. S. Senate. All of this in a mere decade and a
half—not bad for having missed out on the recognition of Sheriff
Schlesinger, who thought he had lassoed all the whoopers and
roarers and locked them up far from the main-traveled roads of
the American mind.

For William F. Buckley is an original article. He has become
Mr. Conservative, while confessing that he is "not of the breed."
He has held to his starchy principles while expounding them in a
racy, gossipy style. He has libeled the liberal code a thousand
times and cultivated warm friendships among its truest believers.
Alone among the celebrated figures of his time, he is recognized
more frequently by reference to his political philosophy than to
his profession of journalism. Thus the winged messengers of our
airwaves will speak of "conservative columnist James Jackson Kil-
patrick" or "liberal economist John Kenneth Galbraith," but it is
usually "conservative William F. Buckley, Jr." All additional ornament is provided by the man himself.

From *God and Man at Yale* to Buckley at the United Nations

winds a path originating in the dogma of One-True-Church Catholicism and Adam Smithian economics, and leading into a jungle of diplomatic bombast. It is a pilgrim's progress which is not yet ended, a metaphor for the growth of a native Toryism in an age of American international grandeur. Its character is expansionist, proceeding from a strong internal structure and engaging a horizon which broadens at every turn. In Buckley's case, as with those thousands who follow his lead, there have been two phases: before *National Review* and after. In his college days, editing the *Yale Daily News,* he had first begun to practice journalism, but the primary concern of his writing was to score points off opponents. The competitive drive has never left him; indeed, it has engineered his journalism. But the withering of liberal verbiage is less prominent a passion than it once was; there are other things now, such as deciding which principles deserve to be defended, and getting a firm enough grip on the world to keep conservatism out of the waxworks. In short, he has become a Leader of Thought: his influence has grown, and he seeks to conduct himself in a responsible manner. That he has managed this, and become more amusing in the process, reflects his personal charm—genius, if we use the word lightly. It is the second phase—from 1956 forward—which is most interesting in all its attributes: Buckley on the Attack, Buckley for the Defense, and Buckley the Man of the World. Slowly, he has shed the debater's mantle for that of the journalist, the man of experience, a most engaging character indeed. But it is useful to revisit those early days of *God and Man at Yale* and *McCarthy and His Enemies,* if only to remind ourselves that spinners of fine lace can begin as undernourished lumberjacks.

II

His first book was written, he confessed, because, "I fell victim to arguments I have so often utilized myself: that the so-called conservative, uncomfortably disdainful of controversy, seldom has the energy to fight his battles, while the radical, so often a member of the minority, exerts disproportionate influence because of his dedication to his cause. I *am* dedicated to my cause." As outlined in

God and Man at Yale, the cause was simple enough: universities should indoctrinate students with the values of their alumni—meaning, in the case of Yale, Christianity and free enterprise. There is no shading given to either of these broad concepts. It is not clear what young Buckley would do about Jews at Yale, and even less certain what he would do about those few Moslems who might take their instruction at the university. Instead, he busies himself with assessments of Yale's professors. Some of them are "straightforward Christians," others "straightforwardly antagonistic to religion," while the rest are either simple "pro-Christians" or "anti-Christians." These stances are balanced against the potential professorial influence on the religious attitudes of students; Buckley does not bother about chemists who may be raving atheists.

"The first duty, of course," he writes, "is to arrive at a judgment as to whether or not there exists at Yale an atmosphere of detached impartiality with respect to the great value-alternatives of the day, that is, Christianity *versus* agnosticism and atheism, and individualism *versus* collectivism." The entire book is written in this crude dialectical manner; obviously, he is not interested in any "atmosphere of detached impartiality," but desires a subtle partiality leaning toward his view of things. He chafes at what he believes to be ill-mannered Keynesians who refuse to give the "individualists" a fair shake in their textbooks. He assigns to the forces of modern history the roles of "truth" and "error" like an old Victorian who has just completed his first examination of a newspaper in fifty years. "The denial of truth in Italy and Germany, coupled with the refusal of Japan to ally herself with truth, resulted in a devastating world war. The continued refusal of Russia to scorn error bids fair to bring an end to truth everywhere in the world." He slaps at the "academic freedomites," perhaps because they are often pushing doctrines as strict as his own, only theirs are propounded in the name of "freedom" while his are in the name of "truth." At his mildest, he seems willing to accept a compromise along the lines of: you pay your money, you take your choice, and let's forget about atmospheres of detached impartiality. In the meantime, he will cry his heart out since, "Individualism is dying at Yale, and without a fight." Sometimes he sounds quite tender in his anguish, and we look upon his arguments as mere pimples to be popped. "If the recent Yale graduate, who exposed himself to Yale economics during his undergraduate years, exhibits enterprise, self-reliance, and independence, it is only because he has turned his back upon his teachers and texts. It is because he has not hearkened to those who assiduously disparage the individual, glorify the government, enshrine security, and discourage self-reliance." Three cheers for young Bill Buckley, who survived his baptism by fire!

III

Toward the end of *God and Man at Yale*, there appears the injunction that "a responsible, reflective man must, soon in life, cast his lot with the Communists or against them." Considering himself responsible for truth and reflecting on the evils inherent in its abandonment, Buckley took up his slingshot in order to engage in a little guerrilla warfare on behalf of Senator McCarthy. It is possible that this genuflection before the Wisconsin Savonarola sacrificed a generation of would-be *National Review* conservatives in the academies. Few were the scholars who were not revolted by McCarthy, and Buckley's journal, founded so soon after the senator's escapade, struggled hard to make known its devotion to the principles of Edmund Burke and Adam Smith. Until the emergence of Barry Goldwater as the political spokesman of the Right, the New Conservatism was perceived as being little more than undiluted McCarthyism, and there were few buyers.

Before McCarthy fell, however, Buckley wrote his apologia. Along with his brother-in-law, attorney L. Brent Bozell, he arrived nimbly at the excuse which he would use in all subsequent references to McCarthy: whatever the senator said about people or did to them, it was not nearly so bad as what his opponents did to *him*. Consequently, the book bore the title *McCarthy and His Enemies*, and the authors drew concentric circles around the politician who moved them to their conclusion about "men of good will and stern morality." For instance, the following is written in defense of the senator's lying about his evidence:

Perhaps McCarthy deliberately sensationalized the evidence he possessed in order to draw attention to the gravity of the situa-

tion. Perhaps, again, the complexities of the Communist problem
were lost on Joe McCarthy in the early days of his venture.
After all, he had seen alarming reports of various investigating
agencies on certain employees of the State Department. And
who, McCarthy may have asked himself, who but Communists
would do and say such things?

Naturally, the standards are much more rigorous when applied
to McCarthy's victims. For example, there was O. Edmund
Clubb, the highly competent diplomat and (later) historian,
whose status as a genuine security risk was argued by Buckley-
Bozell on the grounds that Clubb was an important man on the
China desk in the State Department "in the years we lost
China." On such matters an "unresponsive public" is chastised
for having insufficiently appreciated "the irrepressible efforts of
one man." Things were so bad that "logic in our age must be
strained through the woof of irrationality and the warp of ignorance." Thus, a book written in the nineteen twenties by a youthful Mr. Haldore Hanson, supposedly "favorable" to the Chinese
Communists (I have not read the work in question), made Hanson a security risk twenty-five years later.

The efforts to discredit McCarthy, meanwhile, were viewed as
highly partisan. In screaming italics we are informed, "*The Ty-
dings committee . . . consciously set out to destroy McCarthy and
make of him an example for all who, in the future, might feel
tempted to agree that the Democratic Administration was jeopard-
izing the national security by harboring loyalty and security risks
in sensitive agencies.*" Unfortunately, we are offered no explanation as to why the Democrats should wish to do such awful things.
And McCarthy himself is painted as a man of high moral scru-
ples, only occasionally a bit careless and excesssive in his righteous
zeal. "The essence of McCarthy—and McCarthyism—lies then
in bringing to the whole loyalty-security problem a kind of skepticism with which it had not been approached before," and brave
for that.

Most of the book has even less stylistic distinction than *God
and Man at Yale*, and the collaboration frequently bears the
marks of lawyer Bozell, as in all of the "To sum ups" and "We
concludes" and "It is our judgments." In the summarizing chapters, however, we detect the emerging polemicist in Buckley

which will appear full-blown in *Up from Liberalism*. "The Liberals, in short, want conformity—with Liberalism." "McCarthyism, on the record, is not in any sense an attempt to prevent the airing of new ideas. It is not directed at *new* ideas but at *Communist* ideas, of which the last thing that can be said is that they are new or untried." McCarthy's opponents among the intelligentsia "are confused, . . . have misread history, and . . . fail to understand social processes." To those who griped that McCarthy had ushered in a Reign of Terror, Buckley merely laughed:

> Those who have not felt the Reign of Terror are warned not to take the threat lightly. The professional mourners at the wake of American freedom are unimpressed, in fact angered, by consolations, especially of the empirical sort. They appear to resent any distractions from their gloomy introspections.

And, in those days before he assumed a reputation as the archest of American snobs, he posed as a rootin'-tootin' Yankee patriot:

> A considerable number of Americans support McCarthy not only in his fight to prevent America from becoming Communist, but also in his fight to prevent America from becoming like Europe. For us Communism is the *worst* fate on the horizon; but there are *other* fates that we would avoid, one of them being the fate of Europe, whom we see today as a weary and cynical community of pettifogging nations whose deterioration is not only measured by the strength of her Communist minority but by the weakness of her non-Communist majority.

All in all, *McCarthy and His Enemies* provides little more than flossy lining to cover the deeds of a classic demagogue. The book is mildly amusing when shooting arrows at outraged liberals, weak in its characterization of McCarthy, and pernicious in its examination of the loyalty-security business. In his first two books, Buckley had laid down three bases for the New Conservatism: laissez-faire economics, orthodox Christianity, and anti-Communism. He had not done his work with any great skill, and the establishment of *National Review* two years later encouraged fishy looks from liberals and hesitant applause from those who had hitherto practiced conservatism without benefit of clergy. Conservatism in America had lived so long in the backwoods that its liberal opponents had trouble believing that its new torchbearers did not secretly attend meetings of the Ku Klux Klan once they got off the golf course. Their confusion was understandable. Many of the leading figures at *National Review* were reformed Communists who had seen the error of their youthful ways and now consoled themselves with daily predictions of Armageddon. The New Conservatism grew from sentiment, from an intuition that the United States was going to Hell, resulting in a silent decree to halt America before she reached the brink. The brink of what? *National Review* was trying to find out. Meanwhile, its editor was working harder than ever to try and understand how the other side—the liberals—stood, and *Up from Liberalism*, published in 1959, would be his next report card.

IV

How conservative was this New Conservatism? Why had it arisen? Surely it can be seen as a reaction to Franklin Roosevelt and two decades of Democratic presidential government, but just as surely it was something more than that. When H. L. Mencken founded his *American Mercury* in 1924 he intended that it be a journal of "civilized Toryism"—antagonistic to socialism and the aggrandizement of government, but equally committed to the destruction of prudery, religious dogmatism, and the "booboisie." Democracy was regarded as a delightful farce, while civil liberties were held to be inviolable. In short, Mencken was Mencken, and attempts to paint him as a conservative are as futile as efforts to read a class consciousness into the maxims of Sancho Panza. Yet the mistrust of social planning constituted a large measure of the New Conservatism; as did the attitude of aristocratic condescension and the lack of faith in businessmen as primary agents of social progress.

Then there was Senator Robert Taft, whose steadfast devotion, for half a century, to the principles of his father's presidency lent a consistent old-fogeyism to the conservative movement. Senator

Taft had the advantage of being a man of the cities, without that categorical dislike of urban wickedness which would hamper Barry Goldwater in future years. By his support of such things as Federal Housing and his denunciation of the conduct of the Nuremberg trials, Taft kept alive the notion that political conservatism retained a conscience. He forced liberals to recognize that all relevant debate did not occur within the caucuses of the Democratic Party.

Nevertheless, by the end of World War II, conservatism remained an inchoate movement, lacking much appeal for college-educated Americans seeking a wider world. The political direction of the United States seemed irrevocably fixed by the New Deal, and now the war had thrust America into pre-eminence among Western nations. Worst of all, in the "advanced" thought of the day, was the conservative devotion to American isolationism. The Communists were knocking at the door, and there were still men who cherished the desire to retreat into their own back yards. Britain was weakened, the old empires were breaking up, and who would carry freedom's torch? After some soul-searching, the isolationists reversed themselves, and even Senator Taft came round. Worldwide Communism was designated the enemy, and the conservatives, who had always been formidable in pursuing the domestic version of godless Communism, now steeled themselves for a round of big-stick-carrying. Young William F. Buckley, Jr., arising from his quarrels with Yale professors, offered this historical perspective in *McCarthy and His Enemies:*

For nearly three decades a handful of prophets—an American Resistance—tried to alert the nation to the Communist threat; and fought a lonely and costly fight. After the Second World War, in the dawn of a new realism about international affairs, the prophets began to get a hearing; for it had become apparent that nothing but the integrity of the United States stood between the Soviet Union and world domination. But it was only when one spy scandal after another rocked the nation that the American Resistance enlisted recruits in sizable numbers and fixed our attention on the problems of Communist infiltration. By 1950, a genuine mobilization was under way. And Senator McCarthy—

having fairly recently been mobilized himself—became one of its leaders.

Well, a new realism may have dawned, but not quite in the way that Buckley would have it. The international poker players—Truman, Acheson, Marshall—knew fairly well how the cards were stacked. But those repentent Communists, such as James Burnham and Whittaker Chambers, who gathered around the Catholic romantic editor of *National Review* were rather afflicted by a blinding sunburst which sent them screaming for the shade. As for politicians like McCarthy and the captor of Alger Hiss, it is better said that revelation and ambition were neatly combined for a season of rainmaking in the political atmosphere. There were former Communists and fellow travelers in the government, surely, and perhaps the time had come to rout them. Unfortunately, the inquisitors ended by making more mischief than their victims, the O. Edmund Clubbs and J. Robert Oppenheimers were unreasonably reviled, and the nation lost the services of numerous able men.

But the New Conservatives were inexperienced at this sort of thing. Not since the Red Scare of post-World War I days had the specter of Communism so haunted the nation. That had, in many ways, been a more reprehensible period than the witch-hunting season of Joe McCarthy, presuming the deportation of innocents to be more disgusting than the denial of security clearances and the presentation of false charges. Of course, the intellectuals resented McCarthy more keenly than they did A. Mitchell Palmer, but no one who told McCarthy the truth was assigned a jail sentence, whereas the thousands rounded up by Palmer could only tell their stories to the commissars.

Yet Mencken, who could shout down the "red ink boys," was outraged by Palmer, and a proper conservatism should not have occupied its time in elaborate defenses of McCarthy. The movement was still immature, so much so that Buckley could write, in *God and Man at Yale*, "The conservatives as a minority are the new radicals." A conservatism which cannot see itself defending the status quo must be defined as reactionary, and not conservative. The New Conservatives spent far more time on the attack than on the defense, and Buckley became their chief lancer.

V

It was initially remarked by reviewers of *Up from Liberalism* that its author devoted a whopping portion of his book to detailing our fall, and gave a meager forecast of our resurrection. The liberal is viewed in six guises: "In Controversy," "As Indoctrinator," "In Action," "And the Obliging Order," "And the Silent Generation," "His Root Assumptions." Two chapters are devoted to "The Conservative Alternative." In other words, Buckley's *manner* had not changed from that of his first two books; like a team trying to catch up from behind, these New Conservatives did not devote themselves primarily to the defense of their own position. What had changed since *McCarthy and His Enemies* was Buckley's *style.* The stiff legalisms are gone; so is the point-by-point categorization of *God and Man at Yale.* The new method, devised after three years' practice of weekly commentary at *National Review,* is disarmingly casual. Like the two books before it, *Up from Liberalism* utilizes clips from the daily papers; unlike the first two books, such illustrations are followed by idiosyncratic comments on the "deviationist sallies," "the mystique of the spontaneously generated dollar," and "our age of modulation." Mr. Wilfrid Sheed has remarked, and I have concurred, that in the late nineteen fifties Buckley's perception of the opposition deepened. He also achieved a maturity of style by fusing precisely stated exposition with a somewhat conversational tone—sort of a "well, this *is* jejune!" approach to the world. Huffy liberals are breezily dispensed with in this manner. The device is interesting in that it gives conservative presuppositions, which Buckley himself termed those of a "radical minority," the air of status quo. Liberals find it either powerfully irritating or enjoy it hugely, depending on their individual temperaments.

Up from Liberalism, the first book to present Buckley's style in full blossom, became the prototype for all of his occasional essays in the years to come. To a great degree, it is itself little more than an overlong occasional essay. Its style has great charm, but in several important ways it lacks sufficient force. The basic trouble would seen to be Buckley's politeness, something which is less apparent in a short piece than in consideration of his work as a whole. In the sporting world there is something referred to as the "killer instinct," and Buckley lacks it. He enjoys knocking his opponent down, but then he only rushes over and lifts him up before the count has reached five. Worse still, he proceeds to brush the fellow off, praise his character and talent, and stride merrily away, carrying with him an air of supercilious good cheer, as if to say: "How did such a nice man wind up with such nutty ideas in his head?" Perhaps this inclination to charity is rooted in a deeper instinct for survival; maybe Buckley assumes that hollering and stomping his feet would only make the liberals ignore him completely, rather than come tiptoeing into his verbal spider webs. I think it more likely that the style is indeed the man: that he loves to jab and hates to uppercut. But those who adore the invective of Mencken and Shaw, of Schopenhauer and Nietzsche, of Macaulay and Voltaire cannot help but assign Buckley a middling place in the ranks of those who have gained their celebrity through practicing the art of exquisite defamation.

There is, for example, his inability to hold his attention in one place for very long. He skips like a pebble on water, confronting one small wave after another. In *Up from Liberalism* he moves from Eleanor Roosevelt to Arthur Schlesinger to John Kenneth Galbraith to Earl Warren to Joseph Rauh and so on, and in each case he captivates but fails to devastate. He is most remarkable in his epigrams, which may be found anywhere in the midst of long arguments. Once discovered, they are to be written out, hung on peg boards, and memorized for use at the next meeting of your local salon. "Anybody who showed as much respect for the Pope as the typical liberal now shows for Earl Warren would be considered as a living violation of the separation of church and state." "Cross a liberal on duty, and he becomes a man of hurtling irrationality." "Such facts as the Original Sin cannot be made to disappear, even by action of the General Assembly of the United Nations." "Professor Arthur Schlesinger, Jr., told the *Crimson* that 'it is characteristic of the state of mind of the country to encourage tattling and snooping.' And to give this statement historical depth, as it becomes a professor of history to do, Mr. Schlesinger added: 'This illustrates the typical conservative idea that snooping is the way to get personal freedom'"—an "in" joke turned inside out. It is all satire of a rather gentle sort, foamy but light.

No discussion of Buckley's technique would seem adequate without mention of his use of logic. For purposes of full examination, it is best reserved for our description of his defensive armor. At the same time, logic is among his main offensive weapons, too. He is not exactly the contemporary American version of St. Thomas Aquinas, but he is closer to Thomas than to the writers of confessionals. There is, for example, his practice of taking what he presumes to be some preposterous heresy and then proceeding with a well-mannered strangulation of it. We watch the old debater as he lines up points a, b, and c, reduces his opponent to pygmy size, and then closes by noting cheerfully that, after all, Mr. So-and-So's cockamamie scheme is not likely to be taken seriously anyway, and surely this is not what he meant to say, but just in case . . . An example, from a column of August 19, 1967:

> Now Dr. Martin Luthur King proposes massive "dislocations." Not violent dislocations, understand. Just "massive civil disobedience," like blocking plant gates, highways, government operations, sit-ins in federal buildings, that sort of thing. But not violent, repeat. The man reporting to work at his factory is not expected to press his way through Dr. King's human wall, nor the wife driving her car to pick up her child at school to trample the toes of the *satyagrahi.* No violence, just a national convulsion.

Of course, he then goes on to say, Dr. King "can't bring it off," because the leadership of the Civil Rights movement has moved into the hands of the militants, which only points to the trouble with all forms of social disruption, and clarifies the meaning of repression. It being agreed that the end of the Civil Rights movement must come in the elimination of human hatred and the promotion of mutual love and respect, how can such ends be advanced by the promotion of disorder? And he concludes:

> Such a program will not likely be accelerated by any new, desperate exhortation to chaos. Nor should it. Repression is an unpleasant instrument, but it is absolutely necessary for civilizations that believe in order and human rights. I wish to God Hitler and

Lenin had been repressed. And word should be gently got through to the non-violent avengers that in the unlikely event that they succeed in mobilizing their legions, they will be most efficiently, indeed most zestfully, repressed. In the name, quite properly, of social justice.

It is a mechanism which checks his satiric impulse, but, like the poking of holes in liberal arguments and the burial of epigrams within long paragraphs, it is part of an original style. And, as I have already mentioned, Buckley has attempted to direct his development, and that of his journal, toward greater respectability, and less rambunctiousness. Unquestionably there was a choice involved, and not an easy one. It is more fun to be a sniper than a balancer of scales.

VI

But a balancer of scales he chose to be. In his first two books he had laid down the bases of the New Conservatism by identifying what he thought to be three basic characteristics of the opposition: a bias against Christianity, a hostility toward the free market system, and a softness in dealing with Communism. All three of these complaints are repeated in *Up from Liberalism*, wherein he attempted to expose the complete "failure of contemporary Liberalism." In addition, he wanted to blast the Republican Party, from President Eisenhower on down, for its infuriating lack of principle. In this connection he wrote:

It was the dominating ambition of Eisenhower's Modern Republicanism to govern in such fashion as to more or less please more or less everybody. Such governments must shrink from principle: because principles have edges, principles cut; and blood is drawn, and people get hurt. And who would hurt anyone in an age of modulation?

He regretted that "even in literature, one does not often find oneself concerned with kings and knaves, fair maidens and heroes, treachery and honor, right and wrong"—reflecting his own unshakable taste for absolutes, unchanged since the days of *God and Man at Yale,* despite the adoption of a personally modulated style. Above all, he saw himself living in an age in which the sociologists, the technicians, and the planners ruled. He shuddered at the thought that Communism and atheism were just two ideas to be treated like any others. If the Republican Party could offer no alternative to the pleasant golfer in the White House, then he, self-styled conservative, would give it a try. But first he must identify the "root assumptions" of these liberals, and to this he devoted the most important chapter of *Up from Liberalism.*

He reached the following conclusions: 1) "Method is king—because things are 'real' only in proportion as they are discoverable by the scientific method; with the result that method logically directs all intellectual (to which we subordinate moral and metaphysical) traffic." Therefore, "Isn't the whole of the liberal ideology agglutinated by semantical raids on substantive ideals?" 2) "The commitment by the liberals to democracy has proved obsessive, even fetishistic"—that is, democracy is a process, a method of doing things, and the liberals have tried to endow it with a *substantive* character, which has resulted in the confusion of their thought. "It is part of their larger absorption of Method, and Method is the fleshpot of those who live in metaphysical deserts." 3) The liberals, owing to the mistakes described in points one and two, have denied the economic basis of freedom. Big government reduces freedom by its removal of the power of the individual to choose between alternatives. Here the devotion to democracy as a substance, rather than as a process, is easiest to discern. The liberal will say that the government, being democratic, is a government of the people, and hardly restrictive of choice. But "political freedom is meaningful, I am saying, in proportion as political power is decentralized." The liberals cannot see that centralized government dissolves individual choice in a mere process, handing substantive decisions over to the government. 4) On the greatest social issue of the day—race relations—the liberal has made too much of the issue of suffrage, in accordance with his devotion to Method. "It is more important for a community, wherever situated geographically, to affirm and live by civilized standards than to labor at the job of swelling the voting lists." It is another reflection of the ascendancy of process over substance. "The problem of the South is not how to get the vote for the Negro, but how to train the Negro—and a great many whites—to cast a thoughtful vote." Voting qualification tests should be administered to everyone.

Rather than offer a critique of each of these statements, I prefer to note that Buckley's criticism of the liberal "obsession" with Method would stand as doctrine for some time, only to be expunged in 1973, with the publication of Buckley's *Four Reforms*. In the Introduction to this little book Buckley explained, "I think of my reforms as entirely procedural in character," and suggested, "Let the substantive reforms spring up in the terrain made available by the cleared underbrush." Essentially this says the same thing as the liberals were saying when they suggested assuring black people of the right to vote in Southern states—that a "civilized standard" might include this right, and that this must be set straight before "substantive" changes could arise from the "cleared underbrush." So, as mentioned in the previous chapter, the native conservatives are not quite candid in raising "procedural" arguments against "substantive" questions. Ultimately, they are making empirical arguments in support of an idea or in opposition to it, and they should say as much. *Then* it is left for them to question whether the substantive end of a proposed reform justifies the wrenching procedural revision.

But Buckley's mind was set: the liberals had a thing about Method, and were prone to confuse its purposes. "I have resolved not to read another history of liberalism," he wrote, "unless my mother undertakes to write one." He was repelled by the homage shown toward vague notions of "progress" and "liberty and equality" (the two notions are inherently contradictory, says the conservative); in fact, the only consistent aspect of liberalism seemed its "total appetite for power," and a salient disregard of coherent principles in the pursuit of power:

> I do not understand liberalism as a historical continuum. I refuse to submit to the facile expositions of liberal historians who do not shrink from coopting for the liberal position any popular hero out of the past. Thomas Jefferson, a liberal when he lived, would be a "liberal" were he alive today because, so their argument goes, the principles he then propounded, *mutatis mutandis*, have evolu-

tionized into the principles of the contemporary liberal. Thomas
Jefferson, the humane, ascetic, orderly patrician, countenance the
mobocratic approach to belly-government of Harry Truman and
the Americans for Democratic Action? Why?

Contemporary liberalism requires probing "as a contemporary
phenomenon," as "the reigning secular ideology of the West":

> What is the liberal millennium? So far as I can make out, it is the
> state in which the citizen divides his day equally between pulling
> levers in the voting booth (Voting for what? It does not matter;
> what matters is the vote); writing dissenting letters to the news-
> papers (Dissenting from what? It does not matter; just so he dis-
> sents); and eating (Eating what? It does not matter, though one
> should wash the food down with fluoridated water).

He still had a great deal to learn about his opponents, and even
found mobocratic belly-government to his liking when its practitioners were such as Spiro Agnew. Henceforth his growing collection of liberal folklore would be presented to the public in books
which pasted together occasional writings. There would be no
more *Up from Liberalisms* thrown at us with pretensions to organic wholeness. Buckley is to the liberals of our day as the Im-
pressionists were to the late-nineteenth-century Salon painters: he
turns their perceptions inside out, and lays them before us in
different colors, in a different light. His own commitment to
"Method," or "Procedure," or whatever you choose to call it,
would prove as tenacious as any liberal's. Always he deals at the
level of *ad hominem* argument—always, that is, when he is at his
best. But it is *ad hominem* argument of a superior sort—to use a
reverse paraphrase, strained through the woof of rationality and
the warp of intelligence. He would find that the liberal view of
the individual was as morally based as his own; that a religious
bias is as evident among reformers as among conservatives; that
liberal economic theory differs from conservative-libertarian theory
not because liberals desire inflated currency and more centralized
power for themselves, but because economists have differences of
opinion.

I have said that Buckley is a jabber with a weak knockout

punch. It is pleasant to watch him dance lightly around the ring, inviting all comers, brushing them back with a short punch and a laugh. He is a natural as a writer of columns. The brevity imposed on him by the form forces a refinement of his conservative protest, in order that he may deal with the immediate sensation of liberal enticement.

VII

Looking back over the tumultuous 1960s, Buckley decided that the most significant development of the decade was "the philosophical acceptance of coexistence by the West." "Why 'philosophical'?" asked the *Playboy* magazine interviewer, and Buckley replied:

> Because a military acceptance of coexistence is one thing; that I understand. But since America is, for good reasons and bad, a moralistic power, the philosophical acceptance of coexistence ends up in hot pursuit of *reasons* for that acceptance. We continue to find excuses for being cordial to the Soviet Union; our denunciations of that country's periodic barbarisms—as in Czechoslovakia—become purely perfunctory. This is a callousing experience; it is a lesion of our moral conscience, the historical effects of which cannot be calculated, but they will be bad.

This is an important statement, something of a landmark among conservative snarlings. Obviously, it is a modulation of traditional anti-Communist feeling. At the same time, it is more than that, as it asserts the following: 1) that the Western acceptance of coexistence with Communist totalitarianism is an accomplishment of contemporary liberalism, since Buckley makes it clear that conservatives want no part of this arrangement; 2) that the nature of this acceptance is "philosophical," as opposed to being an exercise in moral tactics, i.e., it is a fundamental matter; 3) that American history is inextricably linked to the national morality, which has now been debased by a dirty compromise, producing "a lesion in our moral conscience."

It is questionable whether or not such a "philosophical" acceptance actually occurred; what concerns us here is that a supposed conservative like Buckley *believes* that it did. Of the three bases of the New Conservatism which I have cited in connection with Buckley's career—a strong partiality toward the unfettered free market, a roaring support for traditional "Christian" religion, and militant anti-Communism—it has been anti-Communism which has most completely set the current generation of conservatives apart from its predecessors. The New Conservatives have achieved an intensity of revulsion from Communism which would have mystified their antecedents, whose devils were domestic and identifiable as human beings. Beginning with a political and economic philosophy employed in different forms around the world, the New Conservatives have sweated their way into abstraction. They have conceived an apparition more gruesomely fascinating than a Transylvanian vampire. History may deny them the medallion of truth, but lovers of literature must concede that *National Review* has serialized one of the great ghost stories of our time. "Worldwide Communism" is what they called it—not just the liberals' political and military demon, but the systematic encroachment on "civilization" of a godless monolith.

From Buckley's writings, we might guess that the initial movement toward our "philosophical acceptance" of coexistence with the monster occurred in 1959, when Nikita Khrushchev visited the United States. "The damage Khrushchev can do to the United States on this trip," he wrote, "is not comparable to the damage we have done to ourselves. Khrushchev is here. And his being here profanes the nation." But there were other signs of degeneration—for example, the liberals actually wavered in their discernment of the rectitude of Chiang Kai-shek! "I leave Taiwan," Buckley announced to a group of Taiwanese, "believing that it may be your mission to liberate the United States." And then there were those who questioned the nobility of the pathological Whittaker Chambers. "For me," wrote Buckley, ". . . his voice had been and still is like Kirsten Flagstad's, magnificent in tone, speaking to our time from the center of sorrow, from the center of the earth." In the early sixties the situation worsened, and Buckley wrote, on May 6, 1962, "Every time the sun sets, our knowledge of Communism evaporates just a little bit. Unless we work hard, day after day, to replenish our dissipating reserves, those of us who have known tend to forget, and those who never knew—the generation coming out of childhood—tend to grow up in ignorance of all those gruesome data about the nature of the enemy we face." They came crawling out of the caves at *Partisan Review* and *The Village Voice*, and at the height of protest over the Vietnam war they presented themselves in their truest colors —as "the new pro-Communists," according to Buckley. On March 18, 1967, he wrote, "They are not so much pro-Communist as anti-American. But since they work at anti-Americanism feverishly and at anti-Communism not at all, the vector of their analysis and passion is pro-Communist." The Democrats confuse the reasons for our participation in Vietnam, and fight the war badly. In 1968, Vice-President Hubert Humphrey "announces that we should make love, not anti-Communism, and calls for a new era of international relations, which presumably would reach a climax of joy under a Humphrey administration." To be sure, "The Soviet Union is, of course, different from the way it used to be under Stalin, and even under Khrushchev . . . unfortunately, in many respects it isn't different. For instance, they are still the most unmitigated liars in the world and care nothing about it; on the contrary it is a way of life." "The difficulty is that for every Communist incredibility there is in the West—a Kennedy." How grotesque and farcical it all would seen, were it not so sad! "Every now and then the Innocents travel to Moscow and, because they are otherwise intelligent, come back and write their stupefactions at what they witnessed. I think, for instance, of Arthur Schlesinger, Jr., and James Reston, who for at least forty-eight hours after each visit to Russia, achieve such a pitch of anti-Communist indignation as years ago Mr. Walter Lippmann condemned as vulgar. Unfortunately, we have not contrived a means of persuading Messrs. Schlesinger and Reston to stay in Russia."

Then the Republicans came to power with Nixon as President, and things really got confusing. At a state dinner honoring the Prime Minister of Australia, Nixon whispered into Buckley's ear that the Australian leader was "one of us." What did he mean by that? After much heavy pondering, Buckley concluded, "Nixon meant to say to me: Gorton is an anti-Communist." But what did *that* mean? Was not Nixon himself preparing to exchange toasts with the Red Chinese? Only the hardhearted can fail to be touched by Buckley's agonizing effort to reach terms with the lies, deceptions, and assorted outrages of the Nixon Reich. "All the restraints one thinks of as decent in suddenly fraternizing with the killers are forgotten: and it becomes basely clear that what matters isn't so much whether a government is vile in its provenance, in its practices, in its ambitions, as whether it is powerful." This, too, is an important statement of the New Conservatism, coinciding with the revolution of American diplomacy in the Peking and Moscow journeys of President Nixon. It is comparable to the epigrammatic critique of the "philosophical acceptance of coexistence": at last the point was being driven home that, if the New Conservatism would insist on the primacy of moral over political order, it must resign itself to practical impotence. It is a critical choice which has not yet been made. In the interim between Cold War and entente, Buckley has fumed. "What makes him [Nixon] think that he can manipulate the nation, as Hitler and Stalin did?" He watched from the press table at the banquet in Peking, as Nixon clinked glasses with Chinese luminaries:

> The effect was as if Sir Hartley Shawcross had suddenly risen from the prosecutor's stand at Nuremberg and descended to embrace Goering and Goebbels and Doenitz and Hess, begging them to join with him in the making of a better world. Never mind the difference . . . all that that difference reminds us of is that history is indeed the polemics of the victor . . . And then . . . and then, he toasted Chairman Mao, Chou En-lai, and the whole lot of them. I would not have been surprised, that night, if he had lurched into a toast of Alger Hiss.

In his fury, his rhetoric ran away from his logic. He is too well-mannered to report whether or not he vomited on his mao-tai, but, reading his account of Nixon's Chinese journey, it would not surprise me to learn that he did. Surely he did not mean to compare Nixon with Hitler and Stalin as manipulators of public opinion? And yet, he did. Had he forgotten that Mr. Goebbels could not possibly have warmed to Sir Hartley's mythical embrace, having already pursued his vision of a better world by escorting Hitler out of this one? It is a small point of fact, and yet somehow symptomatic of a crisis in the anti-Communist conscience which has accompanied the perception of "philosophical acceptance" and politican détente. What are a few petty details concerning *which* Nazis were on trial at Nuremberg, when the question is one of *America's* immortal soul? Toasting the Chinese dictators, was not Nixon mocking his country's moral history, and thereby sacrificing its moral future? The praise of murderers was the praise of murderers, no matter what the time and place.

Yet, Buckley surely *understood* Nixon's conviviality with the Chinese better than he would have understood a toast of Alger Hiss. For Hiss was a domestic political concern, and subject to a different hierarchy of values than the Chinese, a foreign power. One would think that all those years of debate and polemical energy would have made him *understand* this much. Instead, it would seem that the specter of worldwide Communism hovers as menacingly over Buckley's conscience as it ever did, and that its form remains harmonious and unbroken.

Meanwhile, a Nixon could lay aside dogmatic international anti-Communism in favor of *Realpolitik*. That "dawn of a new realism," warming the young Nixon and Joe McCarthy with its rays, had dissolved into a chill twilight. The New Conservatives were left without any response but their clanging rhetoric about the decline of the West, and crude comparisons to the appeasement of Hitler, and even, as I have noted, comparisons with Hitler himself. After Nixon's visits to Russia and China, things quieted down somewhat as the soul-searching of the anti-Communists was left to simmer on the back burner. At *National Review* there was fresh concentration on opposing the specifics of détente, and a growing tendency to relish each exposé of Communist brutality. Editor Buckley even spent an autumn as member of the U.S. delegation to the United Nations, where he cheerfully endured the frustrations of advocating human freedom. How the most hot-tempered of the Cold Warriors will end up is in no way certain. But anti-Communism will never be quite the same again; the issues will never seem quite so clear. The generation of New Conservatives is aging, and it senses that the anti-Communist war has been lost, "that what matters isn't so much whether a government is vile in its provenance, in its practices, in its ambitions, as whether it is powerful."

VIII

"If I felt that I were losing my faith," Buckley wrote in 1968, "I would lie down until I got over it." He was speaking metaphorically, in reference to his political "faith" as well as his religion. Still, the New Conservatism is nothing if not insistent about "transcendence." Max Eastman, one of those erstwhile Communists who confessed and became Conservative, found that he could not swallow *National Review*'s religiosity and resigned from its masthead. But Whittaker Chambers, addressing us from the center of the earth, announced that, "If God exists, a man cannot be a Communist, which begins with the rejection of God. But if God does not exist, it follows that Communism, or some suitable variant of it, is right." And Buckley, who does not profess to be rational in assessing the loftiest affairs of man, compares Chambers' bulbous maxim to the Beatitudes. There are those who remind us that it would seem to be Buckley's nap time, lest the cult of St. Whittaker get out of hand. But it should be noted that he was defending Chambers against some posthumous sniping by an agnostic Socialist; what would he *not* do to help his brother-in-anti-Communist-Christ?

At the same time, he will do quite a bit to assist an atheistic brother-in-conservatism, too:

The reason why Christian conservatives can associate with atheists is that we hold that, above all, faith is a gift and that, therefore, there is no accounting for the bad fortune that has beset those who do not believe or the good fortune that has befallen those who do. The proreligious conservative can therefore welcome the atheist as a full-fledged member of the conservative community even while feeling that at the very bottom the roots do not interlace, so that the sustenance that gives a special bloom to Christian conservatism fails to reach the purely secularist conservatism.

The conflict between "traditionalist" and "libertarian" conservatism was thorniest in the early years of *National Review*, when Buckley was able to write, "I have grounds for optimism, based not merely on *National Review*'s own amiable experiences with all but the most dedicated atheists, but on the conviction that the hideousness of a science-centered age has resulted in a stimulation of religious scholarship and of all of those other impulses, intellectual and spiritual, by which man is constantly confounding the most recent wave of neoterics who insist that man is merely a pandemoniac conjunction of ethereal gases." Such gregarious phrasings would fade away in succeeding years, which would bring wrenching liturgical reforms, slugfests over birth control and abortion, un-Christian quarrels over the "Christian" attitude toward the war in Vietnam, and the rise of Guruism among the young. By the time his collection of articles *Inveighing We Will Go* was published in 1972, Buckley would introduce his religion-oriented pieces under the heading: "The Decline of the Catholic Church."

As always, Buckley's writings on religious matters are on the level of personalities and politics; we find no doctrinal disquisitions or critiques of the *Summa Theologica*. There is, in all of his writing, the presumption of the believer; thus he asserts that atheism renders Sartre "ultimately a dull man"; or, in his essay upon the death of Evelyn Waugh, that Waugh "knew people, he knew his century, and having come to know it, he had faith only in the will of God and in individual man's latent capacity to strive toward it." This presumption should be noted as an honorable prejudice. Superficial commentators have denounced Buckley's arguments for human dignity as nothing more than a transparent shield, protecting a deeper belief in the rectitude of selfishness. I find nothing to indicate that this is the case, and I wish that these commentators would state their own prejudices as baldly as Buckley has stated his own. It is no sham to insist on the "invisible hand" in economics, or express a bias for protecting the victims of crime before worrying about criminals; and at the same time to assert the mystery of God's ways, and the need for obedience to his revealed laws. Indeed, there tends in practice to be something fishy about those who are always shouting for "human dignity" or "the will of God" without paying much attention to the means of joining these ideas in theory. Their "dignity" reduces to a mere sufficiency of possessions—enough to eat, warm clothes, etc. Their "will of God" collapses into monkeyshine and the sermons of a Billy Graham. On the one hand, they are the sort of people who would pluck an argument for the welfare state from the life of St. Francis of Assisi; on the other, they would refuse to perform their daily chores without appropriate counsel from an evangelist or an astrologer.

I can find no better example of the political and aesthetic—and, therefore, traditionally Catholic—cast of Buckley's religious thought than the one he offers himself in *Cruising Speed*, a little book documenting a week's activity in November 1970. Being opposed to the liberalization of the abortion laws, Buckley had written a column expressing his puzzlement over the ranting of his fellow Catholics over the "murderous" character of abortions, while New York's Cardinal Cooke had, only recently, been quite willing to shake hands in public with the leader of the New York State Assembly which had passed the liberalized laws—and at a dinner hosted by the Cardinal, yet! So now he reflects:

> The social problem frames the political problem exactly; if abortion is murder pure and simple, then those who directly expedite murder do not qualify as guests at cardinals' functions. Surely . . . even Catholics must begin to use a word different from "murder," even as we use an assortment of words to distinguish between, say, what an assassin does to his victim, and what a drunken driver does to his . . . The whole subject weighs heavily, and for once I find Catholics to the right of me, notwithstanding my own conviction that abortion is gravely, tragically wrong.

In other words, using words like "murder" loosely is not a conservative thing to do; it does not contribute to the construction of an orderly society, based upon the sense of reverence which religious men feel. To be sure, Buckley has been undiscriminating in his application of labels from time to time. But I find that such pejorative imprecision occurs quite seldom in his religious writings. Indeed, the relative scarcity of such writings, in contrast to the obvious relevance of religion to his daily concerns, indicates a basis of belief so strong that it cannot bear casual scrutiny, and so weighty that it is useless for casual exercise. However, his conser-

vatism is so embedded in his religion that, were his religion suddenly to be pulled out from under him, I would agree with
Buckley that the best thing to do would be to lie down, since he
would have little left to stand on. There are, for example, those
assessments of Sartre and Waugh—meaningless without his faith.
There is the anti-Communism, the nature of which I have shown
to be a matter of absolute dogma. Without his faith, his critique
of Communism would have no more crackle than the average liberal's. Forget those reformed Communists at *National Review*:
they are converts, while Buckley himself never actually tasted the
forbidden fruit. And his complaint about government intervention in the economy is, if only partially so, anxiety over the
secularization of charity. So, by extension, he speaks of those who
are "cut off from the Great Tradition," and he responds to a critic
who was justifiably irritated by Whittaker Chambers' ponderous
invocation of "the West," that "Chambers is intelligible to the
same people to whom 'the West' is intelligible, and the latter are
not, for the most part, running the affairs of the West, although,
happily, they continue to influence the public policy of the West
to a greater extent than they run the book review media of the
West." Despite those outcries against the "hideousness of our
age," Buckley seems merry enough in presenting his minority report; "the West," he would have us feel, is in his bones, and
shame on you if it is not in yours, too.

He is a romantic in celebrating the "richness" of his faith, and
some of his best writing has been done in denigration of what he
sees as perversions of Catholicism—the end of the Latin mass, for
example, robbing church-going of its pageantry. I read one of
Buckley's autobiographical essays on the subject, and I sense that
the whole man is addressing me: to lover of tradition, the hater
of vulgar change, the lover of language for its own sake and of
religion for *its* own sake, who simply cannot abide the invasion of
banality into his beloved liturgy. "One cannot read on," he writes
of the new text, "without the same sense of outrage one would
feel on entering the Cathedral of Chartres and finding out that
the windows had been replaced with pop art figures of Christ sitting in against the slumlords of Milwaukee." He will remain the
obedient son of his beloved Church, but, "My faith is a congeries

of dogmatical certitudes, one of which is that the new liturgy is the triumph, yea the resurrection, of the Philistines."

IX

The New Conservatism's critique of the mixed economy is the most comely aspect of its theoretical cosmetic. Herein conservatism and libertarianism are joined, to good effect: the conservatives force the libertarians to apply their thoughts to the problems of a pluralistic society, and the libertarians inject a dose of original thought into sluggish conservative streams of consciousness. In recent years the libertarian-conservatives have proposed intriguing reforms ranging from the negative income tax for the poor to the voucher system of education, intended to allow private schools to survive. Out of what other group of thinkers could someone arise to offer the following combination of satire, provocation, and suggestion, as Buckley did in his *Four Reforms?* He speaks of our system of taxation:

> Why should it be so complicated? The reason why is that tax reforms seek to improve on tax reforms by arching their provisions, like jungle leaves writhing for the sunlight, towards such rays of justice and equity as are discernible at any given moment of relative composure in American politics, when the pandemonium freezes, as for a photographer, for just long enough to permit one set of claimants to overshadow another. Thus a tax reform is born.

More than once, the New Conservatives have insisted that the worst advocates of free enterprise are those organ-grinding businessmen whose noisy platitudes could send intelligent listeners dashing for the nearest copy of *Das Kapital*. This distinctive criticism would be enough to distinguish conservative-libertarian thought from mere neo-Hooverism, but its adherents have gone a step further: they have committed themselves to the "upward mobility" of those born to unfortunate circumstances. Buckley offers the following explanation:

Over the years the social democrats were thought of as the principal enthusiasts for [upward mobility] because of their social programs which were essentially egalitarian, redistributionist. The
conservatives insisted (quite rightly) that upward mobility was
precisely what the free market system most generously contributed to, and they had the figures to prove it. But having said as
much, the conservatives left it (quite rightly) to human resources, up against the system, to take advantage of the opportunities to rise. Many, many millions did so. But now the need for
that mobility is more acute than ever, so much so that the new
conservatives are giving the free marketplace something of a hand
—for instance, by preferential hiring of Negroes. That is helpful.
More helpful, I think most of them would agree, is a concerted
assault on institutional barriers to the rise of the depressed, to the
victimization of the poor. So? Repeal of minimum wage laws. Destroy antiblack discrimination in the labor unions. Ease the progressive feature of the income tax . . .

It is interesting to learn that the need for "upward mobility" had
become "more acute" by 1969, when Buckley wrote this, than it
had been five years earlier, when beating the liberals at their own
game—procedural reform—was not the primary concern of American conservatism. And ten years earlier, Buckley had outlined his
"program" at the close of *Up from Liberalism* by terming it a
"No-Program, if you will," and arguing, "It is not the single conservative's responsibility or right to draft a concrete program—
merely to suggest the principles that should frame it."

So what happened? First, in 1964, the New Conservatives had
their day in the sun, with Barry Goldwater blasting the Social Security system and monopoly labor unions—and getting clobbered
at the polls. A year later, Buckley took a semi-serious shot at the
mayoralty of New York City. He discovered that concrete proposals were useful things to have in politics, and he has been in
the cement-mixing business ever since, dragging faithful followers
into the quarry with him. To his supreme delight, he also found
that he need not even give up principle-suggesting in order to pursue his exciting new trade. Furthermore, those rude Keynesian
collectivists, whom Buckley had given such a bawling out in *God
and Man at Yale*, seem to have vanished into thin air, making

matters easier all the way around. Indeed, in a column of January 19, 1971, Buckley wrote, "Today, if you say you are a Keynesian, you are either saying: a) nothing at all; or you are saying, b) that you are a reactionary." An explanation follows: "There hasn't been a Keynesian in the entire sense of the word since the feverish Harvard acolytes of the late thirties, who have gracefully disbanded"—which makes one wonder if young Buckley at Yale had not spent too much time at the table down at Mory's, after all.

There is no reason to recount the principles of free enterprise, which are almost the entirety of conservative-libertarian economic theory. Such divagations as are permitted were well summarized by Buckley in the column on Keynes:

The best-known American conservative economist is Professor Milton Friedman, and he most enthusiastically backs the use of monetary policies in order to achieve economic goals. In the ideological wars, the recent battles have been between those who desire to stress fiscal policies, i.e., the rate of taxation, deficit spending—that kind of thing. And those others who believe that the key to the problem lies in the money supply. Both sets of people, should they choose to do so, could call themselves Keynesians, though as professionals, they would be unlikely to do so, because they know too much about Keynes to use him as a particularly useful eponym.

Set beside this, the earlier pieces are conspicuous for the absence of accommodation in their tone. But the desire to be influential is a powerful one, and in America one cannot wield respectable influence without becoming something of a positive thinker. As he toured the country in the early years of his career, singing arias from his *Anti-Communism Suite*, Buckley must have heard, over and over, the grumbles in the audience: why can't he do something traditional; why can't he suggest something better? And in time he was smitten; I cannot pin down exactly when it happened, but, as I have observed, the experience of Goldwater, and his own campaign in New York City, must have played their parts. Respectable influence was not something the New Conservatives required; they could have remained lofty debunkers, and Buckley might have become the Juvenal of America's Imperial

Age. Instead, today we find not only "four reforms," but many more besides; almost weekly Buckley turns his column into a suggestion box. The professional uplifters have discovered an erratic comrade, and in the liberal salons the refrain is often heard: "I don't agree with Buckley much, but I sure have to hand it to the guy . . ." And the closing lines of *Up from Liberalism* fade, slowly but surely, into the dusty archives of literary campanologists: "I will not cede more power to the state. I will not willingly cede more power to anyone, not to the state, not to General Motors, not to the CIO. I will hoard my power like a miser, resisting every effort to drain it away from me. I will then use *my* power, as *I* see fit. I mean to live my life an obedient man, but obedient to God, subservient to the wisdom of my ancestors; never to the authority of political truths arrived at yesterday in the voting booth."

X

Ultimately, any claim to conservative status must rest on a conviction of allegiance to an order of things. In a country like the United States, where nothing stays the same for too long, a genuine conservatism is difficult to cultivate. Numerous writers have pointed out the irreconcilability of the principles of an Edmund Burke, defender of a landowning aristocracy, with those of American business, the agent of perpetual change. So, too, the New Conservatives have found the dichotomy rather uncomfortable; thus we find Buckley fidgeting on behalf of "upward mobility" one day and arguing for "proper repression" the next, as if to ask, "Which way shall we tip the scales today?" Stability can be as difficult to imagine as it is to impose. And in the United States, where every man believes his opinion to be as worthy as the next man's, and contestants insist on invoking morality for their causes, protestations of stability and order are practically without meaning; people worry about what is "right." In most of the world, what is right is what ordained authority says is right—not so in America, where rebellion is listed among the great national traditions. Whatever coherence the nation may enjoy comes by way of law. The laws are legitimized by the Constitution, which the people respect because it allows everything to be changed except for the procedure of change. This, then, is the order of things to which would-be conservatives must adhere: morality as a standard for all personal and political behavior, rebellion as an accepted instrument of morality, and change as the great incorporator of morality, the law of the land. Thus we are presented with the spectacle of "conservatism" which lays claim to its title by asking people to recognize that what they need to conserve is a "moral tradition," and which incites them to conservation by issuing stern warnings of the encroachment of the "liberal establishment"!

Buckley's formidable engineering of the New Conservatives rests on a sound perception that wars of ideology are reducible to wars of words. The English language is the only weapon of attack or defense, and he is master of his arsenal. I have noted his methods of attrition, and have pointed out his cherished precepts. But what of his defenses? How does he proceed to guard his notions of God, Freedom, Tyranny, and the West?

"A society that abandons all of its taboos," said Buckley to the *Playboy* interviewer, "abandons reverence." It was the conservative's duty to aid in the preservation of societal reverence. "Doesn't society abandon something even more precious," pressed the interviewer, "by attempting to preserve that reverence by force?" And Buckley responded:

Again, it depends on the situation. If you have a society that is corporately bent on a prolonged debauch—determined to wage iconoclasm à outrance—then you've got a society that you can't effectively repress. But if you have a society—as I think we still do—in which the overwhelming majority of the people respect their own and others' taboos, . . . then it isn't much of an exertion on the commonweal to implement such laws as have been on the books in New York for generations. My final answer . . . is ambiguous: If you ask simply: Does the individual have the absolute right to do anything he wants in private contract with another party? then my answer is: No, only the presumptive right. A sadist cannot contract to kill a masochist. John Stuart Mill reduces the matter of sovereignty to the individual's right over himself. The state hasn't the right to protect you against yourself—

which is a good argument against my being required to wear a
helmet when I ride my Honda.

I cite this passage from among dozens of possibilities because it
shows Buckley in top form. Here is an excellent example of his defense of a conservative idea, in this case, the extent of the state's
right to assert the communal will against the violation of common
standards. The method involves starting with an a priori, safe, but
intuitive notion—in this case it is reverence, elsewhere it might be
freedom, the West, etc.—and stating the presumption that society, on the whole, approves of it, and wishes to preserve it. After
this intuition, qualified by a presumption, the rest of the way is
pure deduction, peppered with common references to Buckley's
Honda and to sado-masochism. The difficulty, of course, is with
points one and two. The intuition must be substantial enough to
be plausible, and the qualification must be correct. If these first
two hurdles are mastered cleanly, then Buckley can sprint the
rest of the way; if not, then his elegant argument is mere horse-
play. Buckley's minority position and commitment to the growth
of his movement being what they are, he cannot afford too many
instances of the latter. Nevertheless, he is not so clever that he can
avoid getting caught; his "movement" has, at times, been impeded
by Buckley's hastiness and insufficient depth of perception. One
example would be the castigation of Keynesian economics in the
early years, before he had bothered to find out what Keynes actually wrote; another would be the diatribe against the liberals' supposed obsession with Method, only to be forced into retreat on
the question years later, when his own slate of procedural reform
was put forward. Such slips were avoidable.

The problem with the New Conservatism is its commitment to
absolute ideals, empirical critiques, and the accumulation of
power all at the same time. The New Conservatives are too
greedy. Their ideals are sound enough: one God over all, free enterprise and the protection of it properties among men, and a
world relieved of those subversive forces which would undermine
the first two things. Their critique, based on this stance, is quite
substantial and grows, if anything, weightier with the years. People have begun to sense the price they must pay for yielding control of their own destinies to the government, particularly on the

federal level. They are also uneasy about accepting a world half-ruled by Communist dictators. The search for God among reflective people is a perennial matter; surely Buckley, with his demonstration of simultaneous confidence in God and reason, provides an inspiring example to many lost souls. And no one can justly quarrel with the efforts of the New Conservatives to elect people who hold these beliefs to public office.

The trouble comes in orchestrating such various concerns. The analogy I used to describe the New Conservatives when *National Review* was founded—that of a team trying to catch up from behind, and thereby given to reckless errors—applies just as well twenty years later. The truth-and-error school of historiography is going to have a rough time of it in a country which prides itself on skepticism and change (no: I do *not* believe that the "Puritan ethic" is the chief motivating factor in American history; I *do* believe that too many major historians have come out of New England). Yet truth-and-error is where Buckley's—and *National Review*'s—anti-Communism ends up. What is all of that spluttering over Nixon's trip to Peking, if it is not outrage over a course of action which is, in Buckley's view, wrong, morally wrong?—what is tactically correct can still be strategically wrong, since strategy is based on morality in the United States: truth-and-error.

Then there is the idea of God, and the traditional conservative idea that belief in God is not only righteous, but beneficial to the furtherance of communal cohesion. We have seen Buckley reduce this to a matter of some being "gifted with faith," some not, and all being welcome to the New Conservative movement so long as they can swear by Milton Friedman and swear at Communists. This bald concession to the higher principle of enlisting new members is not without charm. But Buckley's journal has not yet assumed the practice of separating on its masthead those who are "gifted with faith" from those who are not. Therefore, the New Conservatives have effectively eliminated religion from their roster of precepts at the same time they are insisting, in however veiled a form, that God is on their side. And, as I noted earlier, take Buckley's faith away from him and his theoretical system falls apart. We might as well start calling in epistemologists for therapy—except that epistemology ends in skepticism, and skepticism is not what the New Conservatives claim to be about.

The concept of "upward mobility" is a troublesome one, too, whether the New Conservatives have adopted it for political purposes (i.e., increased membership in the movement), or whether it is supposed to be an extension of their code of order. If political motives are at work, then the concept is a cynical one, and intended for use only until some other idea can be developed which will crush the liberal vermin. I prefer to think that this is not so. If, then, we consider "upward mobility" as an extension of the moral-political order of the New Conservatism, we find ourselves contemplating arguments which are traditionally libertarian, even liberal—such as that the greatest happiness of the greatest number is a fit object for society, and that such happiness may be promoted by increasing the possessions of the multitude. At this point the libertarian-conservatives argue that this object is best pursued by keeping the government's role at a minimal level. Indeed, say the libertarian-conservatives, led by Professor Friedman, practically all the government need do is properly administer the money supply, and prosperity will perpetuate itself as fast as the laws of supply and demand allow. I am not an economist, and am not fit to speak on such matters in any technical sense. But it is clear from this concept, aside from any consideration of whether or not it is correct, that "upward mobility" is intended to occur as part of a general rise in prosperity. Whether or not one hires someone from unfortunate circumstances, ahead of someone who has had all the luck, is irrelevant when the question concerns whether economic circumstances permit anyone to be hired at all. Destroying anti-black discrimination in labor unions presupposes the usefulness of such unions—in short, the assumption is that the economy is expanding. The libertarian-conservative commitment, then, is to the fair practice of pure capitalism (with a little help from correct monetary policies) in the abstract, and to equal justice before the iron laws in the concrete. There is nothing wrong with that, of course, except that "upward mobility" is a poor term with which to describe it. It betrays, once more, the vulgar mentality of membership-raising. Its beneficiaries could not ever hope to be more than freckles on the invisible hand. And those of us who would understand the New Conservatism must hack our way through terminological haze before settling on this basic point.

Confusion, then, is the order of things to which a would-be conservative is introduced these days. The movement which Buckley leads is still young, and, while it issues periodic reports of its principles and goals, it has not resolved the questions of priority and method. What is the first principle of American conservatism in the final quarter of the twentieth century? Is there such a principle? If so, how is its defense best argued? If not, is there a primary *set* of principles? Are there only conservative intuitions requiring rational defense, or are there fruits of practical wisdom to be borne to market and sold without the counsel of the gods?

At such an impasse stands the political movement which claims to defend the tried and true. It could not have a more interesting leader than the malleable Mr. Buckley, master of the superbly rationalized intuition.

XI

Once upon a time, on their way to a session of skiing in the Swiss Alps, John Kenneth Galbraith and William F. Buckley, Jr., found themselves pondering Buckley's curious career. Wouldn't your contribution to American conservatism be greater, ventured Galbraith, if you became a college professor, like me? Give up all your televised chitchat and newspaper columns and lecture tours, and come to the academy. Only then will you be able to enlarge on your position, and give it theoretical depth. "But—I answer in hindsight—," wrote Buckley in *Cruising Speed,* "the theoretical depth is *there,* and if I have not myself dug deeper the foundations of American conservatism, at least I have advertised their profundity."

I have, accordingly, found myself assessing those advertisements throughout this essay. Occasionally I have indulged a little intellectual *Wanderlust,* and offered commentary on the general tendencies of post-World War II American conservatism. But the job is not done until we linger for a moment over Buckley the man, and take account of that famous, infuriating charm which has placed him among the genuine characters in the current American version of the Human Comedy. It is hard to pinpoint the date of Buckley's conversion into a national legend—the epitome of the snobbish poseur, the clever debater who might cut down an opponent in half an instant, the despiser of anyone so ludicrous as to be born without a million dollars waiting from him in trust. The legend is ridiculous, anyway, and Buckley has been first among those who have tried to debunk it. His book *Cruising Speed*, which might ordinarily be taken as an exercise in *pure* vanity, is in fact an exertion of *applied* vanity; given his celebrity, Buckley wants to keep it in check.

God and Man at Yale fomented a great storm when it was first published, and Buckley has been provoking the Republic ever since. From the perspective of a quarter century, it is hard to see how that incompetent polemic earned its author any attention at all. Apparently its dire warnings of creeping agnostic collectivism touched the national nerve in a manner so aptly described by Buckley in his book about the 1965 mayoral campaign, *The Unmaking of a Mayor*:

> Some crises are of course more modish than others, and they tend to have their day in court . . . The crisis of air pollution in New York, for instance, has occurred partly because the air is dirty and actually dangerous to those who suffer from asthma and emphysema; but partly also because crisis-collectors have discovered it, as they recently discovered the poverty crisis, and can, one gathers, be counted upon to discover crisis after crisis in the Dominican Republic, which seems to have developed as a year-round crisis resort.

McCarthy and His Enemies did not appear until McCarthy was pretty well finished, but *Up from Liberalism* arrived at just about the same time as Professor Galbraith's *The Liberal Hour*, and tempted many people to join in the elegant name-calling. During the Kennedy years, Buckley's viper image assumed full proportions. The column began in 1962; twice weekly, he had readers slobbering over their oatmeal. General public opinion was probably crystallized by Jack Parr, speaking after a session with Buckley on Parr's television program. "What I can't stand," he said, "is that these people when they talk they have no feeling of humanity—they just don't seem to care about people." According to *The Unmaking of a Mayor*, Senator Jacob Javits took Buckley's cam-

paign suggestion that drug addicts be quarantined and twisted it
in order to say that Buckley was planning to put black people in
concentration camps. "I suppose a controversialist reaches the
point," Buckley wrote in the same book, "or goes mad, where he
simply ignores criticism that is genuinely unjust."

But the tide against him was ebbing. When the television cameras gave him his chance for a weekly crooning, the citizenry
started having second thoughts; the equation of Buckley to
George Lincoln Rockwell all but disappeared, except from the
lips of Gore Vidal, who had moved to Rome and had not been
told the news of Buckley's emergent civility. Word leaked out that
Buckley skied with Galbraith at Gstaad, that he sailed with New
Leftist Allard Lowenstein, and really enjoyed the music of Johann
Sebastian Bach. New York City borough bosses welcomed Buckley to full status among the ranks of good citizens. James Buckley
was elected to the Senate, and it was agreed that, contrary to
having no humanity in him, he had too much of it; like his
brother, it was said, he is too honest to be a good politician. And
Bill Buckley himself was getting the "I've got to hand it to the
guy" treatment mentioned earlier. Readers of the morning papers
now discovered that they could take their Buckley straight; that,
gol-dang-it, even oatmeal tasted good while reading the sniggerings
of Mr. Conservative.

As I have written, the changes were slight in Buckley's actual
makeup throughout those years. Generally speaking, his are the
views of a minority, and he knows it well enough. Being a decent
fellow at heart, he could not help but make a good impression as
time went on, and people had the chance to adjust their prejudices. And Buckley began to write more about himself, as a man
of the world, often puzzled by what he saw. If there remained
something standoffish about his person, his journals were thought
to be irresistible.

Nevertheless, he is erratic in these, too. His panegyrics, usually
written on the deaths of eminences, tend toward fulsomeness.
The air of subservience to the recently deceased does not harmo-
nize with the vigorous critical intelligence displayed elsewhere.
His attempts to paint himself in mourning ring false. His eulogy
of Dos Passos, for example, is gaseous nonsense. He cannot bid
farewell to General MacArthur without insisting that the late

gentleman's prose style was among the glories of the age; he quotes from a passage which I find offensive to eyes, ears, nose, and throat, and calls him "the last of the great Americans." In the cases of Waugh and Dos Passos, politics intervenes. Buckley wonders whether they have received their critical due; after all, they were conservatives, and the rabble will not concede genius to a conservative. And he qualifies his admiration for the mountebank Mailer by remarking that not only does Mailer make "beautiful metaphors," but he is also "philosophically, in his own fashion, a conservative. Wrestling in the twentieth century with the hegemonies of government and ideology, the conservative tends to side with the individualist"—such as the Mailer hero. In contrast to his reputation for "aristocratic" tastes, Buckley as a literary critic is really rather crude. His taste in novels sticks close to his ideology. Those who eloquently blast Communism are his favorites —Koestler, Pasternak, Solzhenitsyn. Satirists of liberalism like Waugh suit him well, too. Writers of gross confessionals excite him, and he drinks deeply at the wells of Chambers, Mailer, and, in a lesser sense, Lowell. And of course he will always put in a good word for those books which support his own distinctive views.

His judgment is reliable only with his fellow practitioners of essayistic satire—Galbraith, for example, or Murray Kempton. Here he seems to bring down an iron curtain over ideology and recognize his artistic colleagues in the most fundamental light. The admiration for the confessional writers is, on the surface, more puzzling. But when we look deeper we realize that Buckley is, after all, an egocentric, if not confessional, writer himself. I remarked earlier that he is closer to St. Thomas than to, say, St. Augustine, but it is also appropriate to add that Thomist objectivity is not one of the reasons for it. He is devoted to logic, yes; but not in order to prove what is obviously illogical. Here he succumbs to a basic irrationalism, as I have shown. His enjoyment of the confessors seems to arise from sympathy; others have seen the senselessness of the world, and have sought answers as individuals.

All of this points to his most serious limitation as a writer: much as he might wish it otherwise, he is not at his best in expounding conservative thoughts. His egocentrism makes him best when writing about himself, or when poking fun at someone else's

ideas. Only in recent years has he begun to concede this, and concentrate on the development of his peculiar talents. There is nothing wrong, from a literary standpoint, in being egocentric; if anything, quite the reverse. But it is not particularly valuable if one is
primarily concerned with spreading some doctrine of general
truth. The more one's personality is the subject, the easier it is to
reject that person's thinking as something unique, and not really
worthy of an all-embracing philosophy. The confession by Buckley
that he is "not of the breed" of natural conservatives clarifies his
difficulty: assuming that the advertisement of his product is more
important to him than the advertisement of himself, how can
he convince people that his theatrics should *not* be the center of
attention? Moreover, he has not, out of respect for his doctrine,
pursued either of his talents as far as he might. Earlier I discussed
his politeness in relation to his satire. There is also a reticence to
his self-examinations. There are two reasons for it: a personal conviction of what is in good taste; and fidelity to his ideology. Professor Galbraith, reviewing *The Unmaking of a Mayor*, reported,
"I urged him in this book to forswear all temptation to statesmanship and give full rein to his natural talent for invective, malevolence and humor. He did not entirely reject this sage counsel. There is quite a bit of all three in *The Unmaking of a Mayor*
and they are excellent. But serious purpose does intrude and,
given the purpose, that is too bad." I have not involved myself in
conventional disputes between conservative and liberal ideologies,
as has Galbraith, and have preferred to concentrate on setting
ideas in their order, so that we may see how they hang together
against the backdrop of our times. But I concur in Galbraith's
view of Buckley's journalistic books; that is to say, I find them to
be literary mongrels of uncertain outline. They are neither books
about Buckley himself, nor about ideas or institutions, nor even
about the times generally. They are a little of each of these, and,
despite periodic brilliance, they are unsatisfactory. The briefest
pieces tend to be best; they afford the least opportunity for wander-
ing. I think of the essay on Truman Capote's ball in 1967, or "A
Million and One Nights in Soviet Russia": these are among the
semi-precious gems of postwar American literature, and ought to
be preserved for the Buckley chrestomathy likely to issue from the
dotage of the Great Conservative. But *The Unmaking of a Mayor*

is cluttered with position papers. There is much excellent criticism of John Lindsay's "precociously tasteless" campaign style, but too many allusions and correct comparisons diffuse Buckley's attack. There is a great deal of worthy reflection on the "benumbing cynicism" of politics, but it is scattered to the rhetorical winds. *Cruising Speed* contains too much grumbling about Buckley's letters; its "documentary" manner serves once more to blur the focus. As sheer writing, *United Nations Journal* is the best of all Buckley's books. All of the bluster which is the fuel of that tedious organization is captured perfectly here. In chopping the public addresses of politicians and diplomats down to size, Buckley has no peer, not even Galbraith; his critique of one of Lyndon Johnson's State of the Union messages is the best thing of its kind since Mencken analyzed Gamalielese.

He seems to need some sort of adversary to bring him fully to life. The larger and more abstract the adversary, the better he writes. When the opposition is provided by someone like Galbraith, his friend, Buckley's gentleness wins out. But walking through Leningrad, passing the home of Nicholas and Alexandra, he rises to a vituperative eloquence worthy of Burke contemplating the sight of Marie Antoinette. And rearing his head amid the stream of gossamer words which float through the General Assembly of the United Nations, he is irrepressible:

> Of course, one reason why the South African representative is driven to brevity is that if he gives a speech, the Third World regularly walks out, most ostentatiously. Notwithstanding that some of the delegates are nimble, there simply isn't time to sprint out of the room before a speaker has delivered three sentences . . . It is safe to say that there are more congratulations proffered during sessions of the United Nations every day than at a royal wedding. A few of these are spare and perfunctory; more are gooey; some approach sexual ardor.

Having been exasperated by his failure to receive permission to speak on behalf of his version of human rights, he considered resigning, but, "The principal argument against resignation was decorum, which is the piety shown toward the human relationships that insulate us against the ravages of impetuosity." He is not perfect in his use of the language. Surely I am not the only one to be exasperated by Buckley's predilection to pack epigrams within rolling periods. He can even (God forgive him) write like a hack journalist on occasion, as when he utilizes "Wagnerian" in place of "large" or trots out those heavy catchalls: Freedom, Tyranny, and the West, in order to help him over the rough spots. But there is a spot on our honor roll for a man who can manage the above defense of decorum. One may only hope that he will continue to refine his appreciation of life's little joys and irritations, and our age may have itself a democratic version of La Rochefoucauld. Perhaps the ailments and attendant crotchets of old age will reduce him to this, his natural state. In the meantime, we should be glad to suffer his babblings on "the order of moral reality," for they are spiced with a good deal of lovable meanness. And let us leave him as he found himself, when first receiving the invitation to serve his Republic in the greatest of international counsels; before rude reality would prick him once more into the apprehension of human folly, where he is truest:

It was, I think, the only experience I ever had in pure, undiluted Walter Mittyism. I saw myself there, in the center of the great assembly at the U.N. (which I had never visited in my twenty years in New York), holding the delegates spellbound as I read from Solzhenitsyn, as I described the latest account of concentration camps in Mainland China, as I pleaded the case of the ballet dancer Panov. I would cajole, wheedle, parry, thrust, mesmerize, seduce, intimidate. The press of the world would rivet its attention on the case the American delegate was making for human rights, repristinating the jaded vision of the international bureaucrats.

But it was not to be, and so would Buckley return to the proper study of mankind. May his failed example serve as a reminder to all who follow him into the airy heights; may his ensuing laughter encourage us all.

Arthur M. Schlesinger, Jr.

At birth, Arthur M. Schlesinger, Jr., was named Arthur Bancroft Schlesinger. It is trite but true to say that history was in his blood. Bancroft was the family name on his mother's side, and traced back to George Bancroft, the great early American historian whose association with Jacksonian democracy foreshadowed Arthur's connection with the Kennedys. When he came to write his own histories, young Schlesinger was more interested in establishing another connection, and so he changed his middle name to match that of his distinguished father—"I guess because at that point I wanted to be Arthur Schlesinger, Jr. In retrospect, I sometimes wish I had stuck to 'Bancroft' since I do feel a sort of intellectual and political kinship with old George."[1] The father's temperament was patient, moderate, and wise. His histories displayed rigorous scholarship and little passion; they are useful, interesting books, enriching one's learning without causing a ripple of aesthetic delight. The son supposed

> that my upbringing inclined me—no doubt conditioned me—toward becoming an historian. Also my father, in a quiet way, had always been something of a political activist; and no doubt this legitimized my own excursions into politics. However (and this may well have been an inheritance—and one I prize—from my mother), I was always less detached and judicious than my father,

[1] Letter of July 9, 1968.

more eager for commitment and combat. I think this from time
to time disconcerted him, but . . . he always backed me in everything, no matter how misguided he may privately have thought
my activities to be.[2]

Both the Bancrofts and the Schlesingers traditionally identified
with the Democratic Party and American liberalism. The son
later recalled that his father's "skepticism about extreme views
played an important part in keeping me out of political nonsense
in my youth."[3] Even in the nineteen thirties, when so many of his
contemporaries were warming to the homilies of Comrade Stalin,
he considered himself an anti-Communist. His father's "faith in
reasoned democracy and his dislike of absolutisms inoculated me
at an early point against apocalyptic politics."[4] At Harvard he
concentrated on history and literature, and supplemented his father's counsel with the instruction of such esteemed scholars as
Samuel Eliot Morison, Fred Merk, Perry Miller, Bernard De
Voto, and F. O. Matthiessen. But, appropriately enough, it was
his father who suggested the subject of what eventually became
the first book of Arthur M. Schlesinger, Jr.:

> In the spring or summer of 1937, when I was casting about for a
> subject for a senior honors essay in history and literature at Har-
> vard, my father suggested that I look at the article on Orestes A.
> Brownson in the *Dictionary of American Biography*. I did so and
> discovered that Brownson, a New England editor, a friend of
> Emerson's and Thoreau's, a Jacksonian Democrat, an early Amer-
> ican convert to Roman Catholicism, had lived a diverse and fas-
> cinating life; that his writings, if voluminous, were readily availa-
> ble; and that he had thus far been pretty much overlooked in the
> new surge of interest in the flowering of New England.

The essay was expanded and published in 1939 under the title
A *Pilgrim's Progress: Orestes A. Brownson*. In a later preface, the
author proudly noted that the only other senior honors essay at
Harvard to be published in these years was written "by a young

[2] Ibid.
[3] Ibid.
[4] Ibid.

concentrator in government, two years behind me, whom I then knew only by sight in the Yard—*Why England Slept* by John F. Kennedy, '40." If the one book was written in the accent of a future statesman, the other promised the development of a scholar capable of combining the drudgery of the library with literary vigor. Such men were once commonplace among the ranks of historians, but the supply in this country had dwindled to a mere handful by the time young Schlesinger arrived on the scene.

Despite Schlesinger's enthusiasm, Brownson was not all that promising a figure. Most of his life had been spent in unseemly quarrels over now dead theologies—in the words of Van Wyck Brooks, "He had passed from sect to sect, changing his ministerial coat as many times as the Vicar of Bray, although always in response to a new conviction. Every thinker he read, Lamennais, Jouffroy, Comte, Saint-Simon, Owen, overturned all his previous views, and he rushed from one position to another, with a headlong, headstrong vehemence, telling the world each time how right he was."[5] This constant change of views places a heavy burden on the biographer. Duty requires that he account for or at least describe each change, but this process can consume a great deal of time and space. Schlesinger, mindful that neither he nor his readers could bear too lengthy a book about Brownson, resolved his problem by skimming over the man's private life and personal behavior. In this he was probably justified. Any man with such profound interest in polemical denunciation and the advertisement of sundry creeds could not have had much energy left for more personal matters. And Schlesinger did not fail to remind us of Brownson's crankiness, by all appearances his outstanding characteristic. Still, A *Pilgrim's Progress* is somewhat unbalanced as a biography. The personality of Brownson does not quite come through. This may be because he was such an oddball, given to wild shouting about matters which would drive an intelligent man to sleep today. But, then, we could use an analysis of this case which would attempt to sort out the individual aspects of Brownson's angry faith-searching from those which generally marked his contemporaries, or the puritans of our own time. The problem is that Schlesinger's primary concern was not with Brownson's char-

[5] Van Wyck Brooks, *The Flowering of New England*, New York: E. B. Dutton, 1936, p. 247.

acter, but with his place in what academic historians so depressingly term "intellectual history"—the history of ideas in their social circumstances. Intellectual history is more interested in establishing chains of thought and setting them against a broad background of political history than in discerning the deeper urges, personal and universal, which cause people to end up thinking in their peculiar ways.

Given this limitation, A *Pilgrim's Progress* is a decent book. Considering that its author was only twenty-one, and his first consideration scholarly rather than artistic, its most remarkable quality is its lack of dullness. If the story of Brownson's incessant conversions is not precisely enthralling, it is not boring, either. This may be a negative virtue, but it is a genuine one. Aside from a few awkward moments ("On the Fourth of July 1834 at Dedham he made his chief utterance on social conditions before his removal to Boston") the narrative is clean and direct. Schlesinger's talent for epigrammatic summation is also apparent in this early work: "No one in America surpassed Brownson in his hatred of capitalism, but probably few surpassed him in the hatred of the only forces likely to restrain the capitalists"; "Humility was the one Catholic virtue he found impossible to acquire." Yet there is nothing in Schlesinger's three hundred pages to match the crystalline quality of Van Wyck Brooks's three pages in *The Flowering of New England*. There is also, in A *Pilgrim's Progress*, an initial revelation of some of Schlesinger's weaknesses—for example, his tendency to make his distinctions too fine. I cite in this connection a gratuitous contrast which the author draws up between Brownson and Karl Marx: he awards Marx the trophy as "best systematic thinker," and tosses Brownson a laurel as top "pamphleteer." The problem is that nobody asked; and there is no one so tiresome as an arbiter who must invent disputes. Both in its strengths and its weaknesses, A *Pilgrim's Progress* bears many of the qualities which mark Schlesinger's writing until the present day. I shall refrain momentarily from a detailed discussion of these qualities, as they are better viewed in relation to his major works.

After a "most fascinating"[6] year (1938–39) as a Henry Fellow at Cambridge University, he returned to Harvard and became a

[6] Letter of July 9, 1968.

member of the Society of Fellows, which enabled him "to avoid
the PhD mill and work uninterruptedly on *The Age of Jackson*."[7]
(Aside from several honorary doctorates conferred upon him in
later years, he never took any degree except his Bachelor of Arts.)
On August 10, 1940, he married Marian Cannon, and two years
later she gave birth to twins. By that time, Schlesinger's Jacksonian research had endured several stops and starts. At first, after
finishing his Brownson biography, he intended to do a similar
study of George Bancroft

> with particular attention to the interplay of his careers as histo-
> rian and politician; but an invitation to deliver the Lowell lec-
> tures in 1941 diverted me into a larger consideration of the Jack-
> sonian era. These lectures, somewhat pretentiously entitled "A
> Reinterpretation of Jacksonian Democracy," tried to understand
> why Eastern intellectuals like Brownson and Bancroft were so
> deeply engaged in Jacksonian emotions. They later became the
> basis for *The Age of Jackson*.

Then the Second World War intervened, and work on the history
was slowed, but not halted, by service in the Office of War Information (1942–43), the Office of Strategic Services (1943–45), and
in the Army (1945). By 1945 *The Age of Jackson* was ready. In all
bookish quarters it was received with astonishing interest. Not
only did *The Age of Jackson* move the younger Schlesinger into
the first rank of American historians, establish the connection
between Jefferson, Jackson, and Franklin Roosevelt for which liberals had begun to yearn, and encourage, more than any other
book except perhaps Brooks's *The Flowering of New England*,
the reinvestigation of an entire historical epoch: it also started the
motor running for post-New Deal American liberalism, and became itself a seminal event in postwar history.

II

To begin with, there was the dramatic opening, which could have
been written by Sir Walter Scott: "For the White House the new

7 Ibid.

year began in gloom. The President's wife spent a sleepless and painful night, and Mr. Adams, waking at daybreak, found the dawn overcast, the skies heavy and sullen." The President reaches for his Bible and reads from the Book of Psalms that " 'the Lord knoweth the way of the righteous: but the way of the ungodly shall perish.' " The narrator notes that, "The familiar words assuaged disappointments of four years. To an Adams, the first psalm seemed almost a personal pledge." But, "It was no year for righteous men: everywhere they sat in darkness. Two months before, General Andrew Jackson had been elected President of the United States. The ungodly were now in the ascendancy, and those who walked not in their counsels had little but Scripture for consolation."

It is a superb opening, composed with a stateliness befitting the event, yet maintaining a hushed tone, deferential to the great actors who had arrived at the historic moment when the America of the Founding Fathers passed into the hands of the unruly Westerners, with Old Hickory up front. From this "Prologue: 1829," the picture dissolves, the sonorities are softened, and we are set down amid the dying strains of Jeffersonian America, which "had begun to disappear before Jefferson himself had retired from the Presidential chair." Two chapters of scholarly elegy address "The End of Arcadia" and sketch "Keepers of the Jeffersonian Conscience"—John Randolph and John Taylor of Virginia, Nathaniel Macon of North Carolina—who "were in a sense apostles of futility," preachers of lost evangels, but who Schlesinger finds worthy of a generous farewell: "By refusing to yield an inch on some of the ultimate possibilities of democracy, they made it easier for democracy to aim at these possibilities in the future. They kept alive the democratic soul." Then the author turns his full attention to the new governors in the land, sketching their characters and assessing their ideals. He seeks to defend the Jacksonians within the context of their own era, reproaching those who comfortably denounce the spoils system from the distance of a century. Such people, he writes, "substitute moral disapproval for an understanding of causes and necessities. There can be small doubt today that, whatever evils it brought into American life, its historical function was to narrow the gap between the people and the government—to expand popular participation in the workings of democracy." He tells the tale of the Bank War more clearly than it has ever been told before, debunking the various theological interpretations of past and present:

> Some writers have talked of frontier life as if it bred traits of "individualism" and equality which made Westerners mystically opposed to banks. Actually, like all other groups in the population, Westerners favored banks when they thought they could profit by them and fought them when they thought others were profiting at their expense. The Western enthusiasm for an assault on the Bank came, not from an intuitive democratic *Weltschmerz* born in the American forest, nor from a Jeffersonian dislike of banks, but from a farmer-debtor desire to throw off restraints on the local issue of paper money.

The story sweeps on through Jackson's re-election campaign, pausing to note the presence of young Walt Whitman in the Manhattan crowds, punning on the name of Senator Silas Wright ("Of him it could be said with truth that he would rather be Wright than President"), recounting the argument over hard money versus soft, surveying the situations of the workers, the radicals, and the settled interests, the responses of the intellectuals, and the perpetuation of the Jacksonian heritage throughout the succeeding administrations, fading into the twilight years before the Civil War, and coming to a halt with the unhappy presidency of Andrew Johnson. For every slip into clichés—"humble working people" and "ringing statements" of democratic faith—there are a dozen instances of the dust collected over decades being swept away. The narrative surges forward with a youthful, bouncy pride —no "bleeding heart" liberalism here. The author takes up his scalpel where he pleases, and offers no apologies for the surgery he performs—as, for example, when he retrieves the honor of Adam Smith, whose libertarianism he defines as "a source of inspiration to the Jacksonians," announcing, "Believers in the myth of Adam Smith, as expounded by present-day publicists both of the right and of the left, may find this singular; but the real Adam Smith was rich in ammunition for the Jacksonians, as for any foe of business manipulation of the state."

Artistically, the book is not altogether satisfying. Despite the undisputed designation of Jackson as the central figure of the period, the narrative often seems to focus more sharply on Martin Van Buren than on the heroic figure of the title. The deaths of such eminent men as Calhoun and Clay go unmentioned, despite their prominence in the story while they are alive. Once the Bank War is concluded, we hear nothing of Nicholas Biddle for a hundred and fifty pages, until we are suddenly and briskly informed of his indictment on unspecified charges, his release "on a technicality," and his death "as a broken man." The reader who is insufficiently learned in this period must look elsewhere for details concerning these and other relatively small matters; this is surely a defect in what is otherwise a superlative overview of the age. Then too, there is the author's annoying proclivity to assess literary men only in relation to their political views. This is especially unfortunate, since Schlesinger has for some time shown himself to be one of the few contemporary American historians with any high degree of literary sense. But his intelligence in this area is confined to independent essays; in his histories he is too anxious to stick to his theme, in this case meaning Jacksonian democracy. Thus Emerson, elsewhere a favorite of Schlesinger's, is here denounced as a political "failure"; Thoreau is curiously forgiven for having "lived at a degree of moral tension which imposed responsibilities equivalent to those borne by men who sought to govern"; and Whitman is showered with positively Rotarian congratulations—"Thoreau said Nay to the claims of democracy, but Walt Whitman sent back the thunderous affirmation, echoing off the roof-tops of the world." In *The Age of Jackson* as in *A Pilgrim's Progress*, the weaving of men and their works in and out of general events—the basic stuff of historical writing—is imperfectly achieved.

From the scholarly point of view, the book has been challenged since it was first published.[8] Mr. Bray Hammond criticized Schlesinger for his support of Jackson's destruction of the Second Bank of the United States. Professor Richard Hofstadter denied any genuine parallel between the Jacksonians and the New Dealers: the former wished "to divorce government and business" in order

---

[8] For this discussion of the scholarly debate I am indebted to Professor Charles Sellers for the Introduction to his anthology *Andrew Jackson: A Profile* (New York: Hill & Wang, 1971).

to let the country expand, while the latter desired "governmental ascendancy over the affairs of business" in a country whose frontiers had been reached, he argued.[9] These early critiques promoted countercritiques, and the process continues until the present day. But nearly everyone praised Schlesinger for the depth of his research and the energy of his presentation. In any case, as Schlesinger would write in later years, "One comes to feel increasingly that historians agree only when the issues as well as the people are dead . . ." and American history is still too brief to permit any such relaxed consensus on very many matters.

Amid these scholarly disagreements, and despite its defects in historical portraiture, why does *The Age of Jackson* maintain its strong appeal? There is, to begin with, its freshness. The narrative drives forward with guileless confidence in its own correctness. The author does not stop to deliver stump speeches; he simply pulls the needed facts from his grab bag, and sets them down in such order that the reader is drawn to irresistible conclusions. There is the steadiness of purpose which allows the narrative its uninterrupted flow. Schlesinger's general perception of the Jacksonian period is quite clear, and he makes sure to touch every base; the most typical chapters in the book are Twenty-four through Twenty-nine, which canvass Jacksonian democracy in its relation to all the major intellectual preoccupations of the time— religion, industrialism, the law, literature, utopias—and as an intellectual movement in itself. Such sweeping criticism as this, if anyone would oppose it, demands research of comparable depth and diligence; in thirty years no one has even tried. Then, of course, there is the matter of style. Here Schlesinger, if he is not a Macaulay, is certainly pre-eminent among the American historians of his generation. Despite the disturbing number of unfinished portraits, there are many occasions when the desired effect is brought off. Hundreds of characters walk through these pages, some brightly, some dimly. They come before us as rather charming casual acquaintances. Schlesinger has the agreeable habit of putting us in touch with our national ghosts just long enough for them to become familiar, and then snatching them away before they become contemptible or boring.

All of these qualities—freshness, steadiness of purpose, sophis-

9 Ibid., pp. xii–xiii.

tication in research, a light touch—enable *The Age of Jackson* to reach high degrees of clarity and coherence. All too often these days, the historian is not interested in imagining the past, and prefers either to fit his prejudices into a historical context or to concentrate his energies on erecting a tidy bibliography. The twin devils of tendentiousness and pedantry have practically finished off history as a form of literary art. Throughout his career, Schlesinger has fought—by example and by hortatory—to keep the artistic side of history alive. This in itself would earn him an honored place on our literary rolls. But there is another characteristic which gives life to his histories, and it is first to be viewed in *The Age of Jackson*. I refer to Schlesinger's partisanship.

The partisan historian was the rule, rather than the exception, up until the last part of the nineteenth century. Hume and Macaulay, Guizot and Michelet: one knew where these men stood on the great questions of the day. Yet, at the same time, these writers were committed to history as an art, requiring that they tell their tales in human terms. Thus, while they held to the discipline of their parties (or dogmas), the variety of human nature forced a measure of flexibility on all those who presumed to penetrate historical experience. Our contemporary historians, on the other hand, have no such commitment to history as an art. What is worse, they have abandoned the flexible omniscience of the past, and now will consider human experience only after it has been put through the sausage grinders of sociology, social pathology, psychoanalysis, anthropology, urban ethnology, etc. Still more discouraging is the fact that contemporary historians have not really abandoned partisanship, but have simply wrapped it up and hid it behind all those masks. With all of this passing itself off as history, the critical histories of a Ranke, supposedly the destroyers of romantic historiography, seem positively romantic themselves in comparison! So one is grateful to those who keep artistic, partisan history alive.

Why not one without the other? Why not partisan polemics, which address the issues directly without dressing up in all the finery of the past? Or, why not concentrate solely on fluting the tales of lost times, without taking sides in arguments which should be buried with their advocates? The answer, simply, is that these approaches do not work. History requires perspective as well as empathy. Whether the historian is concerned with moving men through a framework of ideas and events, or vice versa, he must have some underlying conviction of what motivates the changes he describes. Even if the historian believes that all human existence is but a chaos of absurdities, he is bound to write a more interesting work than the man who thinks it his business to avoid all conclusions of a general sort. But beliefs *too* strongly and inflexibly held will expose the polemical nature of such a history, the discriminating reader will discern the distorted quality of this picture of the past, and the work will not survive the fever that has brought the historian's blood to a boil. On the other hand, the completely disinterested historian will find himself unable to bring people, issues, and ideas to life. This is the pedantic approach, involving an unhealthy fascination with bibliography, footnotes, and the methods of research. Another kind of disinterest is reflected in some popular historical fictions, and to a lesser degree in some popular works which appear under the heading of history or biography. In these instances, the author abandons his fidelity to the facts in order to concentrate his attention on a private vision of the historical personality. I could babble on about this subject, but my point should be clear enough; if one regards history as an art, then one should grant that, like any other art, history requires a sense of balance.

Partisanship provides the historian's link to the past he is trying to re-create. Gibbon saw himself as the defender of reason against the forces of religion and barbarism which ravaged the Roman Empire. Carlyle hunkered down on the side of the Hero. Treitschke was moved above all by his vision of the German nation. To move closer to our own time and place, we might observe the case of Will Durant, whose heroic *Story of Civilization* has been much maligned by pedants. Durant's *Story* is nothing if not a profoundly American work; yet it does not deal at all with American history. Its purpose was—and is—to educate the American people in the nature of their inheritance. By taking the side of reason, in the eighteenth-century sense, and incorporating some of the darker visions and realities of the years since the American and French revolutions, Durant related the story of all the years before the modern revolutions in a style of wondrous wit and eloquence. It is no accident that his history appeared during the years when the United States was assuming a prominent role in the affairs of the world; one cannot imagine its appearance, let alone its huge attraction, before the turn of the century. Edmund Wilson's *To the Finland Station* is another example of first-rate partisan history. In order to write it, Wilson had endured his own submersion in the Marxian theology; yet his sympathy with the "Revolutionary Tradition" remained strong, and his book retains a good deal of the Socialist passion while managing to dispose of dogma that Wilson had once more or less accepted. Like Durant's *Story of Civilization,* Wilson's book describes the European experience while remaining deeply American in its inspiration. Its partisanship is what gives the book its unity, and makes it a superior work to the later *Patriotic Gore;* which suffers from diffuseness and lack of central purpose.

When Schlesinger wrote *The Age of Jackson,* he was interested, first of all, in establishing a suitable definition for American liberalism and tying it into the history of the Democratic Party and Jacksonian democracy. Traditionally, the strongest element in this tradition had been the principle of popular rule. But one thing that is conspicuous about *The Age of Jackson* is the paucity of "ringing affirmations," on the part of the author, concerning the idea of government of, by, and for the people. According to this book, the significance of Jacksonian democracy lay in its effort to establish some rough framework of economic justice for an expanding nation. Schlesinger distinguished himself from the earlier historians of the Jacksonian epoch in his change of emphasis. Formerly, the conflict between "democracy" and the patrician government of the Founding Fathers had seemed the salient aspect of the age. The conflict is present in *The Age of Jackson,* but it has been moved to the background. So, too, the slavery question and the effects of expansion—the composition and government of the new territories and states, the expulsion of the Indians—seem peripheral to the central economic issues of the time. Schlesinger could, therefore, write freely of "the tradition of Jefferson and Jackson" because he saw the two leaders united in their mistrust of concentrated commercial power. Among the groups competing for control over the direction of affairs of state, he wrote,

The business community has been ordinarily the most powerful
. . . , and liberalism in America has been ordinarily the movement
on the part of other sections of society to restrain the power of
the business community. This was the tradition of Jefferson and
Jackson, and it has been the basic meaning of American liberalism.

It is a point which political scientists might debate endlessly. The
term "business community" is doubtless too general to describe
the merchants of the Jacksonian period. The American economy
was not dominated by multi-national corporations in those days,
of course, and Schlesinger himself drew some rather neat distinctions between the businessmen of the East and those of the West.
The uniqueness of Jacksonian democracy, according to his history,
lay in its ability to break down the old stereotypes. "Was not Jackson's administration . . . a confession that Jeffersonianism required Hamiltonian means to achieve its ends?"

The ambiguity did not stop there. Schlesinger's sense of the
tenuousness and ultimate foolishness of all cries of Absolute
Truth is very strong; it is perhaps his most attractive quality as a
scholar and writer. *The Age of Jackson*, for all its bouncy partisanship, maintains a healthy skepticism toward all self-righteous
men. For the first time, we are introduced in this book to the two
quotations which appear to be Schlesinger's favorites. We shall
see them appear again throughout the writings of future
years. Both carry the same message: human behavior is relative. In
The Age of Jackson, they provide a kind of verbal biding for the
text. The first, from George Bancroft, precedes the Foreword:
"The feud between the capitalist and laborer, the house of Have
and the house of Want, is as old as social union, and can never be
entirely quieted; but he who will act with moderation, prefer fact
to theory, and remember that everything in this world is relative
and not absolute, will see that the violence of the contest may be
stilled." The second is from Pascal, and comes at the book's end:
"The unfortunate thing is that he who would act the angel acts
the brute," to which Schlesinger adds in closing, "The great tradition of American liberalism regards man as neither brute nor
angel."

Perhaps not, but the generation of liberals which was raised between the two world wars saw rather more of the brute than its predecessors. The closing chapters of *The Age of Jackson* describe a darkened American scene, with the old Jacksonian coalition splitting up. The slavery question set North against South. The waves of immigrants from Europe changed "the people" into "the mass"—"bound together, not by common loyalties and aspirations, but by common anxieties and fears." The immigrants proved susceptible to demagogues, and the most ardent democrats were shaken in their faith. Their doubts have persisted until the present day.

But, as always, they were replaced by others who live in order to hope. Almost imperceptibly, Schlesinger brings his discourse to bear on the interests of his own generation. In these concluding pages, he speaks of "the problem of liberalism" as one involving the preservation of "as much variety within the state as is consistent with energetic action by the government." Momentarily, he sounds as if he is saying that the people exist *in order that* they may govern. But this too is softened, when we find that his actual concern is the prevention of any single force from becoming too powerful. Conflict within the Republic should help to assure freedom, while "world without conflict is the world of fantasy." Then Jefferson is invoked, asking those doubters of self-government if they have found angels in the form of kings to govern, Pascal speaks of the angel and the brute, and Schlesinger, with an endorsement of uncertainty, writes *finis* to this admirable history.

III

Besides his acceptance of an associate professorship of history at Harvard in 1946, two events in Schlesinger's career stand out among those early postwar years. One was the founding, in the winter of 1946–47, of the Americans for Democratic Action (ADA), with Schlesinger as a charter member. The other was his role in the execution of the Marshall Plan and its aftermath, as a consultant to the Economic Cooperation Administration in Paris in 1948, and in a similar role with the Mutual Security Administration in 1951–52. The association with ADA put Schlesinger into the mainstream of postwar liberal thought, and the government posts under the Truman administration solidified his commitment to the Democratic Party. The late forties, as Schlesinger later recalled, were a time of transition in American liberalism, "a time when the liberal community was engaged in the double task of redefining its attitude toward the phenomenon of Communism, and, partly in consequence, of reconstructing the bases of liberal political philosophy." Unlike those who had enjoyed a flirtation with Stalinism, Schlesinger was not tortured by the memories of dreams gone sour. Anti-Communism in those days seemed a relatively simple matter. It was still to seem so in retrospect. When a young historian of the next generation sought to blame postwar liberal anti-Communism for the muddle of later American Vietnam policy, Schlesinger would respond, "If the historians who have rather righteously condemned the 'anti-communism' of the forties were to have used instead the word 'anti-Stalinism,' their writings might perhaps have lost some of their piquant flavor of moral superiority." Yet, if liberals perceived Communism in monolithic terms in the late forties, there were bounds to their apprehension. Stalin, though wicked, was not to be confused with Antichrist; Chiang Kai-shek, though perferable to Mao Tse-tung, was not quite the Chinese Churchill; Douglas MacArthur, however splendid, seemed slightly less distinguished than the Lord God. A good many homespun conservatives were unable to make these subtle distinctions.

If liberals cannot be pessimists, they certainly may be skeptics. The generation of 1945, if I might call it that, was more skeptical than its predecessors. Like most Americans at the time, liberal thinkers were not exactly at ease with all the power that had fallen into the national lap. They had survived a miserable Depression and a nasty war, and were disinclined to take the nation by storm with the proclamation of righteous platitudes. At the same time, liberals took some satisfaction in the New Deal of Franklin Roosevelt, and regarded it as a sound base from which future policies might be launched. They also accepted the pre-eminence of the United States among the nations of the world, thus concluding the quarrel over isolationism-internationalism which had split liberal-progressives since the beginning of the century. Given these points of agreement, however, the most striking aspect of the generation of 1945 was its rejection of the notion that all problems are soluble. Schlesinger stated the matter grimly when he denounced a revisionist theory of the Civil War which held that the whole thing could have been peaceably settled if everyone had kept his cool:

> To reject the moral actuality of the Civil War is to foreclose the possibility of an adequate account of its causes. More than that, it is to misconceive and grotesquely to sentimentalize the nature of history. For history is not a redeemer, promising to solve all human problems in time; nor is man capable of transcending the limitations of his being. Man generally is entangled in insoluble problems; history is consequently a tragedy in which we are all involved, whose keynote is anxiety and frustration, not progress and fulfillment.

Yet the struggle itself was worthwhile to the liberals, if for no better reason than that it made them feel better inside. Something gnawed at the vitals; if the world was not perfectible, so far as it was given to them to envision perfection, then surely there were some things which could stand improvement. In order to achieve such improvement, liberals have always preferred human to supernatural intervention. Through the time of Woodrow Wilson, the habit was to act according to one's moral law, and then ask God for his sanction. If the members of the generation of 1945 were less inclined to ask God for anything, and were consequently depressed by the difficulty of finding an adequate substitute, they need not have worried so deeply. Very soon, Justice and Freedom would materialize in order to lend their sanctions. If the keynote of history was anxiety and frustration, Russian Communism threatened to numb such feelings altogether. It was decided that the preservation of unpleasantness was preferable to its extinction. The relativity of human behavior could provide some consolation after all. So, with their faces suggesting a seriousness beyond their years, with their bearing erect and determined, the members of the generation of 1945 marched forward into the world of the Cold War with enough of the old fire to remind everyone that the partisans of Hope had not vanished with the victims of the concentration camps.

IV

In this atmosphere of keen worries and vague promises, Schlesinger wrote *The Vital Center* during the winter of 1948–49. Of all his books, this one is the least good. For a polemic, the prose is flat and undistinguished. The chapter headings have an orotund, empty quality which is not greatly mitigated by the paragraphs which follow. The arguments lack freshness, and the whole thing reads like a drawn-out newspaper editorial. Some of this is no doubt due to the passage of time; nothing dates so quickly as yesterday's opinion. Yet, the best essays do not stale so quickly; their style extends their appeal to the next generation, which either updates or attacks their central arguments. *The Vital Center* only palls.

The book begins with a conventional obeisance to the Age of Anxiety:

> Western man in the middle of the twentieth century is tense, uncertain, adrift. We look upon our epoch as a time of troubles, an age of anxiety. The grounds of our civilization, of our certitude, are breaking up under our feet, and familiar ideas and institutions vanish as we reach for them, like shadows in the falling dusk.

After this unpromising opening, the book sheds its Audenesque cloak and enters the political world. Schlesinger strikes at the failure of the Right and the failure of the Left, at the revival of radicalism and the rise of Russia. He settles down in the last three chapters to a cozy discourse on freedom, examining its "techniques," its place in the world, and its status as "a fighting faith." One does not disagree with any of this so much as one simply nods off. "This work," Schlesinger writes in his Foreword, "is not designed to set forth novel or startling political doctrines. It is intended rather as a report on the fundamental enterprise of re-examination and self-criticism which liberalism has undergone in the last decade." But the text, in fact, disavows this claim. The re-examination is not fundamental, but tangential. A tailor's altertion is not the same thing as a new suit of clothes. Even the most splendid dandy cannot expect too much praise for having his sleeves shortened or his buttons replaced. So, too, with the claims of postwar liberalism, as argued by Schlesinger; it is nice to see that some of the spots have been removed, but this only reveals the Ivy League tweeds in all their redundant familiarity.

What interest the book retains is due to Schlesinger's ambivalence concerning his position as a member of the liberal intellectual establishment. In *The Vital Center* he assails "Doughface Progressivism," i.e., the movement behind Henry Wallace in 1948, as strongly as he denounces "the neanderthals" of the Right. But this critique of liberalism is spoiled once Schlesinger starts barking in several directions. We lose track of him when he proclaims, "The independent left everywhere has been in a state of moral paralysis at least since 1917," and, "The Equalitarianism of the Declaration of Independence was a spontaneous expression of the American experience." The essay moves along, leaving such statements in its trail, forcing us to contemplate them and discern their precise meanings for ourselves. Once again, we read these things, we do not necessarily disagree with them, but, like justices of a court, we wish to hear further arguments. This is no way to conduct a "re-examination."

What lay underneath all this would seem to be an uneasiness with the process of "re-examination" itself. As a historian, Schlesinger may have felt the need to set his own house in order, to make clear, for example, that liberalism and Communism were mutually exclusive, that the waning of the Age of Roosevelt did not necessitate a reversion to Hooverdom, and that American participation in the Cold War required discrimination as well as strength. But, really, he had not much doubted these things before, so what was the need to start shouting now? And even if the shouting helped to enlist liberals behind Harry Truman at a time when they were inclined to look down their noses at the old haberdasher, what excuse could there be for the pretentious moralizing that opens the book, or marks such a passage as the following?: "We live on from day to day, persisting mechanically in the routine of a morality and a social pattern which has been

switched off but which continues to run from its earlier momen-
tum. Our lives are empty of belief. They are lives of quiet despera-
tion." Such writing is disreputable, because the author clearly
does not regard himself as one of the "we"—he is full of beliefs,
and sounds anything but desperate—and therefore has no right to
assert a general truth which must involve himself equally with
other men.

The anxieties, however, certainly existed. Politically, the postwar world was still unformed. Around the time *The Vital Center*
was written, the daily news featured such events as the Berlin
blockade and airlift, the foundations of the states of India and Israel, and the assumption of power by Mao Tse-tung and Co. in
China. At home, the tensions of the moment were fostering the
emergence as a national figure, one year later, of Senator Joe
McCarthy. One might note, as evidence of the American mood,
that so confirmed a liberal as Schlesinger could quote the writings
of Mr. J. Edgar Hoover for reassurance, noting, "All Americans
must bear in mind J. Edgar Hoover's warning that counter-
espionage is no field for amateurs." One cannot imagine such a
statement coming from Schlesinger in later years, at least not
without a heavy dose of condescension. In those days, however,
Schlesinger's anti-Communism was so fervent that his old tutor in
modern poetry, F. O. Matthiessen, refused to speak to him because of it—quite remarkable, even allowing for the latter's unstable temperament.[10]

Schlesinger's more natural skepticism was nurtured through his
friendship with Reinhold Niebuhr. "Through the years, Niebuhr
more than anyone else I have known has served as the model of a
really great man." He first met the theologian at the time the
ADA was being founded, in the winter of 1946–47, and was
"greatly impressed and charmed by him." Then he began to read
his books. By this time Niebuhr had passed out of his stern earlier
periods, and had grown less certain of his correctness in all matters moral, material, and spiritual. Even so, there was something
in Niebuhr of a twentieth-century version of Orestes A. Brownson, and there is a certain neat symmetry to Schlesinger's intellectual affections. "I suppose," he wrote,

[10] Letter of July 9, 1968.

that *The Nature and Destiny of Man* had more influence on me (and my attitudes toward history) than any other single book. Niebuhr's rendition of the Christian interpretation of human nature, his sense of the frailty of human striving along with the duty none the less to strive, his sense of the tension between history and the absolute—all these things gave form to my own gropings about human nature and history and showed me how skepticism about man, far from leading to a rejection of democracy, established democracy on the firmest possible intellectual basis. *The Children of Light and the Children of Darkness* was also vital in this connection. Niebuhr also articulated and confirmed my sense that irony was the best human and historical stance—an irony which does not sever the nerve of action. The line leads straight from Niebuhr to the Kennedys.[11]

Thus, in religion, Schlesinger favored Unitarianism, whose God is unquestionably a liberal Democrat. Toward the end of *The Vital Center* he wrote, "The belief in the millennium has dominated our social thinking too long." And, as at the end of *The Age of Jackson,* he endorsed the battle of ideals as "basically our central strength." The continued exercise of democracy would keep the muscles of the body politic flexed. The work for "gradual and piecemeal reform" was its own reward. The acceptance of democracy required an acceptance of perpetual imperfection:

Let us not sentimentalize the millennium by believing we can attain it through scientific discovery or through the revision of our economic system. We must grow up now and forsake the millennial dream. We will not arise one morning to find all problems solved, all need for further strain and struggle ended, while we work two hours a day and spend our leisure eating milk and honey. Given human imperfection, society will continue imperfect. Problems will always torment us, because all important problems are insoluble: that is why they are important. The good comes from the continuing struggle to try and solve them, not from the vain hope of their solution.

With such a creed, nothing could come easier than the denunci-

[11] Ibid.; likewise the two preceding quotations concerning Niebuhr.

ation of political opponents; it was rather like whistling while you worked. So, two years after writing *The Vital Center*, Schlesinger joined with Richard H. Rovere and jumped into the thick of the national debate over Douglas the Great. They called their book *The General and the President* (later retitled *The MacArthur Controversy*).

It is partially a biography of MacArthur, partially a polemic against him, partially an examination of certain constitutional questions which he raised, and partially a critique of Truman's conduct of foreign policy. The book comes as a delightful surprise to anyone who has previously read *The Vital Center* and expects the same smell of mothballs. Perhaps Rovere's collaboration was the reason for it, but in any case *The General and the President* has a wonderful mocking quality which makes it not only bearable, but enchanting to the uninvolved reader of a quarter century later. The book deserves to be reissued once again, with appropriate footnotes and explanations for younger and more forgetful older readers. Its outstanding characteristic is its treatment of MacArthur, one of the most amusing figures in all American history. "For him," writes Schlesinger-Rovere, " 'I' meant the whole of the allied forces—even though he should have known that many of his men resisted this neat identification." Of his dispatches: "It was not just the egotism of the communiqués which made them intolerable; it was their inveterate, chronic, ineradicable inaccuracy." After his postwar term as the virtual Occidental Emperor of Japan, "The time came for the Japanese to cast off their crutches and try to walk by themselves. Life with Father was fine, but it could not go on forever. The best opinion is that it went on far too long. If this were not true for the children, it was certainly true for the General." The assessment of Truman is sympathetic but somewhat critical, and deserves recollection in a period which has gone just wild about Harry:

> President Truman had the great virtue of rising to occasions; he lacked the greater virtue of transcending them. His qualities were those of a Polk rather than a Jackson or a Roosevelt, of an Attlee rather than a Churchill. He made all the necessary decisions with great and simple courage; but he lacked the gift of illuminating them so that the people as a whole could understand their neces-

sity. Because he did not succeed in making mid-century America comprehend its place in the great stream of history, however much he contemplated that place himself, he did not dispel deep and agonized popular confusion . . . Senator McCarthy's—and later General MacArthur's success in commanding the public ear were a measure of President Truman's failure to set forth convincingly to the American people why they were in the fix they were in. Above all, he failed to persuade them that they must learn to live with crisis.

The authors add that, "This was not a failure in policy; it was a failure in the communication of policy." They conclude with words which, however obvious they might sound today, were very temperate and wise in a time largely dominated by scoundrels and fools:

In the end, unless the nation repeals all its traditions and sets forth on a course of undisguised imperialism, American influence and power will stand or fall on the impression it offers to the world—not the impression projected in its propaganda broadcasts, but the impression communicated by the spirit, purpose, and actuality of our national life.

A year after writing *The General and the President* with Rovere, Schlesinger joined the presidential campaign of Adlai Stevenson. The Democrats were turned out of the White House for the first time in twenty years. They would remain on the outside for eight years. During this time Schlesinger kept busy in party counsels, joined with his ADA colleagues to formulate liberal policy proposals, and generally enhanced his reputation as a professor-politician. Most important of all, he began work on the major historical work of his career, and before the presidential election of 1960 had rolled around, the first three volumes of *The Age of Roosevelt* were off the presses.

V

"This is, I suppose," wrote Schlesinger in his Foreword to the first volume, "a bad time to be writing about Franklin Roosevelt. As historians well know, the reputation of a commanding figure is often at its lowest in the period ten to twenty years after his death." I doubt that this statement was disingenuous. It certainly was wrong. The year 1956 was a fine one for a book about Roosevelt, and lay readers and academics alike received *The Crisis of the Old Order* with the warm enthusiasm which had greeted *The Age of Jackson*. Here, at last, was a history of the recent past which people could not only recall, but in which they had taken part. More significant, perhaps, was the fact that Roosevelt's death in 1945 had wonderfully enhanced his posthumous reputation. There were many reasons for this. For one thing, his death itself had been truly poignant; like Lincoln's, it gave the impression of a commander in chief who had laid down his life like so many thousands of common soldiers. Furthermore, Roosevelt had been in office so long that people had come to take him for granted; he had become the national papa, grandpapa, uncle, older brother, or whatever. We tend to be most deeply moved by the deaths of those people whom we most take for granted. We are then inclined to repair our previous neglect by warming our memories of the person's life. Thus, the death of Roosevelt became a moment tenderly recalled in people's lives, as the Kennedy assassination became for the next generation; and Roosevelt was quickly fixed as a hero in the collective memory. This fixation, of course, cannot last forever, but it seems to linger for a decade or so. If it is strong enough, it may even pre-empt that period of nasty revisionism which Schlesinger correctly identified as a general rule of historical behavior. Thus Roosevelt's standing as one of the great men of American history has never been seriously disputed, except by blustery right-wingers. And the popular bond of affection was still strong, eleven years after Roosevelt's death, when *The Crisis of the Old Order* appeared.

In addition to the popular bond, there was a historical sentiment involved too. By departing this world in 1945, Roosevelt became symbolic of an older world which seemed to vanish with him. No sooner was he abandoned to the worms than the Atomic Age began. War would never again seem to invite the exploits of heroes. Then, too, the American perspective of the world had changed. No longer underlings, or detached observers, or even equal partners in relation to Europe and its statesmen, we were now masters of all. This was something new, which the American people did not associate with the Age of Roosevelt. Consequently, that age was truly part of the past. It was ready to be cuddled and tickled by the historian. The time had come to retell its tale, in order that it might become part of that larger process in which people try to make sense of the confusion of their lives.

According to the author,

> The Age of Franklin Delano Roosevelt covered much more than the dozen years of his Presidency. The events of 1933–45 climaxed half a century of American life. The nation, in responding to the bitter challenges of depression and war, summoned up the resources, moral and intellectual, of an earlier, progressivism, an earlier war effort, and a decade of business leadership. Roosevelt's administration must be understood against the background of a generation's ideas, hopes, and experience.

This is a presumptive thesis; presumption is the foundation of partisan history. In the first place, it presumes that politics is the central feature of American life; accordingly, it presumes that progressive government is the aspect of civilization in America with which all other matters must be tuned into focus. Moreover, it presumes that Franklin Roosevelt represented the highest embodiment of progressive government, at least during the first half of the twentieth century; hence the title, *The Age of Roosevelt*. I do not wish, at this point, to disagree with any of these presumptions, but they should be indicated at the outset in order to facilitate further discourse. They are no different from the presumptions which marked *The Age of Jackson; The Age of Roosevelt* is painted on a larger canvas, with broader strokes, but with an obvious similarity in colors and chiaroscuro. Schlesinger's approach to history is clearly distinct from that of those who seek the past through its wars, its art, its philosophy, its social customs, or whatever. It is also distinct from those who admit the centrality of politics (and its corollary, economics) but deny the possibility of heroes. It is by insisting on the idea of *progressive* leadership as the locus of the age, and identifying Roosevelt as its finest exemplar, that Schlesinger gives his history its framework.

Roughly, Schlesinger sets the dates for *The Crisis of the Old*

Order at 1919–33. Once again, there is a Sir Walter Scottish evocation of the inauguration. Then early portions of the book retreat to the beginning of the century in order to examine the New
Nationalism of Theodore Roosevelt and contrast it with the New
Freedom of Woodrow Wilson. This contrast will reappear, like a
leitmotif, in the two succeeding volumes, with the New Nationalism assuming the mantle of the First New Deal and the New
Freedom transposing itself into the Second New Deal. In *The
Crisis of the Old Order*, we are led to observe a synthesis between
the initial themes. "War completed Wilson's conversion," Schlesinger wrote. "The requirements of mobilization made him, in the
end, the best New Nationalist of them all." Briskly, we are
ushered through the nineteen twenties, one of the most fascinating periods of American history, but of very little use to a historian for whom progressive government is the center of all things.
We stop momentarily to listen to the pathetic Harding inform
Nicholas Murray Butler, "I am not fit for this office and should
never have been here." We listen to the author succinctly pronounce the significance of Coolidge: "His frugality sanctified an
age of waste, his simplicity an age of luxury, his taciturnity an age
of ballyhoo. He was the moral symbol the times seemed to
demand." Then on to Hoover amid the grumblings of the
farmers, the laborers, and the liberal intellectuals. Of the latter
group, four seemed to play dominant roles: John Dewey, Herbert
Croly, Thorstein Veblen, and Charles A. Beard. "Dewey's instru-
mentalism gave the liberal synthesis its philosophy; Croly's progressivism its politics; Veblen's institutionalism its economics; and
Beard's history its sense of the past and its conviction of the future. Together the four men completed the job of reorganizing
the liberal mind and reconstructing the liberal tradition." Meanwhile, the apolitical atmosphere of the twenties encouraged "men
whose happier medium was politics" to "turn to literature."
Listed among these figures are Donald Richberg, William C.
Bullitt, and Francis Biddle, whose return to politics under Roosevelt is put forward by Schlesinger as symbolic of a change in the
intellectual climate. But this is not until the second volume.
Meanwhile, the country struggled through the first years of the
Great Depression. In little more than a hundred pages of great
sweep and power, the author relates the stock market crash and

the "contagion of fear" which spread over the country, hitting politicians, businessmen, unemployed workers, employed workers, unemployed intellectuals, and even employed intellectuals, for whom fear is always less a contagion than a tribal custom. Schlesinger has never surpassed the quality of these eight chapters, which appear under the sectional heading of "The Valley of Darkness." In rendering the strange and complex national mood of the time, in setting down the frustration which was so widely felt, in soundly analyzing the economic issues which framed the collapse, "The Valley of Darkness" marks a high point in American historical writing. It is followed by an account of the campaign for the Democratic nomination in 1932, an excellent brief biography of Franklin Roosevelt's early years, and a chronicle of the electoral campaign and interregnum leading up to Roosevelt's assumption of the presidency on March 4, 1933. *The Crisis of the Old Order* concludes with Schlesinger reading Roosevelt's thoughts on inauguration eve: "The only thing Americans had to fear was fear itself. And so he serenely awaited the morrow. The event was in the hand of God."

Volume Two, *The Coming of the New Deal*, picks up the story with the Hundred Days. As in all of Schlesinger's Prologues, the tone is one of high and stately drama. The spaciousness of *The Crisis of the Old Order* is still here. But the rest of *The Coming of the New Deal* involves a close examination of the domestic political and economic scenes in the years 1933 and 1934. This entails an abandonment of the sweeping narrative style of the first volume and *The Age of Jackson*. It also means a heavy concentration on the famous bureaucracies which arose in those years: the AAA, NRA, CCC, TVA, etc. Inevitably, the story lags. In compensation, we are given a patient and solid assessment of the largest experiment in "affirmative government" in the history of the United States. Having listened closely to the explanations of his friend Galbraith, Schlesinger offers a limited defense of the NRA: "Its ends—economic stabilization and social decency—were necessary and noble. Its assumption about the economy as more administered than self-regulating was much closer to actuality than the assumption of its critics. If it approached its goals in a clumsy and circuitous way, it did so because in 1933 the choice of roads was exceedingly limited." The other bureaucracies are given

similar sizings-up; likewise the top bureaucrats, who are introduced in Schlesinger's masterly sketches and then woven into the
thread of the narrative. Most notable are the portraits of the
crotchety Ickes and the rococo General Hugh Johnson. These
men are little more than adornments to the national waxworks so
far as the generation of the 1970s is concerned; but in Schlesinger's hands they are wonderfully alive again, grumbling and
bellowing their way through history. As always, there is an overly
fastidious account of the activities of the "intellectual community." Perhaps it is a weakness common to his station, for
Schlesinger takes a lively interest in professorial changes of mind
from one month to the next. He writes of the "Conundrum of
Price" and the "Conundrum of Labor," gives rather too much
space to the problems of monetary policy, and ends the book by
describing the opposition of conservatives, their defeat at the polls
in 1934, and the emergence of Franklin Roosevelt in all his glory.
"He has been all but crowned by the people," wrote William
Allen White. "The essence of Roosevelt," Schlesinger concluded,

> the quality which fulfilled the best in him and explained the po-
> tency of his appeal, was his intrepid and passionate affirmation.
> He always cast his vote for life, for action, for forward motion, for
> the future. His response to the magnificent emptiness of the
> Grand Canyon was typical: "It looks dead. I like my green trees
> at Hyde Park better. They are alive and growing." He responded
> to what was vital, not to what was lifeless; to what was coming,
> not to what was passing away. He lived by his exultation in dis-
> tant horizons and uncharted seas. It was this which won him
> confidence and loyalty in a frightened age when the air was filled
> with the sound of certitudes cracking on every side—this and the
> conviction of plain people that he had given them heart and head
> and would not cease fighting in their cause.

To a much greater degree than either its predecessor or its successor, *The Coming of the New Deal* at times borders on te-
diousness. Nevertheless, it is the anchor of the incomplete series;
it is impossible to absorb the significance of Roosevelt and his
works without sorting out the flurry of government activity in
1933–34. "The tenets of the First New Deal," wrote Schlesinger,

were that the technological revolution had rendered bigness inevitable; that competition could no longer be relied on to protect social interests; that large units were an opportunity to be seized rather than a danger to be fought; and that the formula for stability in the new society must be combination and cooperation under enlarged federal authority. This meant the creation of new institutions, public and private, to do what competition had once done (or was supposed to have done) in the way of balancing the economy—institutions which might well alter the existing pattern of individual economic decision, especially on investment, production, and price.

This was something new in America; or, at least, it was so regarded by its most fervent advocates and opponents. Schlesinger lingered over every detail, it seems, because in retrospect the First New Deal appears as the foundation of modern American government. Once the country emerged from the Great Depression and World War II, it would assume the appearance of "the affluent society." The perceptions of the First New Dealers would be employed in a different situation. In economics, unlike philosophy, theory tends to follow practice. Adam Smith wrote of his "natural order" after it had already come into existence; he was its analyst, not its prophet. Keynes did not predict depressions; he examined and proposed remedies for them. So, too, with the post-World War II theorists: what they proposed was based on the actions of the New Deal, particularly in the years 1933–34. Schlesinger was, therefore, recording the history of American government as it first came completely to terms with modern corporate enterprise. Along with racial questions, this coming to terms would provide the most consistent basis for domestic controversy in the next half century.

In *The Politics of Upheaval*, published on the eve of the 1960 presidential primaries, the narrative once again broadens. By the time we read this volume, we are comfortably familiar with the behavior of Roosevelt and his subalterns. The great bureaucracies of 1933–34 are set in place, and require less frequent attention. So Schlesinger opens his pages to the numerous characters of the thirties. Partially, *The Politics of Upheaval* is a solemn chronicle of American politics in the years 1935–36. But, in addition, it is a catalogue of American political nonsense in an era which fostered it to an unsurpassed degree. Schlesinger treats Roosevelt himself with undue politeness; tossing his head and flashing what Mencken called his "Christian Science smile," the President was a formidable actor. He was hardly the most scrupulous of men. While Schlesinger remarks upon this, he does not adequately dramatize it. In contrast, Huey Long, Gerald L. K. Smith, Father Charles Coughlin, and Dr. Francis E. Townsend are treated with proper contempt. So, to a lesser extent, are those deeply conservative men—often businessmen and Supreme Court justices—who forecast the demise of Western civilization with each passage of New Deal legislation. Even the revered Justice Louis D. Brandeis does not emerge unscathed from Schlesinger's examination of the answer-men of the thirties. The good jurist's religious faith in small-business men, and his boresome incantation that all young men of talent should "go back to the hinterland" and remake their communities, seem as quaint one generation hence as Father Coughlin's odes to silver. It is a cliché of political science that social disorder promotes the rise of demagogues. On this opinion, no doubt correct, Schlesinger bases his narrative of the charlatanry of the Roosevelt era. Less widely accepted among the learned, but equally true, is the fact that "affirmative government," proposing remedies for all social misfortune, tends to galvanize every incipient social philosopher into action. On the level of raw politics, this phenomenon is labeled the "revolution of rising expectation," i.e., you give a man a crumb and soon he wants the whole loaf of bread. On the more refined intellectual level, no convenient label has been worked out. Nevertheless, a Roosevelt coming forth with all sorts of solutions inspires less exalted men to imitation. Some are harmless quacks, who differ from demagogues only in the weakness of their power drive. But there are also many sober, thoughtful men who, under these circumstances, tend to stiffen up. Their convictions, in more relaxed times the stuff of casual conversation, assume an air of righteousness. Accordingly, these convictions are often foolish. "History" (in our case personified by Schlesinger) correctly condemns them, albeit with great reluctance. *The Politics of Upheaval* presents case after case of this sort of behavior. Brandeis has been mentioned. There was also Dr. John Dewey, who complained sourly about the New Deal's failure to realize his ideals. Charles A. Beard was another. Walter Lippmann, Raymond Moley, Alf Landon, the literary Communists: all were moved by the force of "affirmative government" into an orgy of criticism and counterproposal. There is a dialectical elegance to the whole pattern. Schlesinger reports it faithfully. But if his approach were more clinical, he might give his readers a clearer view of this process. Often, when people disagree more hotly than the dispute would seem to call for, the explanation is to be found in the requirements of the contestants' egos. This would seem largely to be the case in the debates reported in *The Politics of Upheaval*. But Schlesinger retains his sympathy, even in disagreement. He ascribes the best intentions to the sensitive hotheads who had no genuine quarrel with Roosevelt but quarreled anyway. *The Politics of Upheaval* is thus a mellow book. "Roosevelt's genius," the author writes in conclusion, "lay in the fact that he recognized—rather, rejoiced in—the challenge to the pragmatic nerve. His basic principle was not to sacrifice human beings to logic . . . He had no philosophy save experiment, which was a technique; constitutionalism, which was a procedure; and humanity, which was a faith." This is very vague—another example of the overfine distinction, already identified as a bad Schlesinger habit. It mades it difficult for us to penetrate toward the roots of this history, which has now lain dormant, like an unfinished monument, for a decade and a half. With the story halted at 1936, it is a long, flawed, and yet quite impressive fragment. Difficult though penetration might be, it certainly seems worth the effort.

VI

In his 1960 essay "On Heroic Leadership," Schlesinger wrote,

> The heroic leader has the Promethean responsibility to affirm human freedom against the supposed inevitabilities of history. As he does this, he combats the infection of fatalism which might otherwise paralyze mass democracy. Without heroic leaders, a society would tend to acquiesce in the drift of history. Such acquiescence is easy enough; the great appeal of fatalism, indeed, is as

a refuge from the terrors of responsibility. A purposeful and vital democracy must rest on a belief in the potency of choice—on the conviction that individual decisions do affect the course of events.

It is this belief in the efficacy of heroism that sets Schlesinger apart from many of his fellow liberals. His mind is less programmatic, more supple. This, indeed, sets him somewhat apart from the mainstream of modern American historiography, which works in the tradition of Charles A. Beard and Frederick Jackson Turner, emphasizing the influence of external forces on the lives of the masses. Schlesinger is not necessarily antagonistic to his colleagues; few historians have so generously praised their inferiors. Rather, he is inclined to incorporate their views, and then write his own books in the tradition of nineteenth-century romanticism. "History has always seemed to me," he wrote in "The Historian as Artist" in 1963, "primarily an art, a branch of literature, a minor branch perhaps, subject to its own rules, concerned with its own issues, but committed nonetheless to the written word, and therefore a literary enterprise." He scorned the claim of history as a science, writing that "if the test of science is predictability, historians who claim to be scientists might as well go out and cut their throats." It is clear that he loves the historians of the early nineteenth century best of all, though he recognizes their errors, and appreciates the improvement in research which has occurred under the technical historians from Ranke until the present day. At the same time, technical history "turned the historian's attention from description to explanation," and "implied the tacit assumption that emotion had no place in history, and this whole conception not only impoverished history but falsified it." Inevitably, historians stopped looking at the big picture in order to perfect their little monographs. This opened the gates to the worst of all breeds of historical thought. With Karl Marx, Arnold Toynbee, and Oswald Spengler particularly in mind, Schlesinger wrote, ". . . I would call attention to what seems to me the gravest problem produced by the renunciation of the technical historian—that is, the rise of the prophetic historian, who has converted the genial visions of the romantic historian into dogmatic, comprehensive, universal, and tyrannical historical theories." As an antidote to prophetic history he proposed, with charming simplicity, that the historian become a more conscientious craftsman. "He must brood lengthily on the question of structure and note the cunning skill with which the great historians constructed their intricate and majestic works." When historians are once more artists, "Rational history will then elevate the popularizers, influence the journalists, and devalue the prophets."

What has all this to do with Schlesinger's history of the Roosevelt era? Simply this: in *The Age of Roosevelt*, Schlesinger's belief in heroes meshes with his belief in the heroic possibilities of history as an art. This permits him to invest his work with its element of grandeur. It gives the narrative its sense of purpose. It raises history above the level of simple chronicle or analysis and brings the whole thing together in something resembling an act of faith. I noted earlier that the ideal of progressive leadership, with Roosevelt as its finest flower, is the foundation of *The Age of Roosevelt*. By his ability to absorb the technical problems of politics and economics into the personalities of the men who dealt with them, Schlesinger gives his work its sense of balance. He establishes the human basis of understanding, which is the first requirement of literary art. And, perhaps most important of all, he restores to history its public importance, redressing the grievance expressed in "The Historian as Artist": "The effect of the progressive separation of history from both art and experience was, in the end, to separate it from the intellectual community. History ceased to matter to the reading public."

The Age of Roosevelt, even in its incomplete state, has commanded the attention of anyone who would debate the national past. This is largely because of its concentration on public affairs. I believe this emphasis is essentially correct. Alexis de Tocqueville, arriving in the United States almost a century and a half ago, found that, "No sooner do you set foot on American soil than you find yourself in a sort of tumult; a confused clamor arises on every side, and a thousand voices are heard at once, each expressing some social requirement." Tocqueville duly noted the people of a district debating over whether to build a church, the farmers planning roads and schools, the temperance ladies denouncing demon rum, and so on. "It is hard to explain," he continued, "the place filled by political concerns in the life of an American. To take a hand in the government of society and to talk about it is his most important business and, so to say, the only pleasure he knows."[12] Has the Republic changed all that much since Tocqueville's visit? Today we are much more inclined to debate the merits of a quarterback than those of a congressman. Politics is surely not the "only pleasure" of the average man in a day when proletarians own sailboats. Almost half the population does not participate in presidential elections. And yet—politics is still the core of American life. If citizens are prone to take things for granted these days, and political behavior is, on the whole, more temperate than in the past, politics in the broadest sense remains a central concern. Americans still believe the preposterous promises of politicians, and grow indignant when they are not kept. They still howl about utility rates and sewage commissioners. They still relish the sport of presidential campaigning. They allow televised newsmen to serenade them at dinner with ballads of political lunacy. They still attack and defend "the system" with great passion, and their passion reflects their undefined but basic faith.

It is this faith which *The Age of Roosevelt* portrays. Throughout this grand, organic history, Schlesinger seems to accept the notion that the American people are in their most natural state when they are conducting and worrying about their government. And although it would really be nice to hear about Prohibition and the New York Yankees and George Gershwin and Ernest Hemingway, it is probably true that Schlesinger is telling the main story, with America looking to its leaders, particularly its President, for its myths and its ideals.

VII

In his book *The Kennedy Legacy*, Theodore Sorensen speaks of Schlesinger's *A Thousand Days* as having "justified JFK's decision to have his own historian in the White House."[13] One wonders if this puts the matter correctly; anyway it sounds a bit cynical. No

[12] Alexis de Tocqueville, *Democracy in America*, tr. by J. P. Mayer, New York: Anchor Books, 1969, pp. 242–43.
[13] Theodore C. Sorensen, *The Kennedy Legacy*, New York: The Macmillan Co., 1969, p. 97.

one has claimed that John Kenneth Galbraith's tenure as Ambassador to India "justified Kennedy's decision to have an economist serve as ambassador to a developing nation." It is also conceivable that, after the passage of years, Schlesinger's career may seem more important than Kennedy's; will it then be said that Schlesinger's subsequent writings "justified" his decision to accept a major public appointment? Or, perhaps, that the effects were harmful for the historian?

The fact is that Schlesinger has produced no major historical work in the decade since *A Thousand Days*, his "personal memoir" of the Kennedy years. Despite having more time for research and writing than in the years at Harvard preceding the Kennedy administration, Schlesinger's creative production has flagged. He has left *The Age of Roosevelt* unfinished, and attempted nothing new on a similar scale. Instead, he has produced workaday film criticism for *Vogue* magazine, edited the works of other writers and a history of American presidential elections, and, most notably, performed as a scholarly and competent pamphleteer. In this last capacity he has opposed American Vietnam policy, analyzed the "crisis of confidence" of the late sixties, and denounced the "imperial presidency" of Lyndon Johnson and Richard Nixon. This is all very honorable, but it is less than Schlesinger's best. Inescapably, one wonders if Schlesinger the public servant destroyed, or at least severely crippled, Schlesinger the historical artist. Before we turn to *A Thousand Days*, then, it is useful to contemplate the Schlesinger-Kennedy connection.

The most pertinent document in this case is an article published by Schlesinger in *Foreign Affairs* in April 1963, while he was still serving as Special Assistant to the President. This is roughly the same time at which "The Historian as Artist" was written. Together, these two pieces, written at the time when Schlesinger was furthest removed from his career as a historian, comprise his most revealing reflections on the nature of his art. "To take part in public affairs," he wrote in "The Historian and History," "to smell the dust and sweat of battle, is surely to amplify the historical imagination." But at the same time he wondered whether or not it might restrict the historian's talent. "To act is, in many cases, to give hostages—to policies, partisans, to persons. Participation spins a web of commitments which may imprison the chronicler in invisible fetters. Macaulay was forever a Whig, Bancroft a Jacksonian, Adams an Adams; and their histories became the servant of their loyalties." Moreover, the historian is made sometimes to feel naked in the presence of power.

Nothing in my own recent experience has been more chastening than the attempt to penetrate into the process of decision. I shudder a little when I think how confidently I have analysed decisions in the ages of Jackson and Roosevelt, traced influences, assigned motives, allocated responsibilities and, in short, transformed a dishevelled and murky evolution into a tidy and ordered transaction.

From the inside looking out, the press now seemed unreliable and often irresponsible: "As for newspaper and magazine accounts, they are sometimes worse than useless when they purport to give the inside history of decisions; their relation to reality is often considerably less than the shadows on Plato's cave."

I do not mean to counsel defeatism in this matter. Tendencies can of course be discerned and identified, and a sequence of decisions may supply the evidence for a clear delineation of conflicting programs and policies. But I do doubt whether specific historical episodes can always be reconstructed with the glib exactitude to which historians are sometimes professionally addicted—and I speak as one who has sinned more than most.

This confession is all very well, but it is most striking in its elaboration of what lay readers of history have always considered fairly obvious. Traditionally, the historian justifying his verisimilitude has been like the great man excusing his peccadilloes. The rule is: never complain, never explain. (Though the historian must have his footnotes in order.) I, for one, have never doubted that the primary tools of the historian include sinuses immune to library dust, a sturdy rear end, and a fondness for prestidigitation. In large part, history involves the discovery of facts to match our dreams. The historian living at the pinnacle of power is a man who watches his dreams transformed before his very eyes. He must confront those things which the uninvolved historian need never face. Whether he is the better or worse for this confrontation, he is certainly changed by it. It is too soon and too difficult, at this short distance in time, to see how Schlesinger was changed by his experience in the Kennedy administration. He is still in the midst of a flourishing career, which unquestionably took a sharp turn after he left the White House. But its evolution is not yet finished, and we must await further developments.

The details of the Schlesinger-Kennedy connection need only be sketched, as my purpose is critical and not biographical. John F. Kennedy was Schlesinger's congressman from 1947–52, his senator from 1953–60. Over these fourteen years, Schlesinger came to know and admire the young legislator. When the 1960 election season approached, he decided to support Kennedy's bid for the Democratic nomination, much to the chagrin of many of Adlai Stevenson's loyalists. This decision was made easier by Stevenson's exasperating refusal to clarify his intentions in 1960. During the presidential campaign that year, Schlesinger spent much of his time trying to convince many of his intellectual colleagues that Kennedy was a genuine liberal. Lyndon Johnson's nomination for the vice-presidency was a particularly difficult moment. Liberal academicians had acquired the habit of regarding Johnson as a conservative. When it comes to political labels, professors are more stubborn than longshoremen. Johnson's nomination thus presented itself as a betrayal of liberal principles. Schlesinger's personal crisis passed when Reinhold Niebuhr came round and convinced him, in practical terms, that Johnson was indeed a good choice for the vice-presidency. Besides, there was Nixon to beat. Schlesinger composed a pamphlet, *Kennedy or Nixon: Does It Make Any Difference?*, which blasted Nixon more eloquently than it defended Kennedy.

Ten days after the inauguration, Schlesinger was installed as Special Assistant to the President. His duties were not specified. Galbraith found him at first "unhappy and uncertain concerning his White House assignment. He has a good address but no clear function."[14] Appropriately enough for this rangy-minded man, his function was never really clarified. Theodore Sorensen writes that Schlesinger "served as a constant contact with the liberals and in-

[14] John Kenneth Galbraith, *Ambassador's Journal*, Boston: Houghton Mifflin Co., 1969, p. 28.

tellectuals both in this country and abroad, as an advisor on Latin-American, United Nations, and cultural affairs, as a source of innovation, ideas, and occasional speeches on all topics, and incidentally as a lightning rod to attract Republican attacks away from the rest of us."[15] The initial disappointment faded quickly. By March, "One could not deny a sense of New Frontier autointoxication; one felt it oneself." He first distinguished himself in administration counsels by his opposition to the CIA-sponsored invasion of the Bay of Pigs. "Arthur wrote me a memorandum that will look pretty good when he gets around to writing his book on my administration," said Kennedy. His quarrels with conservatives were among the more amusing aspects of the Kennedy presidency. Some of them are reported in A Thousand Days. The "Harvard eggheads" were not without willing sparring partners, and Schlesinger relished the controversy more than most. At one point, though, the heat became hard to bear; Schlesinger wondered sheepishly if he should resign; the President told him to forget all about it. Schlesinger neither forgot nor resigned, but did what any smart writer would do—he saved his revenge for his memoirs. One time in Boston Schlesinger engaged William F. Buckley, Jr., in debate. He began by offering traditionally unctuous praise of his opponent. Buckley impishly snatched the statement from its context and slapped it on the jacket of his next book. Infuriated, Schlesinger had his lawyers demand an apology and threaten a lawsuit. Eventually, the quotation was removed from the jackets of succeeding editions of the book, and the smoke cleared. Conservatives meanwhile rejoiced at seeing Schlesinger so red in the face. Buckley's prank was mean but essentially harmless, and Schlesinger's indignation was somewhat exaggerated. It was not his finest hour, and failed to earn a spot in his memoirs.

Elsewhere, Schlesinger's wit and high-spirited partisanship were a credit to the administration. With Galbraith away in India most of the time, Schlesinger became the prototype of the bookish activist, the quintessential New Frontiersman. Walt Whitman Rostow and McGeorge Bundy had been read by their fellow scholars; Schlesinger had been read by half of literate America. The eminent historian in the White House was not

[15] Sorensen, Kennedy, New York: Harper & Row, 1965, p. 296.

without his effect. Liberals could not easily question Kennedy's liberalism when a man like Schlesinger lent his imprimatur.

Amid the ombudsmanship, Schlesinger found time to praise the state of the nation which had so rewarded him. In the Introduction to *The Politics of Hope*, his collection of essays published in 1962, he wrote, "We are Sons of Liberty once again; or, at least, we admit this as a legitimate ambition. We have awakened as from a trance; and we have awakened so quickly and sharply that we can hardly remember what it was like when we slumbered." It is nice to see him so enthusiastic, but it is hard to avoid feeling that there was something a little fatuous about Schlesinger wrapped in a flag like that. He is more natural in the traditional historian's role, extolling the past, griping about the present, and worrying about the future. Anyway, it was all over soon. A few days after the assassination, Galbraith found Schlesinger "party reconciled to the thought of coming back to Cambridge. But not completely reconciled."[16] Lyndon Johnson asked him to stay at the White House. He agreed, only to discover that his counsel was rarely sought. After two months of restless inactivity he resigned. Instead of returning to Cambridge, he stayed in Washington and set to work on *A Thousand Days*.

VIII

All of Schlesinger's major works are, in part, acts of hero worship. They represent a modernized, temporized version of this ancient attitude, but there is no mistaking the faith which moves the verbiage. Accordingly, readers find Schlesinger's histories attractive or repellent in correspondence to their own feelings about the hero.

A Thousand Days is, however, a more complicated case than *The Age of Jackson* and *The Age of Roosevelt*. It concerns itself with individuals who were still active in the government at the time the book was written. Schlesinger's scorn for Secretary of State Dean Rusk, a dominant theme in the book, did not encourage universal enthusiasm. The revelation that Kennedy intended to fire Rusk at the start of his second term created a national scandal. The original controversies have abated in the last ten

[16] Galbraith, *Ambassador's Journal*, op. cit., p. 599.

years, only to encourage a fresh round of questions. A *Thousand Days* remains one of the central political books of our time. One cannot read it without becoming engaged in the great debates concerning the Kennedy administration, contemporary liberalism, and the history of the United States since World War II. "Everything written about the Kennedy years from now on will be influenced by this history," wrote John Kenneth Galbraith enthusiastically; "the best political novel since *Coningsby*," snapped Gore Vidal.[17] After another Kenilworthy opening ("It all began in the cold"), the story chugs along at the pace of a page a day. As Vidal commented with typical exasperation, "From this point on, the thousand days unfold in familiar sequence, and . . . the story possesses the quality of a passion play: disaster at Cuba I, triumph at Cuba II; the eloquent speeches; the fine pageantry; and always the crowds and the glory, ending at Dallas."[18] There are also several snippets of autobiography: Schlesinger informing us that he had begun to think of such-and-such a problem so many years ago, Schlesinger meeting up with old friends from the ADA, Schlesinger recalling his first interview with LBJ, etc. It is common to find characters introduced by having their relationship with Schlesinger sketched: one fellow goes back to the Army and OSS days, another is an old Harvard colleague, and so on. At the same time, there is a detached quality to this book, and the author seldom discusses his innermost thoughts, fears, and dreams. A *Thousand Days*, despite the disclaimer in the Foreword, is more an informal history than a memoir.

Schlesinger may begin his ruminations on a subject with the personal pronoun "I," but before long "I" becomes "one." Events are not described with the ironic and idiosyncratic eye of the participant, as they are, for example, in Galbraith's *Ambassador's Journal*. Instead, they are elevated to the Olympian plateau favored by historians. The lively portrait of Kennedy is the most remarkable aspect of A *Thousand Days*, and Schlesinger really seems to be serving up the main dish with all the trimmings. Yet, later books, such as Benjamin Bradlee's *Conversations with Kennedy*, show the President to have been a man not without his vul-

---

[17] Gore Vidal, *Homage to Daniel Shays*, New York: Random House, 1972, p. 238.
[18] Ibid., p. 237.

gar, petty streak. As with Roosevelt, Schlesinger prefers to excuse the less noble qualities with a wave of the hand, and then resume his epic to the sound of ruffles and flourishes. I submit this passage:

> Of course there was an element of legerdemain in all this. Every politician has to fake a little, and Kennedy was a politician determined to become President. He was prepared to do many things, to cut corners, to exploit people and situations, to "go go go," even to merchandise himself. But many things he would not do, phrases he would not use, people he would not exploit (never a "Jackie and I"). Even his faking had to stay within character. This sense of a personality under control, this insistence on distancing himself from displays of emotion, led some to think him indifferent or unfeeling. But only the unwary could really suppose that his "coolness" was because he felt too little. It was because he felt too much and had to compose himself for an existence filled with disorder and despair.

What does this really say? Nothing more than that Kennedy perceived that he could serve his own ambitions best by adopting a statesmanlike, patrician manner. It is only natural that a politician should choose a style which suits him best. There was calculation behind the salty twang of Harry Truman and the thumping vigor of the Roosevelts. Every politician is part actor: the trick is to choose the role to fit the performer. The choice reflects the politician's craftsmanship, not his character. Consider Schlesinger's statement that Kennedy would not exploit his wife. This is untrue. Jacqueline Kennedy was the most subtly exploited "First Lady" in modern times; that is, she was made to seem symbolic of many of the graces and charms which Kennedy wanted his administration to represent. There is nothing at all wrong with this, so long as the partner is willing, and there seems little point in praising the President's character because of it. There is even less sense in denying it, which is what Schlesinger does. This is not even one of those instances where the demands of history and courtesy conflict. The facts, like a lady's nose, are better left unshined.

Similarly, high affairs of state occurred too close to the writing of *A Thousand Days* to be seen in proper perspective; much eloquence is wasted on the footnotes of the future. The long debate over the structure of the nuclear deterrent in Europe, for example, is of minor interest today. The precise nature of the situation in Laos in the early sixties now seems less significant than the situation in Vietnam. This is not Schlesinger's fault. As he is the first to admit, the true history of the Kennedy years can only be written by a younger man. His is the viewpoint of one who worked in the White House at the time of the events described.

But the attempt to combine the intimacy of the Special Assistant with the detachment of the historian is not all that successful. There are moments when the grandiloquence seems rather stilted. One time Schlesinger recounts standing on the beach at Hyannis Port, watching John and Jacqueline Kennedy return from a stroll. He writes: "One could only think: What a wildly attractive young couple." What is this "one could only think"? Did Schlesinger think this, or didn't he? And, if so, why would Schlesinger, himself a few months younger than Kennedy, think of them as such a "young couple"? He sounds more like a doting old uncle than a friendly contemporary of the President-elect. I am many years younger than Schlesinger and Kennedy were at the time, and I know that I do not think of my own contemporaries as young: I think of them as contemporaries. It is this sort of writing which Vidal must have considered when he spoke of A *Thousand Days* as a "political novel." At such moments Schlesinger really does seem to be reconstructing a Camelot filled with sand castles. Likewise, there is a passage concerning the funeral of Eleanor Roosevelt which seems to me worthy of nomination as the worst moment in the complete writings of Schlesinger. He has just finished listing all the old warriors who attended the funeral, and then he mentions that the New Dealer Tom Corcoran has turned to him:

"This is the last assembly," Corcoran whispered to me. "There will never again be an occasion on which all these people will gather together." By the time we reached the grave site, a gentle rain had begun to fall. Later we went over to John Roosevelt's. All the Roosevelt children were there. Thinking of the young Roosevelts, lost suddenly in middle age, and of the young Kennedys, so sure

and purposeful, one perceived an historic contrast, a dynastic
change, like the Yorks giving way to the Tudors.

Did "one" indeed? If so, we are slapped with a sobering reminder
of why romantic history went out of style. This sort of blowzy
daydreaming is more appropriate to the "journalism" of a Norman Mailer than it is to a professional historian who prides himself on realism. (It does, however, help to explain why, when Kennedy said of Mailer's windy "Superman Comes to the
Supermarket," "It really runs on, doesn't it?," Schlesinger thought
this comment "enigmatic.")

Besides its author's fantasies about wildly beautiful young couples and dynastic changes, A *Thousand Days* reveals a few blind
spots. The most notable of these is to be found in the treatment
of Rusk. In chapter after chapter, Schlesinger is interested in exposing the Secretary of State as a boob. This is accomplished
quite elegantly. A particularly effective device is the description of
meetings during times of crisis, at which Rusk, apparently, either
sat in glum silence or mumbled platitudes. Then, of course, there
is the famous indiscretion at the book's end: Kennedy ultimately
turned thumbs down on Rusk, and had decided to boot him out.
Now, it is impossible to read A *Thousand Days* and emerge with
a feeling of satisfaction concerning the conduct of the State Department during the Kennedy administration. But Schlesinger,
very oddly, never blames Kennedy for any of this. He simply excuses it: bureaucracies are tough to change (true, but all the more
reason to provide them with strong leadership); Kennedy was really his own Secretary of State (a practical impossibility, as A
Thousand Days itself amply demonstrates); dismissing Rusk
would make it seem that Kennedy had made a poor choice in the
first place, and injure administration prestige (correct, but bad diplomacy is even worse for prestige); and, of course, Rusk was to
be fired before the start of the next term, and that would finally
settle the problem (but the damage had already been done). This
is not very rigorous as analysis, but is certainly compelling as a
study in loyalty. If Rusk was half as bad as Schlesinger portrays
him to be, and the State Department so bungling under his direction, there is little reason why he should have remained so long in
high office. A first-rate leader does not serenely tolerate a ministe-

rial dunderhead for three years, and then agree to rid himself of the fellow only after another year has passed.

But Kennedy, however superior to his bland predecessor and his two ghoulish successors, was not quite a first-rate President. Perhaps that is because he needed more time; this is at least the nicest way to remember him. As Walter Lippmann put it, although he had often been "skeptical" and "disappointed" during the Kennedy years, "now in retrospect, I am glad of the legend and I think it contains that part of the truth which is most worth having."[19] Schlesinger insists on placing Kennedy high in the first rank of American Presidents. That is his privilege; maybe he even thinks it his duty. But A *Thousand Days* suffers under the burden of this overwrought evaluation. Perhaps it is best if we regard this book as an enormous group portrait. Kennedy is at the center, but he is flanked by an entire generation. The ideals and the spokesmen of postwar liberalism are set down here in indelible ink. The Kennedy years proved the only time when these men and ideals would come to power. Kennedy himself, in his short term, embodied Schlesinger's dream of the progressive leader, and so all America seemed fully alive again. Nevertheless, Schlesinger writing about his own time and his own President is less good than he is when writing about the ages of Jackson and Roosevelt. Many critics regarded A *Thousand Days*, at the time of its publication, as the best of Schlesinger's histories. They, too, were still ensnared by the terrible poignancy of the assassination only two years before. Their judgment seems faulty with the passage of a decade. A *Thousand Days* is a good book, with moments of excellence, but more of it is boring and irritating than is the case with its predecessors.

IX

The publication of A *Thousand Days* marked the peak of Schlesinger's career. *Time* magazine featured his beaming face on its cover. Book clubs rushed copies to their subscribers. The Pulitzer Prize and National Book Award were offered in celebra-

[19] Quoted in John Luskin, *Lippmann, Liberty, and the Press*, University, Alabama: University of Alabama Press, 1972, p. 217.

tion. Kennedy himself seemed on the verge of secular canonization; the Congress rendered homage unto his memory by passing the legislation which would convert the United States into the Great Society. Nothing better suited the mood of the country than a book warmly faithful to his memory. Schlesinger decided not to return to Harvard, after all. At first he went up to Princeton in early 1966 as a Visiting Fellow, and then, in the fall of that year, settled down in New York City as Albert Schweitzer Professor of the Humanities at the City University. He made the move, he says, "partly because the Schweitzer chair offered me more opportunity for my own research and writing and partly, I guess, because I had already lived nearly forty years of my life in Cambridge and felt that the time had come for a change."[20] He has held the same post ever since.

As I have already mentioned, his literary output over these years has been spotty. Perhaps, years from now, it will seem that this decade—from the mid-sixties to the mid-seventies—was a period of great re-evaluation—for Schlesinger, for American liberalism, and for America itself. Unlike Galbraith, his friend and fellow veteran of the ideological wars, Schlesinger never seems altogether independent in his thoughts. He is deeply sensitive to the intellectual atmosphere surrounding him. When he feels a stiff wind at his back, he can ride a fresh idea until spectators have gathered to discover what all the fuss is about. Left alone to argue small points or whip aberrant colleagues into line, he tends toward nervous strain and irritability. Alfred Kazin, observing the liberal *Dioskouren* at a rally for Robert Kennedy's Senate campaign in 1964, noted:

> In public, our Gulliver is always a humorist. He sees life with irony natural to another species. Schlesinger, God knows, does not. New York, at least the West Side of it, irritates him powerfully. "New York intellectuals," though they had gathered to hear him, provoked all his scorn as he lashed "those who had been wrong about Jack Kennedy, and are now wrong about Bobby."[21]

After three years in the White House, and two years spent reliving the three years, Schlesinger found, sadly, that America had

[20] Letter to the author, December 3, 1973.
[21] Alfred Kazin in *New York* magazine, August 1973.

changed. It was not the proud, confident land he had envisioned from his high office. The well-polished phrases about "American purpose" now seemed worn and out of date. The interpretations of right and wrong were subject to new standards. The ideal of service was being discredited by the draft of thousands of young men for duty in Vietnam. Official business was conducted by lying. The citizenry responded by shouting—at officials and at one another. Things seemed to be spinning out of control. By June 1968, in the aftermath of Robert Kennedy's assassination, Schlesinger would ask, "What sort of people are we, we Americans?" And he ventured to say that much of the world might respond that we are "the most frightening people on this planet."

The year 1968 marked the nadir of this mood of despair. The descent began, for Schlesinger as for so many others, with the first Kennedy assassination; Lyndon Johnson's expansion of the Vietnam war accelerated the downward spiral. In the spring of 1966 Schlesinger met for lunch at the Quo Vadis restaurant in New York with Galbraith and Richard Goodwin. In those days a few people considered that the Vietnam war might escalate into the ultimate catastrophe, and it was this unpleasant topic which dominated the table conversation. "Before they left the restaurant each of the three friends promised to do what he could to end the war."[22] The event signaled the end of Lyndon Johnson's support among the liberal intelligentsia. Schlesinger's contribution to the cause was contained in the little book *The Bitter Heritage: Vietnam and American Democracy 1941–1966* (this was the first edition, with succeeding paperback editions carrying the frame of reference up to 1968). From the start, Schlesinger specified his polemical intentions. "Why we are in Vietnam," he wrote, "is today a question of mainly historical interest. We *are* there, for better or for worse, and we must deal with the situation that exists." Unlike those who chanted the glories of Ho Chi Minh, Schlesinger cautioned, "It is important not to become romantic about the Viet Cong. They did not simply represent a movement of rural organization and uplift . . . The systematic murder of village headmen . . . could be an effective weapon, especially when the people of the countryside had been given little reason to pre-

[22] Lewis Chester, Godfrey Hodgson, and Bruce Page, *An American Melodrama*, New York: The Viking Press, 1969, p. 52.

fer the government in Saigon to their own survival." And, on the domestic front, he disdained the inclination to chase after villains. Perhaps this is because in 1961 he had himself recommended to Kennedy that the administration aid President Diem. At the time, Vietnam seemed a minor problem; certainly it is not a dominant subject in *A Thousand Days*. As late as 1965 Schlesinger publicly defended the American intervention. "In retrospect," he now wrote, "Vietnam is the triumph of the politics of inadvertence. We have achieved our present entanglement, not after due and deliberate consideration, but through a series of small decisions. It is not only idle but unfair to seek out guilty men." But he denounced the current strategy, which emphasized heavy bombing raids, as "trying to weed a garden with a bulldozer. We occasionally dig up some weeds, but we dig up most of the turf, too." He feared a revival of McCarthyism due to the strains induced by the war, and here he was certainly prescient, although this time the disease occurred in the form of Watergate. He also detected the misuse of historical analogy, specifically in Dean Rusk's employment of the appeasement of Hitler as a precedent to be avoided in Vietnam. He proposed a "middle course" as a solution—a negotiated settlement of the sort which Nixon and Kissinger eventually achieved, although by that time Schlesinger had accepted the view of presidential candidate George McGovern that the only term for American withdrawal need be the return of American prisoners. His constant interest was "to preserve mutual trust among ourselves as Americans." "The war began as a struggle for the soul of Vietnam: will it end as a struggle for the soul of America?"

The questioning continued in *Crisis of Confidence*. "Heaven knows that Americans have faced tough problems in the last forty years," he wrote, ". . . yet, until recently, we have always felt that our leadership and our resources—moral and psychological as well as economic—were equal to any conceivable challenge. Are we so sure of that now?" By this time the country had endured the tumult of 1967–68, and 1969 was only slightly quieter. The essays in this book were written during that period. Here, as in *The Bitter Heritage*, Schlesinger attempts to poise himself between the rival fanaticisms of Left and Right. The first of the six essays, "Violence as an American Way of Life," is a rather confused meditation which fails to answer the central historical question: how deeply embedded a tradition is violence in America? There are admissions, such as, "Violence, for better or worse, *does* settle some questions, and for the better," with such illustrations as the War for Independence, the freeing of the slaves, and the demise of Hitler; "reason cannot always disentangle the log-jam into which history may thrust the structures of society, nor can it pacify a gangster or placate a madman"; and, "If we are to survive as a community, we must acknowledge the destructive impulse." All sorts of learned authorities are quoted, statistics are cited, and Herbert Marcuse is effectively denounced, but the whole discussion is conducted on an abstract level. We are no better informed on the subject of American violence at the conclusion of this essay than at the start.

The second piece, "The Intellectual and American Society," sketches the history of relations between the men of ideas and the men of power in America. This is a subject on which Schlesinger is one of the world's foremost experts. The chief delight in this essay, however, is the dissection of Dr. Noam Chomsky's opinions concerning American foreign policy. Though he makes his living as a professor and philosopher of linguistics, Dr. Chomsky moonlights as one of the stupidest political analysts in the history of the Republic. It is a good thing to find a liberal who is not afraid to confront this boor with a hatchet. Elsewhere, Schlesinger is less inspiring. He argues, for example, that in the late sixties college students came to constitute a national constituency on a par with farmers and laborers. This is nonsense for many reasons, the most obvious among them being that most students are students for only four years, and laborers and farmers are such for the greater part of adulthood. Returning to his original theme (the essays in *Crisis of Confidence* tend to digression, perhaps because their subjects are a bit vague), Schlesinger concludes that "in a true partnership of ideas and responsibility the intellectual must remember that his abiding obligation is neither to power nor to ideology but to the integrity of reason." If the intellectual can manage this, "he need not fear his capacity to move and live in the world of power."

"The Origins of the Cold War" was originally written for the October 1967 edition of *Foreign Affairs*, which examined Russia

fifty years after its revolution. This is the best essay in the book. It
is also the only one directly concerned with historical matters; the
others utilize history in order to moralize about current events.
Even so, Schlesinger is aware of New Leftists creeping up behind
him, and he denounces those who would blame the Cold War on
American aggression:

> The Cold War could have been avoided only if the Soviet Union
> had not been possessed by convictions both of the infallibility of
> the communist word and of the inevitability of a communist
> world. These convictions transformed an impasse between na-
> tional states into a religious war, a tragedy of possibility into one
> of necessity. One might wish that America had preserved the
> poise and proportion of the first years of the Cold War and had
> not in time succumbed to its own forms of self-righteousness. But
> the most rational of American policies could hardly have averted
> the Cold War. Only today, if Russia begins to recede from its
> messianic mission and to accept, in practice if not yet in princi-
> ple, the permanence of the world of diversity, only now can the
> hope flicker that this long, dreary, costly contest may at last be
> taking on forms less dramatic, less obsessive and less dangerous to
> the future of mankind.

In "Vietnam: Lessons from the Tragedy," he elaborated on the
conclusions of *The Bitter Heritage* and predicted, "In the period
ahead the world will heed America less because of our armed
might than because of our capacity to heal the disruptions and
fulfill the potentialities of the electronic society." In "Joe College,
R.I.P." he appraises the American student in the age of the great
demonstrations. This is done by quoting obscure and sometimes
anonymous specimens, many of whom he has apparently interviewed, and then by drawing generalizations from their remarks.
The result is, in large part, insufferable. For example, Schlesinger
writes that the current wave of youth differs from its parents in
their relationship to violence. "For their parents," he notes, "had
been through depressions, crime waves, riots, and wars; but for
them episodes of violence were still exceptional. For the young, violence has become routine." The standard references are cited:
Hiroshima, Korea, Vietnam. He comments, "The war in Vietnam

seems to them particularly odious and brutalizing." Now this is
surely inconsistent. If violence is so routine, it is not likely that it
will also seem "odious" and "brutalizing"; routine requires acceptance, and it is obvious that we do not rebel against what we accept. There is also the strong presumption in this essay that "the
young" are, in the natural order of things, liberal. It is no doubt
true that highly educated young people are often more idealistic
and less practical than their elders. But it is also true that most
young people are not educated at the universities where Schlesinger conducted his interviews, and that a great many are not at
all highly educated. Among those who are fashioned more or less
in the Schlesinger mold, there is a tendency toward idealism of a
highly self-centered sort; adopting a pet cause becomes part of the
search for identity. It is useful to remember that most of the demonstrations of the late sixties concerned campus issues such as dor-
mitory policy and discounts at the student bookstore. This is
somewhat different from the liberalism practiced by Schlesinger,
who did not howl about the Vietnam war because he was afraid
he might have to fight in it. There are moments when he seems to
sense the difference, as when he writes in conclusion, "One can
hardly doubt that a good many—perhaps most—of these defiant
young people will be absorbed by the System and end living
worthy lives as advertising men or insurance salesmen." But the
primary impression is one of sympathy diffused into muddlehead-
edness.

The final essay in *Crisis of Confidence* discusses "The Prospects for Politics." It is also a botched job in that it disguises
a eulogy for Robert Kennedy as an analysis of current American
politics. There are, as always, some insightful moments, as when
Schlesinger remarks upon the curiosity of Richard Nixon's obsession with his own performance in times of crisis. But mostly he is
interested in arriving at synthetic judgments which are of dubious
value. There is much ponderous discussion, for instance, concerning the "issues" which supposedly divided Eugene McCarthy and
Robert Kennedy in 1968. In fact, the single overwhelming "issue"
which divided them was mutual dislike, and this is not mentioned
at all. In private, Schlesinger did not hesitate to express his view
that McCarthy was a "somewhat indolent and frivolous

man."[23] But in public, through some curious code of political honor, he preferred to invent matters of contention. Indeed, much of "The Prospects for Politics" seems to be written in code language: when Schlesinger starts talking about the reaction of "the intellectuals," the temptation is strong to read this as "a few friends and I."

What is wrong with *Crisis of Confidence?* Basically, it seems that Schlesinger is uncertain of his bearings, and so he loses his co-ordination and adopts the occupational bad habit of historians: the dialectical fiction. We have witnessed another case of this sort in Henry Kissinger, and so it is not necessary to detail every symptom here. In *Crisis of Confidence* there are two very noticeable tendencies: one is the elevation of casual observation to the level of abstraction; the other is the making of too many distinctions, which results in a blurred focus. Historians are inclined to commit these errors simultaneously, much as in baseball a batter who puts his foot "in the bucket" is likely at the same time to spoil his wrist motion. There is an either/or manner of thinking here, even though Schlesinger shies away from either/or solutions. It is true that the historical mind is naturally dialectical. Human experience, in order to be digested, must be organized into strains of development. These lead to contradictions which, if not inevitable, must still be resolved. The attempt to resolve them is the material of history. The problem for the historian arrives when he must decide how to interpret his material. Too much generalization leads to what Schlesinger terms "prophetic history." This is what happens when historians start talking like sociologists. They do this when their intuitions surpass their factual resources. Books like *Crisis of Confidence* result.

Aside from his edition (with F. L. Israel) of a *History of American Presidential Elections,* Schlesinger required four years to publish another book. It is possible that "the crisis of confidence" afflicted him personally more than it did the Republic at large. The assassination of Robert Kennedy was a powerful blow. The presidency of Richard Nixon (for whom, as he wrote, "my enthusiasm has always been well under control") could only be a depressing era for anyone whose liberalism was a way of life, and

[23] This was in a letter to Kennedy written on November 3, 1967, and quoted in Chester et al., *An American Melodrama,* op. cit., p. 114.

who had tasted too much of the high life of poetry and power to share in the exalted self-righteousness of the protesters. His marriage was another casualty of these years, and on November 16, 1970, Arthur and Marian Schlesinger were divorced. Their bond had lasted thirty years.

By the time *The Imperial Presidency* appeared, in the autumn of 1973, there were signs of rejuvenation. Less than a year after his divorce, he had married Alexandra Emmet, a woman young enough to be his daughter. A year later, nearing the age of fifty-five, he found that he was once again a father. The child was named Robert Emmet Kennedy Schlesinger. The McGovern campaign, though it proved disastrous, at least provided Schlesinger with a candidate he could warmly support. The two men were old friends from the Kennedy years, and Schlesinger had written affectionately of McGovern in *A Thousand Days*. And, perhaps not least pleasant, the dissolution of the Nixon presidency began in early 1973. Schlesinger was revealed to be among the people who had earned lasting distinction through their placement on the Nixon "enemies list." By this time work on *The Imperial Presidency* had already begun. Watergate fueled the scholar's fire. The last stages of American involvement in the Indochinese wars had driven Schlesinger to inquire into the warmaking power of American Presidents. The abuse of presidential power under Johnson and Nixon sent him searching for the roots of their evils. "Though such a book inevitably has its topical and polemical aspects," he noted, "I hope this will be taken as a serious historical inquiry."[24] Serious it certainly is, and *The Imperial Presidency* joined several law school textbooks on impeachment as the unlikely best sellers of a season.

This is one of those thick books which rest upon a small set of fairly simple ideas. All of these are set out in the Foreword. "The American Constitution was established," it begins, "for better or worse, on an idea new to the world in the eighteenth century and still uncommon in the twentieth century—the idea of the separation of powers." However, "The Founding Fathers were good Newtonians, and their system of checks and balances, conceived almost as a mechanism, contained an inherent tendency toward inertia." Inevitably, institutions must come into conflict; the sys-

[24] Letter to the author, October 23, 1973.

tem would not work "unless one of the three branches took the initiative." The most effective of these, it was found, was the presidency. But now the presidential power has grown out of all proportion to the intentions of the Founding Fathers and had become dangerous. "In the last years presidential primacy, so indispensable to the political order, has turned into presidential supremacy. The constitutional Presidency—as events so apparently disparate as the Indochina War and the Watergate affair showed—has become the imperial Presidency and threatens to be the revolutionary Presidency." It was particularly in foreign affairs that this inflation was evident. "By the early 1970s the American President had become on issues of war and peace the most absolute monarch (with the possible exception of Mao Tse-tung of China) among the great powers of the world." In correcting this problem, it is important not to weaken the President too much. Again, the value of a "middle ground" is invoked:

> The answer to the runaway Presidency is not the messenger-boy Presidency. The American democracy must discover a middle ground between making the President a czar and making him a puppet. The problem is to devise means of reconciling a strong and purposeful Presidency with equally strong and purposeful forms of democratic control. Or, to put it succinctly, we need a strong Presidency—but a strong Presidency *within* the Constitution.

Over four hundred pages are required for the elaboration of these points. All sorts of historical and legal vignettes are employed in order to fasten down an argument. Here, as never before, Schlesinger sounds truly professorial. The pace is quite leisurely, the author occasionally filling in the blank spaces with personal anecdotes featuring Schlesinger's one-I combinations. There is even a spot of shoptalk here and there, as when Schlesinger devotes several pages to discussion of when presidential documents might best be opened to historians. The book concludes with a chapter on "The Future of the Presidency" in which Schlesinger admits that, all institutional remedies aside, the best way for the American Republic to assure itself of decent presidencies is to elect decent men to the office. There is also an amiable warning to those who might be alive at the end of the first quarter of the next century: they had better be alert for crooks at the top. About every fifty years, it seems, something goes rotten. "This suggests," he writes, "that exposure and retribution inoculate the Presidency against its latent criminal impulses for about half a century. Around the year 2023 the American people would be well advised to go on the alert and start nailing down everything in sight." In contrast to *Crisis of Confidence*, which tries to say too many things on the basis of too little evidence, *The Imperial Presidency* is rich in evidence but does not say all that much. Its essential points are well stated in the Foreword, and they are not of terribly astonishing character. All the same, this is a healthier book than its predecessor. It exhibits few inclinations toward morbid generalization. Its many digressions seem more closely related to Schlesinger's fascination with American history than to any craving for moralistic certitude. There is every sign of an intelligence ready to confront the present and past squarely. These things cannot be said of *Crisis of Confidence*. Even so, it is not certain in *The Imperial Presidency* that the historian of the ages of Jackson and Roosevelt retains the richness of imagination to enable him to resume the glory of former days.

X

The Age of Jackson, The Age of Roosevelt, and *A Thousand Days* speak in confident tones of a nation which Schlesinger thought he understood. It was a nation which displayed every variety of man to the world, and where almost every impulse found its outlet in the political process. Its presidential heroes were brave, confident men who survived the rigors of office to win a lasting place in the affections of the people. They did this by pursuing progressive policies and displaying attractive personalities. The people themselves acquired nobility and grace through the election and support of great men. Together, the citizen and his President (aided by a lusty band of devoted ministers) could crusade against the injustices of the earth. Apart, the people's finer talents were submerged: citizens grew self-indulgent, and in a puritanical land, this most often meant that undue energy was devoted to mere money-making. Such was the myth of Schlesinger's America.

The three post-Kennedy books were written in, and about, a time when such leadership was clearly absent. These books asked questions which Schlesinger-style leadership would tend to squelch: Is there something wrong with the country's character? With its institutions? With its assumptions about itself? These books do not answer those questions, though sometimes they try. Such answers are at best tentative; Schlesinger is still looking for models of great leadership against which he might measure the gabble of the age.

His next book is to be called *Robert Kennedy and His Times*, and will no doubt attempt to restore the grand perspective of the early histories. "This will be in part a biography of Robert Kennedy drawn from his letters and diaries," he writes, "and in part a fresh look at some of the issues of the Kennedy Presidency; it will thus be in a sense a sequel to *A Thousand Days*."[25] It will be interesting to see if this book regains the sweep of the early histories; or if it continues the long, useful, but uninspired arguments of *The Imperial Presidency*; or if it reverts to the sand-castle construction of the worst moments of *A Thousand Days*. It will also be intriguing to discover the degree to which Schlesinger has become the servant of his loyalty. Afterward, he intends to resume *The Age of Roosevelt*. "I am consoled by the memory of my remote ancestor George Bancroft who published the first volume of his *History of the United States* in the 1830s and the last volume in the 1880s."[26] Here we will see how the experiences of the past two decades have changed his perspective on the America of the Roosevelt years.

Meanwhile, nearing his sixtieth year, Schlesinger seems more uncertain of himself and his convictions than when he published his first big book at the end of World War II, or when he went to Washington to work for John Kennedy in 1960, or even when he said farewell to the Kennedy years in *A Thousand Days*. Throughout much of *The Imperial Presidency*, Schlesinger seems to be conducting a discussion with himself on the nature of the presidential myth he has helped to create. He has not, as we have seen,

[25] Letter to the author, March 11, 1975.
[26] Letter to the author, October 25, 1973.

found the reconstruction of the past more compelling than the disputation of current events in recent years. Now he appears eager to complete unfinished business. There is a tension which runs through all of Schlesinger's work, and he is himself aware of it. This concerns the nature of the "tough-minded idealism" on which his generation has prided itself. Inevitably, the toughness and the idealism are bound to conflict. No one who moves freely between the worlds of politics and letters can help contradicting himself. This in large part explains why, in the world of affairs, one's enemies so deeply desire that one will write a book. Authorship sets a man on a higher standard, and men in the unreflective and forgetful world find an easy target at which to aim their slingshots. Likewise, those in the world of books are fond of lowering their noses at those who muddy their hands with the common lot. It is impossible to enter politics without getting a little bit dirty. It is impossible to leave politics without wanting to look clean. So there are times when tough-minded idealists—or "idealists without illusions," as John Kennedy liked to characterize himself—want to sound more tough than idealistic, and vice versa.

A writer of history is a creator of myths. Schlesinger's problem has been less with his personal reputation than with maintaining a vision of history which incorporates the realities of power. Doubt intervenes: is this really the way it was? So he lays aside his creative work and concentrates on the immediate issues which don't require such a long perspective. This is a rather refined version of the dispute between toughness and idealism, but Schlesinger has always exhibited a highly refined talent. It remains to be seen whether he can stay far enough away from politics to write books of enduring value in his final years. At the same time, he must stay close enough to politics to give his books their peculiar, partisan edge. How he might achieve such a balance is unclear to me, but he did it in his early years, and has lost it more recently.

John Kenneth Galbraith

By what rule of historical behavior does it occur that an economist should rank among the finest literary artists of the age? By none, according to those academicians who have spent their careers poring over monographs on *The Waste Land* and *Finnegans Wake* and have ignored the strongest forces currently acting on the American mind. Thus, John Kenneth Galbraith has been ignored in the English departments of our universities. Officially, in the groves of academe, he has been abandoned to the expositors of the dismal science. And his jealous colleagues, watching Galbraith's books ascend the best-seller lists, have addressed his style as if it were something sinful; out of a mixture of professional decency and professorial contempt, they have sought to separate the aphorisms from the ideas.

This cannot be done. When such a style treats such important subject matter, the result is literature. The dictates of professors of English to the contrary, it must be considered in its full dignity. As the great Hippolyte Taine had no difficulty in stuffing a hefty chapter on John Stuart Mill into his *History of English Literature*, so should we not trouble ourselves about setting Galbraith at the front of contemporary American literature. The great mass of American readers understands this, I think, but professors are sometimes a little slow to catch up. In any case, Galbraith is too important to be left to the economists for serious discussion.

II

He is the oldest of our literary politicians. His books are entirely the product of the postwar years, but Galbraith was thirty-seven years old in 1945. His first influential book, *American Capitalism*, was published in 1952. In a country where literary fame tends to strike the young in a blazing moment, only to slip away slowly and tortuously, Galbraith's prominence came later in life and endured.

He was born in 1908 and raised in a community of Scottish-Canadian farmers (they called themselves "Scotch"; Galbraith called his book about them *The Scotch*; and I shall henceforth conform to custom) on the north shore of Lake Erie. According to his son, the senior Galbraith was a man of standing among these people, and was appointed county auditor. In fact, all the Galbraiths were treated as aristocrats in this isolated sect. "We were strongly cautioned against suggesting our superiority," the mature economist recalled, "and, as a youngster, I found this a baffling restraint. For a long while, I swung between disavowing it and apologizing for it." Once freed from the clan, he decided it was better simply to proclaim it. The Galbraiths were tall men, and this was important in establishing their superiority. Later in life, grown to six feet eight inches, Galbraith congratulated himself and composed a maxim: "The superior confidence which people repose in the tall man is well merited. Being tall, he is more visible than other men and being more visible, he is more closely watched. In consequence, his behavior is far better than that of smaller men." (General Charles de Gaulle was much taken with this pronouncement, and added ominously, "It is important that we be merciless with those who are too small.")

Father introduced son to humor and politics. When John Kenneth was six, the older Galbraith brought him along to a bucolic political rally. He began his speech by mounting a manure pile, and promptly apologized for speaking from the Tory platform. Like all the Scotch farmers, the Galbraiths were Liberals. This was mainly because the nearby townspeople were mostly Tories. They were also of English extraction. Friction was intensified among the young Scotch by their schooling, which took place in town. Galbraith's recollection of his high school principal clarifies his feelings about one caste of men: "In any calling Old Tommy would have been counted a man of remarkable ignorance but as an educator he excelled." Between the Scotch and the English,

> Mostly the conflict resolved itself, as most such conflicts do, into a difference of opinion as to who was superior. The Scotch believed, I have always thought rightly, that they were. They considered agriculture an inherently superior vocation. It placed a man in his fit relation to nature; it abjured the artificialities of urban existence. It gave him peace and independence. It was morally superior for it required manual labor. The finest aphorism of the Scotch was: "A good man wasn't afraid of work." Not one of them believed that clerking in a store or weighing in at an elevator was work.

The Scotch love of money also assisted in the breeding of an economist. "This was, I think, pure love. Some have always wanted money for what it would buy. Some have wanted it for the power it conferred. Some have sought it for the prestige it provided. The Scotch wanted it for its own sake." Sexual frolicking among the Scotch was inhibited by the climate and the nosy neighbors. But "the love of money meant that a man's emotions were reliably engaged until the day he died." So the cant of more sophisticated men would in time meet with at least one skeptical listener.

Young John Kenneth was thus raised in humble (if not humbling) circumstances, doing the chores expected of a farmer's son. He may think that this mode of life was morally superior; he has not, however, stated whether or not he found it pleasant. Years later, having gained much esteem through his writings, he returned home for a gathering of the clan. "Most asked me whether, in all my travels, I had found a place as good as this. I said no for this could have been the truth and, when I faced up to it, I found I did not wish to have people think me irresponsible." (A few months later President Kennedy appointed Galbraith to a high diplomatic post, perhaps in recognition that such talent for hedging should not go unused.) He was reared as a Baptist, and lost his faith at an early age. The sermons of the local elder were excruciatingly boring, and left deep scars. "For thirty years I have not been in a church for other than architectural reasons or to witness a marriage or funeral," he wrote in 1964, "and it is partly because I associate them to this day with torture." He adopted the habit of reading books, and made himself a slightly suspect young man. The novels of Anatole France helped guide him through the perils of puberty. These "made unlicensed sexual transactions, especially if blessed by deep affection and profound mutual understanding, seem much more defensible than I had previously been allowed to suppose." One summer young Galbraith found himself deeply in love with "a compact golden-haired girl." Upon an afternoon the two of them walked out into the fields and observed a bull serving a heifer. "I think it would be fun to do that," said John Kenneth; his inamorata replied, "Well, it's your cow." He matriculated at the Ontario Agricultural College at Guelph. Here,

> leadership in the student body was solidly in the hands of those who combined an outgoing anti-intellectualism with a sound interest in livestock. This the faculty thought right. Anyone who questioned the established agricultural truths, many of which were wildly wrong, was sharply rebuked and if he offended too often he was marked down as a troublemaker.

Galbraith does not say so, but we may safely assume that he was marked down as a troublemaker. After four years of unsound instruction in animal husbandry and related crafts, aged twenty-two, he departed Ontario for the University of California at Berkeley. Earning $720 annually as a research assistant in agricultural economics, he found himself enchanted. "At Berkeley I suddenly encountered professors who knew their subject and, paradoxically, invited debate on what they knew." Student life was also more interesting:

> The graduate students with whom I associated in the thirties were uniformly radical and the most distinguished were Communists. I listened to them eagerly and would like to have joined both the conversation and the Party but here my agricultural

background was a real handicap. It meant that, as a matter of formal Marxian doctrine, I was politically immature. Among the merits of capitalism to Marx was the fact that it rescued men from the idiocy of rural life. I had only very recently been retrieved. I sensed this bar and I knew also that my pride would be deeply hurt by rejection. So I kept outside. There was possibly one other factor. Although I recognized that the system could not and should not survive, I was enjoying it so much that, secretly, I was a little sorry.

There was time to have fun—or at least so it seemed until one girl doing graduate work in anthropology asked Galbraith, on their second or third date, "if I thought it right, as an economist, to be wasting both her time and mine. Nothing in my Canadian or Calvinist background had prepared me for such a personal concept of efficiency."

In 1933 he completed his doctorate in agricultural economics, and the following year moved to Harvard as an instructor. He absorbed the new Keynesian theories, as expounded by Professor Alvin Hansen and Professor Seymour Harris. In 1936 he crossed the Atlantic for a year's study of Keynes at closer range (though the two men did not meet until several years later). His economic interests broadened. Back at Harvard, Galbraith and H. S. Dennison combined to publish *Modern Competition and Business Policy* in 1938. According to at least one critic, the book "adumbrates some of Galbraith's later views"[1] in its skepticism toward the competitive model of the economy and the anti-trust laws. In 1939 he moved to Princeton in order to teach there, but found himself accepting several assignments from the government. When World War II broke out, he became Franklin Roosevelt's deputy administrator of the Office of Price Administration. Eventually his staff grew to sixteen thousand. He endured the taunts which would come the way of any price fixer. In 1943 he resigned, without any discouragement from Roosevelt. The experience not only failed to leave him disconsolate, Galbraith emerged with a

[1] Charles H. Hession, *John Kenneth Galbraith and His Critics*, New York: Mentor Books, 1972 (paperback), p. 24. This is an enormously useful book for any student of Galbraith's writings, particularly *American Capitalism*, *The Affluent Society*, and *The New Industrial State*.

heightened respect for the fixer's role, and began to think about how it might be engaged in peacetime. Too tall to join the Army, he took a job as staff writer for *Fortune* magazine. Galbraith credits Henry Luce with teaching him how to write, but surely he learned a few things on his own; his mature style is leaner, wittier, and more precise than anything to emerge from the offices of Time, Inc. In 1944 Galbraith returned to the government as a director of the United States Strategic Bombing Survey, organized by Roosevelt to allay his suspicions about the glowing reports generals were sending him about their own achievements. In this capacity he interviewed Albert Speer, among others, providing the material for an excellent retrospective essay when Speer's *Inside the Third Reich* appeared a quarter century later. After the war he returned to *Fortune,* where he stayed until 1949, when Harvard offered, and Galbraith accepted, a professorship in economics. He stayed there until his retirement in 1975.

In the late thirties he had married, apparently finding at last a lady whose wit could not thwart his intentions. She was Catherine Atwater, daughter of a New York family, Smith College valedictorian, and future professor of German at Radcliffe.

His economic ideas began to assume an original form in the postwar years. Galbraith had quickly earned distinction (or notoriety) as one of the "young Keynesians," helping to write a book entitled *Toward Full Employment.* It is questionable, however, whether or not he should be classified among the "feverish Harvard acolytes" of the late thirties, in William F. Buckley, Jr.'s description. By his own account, Galbraith quickly realized that Keynesian theory may do wonders for depressions, but offers little insight into the causes of, or remedies for, inflation. Galbraith surveyed developments in the wartime scholarship on "Monopoly and the Concentration of Economic Power" for the American Economic Association. According to Charles Hession, "His assessment of this subject was thorough, provocative, and in accordance with the highest standards of the profession."[2] He also published his "Reflections on Price Control," which included a report on "The Disequilibrium System." These last two were combined with fresh material to make *The Theory of Price Control,*

[2] Ibid., p. 25.

published in 1951. Its reception recalled that given David Hume's *Treatise of Human Nature*, of which the author noted, "It fell dead-born from the press, without reaching such distinction as even to excite a murmur among the zealots." Galbraith was embittered. Years later he said:

> I think most people who have read it would say that it is the best book I have ever written.[3] The only difficulty is that five people read it. Maybe ten. I made up my mind that I would never again place myself at the mercy of the technical economists who had the enormous power to ignore what I had written. I set out to involve a larger community . . . I would involve economists by having the larger public say to them, "Where do you stand on Galbraith's idea of price control?" They would *have* to confront what I said.[4]

He summoned his powers, and the next year issued *American Capitalism*. Half of literate America read the book; some economists read it, too. Six years later came *The Affluent Society*, which respectable academicians found they could not ignore. Galbraith rose to international fame. Nine years passed amid diplomacy and politics. *The New Industrial State* (1967) became the most celebrated and defamed of all Galbraith's books. Six years later, the aging theoretician announced that he had brought his system to completion, and would henceforth spend his energies on less taxing problems. *Economics and Public Purpose* (1973) thus became the coda of Galbraithian economics. It is reasonable to suppose that this matinée idol among figure filberts will favor us with a succession of farewell tours. Already, in *Money: Whence It Came, Where It Went* (1975), we find him flexing some of his earlier arguments. Even so, the core of his system remains in place, and is likely to stay so until the end of Galbraith's days. I am pledged to assess Galbraith the writer, not merely Galbraith the economist, and therefore it is best to summarize and analyze his system as a whole, rather than try to set each book in chrono-

[3] At least one sympathetic student of Galbraith, Myron E. Sharpe, agrees in *John Kenneth Galbraith and Lower Economics*, White Plains: International Arts and Sciences Press, 1973.
[4] Quoted in Hession, op. cit., p. 25.

logical order, alongside novels, satires, diaries, and polemics. There are changes from one book to the next, and I shall try to note them; it is too much to expect any man to hold to every aspect of a theory of worldly affairs for two decades; it is probably not desirable that he should do so—at least not if he professes to skepticism toward all established truths.

III

Galbraith, according to Myron Sharpe, is a "revolutionary in economics because he is not simply dissatisfied with this or that aspect of theory, but with its very core. His analytical starting point is the opposite from neoclassical theory. He begins with planning, not the market; the large firm, not the small; producer sovereignty, not consumer; the composition of output, not its magnitude."[5] In his first major book, however, he was less dissatisfied than later. "The task of *American Capitalism* is to explain why it works; the task of subsequent books is to explain why it fails."[6] It is worth quoting the opening of this book at the start of our survey, if only to illustrate the amiable skepticism with which all of Galbraith's ideas are presented:

> It is told that such are the aerodynamics and wing-loading of the bumblebee that, in principle, it cannot fly. It does, and the knowledge that it defies the august authority of Isaac Newton and Orville Wright must keep the bee in constant fear of a crackup. One can assume, in addition, that it is apprehensive of the matriarchy to which it is subject, for this is known to be an oppressive form of government. The bumblebee is a successful but an insecure insect. If all this is true, and its standing in physics and entomology is perhaps not of the highest, life among the bumblebees must bear a remarkable resemblance to life in the United States.

Everyone argues that the American economy is a fragile and crumbling thing, and yet no one disputes that the performance of

[5] Sharpe, op. cit., p. 77.
[6] Ibid.

the economy since World War II has been excellent. "It was the ideas which were the source of the insecurity—the insecurity of illusion." Liberals and conservatives alike uphold a "competitive model" of the economy which does not in fact apply—conservatives through their espousal of laissez faire, liberals through their trust in anti-trust. If these are the ideals which are cherished, it is no wonder that the economy seems in such bad shape: the ideals have no relation to the present reality, nor to any possible reality of the future. Among large firms, price competition has all but disappeared.

> With price competition ruled out, competitive energies are normally concentrated on persuasion and, especially in consumers' goods, on salesmanship and advertising . . . This is competition but no longer the kind of competition that is eligible for the liberal's defense. On the contrary, the very instrument which once rewarded the community with lower prices and greater efficiency now turns up assailing its ear with rhymed commercials and soap opera and rendering the country-side hideous with commercial art. Competition becomes an exercise in uniquely ostentatious waste. What hath Adam Smith wrought?

Meanwhile liberals, trained to seek out and destroy monopoly, are left helpless by the pervasive presence of oligopoly (i.e., the domination of the market by a few firms). "The liberal, who still searches for old-fashioned monopoly in the modern economy, has been made to feel that his is a search for poison ivy in a field of poison oak." Everyone suffers from what Galbraith terms "the Depression psychosis." The fear and expectation of Depression has become, on the basis of experience, a normal aspect of peacetime life; hence, the great quarrels over Keynes, the doctor of depressions. Likewise, the meaning of the term "Keynesian" has taken on a peculiar connotation in the heat of the moment: "It is always for his prodigality that a man is known—Henry VIII for his wives, Louis XV for his mistresses and General Douglas MacArthur for his prose. The Keynesian has been forever associated with public spending."

How many of these notions are correct? Galbraith dispenses with one problem of analysis:

Pessimism in our time is infinitely more respectable than optimism: the man who foresees peace, prosperity, and a decline in juvenile delinquency is a negligent and vacuous fellow. The man who foresees trouble—except perhaps on the stock market—has a gift of insight which insures that he will become a radio commentator, and editor of *Time* or go to Congress. Recognizing the risks in running counter to our national preference for gloom, it may still be worth while to inquire why the years of peace after World War II proved tolerable.

Too many myths obstruct understanding. "There is no more pleasant fiction than that technical change is the product of the matchless ingenuity of the small man forced by competition to employ his wits to better his neighbor. Unhappily, it is a fiction. Technical development has long since become the preserve of the scientist and the engineer." This means that it occurs only in large firms with substantial resources of capital. "The market concentration of American industry that is affirmed by the statistics and condemned by the competitive model turns out on closer examination to be favorable to technical change." No one would really want the competitive ideal. The importance of salesmanship and advertising in spurring the economy have been underrated; this is because they are by-products of opulence, and it violates the puritanical conscience to admit to great wealth. "It is permissible to concede, even with a certain amount of pride, that the United States is a wealthy country. But to conclude that in peacetime this opulence excuses a certain amount of social waste is to invite the divine fury that immolated Sodom and Gomorrah." Yet, it is national wealth which provides for a margin of error in national economic policy, and it is wealth which permits us to elevate the unfortunate from their station without causing undue strain on the lives of the prosperous.

The balancing forces brought to bear on the economy are summed up by Galbraith in the term "countervailing power"; specifically, these are seen as restraints on private power. Countervailing power acts as a "counterpart of competition." At the same time, it is something more than the state's enhanced ability to regulate the affairs of great corporations—though this is not to be discounted. The rise of large retail chains is an example of countervailing power. These firms (to be found, for example, among food and department stores) are powerful enough to restrain the pricing power of suppliers. As a rule, wherever the American economy is most progressive and prosperous is where such firms have become prominent. Their absence in the housing industry explains the poor performance of that sector of the economy. "What is needed," Galbraith writes, "is fewer firms of far greater scale with resulting capacity to bring power to bear upon unions and suppliers." At times when demand is limited and "not pressing upon capacity," in industries where management and labor both are strong, countervailing power may be seen in the union's insistence on wage increases and in management's resistance:

> When demand is limited, we have, in other words, an essentially healthy manifestation of countervailing power. The union opposes its power as a seller of labor to that of the management as a buyer: principally at stake is the division of returns. An occasional strike is an indication that countervailing power is being employed in a sound context where the costs of any wage increase cannot readily be passed along to someone else. It should be an occasion for mild rejoicing in the conservative press. The *Daily Worker*, eagerly contemplating the downfall of capitalism, should regret this manifestation of the continued health of the system.

But when demand presses industry to full capacity, and the firm's advantage in resisting wage increases is offset by the disadvantage of a strike, the resistance is dropped. Countervailing power is dissolved. The inflationary spiral—wages chasing prices chasing wages, etc.—begins.

Countervailing power does not always result in a reduction of prices for the consumer; most notably, as the lot of farmers and laborers has improved, prices have risen. But, by strengthening the bargaining position of laborers and subsidizing farmers, a certain "social serenity" is achieved. The importance of this should not be dismissed. Nevertheless, it is a debatable point, and should be expected to dominate American political discussion for some time. "Liberalism will be identified with the buttressing of weak bargaining positions in the economy; conservatism—and this may well be its proper function—will be identified with the protection of positions of original power . . . On the whole, the appearance of countervailing power as a political issue cannot be considered especially unhealthy although it almost certainly will be so regarded." The cases for and against increased public regulation of industry will assume a more realistic character. The incantations of Socialists and free-enterprisers will become rarer. Thus Galbraith may argue:

> Although little cited, even by conservatives, administrative considerations now provide capitalism with by far its strongest defense against detailed interference with private business decision. To put the matter bluntly, in a parliamentary democracy with a high standard of living there is no alternative to the decision-making mechanism of capitalism. No method of comparable effectiveness is available to decentralize authority over final decisions.

. . . and at the same time urge the public sector to take the lead in those areas of the economy where private capitalism is not working. *American Capitalism* closes on a note of warning. The postwar economy, Galbraith writes, had been so successful because policy had been guided by the fear of another Depression. "For years we have talked of the virtues of confidence. In fact, we have been blessed by the fruits of caution. But this is a wasting resource. With time and prosperity the fear of depression is bound to fade." The greatest risk is now inflation. "Nothing so develops the latent fatuousness in a community as a speculative boom." Capitalism being "an arrangement for getting a considerable decentralization in economic decision," inflation threatens capitalism by compelling centralized authority over wages and prices. This has already happened in wartime; it may now occur in peacetime. Galbraith does not yet advocate the implementation of such controls, but he counsels that circumstances may force them into existence. Conservatives have worried about the Keynesian antidepression policies, but these have "little effect on essentials. Boom and inflation, in our time, are the proper focus of conservative fears."

This worry, however, is not central to the argument of *American Capitalism*. Despite all of Galbraith's pinpricks, the book offers a pleasant and well-tempered account of how well things are working. Now, according to Myron Sharpe, "The whole tidy world of *American Capitalism* comes apart at the seams in *The Affluent Society.*" This is an exaggeration; few arguments in the later book would shock the reader of the earlier; in many respects *The Affluent Society* draws out and elaborates the latencies in *American Capitalism.* Each book reflects the time in which it was composed: *American Capitalism* while the Democrats held power under Truman, *The Affluent Society* while Eisenhower was President. As Galbraith puts it, certain ideas which had attracted or repelled him for some time now seemed ripe for examination:

> They were ideas, both the market revival and the Keynesian pre-
> occupation with employment *qua* employment and production *qua*
> production, that seemed to me damaging. As the Eisenhower ad-
> ministration ensconced itself in Washington after 1953, I set to
> work on the opposing case. Among the largely unnoticed contri-
> butions of Republican administrations is that to scholarship or any-
> how writing. It comes about from not employing the scholars or
> scribes.

The book opens with typical irony: "Wealth is not without its advantages and the case to the contrary, although it has often been made, has never proved widely persuasive." Throughout history most nations have been quite poor. Now the United States has emerged as the richest nation in the world, an "affluent society." Economic thought, however, is still based on the experience of those days when mankind was relatively impoverished.

"The rich man who deludes himself into behaving like a mendicant may conserve his fortune although he will not be very happy. The affluent country which conducts its affairs in accordance with the rules of another and poorer age also forgoes opportunities. And in misunderstanding itself, it will, in any time of difficulty, implacably prescribe for itself the wrong remedies." Galbraith coins the term "conventional wisdom" in order to describe the illusions under which economic thought labors. "Ideas come to be organized around what the community as a whole or particular audiences find acceptable . . . A 'good liberal' or a 'tried and true' liberal or a 'true blue' liberal is one who is adequately predict-able." "The enemy of the conventional wisdom is not ideas but the march of events." Galbraith intends to beat the drums in this big parade.

A brief history of economic ideas is introduced, with emphasis on the "tradition of despair"—the tendency of economists to think ill of the prospects of the common man. There is a brief digression on Marxism which earned Galbraith few friendships with his brothers on the left. What is the cause of the Marxian attraction to intellectuals? "Much of Marx's strength has always been in the contention of his followers that those who thought him wrong were really themselves obtuse, simple- or literal-minded. These are terrible charges; innumerable intellectuals have been unwilling to risk them." The sum of all creeds of economic thought until the 1930s "could not but leave a man with a sense of the depth, pervasiveness and burden of the economic problem and, on the whole, with the improbability of a happy outcome."

But one of the prime symptoms of the current condition is the *lack* of interest in economic inequality. It must be that wealth is being fairly equitably distributed, since "to comment on the wealth of the wealthy, and certainly to propose that it be reduced, has come to be considered bad taste. The individual whose own income is going up has no real reason to incur the opprobrium of this discussion. Why should he identify himself, even remotely, with soapbox orators, malcontents, agitators, communists, and other undesirables?" There are three basic benefits from wealth. "First is the satisfaction in the power with which it endows the individual. Second is that in the physical possession of the things which money can buy. Third is the distinction or esteem that accrues to the rich man as the result of his wealth." In the last fifty years, these "returns to wealth have been greatly circumscribed" and in such a manner that envy and resentment have been minimized. With a few exceptions, the rich do not run the great business concerns any more; these have been taken over by a new class of managers. Thus the first benefit of wealth has disappeared. As for the second, "The enjoyment of physical possession of things would seem to be one of the prerogatives of wealth which has been little impaired . . . But enjoyment of things has always been intimately associated with the third prerogative of wealth which is the distinction it confers. In a world where nearly everyone was poor, the distinction was very great . . . As the rich have become more numerous, they have inevitably become a debased currency." "Prestige and power" are now in the hands of the high corporate official, who is "inevitably a man of consequence. The rich man can be quite inconsequential and often is." The issue of economic security is another one to which the competitive model is inapplicable. It is believed by those who lead cheers for the free market that insecurity is a necessary component of the economic system. Wages must waver and prices must leap and fall; this is the means of progress. Yet, in recent decades, all movement has been toward insuring the economy with higher degrees of security—pension plans, Social Security, unemployment compensation, etc.—and progress has not suffered. Productivity has expanded beyond the dreams of past generations:

> Why is it that as production has increased in modern times concern for production has also increased? Production has become the center of a concern that had hitherto been shared with equality and security. For these reasons . . . it has managed at least superficially to retain the prestige which inevitably it had in the poor world of Ricardo.

This is both irrational and wrong. In calculating the Gross National Product, "No distinction is made between public and privately produced services. An increased supply of educational services has a standing in the total not different in kind from an increased output in television receivers." At the same time, the conventional wisdom looks upon any increase in the production of private services—say, automobiles and television sets—as inherently a good thing, while any increase in public services is borne as a burden. Yet, "Our preoccupation with production . . . may be a preoccupation with a problem of rather low urgency." In a commercial world where the exchange of goods requires the heavy employment of advertising, the goods must be of marginal importance. A hungry man need not be exhorted to buy a loaf of bread. There is an "elaborate myth with which we surround the demand for goods. This has enabled us to become persuaded of the dire importance of the goods we have without our being in the slightest degree concerned about these we do not have. For we have wants at the margin only so far as they are synthesized. We do not manufacture wants for goods we do not produce."

> Because the society sets great store by ability to produce a high living standard, it evaluates people by the products they possess. The urge to consume is fathered by the value system which emphasizes the ability of the society to produce. The more that is produced, the more that must be owned in order to maintain the appropriate prestige.

And "if production is to increase, the wants must be effectively contrived." Meanwhile, public services decline, since according to the conventional wisdom, "The individual has an instinct for good living that should be encouraged; the government for prodigality against which all must be protected."

Economically, the bane of affluence is inflation. Here Galbraith offers an expansion of the warning voiced in *American Capitalism*. Wages affect prices, which in turn force wages to increase. This especially affects the economic health of people on pensions and fixed incomes; small businessmen are also adversely affected. The large unions and corporations which negotiate the wage settlement and set prices fare better for a while. Eventually, these also suffer as high prices curtail demand, forcing management to reduce production and lay off workers. The economy is thrown into recession, for which the advised cure is increased production; the wage-price spiral resumes; the problem of inflation persists. Efforts to assist recovery through prudent management of the money supply are dubious. "There is no magic in the monetary system, however brilliantly or esoterically administered, which can reconcile price stability with the imperatives of production and employment as they are regarded in the affluent society. On the contrary, monetary policy is a blunt, unreliable, discriminatory and somewhat dangerous instrument of economic control." It favors those who need its help least; the great corporations are able to invest their own profits, while the small-business men, builders, and farmers who must borrow from banks are already the ones suffering most from inflation. "We are impelled by present attitudes and goals to seek to operate the economy at capacity where, we have seen, inflation must be regarded not as an abnormal but as a normal prospect." So long as increased productivity is the main goal of economic policy, perpetual inflation is inevitable, and the means for its prevention are denied. Galbraith now directly advocates the implementation of wage and price controls in those sectors of the economy where the wage-price spiral is evident.

"The final problem of the productive society is what it produces," begins the chapter on "The Theory of Social Balance." Shortly thereafter appears what is probably the most famous paragraph in *The Affluent Society:*

> The family which takes its mauve and cerise, air-conditioned, power-steered and power-braked automobile out for a tour passes through cities that are badly paved, made hideous by litter, blighted buildings, billboards and posts for wires that should long since have been put underground. They pass on into a countryside that has been rendered largely invisible by commercial art. (The goods which the latter advertise have an absolute priority in our value system. Such aesthetic considerations as a view of the countryside accordingly come second. On such matters, we are consistent.) They picnic on exquisitely packaged food from a portable icebox by a polluted stream and go on to spend the night at a park which is a menace to public health and morals. Just before dozing off on an air mattress, beneath a nylon tent, amid the stench of decaying refuse, they may reflect vaguely on the curious unevenness of their blessings. Is this, indeed, the American genius?

People consume more and discard more; appropriate sanitation services must be provided. "The greater the wealth, the thicker will be the dirt." In a city such as Los Angeles, people for many years consumed goods in large quantities, and yet denied themselves a municipal trash collection service. So they burned rubbish in incinerators at home, and the air became unbreathable a large portion of each year. This represents what Galbraith terms "the problem of social balance"—so much attention is given to private production that public needs are either ignored or inadequate. In communities where schools are insufficiently financed, the quality of education tends to be poor. "Schools do not compete with television and the movies. The dubious heroes of the latter, not Miss Jones, become the idols of the young. The hot rod and wild ride take the place of more sedentary sports for which there are inadequate facilities or provision." "The scientist or engineer or advertising man who devotes himself to developing a new carburetor, cleanser or depilatory for which the public recognizes no need and will feel none until an advertising campaign arouses it, is one of the valued members of our society. A politician or a public servant who dreams up a new public service is a wastrel. Few public offenses are more reprehensible." It is no accident that the quality of the public services has declined since inflation became endemic to the economic system; indeed, "Discrimination against the public services is an organic feature of inflation." And whenever the rate of economic growth slows down, the first proposal of those who espouse the conventional wisdom is that taxes be reduced and public expenditures curtailed.

What is to be done? To start with, change should be accepted as a fact of life. This is not likely to happen, however, as "it would destroy an engaging, almost Oriental, quality of our political life which leads us to drape the urgencies of the present in the symbols of the past. Though production has receded in importance, we shall doubtless continue to pretend it isn't so." Yet, "Much more than decisions on economic policy are involved. A system of morality is at stake." Full employment must cease to be the primary aim of economic policy; social balance should replace it. Unemployment compensation should be made adequate, in order to care for people who are unable or incapable of finding jobs; these people should not be looked upon as insidious idlers, but should be recognized as being, in the main, victims of circumstances under which they have minimal control. Their compensation should not, in any case, become so substantial as to discourage them from seeking work. In regard to public services, it should be seen that "to a far greater degree than is commonly supposed, functions accrue to the state because, as a purely technical matter, there is no alternative to public management." An automatic pro rata share of increasing income should be made available "to public authority for public purposes"; this means a revision of the tax code, but, "Schools and roads will then no longer be at a disadvantage as compared with automobiles and television sets in having to prove absolute justification." "So long as social balance is imperfect, there should be no hesitation in urging high [sales tax] rates" in states and localities; this may not impress liberals as the best way to do things, but it is better than the current stalemate over which form of taxation is fairest:

> Thus does affluence alter the case against sales taxation. It will be argued that some people are still very poor. The sales tax, unlike the income tax, weighs heavily on the small consumption of such individuals. But if the income tax is unavailable or in service of other ends, the only alternative is to sacrifice social balance. A poor society rightly adjusts its policy to the poor. An affluent society may properly inquire whether, instead, it shouldn't remove the poverty . . . moreover, increased social balance is one of the first requisites for the elimination of poverty. The modern liberal rallies to protect the poor from the taxes which in the next generation, as the result of a higher investment in their children, would help eliminate poverty.

Finally, "the greatest prospect that we face . . . is to eliminate toil as a required economic institution." In large part, this has been accomplished. Work is now something which is supposed to be enjoyable, as well as profitable. People have more leisure time. It is to be hoped that they will use this time wisely. This is more likely to occur if expenditures become more generous in the public services, most notably education:

> To furnish a barren room is one thing. To continue to crowd in furniture until the foundation buckles is quite another. To have failed to solve the problem of producing goods would have been to continue man in his oldest and most grievous misfortune. But to fail to see that we have solved it, and to fail to proceed thence to the next task, would be fully tragic.

In the last stages of writing *The Affluent Society*, Galbraith found, "Presently another and larger world began obtruding itself on my thoughts. This was a world of great corporations in which people increasingly served the convenience of these organizations which were meant to serve *them*." Many characteristics and relationships seemed imperfectly related to their depictions in economic textbooks. A preliminary draft of the new book was completed when President Kennedy summoned Galbraith to his country's service. Before assuming his position as Ambassador to India, "with some misgiving," he put the manuscript in a bank vault. "I worried lest the world were exchanging an irreplaceable author for a more easily purchasable diplomat." But while in India his thoughts matured; by the time *The New Industrial State* was published in 1967, his concern seemed poorly founded. He advised, "Let every writer, if he cannot arrange a tour as ambassador before publishing, at least take a long reflective holiday." His new book now appeared related to *The Affluent Society* "as a house to a window. This is the structure; the earlier book allowed the first glimpse inside." (The Preface to *Economics and Public Purpose*, six years later, would say much the same thing concerning *The New Industrial State*.) *The New Industrial State* benefited from its opposition to the current order, in this case meaning Lyndon Johnson and the American involvement in Vietnam. Had Galbraith published it when things were running fairly well, its indictment would not have been so sharp.

It begins with a chapter on the role of change in what is termed "the industrial system." (Others might call it the "corporate world" or the "corporate state" or something else depending on the pleasant or sinister connotation they wish to evoke; Galbraith seems bland enough and eminently fair in his terminology, if indeed it might not be said that "the industrial system" is a solid, affirmative-sounding phrase.) Change "is imagined to be very great; to list its forms or emphasize its extent is to show a reassuring grip on the commonplace." Yet "the economic system of the United States is praised on all occasions of public ceremony as a largely perfect structure . . . It is not easy to perfect what has been perfected." So this book becomes an effort to resolve the paradox:

I am concerned to show how, in this larger context of Change, the forces inducing human effort have changed. This assaults the most majestic of all economic assumptions, namely that man in his economic activities is subject to the authority of the market. Instead, we have an economic system which, whatever its formal ideological billing, is in substantial part a planned economy.

The consumer is not sovereign; rather, the authoritative force is "the great producing organization which reaches forward to control the markets that it is presumed to serve and, beyond, to bend the customer to its needs." Technology, as it has grown more sophisticated, has led to more planning. "But technology not only causes change, it is a response to change. Though it forces specialization it is also a response to specialization." So the great corporation learns that "it must exercise control over what is sold. It must exercise control over what is supplied. It must replace the market with planning." Because it is large enough to absorb the occasional planning failure, the great corporation is able to regulate its prices. Also because of its size, it is able to control its capital supply. As great corporations occasionally save too much, the economy is subject to periodic recessions and the intervention of the government. Power, meanwhile, has passed to an "association of men of diverse technical knowledge, experience or other talent which modern industrial technology and planning require. It extends from the leadership of the modern industrial enterprise down to just short of the labor force and embraces a large number of people and a variety of talent." Galbraith terms it the "technostructure." Innovations and decisions take place in groups. Too much indvidual power may render the group ineffective; thus the Ford Motor Company, after it had grown to maturity, was severely. hampered and nearly destroyed by the senior Henry Ford. What is best for the company in its youthful, or entrepreneurial, stage, is unacceptable in maturity. Galbraith interjects a note of caution, aimed at those who presume all corporations to be alike:

. . . there is no such thing as *a* corporation. Rather there are several kinds of corporations all deriving from a common but very loose framework. Some are subject to the market; others respect varying degrees of adaptation to the requirements of planning and the needs of the technostructure. The person who sets out to study buildings in Manhattan on the assumption that all are alike will have difficulty in passing from the surviving brownstones to the skyscrapers. And he will handicap himself even more if he imagines that all buildings should be brownstones and have load-carrying walls and that others are abnormal. So with corporations.

The great corporations are distinguished by their large size, by their oligopolistic position, and by the autonomy of their techno-structures. Stockholders, though they are often invoked as the in-spiration behind price increases, have no power at all. Boards of di-rectors are controlled by management. Losses are an infrequent occurrence, considering that ours is said to be a profit-and-loss economy. The controlling mechanism of the market is replaced by planning. "Prices, costs, production, and resulting revenues are es-tablished not by the market but, within broad limits . . . by the planning decisions of the firm." Though it is regularly proclaimed by corporate officers that the firm's aim is to maximize profits and reward stockholders, this is not the case. Were it so, it would require a most unusual psychology, which Galbraith examines:

> The members of the technostructure do not get the profits that they maximize. They must eschew personal profit-making. Accord-ingly, if the traditional commitment to profit maximization is to be upheld, they must be willing to do for others, specifically the stockholders, what they are forbidden to do for themselves. It is on such grounds that the doctrine of maximization in the mature corporation now rests. It holds that the will to make profits is, like the will to sexual expression, a fundamental urge. But it holds that this urge operates not in the first person but the third. It is de-tached from self and manifested on behalf of unknown, anonymous and powerless persons who do not have the slightest notion of whether their profits are, in fact, being maximized. In further anal-ogy to sex, one must imagine that a man of vigorous, lusty and reassuringly heterosexual inclination eschews the lovely, available and even naked women by whom he is intimately surrounded in order to maximize the opportunities of other men whose exist-ence he knows of only by hearsay. Such are the foundations of the maximization doctrine when there is full separation of power from reward.

What really interests the technostructure is the preservation and enhancement of its own power. Members of the technostructure seek to identify themselves with the technostructure's goals, and in turn, adapt the technostructure to their personal goals. "Above a certain level these may operate independently of income." Identification helps to motivate men for obvious reasons. "The organization man has been a subject of much sorrow. But all who weep should recall that he surrenders himself to organization because organization does more for him than he can do for himself." As an example, "The question automatically asked when two men meet on a plane or in Florida is, 'Who are you with?' Until this is known, the individual is a cipher. He cannot be placed in the scheme of things; no one knows how much attention, let alone respect, he deserves or whether he is worthy of any notice at all." And adaptation is strongest as a motive when the individual is closest to the center of power. "To the desire of the individual to mold the world to his goals, a thoughtful Providence has added the illusion of a great ability to do so."

As the individual relates to the technostructure, so the technostructure relates to the society. The technostructure is convinced that its desires are those of the society, and that, therefore, what is good for the company is good for America. Prices are set not by the violation of anti-trust laws, but by the firm's careful study of its few competitors in an oligopolistic market. This allows the arrangement of common prices in a courteous and legal manner. Demand is managed through heavy investment in advertising. The consumer may think that he is paying his money and taking his choice, "But this is superficial and proximate, the result of illusions created in connection with the management of his wants." "It is possible that people need to believe they are unmanaged if they are to be managed effectively."

The great social divide in modern America is not money, but education:

In the United States suspicion or resentment is no longer directed to the capitalists or the merely rich. It is the intellectuals who are eyed with misgiving and alarm. This should surprise no one. Nor should it be a matter for surprise when semiliterate millionaires turn up leading or financing the ignorant in struggle against the intellectually privileged and content. This reflects the relevant class distinction of our time.

Likewise, employment and unemployment often rely upon the relationship between an individual's level of education and the proffered form of work. The great *economic* divide is corporate power—between the great corporations which deal with great unions, and the smaller firms of the "market sector" of the economy, which more closely approximate the competitive model. Labor and management, in the great firms, get along much more amiably now than before; but, "Behavior is not better; it is merely that interests are concordant"—hence the wage-price spiral and the contemporary problem of inflation, which originates in these great firms. Government subsidies to failing corporations are part of a policy of "full employment," and assist corporation and union alike. Unions are less powerful than they once were, but they are more comfortable. The potential conflict of our time lies not between labor and management, but between the technostructure and "the educational and scientific estate." The technostructure represents the new conservatism, the educators and scientists represent the new progressivism. Between these parties the future of society will be debated, bartered, and brokered.

The relationship between business and the State has assumed a fresh appearance. In the days when the entrepreneurial corporation was building the country, the businessman sought his partnership with the legislator, at times by buying him off, at other times by less drastic methods. The Executive represented the public interest. Today, the situation is reversed. The technostructure of a great corporation is more comfortable in dealing with the Executive—particularly the relevant bureaucracy—while the educational and scientific estate must force its views on the legislature. It is unseemly that a corporation should bribe a senator, and unthinkable that a professor might persuade a bureaucrat. There are occasional reversions to the old era, but they are exceptional. Together, the technostructure and the bureaucracy motivate our economic activity to a powerful degree:

> The management to which we are subject is not onerous. It works not on the body but on the mind. It first wins acquiescence or belief; action is in response to this mental conditioning and thus devoid of any sense of compulsion. It is not that we are required to have a newly configured automobile or a novel reverse-action laxa-

tive; it is because we believe that we must have them. It is open to anyone who can resist belief to contract out of this control. But we are no less managed because we believe we are not physically compelled. On the contrary, though this is poorly understood, physical compulsion would have a far lower order of efficiency.

The industrial system has absorbed class interest and created new questions. For instance, has not the industrial system had a pernicious influence on the conduct of American defense policy? Generals still in full bristle retire from the military in order to take lucrative positions with weapons-manufacturing firms; executives with the firms assume positions as consultants to the Department of Defense; the Department is not only the firms' exclusive client, but the government grants the firms subsidies, and encourages increased weapons manufacture in order to implement its Full Employment policy. How great, truly, is the difference between American and Russian forms of economic management when such a situation exists?

Both systems are subject to the imperatives of industrialization. And while each uses different techniques for dealing with the individual who contracts out of the planning, planning in all cases means setting aside the market mechanism in favor of the control of prices and individual economic behavior. Both countries, quite clearly, solicit belief for what serves the goals of the industrial mechanism. Instead of contrast leading to implacable conflict, a more evident economic tendency is convergence.

Let us, Galbraith urges, begin to introduce an aesthetic dimension to our economic planning considerations. The glorious cities of pre-industrial civilization were much poorer than any of our modern industrial citadels; the reason they are lovelier is that they "included, as part of life, a much wider aesthetic perspective." It is too much to expect the technostructure to acquire this perspective; but once the State is liberated from the dominance of the technostructure and its myths, it might reassert aesthetic priority. "That one must pause to affirm that beauty is worth the sacrifice of some increase in the Gross National Product shows how effectively our beliefs have been accommodated to the needs of the industrial system." Although there is no assurance that the State will exercise good taste, there is no alternative to the State. Mayors, governors, Presidents, and Prime Ministers should be compelled to pass a test; have they left their cities, states, or countries more beautiful than when they entered office? "Few if any in this century would have passed." Another recommendation is to develop "a planning authority of adequate power. Only strong and comprehensive planning will redeem and make livable the modern city and its surroundings." Public authority must replace private industry in those areas of the economy, such as housing and transportation, where private industry has not met the needs of social balance. In accordance with the new availability of leisure time, people should be offered the option of taking several months' paid vacation, in exchange for a lower annual pay. This should help weaken the grip of the technostructure on its constituent members. The educational and scientific estate should impose its progressive standards on the Democratic Party, and thence on the nation at large. "The industrial system, in contrast with its economic antecedents, is intellectually demanding. It brings into existence, to serve its intellectual and scientific needs, the community that, hopefully, will reject its monopoly of social purpose."

Economics and Public Purpose was written and published during the Nixon years. Its purpose was to integrate what Galbraith now called "the two systems"—the market system and the planning system—into one harmonious whole. Plumbers, doctors, and small manufacturers are now seen to receive treatment befitting their place in the economic system; fully one half of the economy is seen to be outside the world of the great corporations. Much of *Economics and Public Purpose* is review; reading Galbraith from end to end means meeting up with old acquaintances. Sometimes one feels exasperated; hearing about the wage-price spiral assumes the character of being introduced to the same person a dozen times, as if each introduction were the first.

An early digression in this book is "Consumption and the Concept of the Household," which describes the role of women in the economy. This is the "crypto-servant role of administrator" which makes "an indefinitely increasing consumption possible. As matters now stand (and for as long as they so stand), it is their supreme contribution to the modern economy." The section on the market system is quite brief, and reveals a lack of interest in the subject. A most significant aspect of this system, Galbraith argues, is "its ability to reduce the reward of its participants." The farmer and small-business man contentedly work harder than major corporate officials and make less money. This is due to what Galbraith calls the "convenient social virtue"—i.e., the high moral regard of society. There exists an inequality between the two systems which is not only tolerated, but encouraged by the consuming public:

> In the large corporation no one doubts that there should be limits on hours of toil, on the effort that must be expended and on all other conditions of work. The role of the unions in bringing and defending such humanizing rules is applauded. But in the market system the small entrepreneur who rises early and works late, is available to his customers around the clock and is unremitting in the intensity of his toil, is the man who merits praise. No tedium marks his efforts; he is a public benefactor and a model for the young. Especially stalwart is the farmer who holds a job in town, works evenings, Sundays and holidays on his land and engages his wife and children likewise. Not only does he receive credit himself, but additional praise for his industry is assigned to the relevant Swedish, Danish, Norwegian, German, Scottish, Finnish, or Japanese provenance. That such toil is compelled by the circumstances of the market system is not remarked. That it may damage the health of children and that in agriculture it involves the denial of unions, minimum wages, even workmen's compensation, to those who need their protection the most is unmentioned. Such is the authority of the convenient social virtue.

The market system also survives because certain tasks—"much agriculture, geographically dispersed services, those involving the arts," lists Galbraith—"do not lend themselves to organization."

The Planning system which was the world of *The New Industrial State* is revisited, with special emphasis on "Bureaucratic Symbiosis"—"the tendency for the public and private organizations to find and pursue a common purpose." The most interesting manifestation of Bureaucratic Symbiosis is found in the multinational corporations which comprise the Transnational System. Its function "is, simply, the accommodation of the technostructure to the peculiar uncertainties of international trade. It transcends the market internationally as it does nationally." "The most notable feature of the modern corporation and thus of the planning system is the uniformity of its cultural impact, regardless of its national origin. Its hotels, automobiles, service stations, airlines are much alike not because they are American but because all are the products of great organizations." The notion of cultural imperialism is a myth. "A Frenchman who is employed by Simca and thus by Chrysler in France (is not) less French than one employed by Renault."

The two systems, forced to live together, do so in an unstable environment; the market system gets much the worse of this instability. Earlier books illustrated powerful unions and corporations forcing inflation through the wage-price spiral; the dispersed parts of the market system, lacking this concentrated power, cannot hope to keep pace. And "when demand in the planning system fails, demand for the products and services of the market system is reduced. Since there is no protective control, prices, entrepreneurial incomes and some wages fall. Hardship for the small businessman is severe."

Finally, Galbraith offers "A General Theory of Reform," much of it repeated from, some of it implied in, the earlier books. We must begin with an "emancipation of belief" from the goals of the planning system. At the same time, it should be recognized "that escape from the discipline of the planning system involves escape not from discipline altogether but a transfer to the greater discipline of self." If more women decline the life of housewifely consumption in favor of work for remuneration, the American economy will change; "there will be a substantial shift in the economy from goods to services. This means, pari passu, a shift in the economy from the planning system to the market system." The State should undertake to enhance the power of the system, providing such things as housing, transportation, and medical care, which are not profitable but are still necessary. It should also expropriate the weapons industry, and any other where Bureaucratic Symbiosis has rendered all claim to private authority laughable. These actions are to come under the aegis of a "new social-ism," the "old socialism" being obsolete because "the monopoly behavior which was its original raison d'être does not exist." The new socialism "searches not for the positions of power in the economy but for the positions of weakness." The people should choose candidates, and particularly Presidents, on the basis of "whether the candidate distinguishes the planning from the public interest and is committed to the latter." There should be much slighter reliance on monetary policy, and stronger support of fiscal measures to manage the economy. Tax policy should be reformed to meet the standards of straightforward progressive taxation; no distinction should be made between earned and unearned in-come. Wage and price controls should become a permanent fea-ture of the economy, but, "The controls need apply only to wages that are set by collective bargaining and to the prices of firms that are in the planning system."

> Fortunately the rules that reflect the public interest are rather sim-ple. If public expenditures are increasingly for public purposes, if taxes are increasingly progressive, if monetary policy is passive, if expansion of demand is accomplished by increased public expend-iture and contraction of demand by increased taxes, if wage in-creases are kept in accordance with productivity gains, if increased equality is a major consideration in making wage adjustments and if price increases are allowed only in response to hardship result-ing from the evening-up of wages and productivity gains—then an essentially public management is being achieved.

IV

Paul Samuelson, Nobel Laureate in economics, has written that, with the appearance of Galbraith's books, "The objective scholar must assert that economics will never be quite the same."[7] This is because he rearranges patterns of thought. "When will economists and the public accept Galbraith's frame of reference?" asks Myron Sharpe, who ventures, "When the social tensions caused by the failure to accept it become untenable, just as

[7] Quoted in Hession, op. cit., p. v.

Keynes' frame of reference became acceptable when tensions generated by the Great Depression rendered the previously held theory of unemployment obsolete."[8] "He reminds us," writes Charles Hession, "of the famous toast that J. M. Keynes gave to economists as 'the guardians of civilization.' He points to the neglected dimensions of life and urges us to move beyond a business civilization toward what humanists have called the fulfillment, or fulfilling society—one in which the whole range of human potentialities may have expression."[9] "People listen to Galbraith," observes Robert Lekachman, "because he talks about important subjects in imaginative and iconoclastic terms. Two of these subjects, power and culture, have steadily engaged his mind, as seldom have they interested most economists."[10]

The concern for power, especially, is dominant from the first page of *American Capitalism* to the last page of *Economics and Public Purpose*. Ask the questions: Who is in control of things? Why? Should it be this way? If not, what is a better way?, and the pattern of analysis becomes clear. Galbraith equates power with large size, and these things with conservatism. In contrast, he presents himself as a lone iconoclast, armed only with the weapon of his pen, upholding the tattered banner of liberalism. The personal pronoun "I" appears infrequently in these four books, but there is no mistaking the evidence of a David, firing slingshots at the Goliath which he calls the conventional wisdom. His books become battles, and we read them as we would the memoirs of a famous warrior.

How often is he on target? A layman can only consult the experts, distinguish between major and minor disagreements, and rely on his own common sense. Galbraith seems deficient as an analyst of history, and erratic as an economic psychologist. Yet in each of these areas he has made sound contributions. Thus his idea of countervailing power in *American Capitalism* appears useful and at least partially correct, but, as Myron Sharpe noted, "*American Capitalism* leaves the reader in doubt about what countervailing power countervails and what it does not counter-

[8] Sharpe, op. cit., pp. 79–80.
[9] Hession, op. cit., pp. 223–24.
[10] Ibid., p. x.

vail."[11] Also, it is quite imperfect as an explanation for national economic behavior from 1945-52. "Other analyses that point to the backlog in consumer demand and the massive monetary liquidity in the economy seem equal or superior to countervailing power as explanations."[12] Let me, then, pick out the flaws in the Galbraithian system as I have come to see them through the guidance of those more learned in economics than myself, and through my personal judgment.

Foremost among these is Galbraith's strong belief in the power of institutions to shape the ways of individuals. Sometimes he views this power as direct, as in the case of the "military-industrial complex" and its relation to American defense policy; at other times he suggests that the power is indirect, as when he writes that outmoded ideas are causing people to shape bad policies; then there are such things as advertising, which involve persuasion and fall somewhere between direct and indirect power. Galbraith tends to be too categorical and exaggerates his way to error. The idea of countervailing power is one such instance. The opposition to anti-trust laws is another: if there are indeed two sectors of the economy, and one of them relates closely to the competitive model, then are not anti-trust laws applicable to this sector?

Galbraith's theory of Social Balance presumes that more money spent on public services will improve the quality of those services. In many cases he is obviously right; in other cases he is merely obvious. Clearly more money spent on mass transit systems or highway systems will improve the quality of those systems. But this does not come very sharply to the point: choices must be made, and it is often difficult to discern what is in fact the public interest. In the Preface to *Economics and Public Purpose*, Galbraith confesses that he did not pay much attention to this difficulty in *The Affluent Society*, which is mainly concerned with the problem of Social Balance. Money for public highways might seem an excellent idea, until it is compared with the value of money spent on mass transit. Each of these might seem worthy of the support of all forward-looking men, until contrasted with the damage which might be done to the regional environment. Social Balance appears, on balance, to be a rather unbalanced

[11] Sharpe, op. cit., p. 19.
[12] Hession, op. cit., p. 63.

proposition. In the field of education—along with transportation and medical care, his major concern—Galbraithian Social Balance is impressively muddleheaded. Perhaps his own boyhood in grim Ontario schoolhouses led him to believe that more money meant better education; he was wrong. The most serious failure of contemporary education occurs in the centers of our large cities. Teachers are well paid; libraries abound; facilities are certainly superior to the one-room schoolhouses of rural yesteryear. Yet thousands graduate from high school each year after achieving the barest degree of literacy. Galbraith writes, "Schools do not compete with television and the movies" in "under-financed" school systems, but he does not explain why they should be expected to compete, and he does not admit that this is no less the case in affluent than in impoverished communities. Although "lack of funds" is the most frequent excuse of educators for the inadequate performance of so many students, it is clearly a false and self-serving explanation. Social Balance is, like countervailing power, a catchall phrase, intended to cover a complex of situations which requires separate study. And if the idea of Social Balance is rejected as vaguely dubious, then all of its manifestations—and supposed virtues—must also be called into question.

Galbraith's respect for the power of advertising is too great; his theory of producer sovereignty suffers from this heavy emphasis. Sometimes he sounds as if he would prefer people to exist in ignorance of inventions designed to make life more pleasant for them. Even so, a washing machine remains a distinct improvement over a scrubboard. Refrigerators and automobiles are really quite desirable once they are known to exist; people require, as Myron Sharpe indicates, "an assist from advertising only to familiarize them with the possibilities and jar them out of set patterns of thought . . . Consumer sovereignty might best be regarded as a doctrine of limited monarchy rather than divine right, with the producer in the role of a persuasive Prime Minister."[13]

Galbraith exaggerates the role of corporate planning in the market; his theories actually suggest that economists need to revise their concept of oligopoly more than their concept of the market. "Planning does not replace the market unless the activities of enterprises are coordinated from one center in accordance

[13] Sharpe, op. cit., pp. 32–33.

with one internally consistent budget."[14] The automobile industry, for example, is intensely competitive, as is palpably evident to anyone who has spent much time around Detroit. It is true that price is not the only, or even the primary, form of competition, as it would be according to the competitive model. Yet price competition is not altogether absent, and advertising is but one of several forms that competition takes. There are also such things as styling, fuel efficiency, storage space, safety, and other engineering factors which the customer considers before he buys a car. The competitive process is now subtler than either Galbraith or many conservative economists will allow. It may be that his analysis of planning is more applicable to the primary industries (producers of basic resources such as oil, gas, coal, and metals) than to the secondary industries, such as automobiles, which rely on primary industries for raw materials; size may *not* be the salient factor. Sharpe astutely observes of Galbraith's ideal of planning, "His cardinal error is to abandon the market as the organizing principle of the industrial system . . . Mature corporations . . . plan of course, but what they plan is not how to replace the market but how best to compete in it."[15]

I find the idea of Bureaucratic Symbiosis unclear. Legislators still seem more susceptible than Executives to the enticements of businessmen. Major corporations spend large sums of money lobbying members of Congress; sometimes the lobbying approaches old-fashioned bribery. And the great corporations do not yet seem to get along famously with their regulators in the federal bureaucracy. Not a week passes in which I fail to lift up a Detroit newspaper and read the remarks of an auto industry executive concerning the bureaucrats; I am rarely struck by the cordial tone. Also, the illegal contributions to Richard Nixon's 1972 presidential election campaign do not suggest that corporate bosses were much impressed by Galbraith's arguments about the unseemliness of this sort of activity.

His analysis of the market system, and particularly the convenient social virtue, is poorly done. The passage I quoted earlier, portraying the farmer who holds a weekday job in town and labors on his farm evenings, Sundays, and holidays with his wife

[14] Ibid., p. 45.
[15] Ibid., p. 77.

and children, is supposed to represent the ideal representative of the convenient social virtue. Yet this man is a pitiable caricature and would not be widely admired in today's society. Indeed, the neighbors would remark of such a man that he is working himself toward a heart attack, his wife toward a nervous breakdown, and his children toward open rebellion. They would be right. Prosperous small-business men are not prosperous because they can cut their salaries and those of their employees, but rather because they, like large corporations, plan well to compete in the market. The successful small manufacturer is someone who is able to care for his employees in a manner which makes unionization unattractive; salary-cutting in times of recession is, at most, a minor aspect of his program. Likewise the retailer—say, the local chain-store operator—tends, if successful, to be someone who can out-bargain any union for his employees' affection. It is not, as Galbraith says, that the work of these firms does not "lend" itself to organization to continue within the family, as it were. The weaker parts of the market system have begun in recent years to show signs of strain. The movement toward Social Balance seems to have landed us in a quagmire of public service employee strikes. The unionization of schoolteachers, garbage collectors, police, and firemen has resulted in higher pay for the workers in these fields. It has also cramped efforts to achieve a higher measure of social serenity. The public properly regards strikes by public employees as intolerable: there must be police and fire protection, school must start in September, the garbage must be picked up. The Galbraithian solution to this problem is to supply more money through higher taxation: strengthen the weaker parts of the market system. This is a fine idea, until the demands of workers become untenable and the public refuses to pay more. This has already begun to happen. What occurs at this point is one of two things: chaos or arbitration. The latter is more likely to be the choice of a sane populace. The State is the obvious arbiter: Galbraith would do better to dust off and refinish his theory of countervailing power than to pursue his theory of the two systems.

Finally, it seems that Galbraith's economic thinking suffers from too much rigidity and an overdose of abstraction. While price competition is supposedly the signal feature of the market system, among doctors, lawyers, and unionized skilled workers there is even less price competition than in the planning system. Perhaps this is an inevitable effect of trying to think systematically; perhaps it is the price to be paid for a fresh point of view —qualification and modification may be the work of those who succeed him. But Galbraith is, above all, a moralist: he describes in order to suggest what is right and what is wrong. And morality, grown stiff, may repel the skeptical mind. Preacher Galbraith is usually saved by his wit—but not always. He argues for Social Balance, and implies that money is less likely to be wasted if spent on public schools than on television sets. How does he know? He analyzes the technostructure, and insists that an independent "Educational and Scientific Estate" is abler to decide the public interest than the technostructure itself. Why? He would like economic growth to slow down, or in some cases even cease, but he sees no problem in financing an enormously enhanced program of public services. How high would he like taxes to rise?

Might not a privately produced good serve an individual as well as a public service? Is there not some reason, aside from advertising, for the continued purchase of television sets? Is there not some explanation, aside from the lack of advertising, for the local community's fickleness in voting for school millage increases? Is it not possible that the industrialist, or technostructure, might better perceive the public interest than an academician who is detached from the operations of the firm? Or are we now to set aside Galbraith's argument, in *American Capitalism,* that the autonomy of the firm constitutes the best excuse for the continuation of private capitalism? Is there not a point when initiative is sapped by high taxes, whether on the individual or the mighty corporate level?

All of these questions—and others—persist after a reading of Galbraith's four major books on economics. I prefer systems whose creators are not afraid to expose their holes, and there are times when I am tempted to dismiss more of the Galbraithian system than I ought. Nevertheless, his contribution to contemporary thinking is of the very first order, and books will be written to celebrate it. Once again, I can only submit a layman's notes.

Most formidable is his appreciation of the importance of *size* in contemporary society. Of course he exaggerates and attaches excessive weight to this factor. Of course he fusses too much about the difference between businessmen in large and small firms, and whether they are maximizing profits for themselves or for invisible stockholders. But this is to be excused, since Galbraith has got hold of a larger truth: he understands the drift of our times toward centralization in all forms of human endeavor, and he wants to start dealing with the problems this involves. Unlike the conservative, who sees the centralization of government but is blind to the centralization of commerce, or the average liberal, who sees the reverse, Galbraith acknowledges both. Unlike either liberal or conservative, who rails at centralization where he finds it, Galbraith nods his head and urges that it go forward. Centralization is the inevitable consequence of technology; it brings in its train whole wagonloads of specialists; it creates a grander and more sophisticated world, and meets it on its own terms. Now, Galbraith argues, it is time that the affluent society, crafted by the industrial system, be put to work for the good of society at large. This can only be done if we accept this new situation and rearrange our beliefs so that they are consistent with its reality. "He does not propose to replace it with something else. He would have society use the industrial system rather than have the industrial system use society."[16] In acknowledging the power and usefulness of great institutions, he steps beyond those whose yearning for the past finds expression in undue nostalgia.

From the acceptance of large units proceeds his assessment of strong and weak positions in the economy, and his judgment that the weak must be helped and the strong must be tempered. As I have noted, his examples are sometimes mistaken, his concern occasionally misguided. Too often his proposal for improvement is little more than a rearrangement of wealth, and his analysis of economic psychology does not penetrate outside the stale air of the board room or the union hall. As Sharpe perceived Galbraith's critique of advertising, "Auto manufacturers advertise in England, France and Japan almost as stridently as they do in the U.S., but the public transportation systems of those countries are embarrassingly superior to ours. The explanation must lie not exclusively in advertising, but in broad social attitudes, the causes of which lie

[16] Ibid., p. 72.

outside the realm of Galbraith's analysis."[17] But Galbraith understands the basic point, which is that almost every member of a free society is interested in the enhancement of his power. This power may come in the form of profits, a new home or car, an important position, a tighter control over the immediate environment, or any combination of these or other things. With power blossoms pride—not least of all in the set of beliefs under which the individual labored in order to secure his power. With pride comes the instinct for preservation—of one's possessions and of one's means of obtaining them. Consequently, a prosperous society is bound to operate under a set of conservative impulses.

Not all of them are wrong, and Galbraith does not so argue. But the danger arises when too much power is ceded to too few people—or economic interests. Mere pride then sways national policy; the conservative instinct is too strong; petrifaction seeps in. This can be seen in the relative weakness of certain parts of the society and the economy. Although the importance of these parts is widely accepted, they still do not work well. Something must be done; the power balance must be adjusted; social harmony must be the goal.

Finally, I am not sure exactly how much I agree with Galbraith's analysis or his proposed reforms. But I know that I find his attitude congenial and heartening. It is possible that Galbraith's critics are right, and he is willing to entrust the state with too much power. But at least he provides a tonic to those conservatives who insist that all progress flows from corporate enterprise and pretend that this enterprise manifests individualism; and to those liberals who perfunctorily assume every grasping union to be on the side of righteousness. The dominant mood of Galbraithian economics is mordant skepticism. Our subject sees economic life as a perpetual lust after gain, and he thinks this is so because people are taught to believe that it is good. He proposes that we adopt limits for our production and consumption, lest one of the least endearing traits of human nature be allowed to run riot. While reserving the right to question each specific application of this proposal, I find myself highly sympathetic. And I denounce those who would denounce Galbraith as a mere moralist, and not a sensible thinker. He is one of the most sensible men of our time

[17] Ibid., p. 64.

and he is a moralist because he happens to live in a highly moralistic society. He accepts its rules, and desires only that we do better by them.

V

Whatever the end result of his proposals, his method of presentation marks one of the high points of contemporary civilization. "It has been my conviction for years," wrote William F. Buckley, Jr., "that history may not forgive Galbraith the evangelist, but that literature will add him to the roster of the saints."[18] Writing on "Sound and Substance" in his little book on *Economics and the Art of Controversy* in 1955, Galbraith said, "There is no reason for democracy to partake of the nature of a barroom brawl." Nearly every one of his major books is prefaced by an appeal, expressing the hope that the reader will not find the author ill-tempered. American literature has produced a Mencken and a Mark Twain, rascals with a taste for making everyone look ridiculous; it has spawned Emerson and his (conscious or unconscious) disciples, who have regarded the sermon as the highest form of human thought and art; it has nurtured and tolerated a Thorstein Veblen, grunting and stuttering his way through volumes of bilious economics. But not until Galbraith has it come forth with a preaching man whose sense of humor rivals the masters, and whose passions are aroused by the facts of economic life. His career is without precedent.

Beneath the façade of economics, Galbraith probes psychology. He achieves charm through ironic detachment. The aforementioned *Economics and the Art of Controversy* is an excellent introduction to Galbraith's method. Here we find him arguing not about economic issues, but about the means people employ to argue about economic issues. This, in turn, reveals deeper truths about our way of life. So we learn of the mounting vituperation which seems to accompany the last stages of contract negotiations:

[18] William F. Buckley, Jr., *The Governor Listeth*, New York: Putnam-Berkly (paperback), 1971, p. 228.

One indication of the partly synthetic character of the normal labor crisis is its inability to sustain conversation after the fact. Murder, rape, fire, flood, and other such legitimate catastrophes can be savored for many weeks. So to some extent can such exercises in organized or spontaneous belligerency as a prize fight, a World Series, or a local knife battle. But all discussion of a strike normally dies on the day a new contract is signed. The sound and fury which so commonly mark our collective bargaining tell nothing of the state of rapport in our labor relations. They show only that the process of collective bargaining is being conducted normally.

The core of Galbraithian thought is found in the four books upon which I have dwelled at length: these each required the labor of several years, and sustained Galbraith's imagination while he flirted with a hundred polemical fancies. But other works—histories, memoirs, diaries—have issued from his hand over the past quarter century. It is possible that in these may rest his enduring reputation among the writers of our time; it is certain that they bring us closer to the man himself.

His interest in manners is as deep as any nineteenth-century novelist's: How do people argue? How do people establish and maintain their positions in society? What motivates the acts of politicians? How are decisions of high finance reached? How is power distributed in a community?—these are the questions which tease Galbraith's brain, and he has something interesting to say about all of them.

There must always be controversy, because this is the way political careers are built. Aside from those men who earn reputations as mediators, "Peace for one genus of politician means political destruction." On public policy toward architecture: "St. Mark's might well lose some of its charm were the Piazza San Marco surrounded by Gulf, Esso and Texaco stations, a Do-nut shop, with Howard Johnson's at the end. But such grotesque arrangements are strongly defended by the competitive ideology." On the selectivity involved in historical study:

It is known that the palace of the great Louis at Versailles was notably deficient by any modern standards in its plumbing. Yet peristalsis in that noble and well-nourished court was normal. And the inevitable expedients led to a horrid stench everywhere about the glittering grounds. When the orangery was planted it was hoped, alas in vain, that its fragrance would overcome the terrible smell. All this has been lost in the idealization. Of the court of Louis XIV we know only of the pomp, the wit, and the love. Of features which would have made life there impossible for a fastidious American nothing is remembered.

On the mechanization of modern life: "Man has not retreated before the machine; rather the machine has become desperately dependent on the improvement of man. And our economy is still arranged to supply machines rather than to improve men." On economic reform: "An angry god may have endowed capitalism with inherent contradictions. But at least as an afterthought he was kind enough to make social reform surprisingly consistent with improved operation of the system." On big shots: "The [1929 stock market] crash blighted the fortunes of many hundreds of thousands of Americans. But among people of prominence worse havoc was worked on reputations. In such circles credit for wisdom, foresight, and, unhappily also, for common honesty underwent a convulsive shrinkage." On the national diplomacy: "The most persistent error of American foreign policy is the tendency to identify our fortunes with dictators in their brief moments of glory." On bureaucratic manners:

The Washington protocol that requires the lesser of two officials to get on the line [during telephone calls] and await the pleasure of his superior in rank is, on the whole, more binding than any legislation enacted by the Medes, the Persians or the combined empire of the two. And it is enforced not by the illiterate and often incompetent police but by highly skilled secretaries who can call to mind, with a speed and accuracy unapproached by any computer, the most minute gradations in official precedence. They have reason. Their own position on the Washington ladder is derived from that of their employer.

On sport, "If table tennis is to succeed as a spectator sport, an arrangement must be made to play it behind magnifying glasses.

Otherwise the general impression is of two watchmakers at work in the next town." On governing in the midst of a Depression: "Economic hard times invite recourse to a line of remedial action that has always been favored. This is to seek to exorcise economic misfortune by affirming that it does not exist." And these are but random samplings of a mind which has considered the various economic and political arrangements devised by man over the course of centuries. Most notably, however, Galbraith has concerned himself with the affairs of the English-speaking peoples of North America. And, with only an occasional glance over his shoulder at the old folks at home in Canada, he has found the United States more than adequate for the purposes of his study of the human comedy. He enjoys a comfortably universalist view of world affairs, and assumes the United States to be the prototype of modern industrial society. I have quoted Galbraith on the "cultural imperialism" of the great corporations: he insists that no such thing exists, that technostructures are the same everywhere; he hints that the peculiarities of individuals and peoples are overwhelmed by the similarities.

His "supplementary" books (i.e., those which do not directly expound economic theory) reinforce this view; they involve a subtler application of the same perceptions which guided him throught the four major books on economics. *Economics and the Art of Controversy*, already mentioned, deals with the institutional arrangements of public debate; crammed into its hundred pages is more wisdom, more lightly borne, than in a hundred vast tomes on American government. *The Great Crash* (1955) deserves at least passing attention here, since in two decades it has become a minor classic of American historical writing. This narrative of events in the financial world in autumn 1929 is unsurpassed in its ironic tone by any of Galbraith's books. The Diogenes of the market was never more amused than in contemplating the buffoons of Wall Street. "I never enjoyed writing a book more," he recalled; "indeed, it is the only one I remember in no sense as a labor but as a joy." Forecasters, Presidents, and scoundrels pass in review; strange companies rise and fall; bankers babble foolishly in order to protect their prestige. Rarely has so lovable a book offered such a grim view of human nature. Even the conclusion of *The Great Crash* is unsettling. There are likely to be future crashes, Galbraith writes, because although there are controls available for the prevention of such unpleasantness there are

> . . . a hundred reasons why a government will determine not to use them. In our democracy an election is in the offing even on the day after an election. The avoidance of depression and the prevention of unemployment have become for the politician the most critical of all questions of public policy. Action to break up a boom must always be weighed against the chance that it will cause unemployment at a politically inopportune moment. Booms, it must be noted, are not stopped until after they have started. And after they have started the action will always look, as it did to the frightened men in the Federal Reserve Board in February 1929, like a decision in favor of immediate as against ultimate death. As we have seen, the immediate death not only has the disadvantage of being immediate but of identifying the executioner.

No summary can convey the quality of Galbraith's digressions—for example, his examination of the "no-business meeting," at which executives solemnly gather not in order to accomplish anything, but to reassure themselves of their own importance. The significance of such meetings is psychological rather than practical —but the reader will have to discover this passage for himself.

Beneath the surface of the essays collected in *The Liberal Hour* (1960) runs an undercurrent of concern for the role of public relations in contemporary life. As elsewhere, Galbraith respects power wherever he finds it, and urges only that it be put to better uses. Thus he writes of the propaganda war involved in "peaceful competition" with the Russians, "In the months and years ahead, we will certainly be told that our superiority turns on better filter tips, the preservation of highway billboards, resistance to pay television, and the consumption of more aged whiskey. We should treat this idiocy with the contempt that it deserves." Another piece deals with "The Build-Up and the Public Man" and counsels, "To build extravagant images of [public men's] wisdom renders no more service than the other modern habit of asserting their total venality. If we foster great expectations, we must count on deep disillusion." In the following essay he asserts, "Some of the sharpest political conflicts of our time are between liberals who seek change to a nostalgic goal and conservatives who defend the status quo." Yet another article dismisses as fraudulent the legend of Henry Ford I, the canny enterpriser. The charming piece which closes the book recalls the visit of the Prince of Wales (later King Edward VIII and the Duke of Windsor) to Canada during Galbraith's boyhood, and attempts to sort out the legendary from the true aspects of the situation.

Economic Development, written and published while Galbraith served as Ambassador to India, is as formal as the four major books on economics. Here, addressing himself to the problems of the developing nations, he confronts the obverse side of affluence. He examines and at least partially rejects all of the common explanations for national poverty, but finds "one generalization that is reasonably safe. People are the common denominator of progress. So, *paucis verbis,* no improvement is possible with unimproved people, and advance is certain when people are liberated and educated." So once again he finds himself in conflict with the technocrats, whose idea of education he finds sterile in an affluent society and even worse in an underdeveloped one. The value of factories, paved roads, and railroads is not to be discounted. But the people they are supposed to help must feel that they have a stake in their functioning; this cannot be done unless they can participate; they cannot participate without receiving a certain amount of education. There must be a fair distribution of wealth. Colleges and universities must operate with a view toward leading the community. Industrial planning whether public or private must maintain a significant autonomy from the pressures of politics, domestic and foreign. The goal must be the development of the community, not the development of the firm. The irony in *Economic Development* lies in Galbraith's contrast between his own emphasis on the practical and the rhetoric of Westerners and natives, who differ in their proposals but achieve a mutuality of righteous self-assurance.

In *The McLandress Dimension* and *The Triumph,* the sluice gates are once again opened, the irony comes rippling to the surface, and we witness the flow of some of the most amusing prose of our time. *The McLandress Dimension* is a slim volume of barely a hundred pages, written under the pseudonym of "Mark

Epernay" during Galbraith's tour as Ambassador. It consists of seven vignettes, related in the manner of tall tales, which undermine several American pomposities. Even the reviewer for that somber journal *The Nation* found the book "authentically funny." Most of the stories involve the exploits of Dr. Herschel McLandress, "former Professor of Psychiatric Measurement at the Harvard Medical School and now chief consultant to the Noonan Psychiatric Clinic in Boston." In "The McLandress Dimension" he invents a coefficient which is used to rate the behavior of individuals according to the length of time they are able to concentrate upon something other than themselves. In "The Fully Automated Foreign Policy" he contrives a computer which produces automatic responses for the daily crises of the State Department, thereby eliminating the need for all State Department employees. In "The Confidence Machine" he produces, with the help of his friend Professor Detweiler, a method of therapy for business executives suffering from shaken confidence. "He asked them to spend several hours listening to speeches of Herbert Hoover and to speeches and selected press conferences of Dwight D. Eisenhower. They were then subject to detailed psychological tests. Over half the executives showed a positive response. A few even emerged from the experience exuding confidence." In "Allston Wheat's Crusade" the gentleman of the title, a drug wholesaler in rural Pennsylvania, mounts a nationwide campaign for the abolition of team sports. He claims that they are contributing to the collectivization of American life, and he finds ardent supporters among citizens committed to rugged individualism. In these and the other tales in *The McLandress Dimension*, the joke is on institutions and ideologies, rather than individuals. The narrative tone is purposely flat and understated, enriching the irony. The characters are at once larger than life and banal; our laughter does not exclude recognition.

The Triumph carries this approach on to a larger stage. It describes a Latin American revolution in which nothing happens the way it is supposed to happen. It is not first-rate fiction; characterization is accomplished through the narrator's barbed commentaries, rather than through the actions of the people of the story. Nevertheless, Galbraith carries out his mission, which is to ridicule the pomposities of public men. The soon-to-be-deposed, despotic old President, having viewed the Spanish version of *A Farewell to Arms* several times, now imitates the Hemingway manner of speech: "It seemed right for a roughhewn man of authority as, with very little effort, he saw himself." The narrator dryly observes, "A government crisis has this in common with a sex orgy or a drunken bat: The participants greatly enjoy it although they feel they shouldn't." U. S. State Department officials debate to exasperation on the advice they should give the President. "Once the basic decision had been reached to recommend that the policy of watchful waiting be continued on an interim basis, Worth Campbell moved fairly promptly to communicate it to the President." The worry, of course, is that the upstarts may be Communists, and Campbell, Assistant Secretary of State, for Inter-American Affairs, has earned his reputation for hard-nosed anti-Communism. Eventually a plan is devised whereby the son of the deposed President is retrieved from his studies at the University of Michigan in order to assume his father's mantle. The rebels, who are not, in fact, Communists, are overthrown. Once in power, the young leader proceeds to socialize the entire country, employing many of the ideas he has picked up in Ann Arbor. "And while Worth Campbell regrets as much as any man the developments in Flores, they are also proof that he, and not the young men of uncertain mission, has the correct view of the Communist menace. It has been shown to exist." The State Department seems to work in a self-made haze of terminology; it does not mean to do what it does, and it does not do what it means.

A little book on *Indian Painting: The Scene, Themes and Legends*, written in collaboration with Mohinder Singh Randhawa, followed *The Triumph*. In 1969 Galbraith published *Ambassador's Journal*, "A Personal Account of the Kennedy Years." This is one of the richest of Galbraith's works. It contains his most extended self-portrait, covering the three years between John F. Kennedy's election and his assassination. It contributes to historical understanding, dealing with important events at the highest political level. Perhaps most important, it reveals the full range of Galbraith's mind as he conducts the affairs of the Embassy, writes letters to the President, observes the Indian landscape with its human tumult and obstreperous leadership, advises the world on its economic problems, and amuses himself by perceiving the

affairs of man well beneath his high head and well within his
steady gaze. I think it likely that, among Galbraith's books, *Ambassador's Journal* is the most likely to be cherished by future generations. When he assumed his duties in New Delhi, America
gained a highly competent diplomat and one of its greatest
diarists. Patronage should always be so kind to the public which
must suffer it.

Ambassador's Journal was written during the same period of
time as *Economic Development* and *The McLandress Dimension*, and it is not surprising to find the journal's intellectual concerns to be similar to those of the other two books. The Ambassador reflects on how to make a poor country richer, and on how to
make it work. He discusses the situation with Nehru through an
exchange of one-to-one lectures; he tours the universities and the
farmlands; he wipes his brow in India's steamy cities, and suffers a
bout of amoebic dysentery. And—perpetually, it seems—he quarrels with the sour punctilio of the State Department. Almost incidentally, *Ambassador's Journal* contains some of the finest natural
descriptions in American literature—smooth and factual, bright-
ened by an occasional turn which makes one sit up and take account of the whole passage, like Dickens' descriptions of so many
aspects of Victorian England. Its highlight is probably Galbraith's
account of the India-Pakistan war over Kashmir, and his assessment of the martial enthusiasm of middle-age intellectuals. Otherwise, the delights in the book are too numerous to mention; I am
personally enchanted to read the notation of a diplomat at the
end of a day that "Not much business came in and I can't see
that the world was any the worse for it."

In succeeding books, most notably *Economics, Peace and
Laughter* (1971), *A China Passage* (1973—a diary of a one-
month trip to the Chinese Mainland in September 1972, and on a
smaller scale as good as *Ambassador's Journal*), and *Money:
Whence It Came, Where It Went* (1975—a short history of
money, and a polemic against contemporary American monetary
policies), Galbraith has continued to weave his own peculiar
product. He is a fine storyteller, so long as he has a message to
convey. His satire tends to be rather broad: he is without mercy
when thrusting at stuffy institutions or conventional ideas, but he
is gentle when he disagrees with a fresh idea, and he is slow to

denounce the most contemptible character. I think it is because his ironic mind enjoys any novelty, at least until it becomes dangerous. So he can make more fun of sameness than of eccentricity; he is better able to characterize a Worth Campbell than a Nehru. Exceptional men, except himself, are beyond the reach of his art. His personality (or at least his literary persona) is stamped onto nearly every page he writes; the reader has trouble deciding whether the author is more interesting than his subject.

VI

The epigram is the ideal form for a moralist of wit; Galbraith is almost as quotable as Alexander Pope. His description of the wage-price is no more likely to be remembered than his revelation of a sinus attack: "These are headaches, nearly disabling, that leave me stranded between fear that I will die and alarm that I will not." The Galbraithian style at its best is hard and glossy, straddling a line between contemptuous wit and gentle humor. At its worst it descends merely to the average level of his colleagues and tires us with professorial persistence. He is one of a handful of contemporary authors who are rarely a chore to read.

What lies beneath this brilliantly polished surface? If he is a moralist, then what is his morality? The first question is more difficult than the second. An art such as Galbraith's is expected to have emerged from tortuous origins, betraying the confidence it radiates. Yet, there is no evidence that this is the case here. Galbraith presents a picture of normality, rising from his boyhood on the farm, thriving in the academy, learning the social graces and marrying into a family of good stock, writing books which feature a humorous and graceful intelligence, and committing himself to use his talents in order to serve the public interest. The anomalies are only strong enough to set him slightly apart; a Canadian who crossed the border, a farm boy who charmed the city slickers, an economist who determined to write well, a tall man looking down on shorter men. He has proven himself remarkably prolific, and yet admits to the presence of no demon within him. Something is lacking in the picture.

Or is it? Is it not possible that the lack is in ourselves, and in the way we perceive talent and genius? Have we not been blinded by the Romantic tradition, with its way of looking at the individual as something absolutely special, possessed of unique injuries and founded upon an incontestable pride? Galbraith, it seems to me, belongs to an older tradition, with which Romantic criticism and all its Freudian vagaries are ill-equipped to deal. Because of this ineffectiveness, it has ignored the tradition to which Galbraith belongs. It has bypassed the more exact forms of writing which this tradition employs—economics, history, political polemics, journalism, the informal essay—and concentrated on the more fantastic forms which are congenial to the Romantic imagination—the novel, the drama, the lyric verse. A large gap has developed in our appreciation; it has made difficult the full enjoyment, as literary artists, of the authors included in this study. Galbraith is the greatest among these, and so his case is the most remarkable. *The Scotch, The Great Crash,* and *Ambassador's Journal*—to name only the three most obvious examples and to avoid, for the moment, the controversies which swirl about Galbraithian economic theory—are more likely to be read with delight a generation hence than most American novels of our time. Yet, look for some recognition of this fact among the professors of literature, and you look in vain. Our poetasters, though deeply ignorant of the fact, are directly responsible for the decline of contemporary style, and contemporary taste. In a time when Norman Mailer's "The White Negro" can earn esteem as an outstanding example of the essay form, we can observe how far the decadence has penetrated.

For Galbraith belongs to the tradition of reason, and we are foolish to deny this tradition its place. Literary politicians, in our day as in earlier ones, are significant because they force public notice of this old tradition. Without them, our literature would be completely overwhelmed by the men of fantasy, and our politics would never rise above the gabble of the cloakroom. The first development, alas, already threatens, with the increasing exclusion of the literary politicians from serious consideration in literary ranks. On the second count, of course, developments are more encouraging, as evidenced by the careers of Buckley, Schlesinger, and Galbraith.

The Romantic tradition likes to identify the tradition of reason with the eighteenth century, which is by way of setting it against the Romanticism of the nineteenth century; this allows the line of conflict to be easily drawn. In fact, both traditions are much older than that, but the Romantics prefer this distinction because reason was much the stronger of the two before the eighteenth century. Montaigne may have spent his lifetime searching for himself and emerged with all the appropriate contradictions, but he refused to forsake reason in the process. Erasmus is indubitably a distinguished character, but not for his neuroses. The passion of Thomas Aquinas was to make Christianity reasonable.

Yet, if we seek a place in the tradition for Galbraith, it is among the men of the eighteenth century that he fits best. Of the classic authors, he best recalls two of his fellow Scotsmen, David Hume and Adam Smith. In Hume we find the relentless skepticism, the worldly manners, the sunny temperament, the joy of living in a world of irreconcilable discrepancies. In Smith, of course, there is the fundamental attachment of morality to economics, the passion for reform, the love of illustration, and the insistence on relating theory to current conditions. One can imagine Galbraith writing like Hume at the end of his life, in an imaginary dialogue between himself and Charon, "If I live a few years longer, I may have the satisfaction of seeing the downfall of some of the prevailing systems of superstition." And we might make the same prediction of Galbraithian economics that one admirer made of Smith's work; that it "would persuade the present generation and govern the next." Like the two luminaries of the Scottish Enlightenment, Galbraith strips Calvinism of its horrors and represents it with dignity, and even elegance.

His book on *The Scotch* is the best introduction to Galbraith himself, even though it is more of a generalized memoir than an autobiography. Here we find the attitudes which pervade the formal treatises on economics as well as the journals. The book was written while Galbraith was in his middle fifties, and at the time he was most insistent that readers not assume he was now turning to memoir-writing in order to comfort his declining years: "I am more than normally resistant to the idea of advancing age and I intend, so far as possible, to have no part of it. I would rather see this manuscript join Carlyle's in the fireplace than encourage anyone to hope that I am now turning to personal history and retrospection." Yet the book revealed more of himself than perhaps he suspected. It portrayed a community which operated under a set of severe standards, and raised its young men to adopt its severity, if not its standards. The mature Galbraith is very much a product of his rural Canadian origins. For all the liberal idealism with which he is identified, he is most distinguished for his suspicion of human nature. Everywhere he detects a wildness which requires taming. "Most of the Scotch," he recalled, "were content to be considered ordinary citizens so long as they could determine who, because of being better or worse, were not. This they addressed themselves to assiduously." So, too, Galbraith has perceived Planning Systems, Market Systems, technostructures and Bureaucratic Symbiosis, and he has judged the value of each according to his own intractable model. As a McCrimmon might observe a Graham, so Galbraith looks at corporate or national leaders; a sense of superiority becomes the basis of judgment. Calvinism assumes unwontedly aristocratic airs.

His political image, and in large part his political function, has been over the years to adorn fresh ideas with his arrogant support. So he righteously admonished Democrats in 1970, "The function of the Democratic Party, in this century at least, has, in fact, been to embrace solutions even when . . . it outraged not only Republicans but the Democratic establishment as well. And if the Democratic Party does not render this function, at whatever cost in reputable outrage and respectable heart disease, it has no purpose at all." Of course this has not been *the* function, as Galbraith would have it, but it has been *a* function, and it is the one of which he would like to remind his colleagues. So he dresses it up, powders its face, and sends it out into the world for everyone to notice. Whether working with Adlai Stevenson, John F. Kennedy, Eugene McCarthy, or George McGovern, Galbraith has served as something of a front man, and sometimes his political colleagues have not even understood this. Galbraith will send an idea sailing into the political atmosphere; respectable men will quickly denounce it as preposterous and radical; meanwhile, the real value of the proposal will begin to make itself clear to political men, and over a period of time it will come to seem less preposterous and radical. There are many examples of this in Galbraith's career, but one of the most notable is the case of wage and price controls, for years advocated almost alone and in vain by Galbraith, at last adopted in 1971 by Richard Nixon, a Republican President. Said Galbraith of Nixon, who had worked under him in the Office of Price Administration in World War II, "That he should have gone on from regulating the economy to being an apt student of *The Affluent Society* was entirely to be expected."

But it would be wrong to exaggerate the prominence of this self-assurance among Galbraith's virtues. No man could insist on the correctness of his ideas to the point of true self-righteousness and still remain so funny. Again, his heredity was helpful. The Scotch may be as hardheaded as the Germans or Scandinavians, but they are much less mystical. Too much importance is doubtless attached to ethnic and racial origins in determining a man's character; still, it is worth a thought that Galbraith avoided the fate of Thorstein Veblen by being born Scotch instead of Norwegian. "Our neighbors made no fetish of land," he wrote; "none was ever seen holding the good earth in his cupped hands and gazing soulfully at the sky, and any such behavior would have been taken as indication of incipient mental disorder."

His journals, with their abundant discussion of his own little weaknesses, keep us wondering about the man. He seems too forthright to be honest, and yet there is no reason to believe he is anything else. His incidental reflections must often surprise his most cherished theories. He gives the same impression as so many first-rate writers: of being delighted to find that things are not the way they are supposed to be. In prose which combines the virtues of polish and simplicity, he conveys this delight to the reader, and therein is the source of endearment between Galbraith and the literate public. This marks an aspect of American life, and probably all civilized life, which is too little noticed: people love to be stunned, and kept on their toes, so long as it does not hurt too much. We hear so often of our complacency and resistance to change that we are amazed to find that it is not a banished commodity. It is not, because we are more alert and healthier as a people than we suppose. And so Galbraith may pursue his practice, in the great tradition of reason, without fear that his preachments will fall upon deaf ears. "For to what purpose," asked Adam Smith more than two centuries ago in the *Theory of Moral Sentiments*, "is all the toil and bustle of this world? What is the end of avarice and ambition, of the pursuit of wealth, of power, and pre-eminence?" He might have guessed that his question would be rephrased and asked again and again by his successors in the field of political economy. And so Galbraith resounds, in a voice per-haps destined to be heard down the decades, "The question now is *what* we produce and *for whom* and *on what* terms"—and intel-ligent people start shouting at each other and stamping their feet. This is not because any of them are necessarily wrong, but be-cause Galbraith is stating the correct question, with which they all must deal.

PART TWO

◆

The French have been the leaders in combining careers in politics and imaginative writing. No two twentieth-century writers have stood out more strikingly than Sartre and Malraux. All German writers became literary politicians for a spell in the thirties, but most did so out of necessity, not temperamental affinity. Only Brecht, among the past masters, retains a strong political tint today. Although it arrived late, the tradition in Germany now flourishes in the person of Günter Grass, whose *Diary of a Snail* is the testament of a political man unwilling to part with literary artifice. England had Orwell, whose successors have composed a pack of neo-nineteenth-century novels, lacking bite.

In the lands of the totalitarians, the most interesting writers tend to be literary politicians. Even a third-rater like Yevtushenko is of the breed. An unremarkable play set off the Great Proletarian Cultural Revolution in China. Meanwhile the exiles cluster and seethe at the rulers who cast them out. The West is for them a refuge, never a home.

American writers are normally ill-suited to the hustings, and feel better staying home and complaining about the national inhospitality toward genius. Occasionally they venture out, asserting their independence from partisan conformity. But if they like politics, they will find some platitudes and make themselves comfortable.

The present collection includes three interesting specimens

from a generation's harvest. All were born (Mailer, 1923; Lowell, 1917; Vidal, 1925) to that group which came of age with the second of the great wars. Lowell began with conscientious objection and a jail term, Mailer and Vidal with military service and war novels. All have been public figures ever since. Mailer linked arms with Henry Wallace and associated innocents, listened to harangues from Socialists and served up some of his own. Eventually he ran for mayor of New York City and lost. All the while he developed a political vocabulary suitable to astrological speculation, and devised a journalism which he employed to bless or curse the men in the arena.

Vidal moved from being suckled at the breast of Anaïs Nin to bathing in the lava gushed forth by Eleanor Roosevelt. He ran for Congress, lost, partied at the White House, got booted out by Bobby Kennedy, and poured out a stream of vituperation at Kennedys, conservatives, heterosexual moralists, and rich men.

Lowell has been less conspicuous, while writing editorials in verse form. Even so he pops up now and again, reading Dante, for instance, to the same Kennedy who showed Vidal the White House door. In 1968 he played troubador to Eugene McCarthy during the crusade to usurp the presidency from Lyndon Johnson. His role was unusual. Wilfrid Sheed found him alone with McCarthy at the end of the California primary. "They talked about which of his own poems he should read tonight, if the mood was on him; Lowell had helped him with one or two of them and made his recommendation meticulously; liking the rhythm of this one, the imagery of that one."[1]

Their political adventures have enforced their penwork. It is, of course, the writing that gives the politicking a passing interest. All three are Democrats, more or less. None would care to be so stamped, but that is typical of American writers. Moreover, all are politicians in the sense that they have used politics to enhance their literary careers, lifting them beyond the realms of meditation and entertainment where most writers dwell. They are seen engaging great issues, sparring with great personalities, giving no quarter to those who would claim superior wisdom because of their "practicality." Because of this, and despite the frequent

[1] Wilfrid Sheed, *The Morning After*, New York: Warner Books, 1972, p. 134.

bumbling that ensues, Mailer, Lowell, and Vidal are all chal-
lenging figures. Their presence forces the reader to take sides, not
so much on their politics, which are rarely original or even remarkable, but on their careers. Here they stand apart from their contemporaries in letters, who start us asking whether or not we like
their books. Mailer, Lowell, and Vidal cause us to ask what we
think of them as men. In this they achieve the stature of politicians, demanding that they be recognized as historical figures on
the current scene.

Norman Mailer

Two thirds of his way through life's journey, Norman Mailer has compiled a body of writing which at first glance appears as chaotic as his personal life has been. The latter has included five marriages, children ranging a generation in age, prison sentences for matters as straightforward as conscientious civil disobedience and as twisted as the stabbing of a wife, and critical and popular reception ranging from garish cover stories in *Time* magazine to vindictive charges of plagiarism by obscure free-lance journalists. Where and how does one begin to discuss such a career? Amid the perpetual backbiting of the literati and the boosterism of lobbyists for a Mailer Nobel Prize, amid the jealous debunkers who would have this laborious writer decried as a common huckster, how does one explore his lengthy catalogue of books without facing verbal assault in the obscene manner which Mailer himself has done so much to popularize? Before opening one of our subject's books to analysis, we must note as a caveat that Mailer has done his damnedest to introduce the ethical habits of angry longshoremen to the study of literature. And yet . . . the professors have already begun their lobotomies, determined to entomb Mailer among the American classics. And, if the hour is not already too late, it is time for those who dissent from this whole proceeding to be heard.

II

I say his career gives the initial appearance of chaos, because the observer need only stand back a bit to note a certain shapeliness in the entire affair. The professors who have a special aptitude for such things might even find Mailer's work divisible into three periods. The first, dating roughly from 1948–55, from *The Naked and the Dead* to *The Deer Park*, might be dubbed Mailer's early period, in which the author earned for himself the professional stamp of "Novelist" which he has carried with him on his various adventures ever since. The middle period, rising out of the ashes which the reception of *The Deer Park* had left in its author's mouth, was first punctuated by the appearance of *Advertisements for Myself*, a title which aptly describes this entire phase of close to twenty years. This second period proved far more prolific than the first. Besides the hasty composition of two novels, the author poured out reams of an exotic fashion of journalism, and a tittle of philosophy. He even produced, directed, and starred in three motion pictures. With the announcement in 1974 of a $1 million contract for Mailer's long-awaited "big novel," a third period seems to have begun. This, we may guess, is to be the period of crowning achievements, involving Mailerian labor on large canvases which will assure him of immortal glory.

It is an elegant scenario; so much so, in fact, that I shall momentarily leave it for the professors. I trouble myself to mention it at all because Mailer, in a sense, insists upon it, with his ridiculous proclamations of candidacy for a mythical "literary presidency." We are tempted at every turn to look upon the critical notices posted by the lady critics of the newspapers as if they were endorsements by power-breaking precinct bosses. We are all but asked to check the best-seller lists of the past quarter century in order to find out which "serious" writer has chalked up the most sales. Hear the author's testimony on the first stirrings of literary ambition within his breast:

. . . I may as well confess that by December 8th or 9th of 1941, in the forty-eight hours after Pearl Harbor, while worthy young men were wondering where they could be of aid to the war effort, and practical young men were deciding which branch of service was the surest for landing a safe commission; I was worrying darkly whether it would be more likely that a great war novel would be written about Europe or the Pacific . . .

Is this "confession" apocryphal or true? With Mailer we can never know for sure. In either case, its inclusion in a book entitled *Advertisements for Myself* bespeaks a temperament highly unusual in American letters. Henry Adams, in his *Education*, displays something of this sentiment: that history awaits each successive labored breath. The journals of Emerson have something of this moral vanity. But Adams, for all his indulgence in third-person autobiography, was writing autobiography in the conventional sense: as an old man looking back over the years of a lifetime. And Emerson's journals were not written for publication at all—at least not during the author's years on earth. We may look to Mailer's immediate predecessors for comparison. Hemingway, who inspired Mailer with his efforts to live out his ideas, never discussed his inner turmoil in the manner of the younger man. Fitzgerald, perhaps, came closer, with his example of overnight success and eventual disintegration; but Fitzgerald had none of Mailer's passion for politics and metaphysics, and even less interest in Mailer's peculiar combination of the two.

It is a fruitless exercise. Even the professors, I daresay, have been confounded in it.

Let us, instead, plod our way through the gushings of nearly three decades.

III

The Naked and the Dead is often praised as "the greatest novel to come out of World War II" and "the announcement of a bold new voice in American literature." Of all Mailer's books, it has been the one most immune to serious complaint. Even his detractors cite this first novel as a signal of "promise" which has gone sadly unfulfilled. Those who have been lukewarm to the book have been somewhat reticent in stating their objections—such as

Professor Alfred Kazin, who found *The Naked and the Dead* a trifle "too literary," whatever that may mean. The rule, however, has been to honor this novel with heaps of critical whipped cream, and begin one's arguments over Mailer from there. As an example, I offer the following deposition from Professor Robert Solotaroff, author of one of the more recent theses on Mailer. The talmudists of a later age will be impressed by the forty pages of analysis which open Professor Solotaroff's gospel on Mailer and address the forbidding subject of *The Naked and the Dead*. Here, the dark matter of a novel set in the jungles of a Pacific island is further obscured by such doctoral balderdash as:

> When the freedom of a character in a novel is most severely curtailed, when the author makes him no more than the point upon which the vectors of his society, heredity, and unconscious converge, freedom still exists but is transferred to the author himself and to the reader. In a thesis novel which attacks the inevitable effect of certain social malignancies, the author is asserting his own free will in writing the book and tacitly demanding that the reader exercise his free will to resist, change, or eliminate these malignancies. With its attack upon American society and its warning of the coming of fascism, *The Naked and the Dead* is in part a thesis novel, but we need not look this far for assertions of free will.[1]

Professor Solotaroff, having posited his windy notation on the psychology of reading novels, goes on to add that, within the pages of *The Naked and the Dead* itself, there exist such characters as actually *speak* for the author-reader in their battle against the insidious atmosphere of the book!

Against such learning, what rebuttal? I found *The Naked and the Dead* to be the dullest of all Mailer's books, excepting *Of a Fire on the Moon*. There is no coincidence here: a disagreeable author is most disagreeable at great length. His other books have their obnoxious features, but these two left me with a distinctive feeling of relief at having done with them. "Poor cheese, pretentiously wrapped," groused Hemingway, stopping after the second chapter of *The Naked and the Dead*. The temptation is to echo

[1] Robert Solotaroff, *Down Mailer's Way*, Urbana, Ill.: University of Illinois Press, 1974, p. 11.

the eminent Papa, and move on to other matters. But duty compels us to detail our grievances.

The Naked and the Dead is a simple story. A reconnaissance platoon lands at the invasion beach of Anopopei Island in the Pacific. It is sent on a dangerous patrol, suffers heavy casualties, and, in the end, discovers that the Japanese have been driven from the island independently of the labors of the platoon. The heart of the book is in the characters of the platoon, who come from backgrounds divergent enough to suggest a cross section of America. Hovering over the island, and the action of the book, is Mount Anaka, the symbolic importance of which was volunteered by Mailer: "I suppose the mountain was Moby Dick."

The story is couched in a setting of extremes. It is not enough that we have a war in the twentieth century, with all its horrible weapons; we must see the war as conducted on a tiny, stifling, malarial island. It is not enough that the commanding general recite the typical philosophical flubdub of American generals; no, he must be subject to dark latencies in politics and sexuality, too. It is inadequate that the platoon sergeant be a Texan of the up-an'-at-'em school; no, he must be so dreadful a man as crushes harmless birds in his hand for no better reason than spite. It is not satisfactory to have a lieutenant who is a graduate of Harvard and an upholder of liberal sentiments; no, this liberal must be of the sort who mixes high hopes for humankind with a Pecksniffish disdain for every individual human being with whom he comes into contact. Etc., etc.

Not since Carlyle concocted his Everlasting Yea has so irritable a pessimism in so young a man crawled beneath such woolly blankets of prose. To be sure, it is nothing when set against the books which follow. But it is here, for the first time, that we observe adjectives drawn from hither and yon as they are sent marching in dreary file. Behind them slosh thick catalogues of nouns. On the very first page a soldier removes from his bunk for an extended sitting upon the latrine box, because "it is cooler here, and the odor of the latrine, the brine, the chlorine, the clammy bland smell of wet metal is less oppressive than the heavy sweating fetor of the troop holds." The flashback on the life of Lieutenant Hearn concludes with Hearn contemplating "all the bright young people of his youth . . . A bunch of dispossessed . . . from the raucous

stricken bosom of America." Likewise, the other leading charac-
ters think in symbols so grand as to affect their deepest emotions.
The perverse Sergeant Croft, failed in his effort to climb Mount
Anaka,

> was feeling the anxiety and terror the mountain had caused on the
> rock stairway . . . Croft kept looking at the mountain. He had
> lost it, had missed some tantalizing revelation of himself.
> Of himself and much more. Of life.
> Everything.

Sometimes the author intrudes with commentary upon his narrative of all-consuming symbols. We are informed that the internal rhetoric is only partially that of the contemplative character,
while the rest is supplied by Mailer for the reader's more thorough
comprehension. So General Cummings hears an explosion in the
jungle, and reflects:

> The war, or rather, *war*, was odd, he told himself a little inanely.
> But he knew what it meant. It was all covered with tedium and
> routine, regulations and procedure, and yet there was a naked quiv-
> ering heart to it which involved you deeply when you were thrust
> into it. All the deep dark urges of man, the sacrifices on the hill-
> top, and the churning lusts of the night and sleep, weren't all of
> them contained in the shattering screaming burst of a shell, the
> man-made thunder and light? He did not think these things co-
> herently, but traces of them, their emotional equivalents, pictures
> and sensations, moved him into a state of acute sensitivity. He felt
> cleaned in an acid bath, and all of him, even his fingertips, was pre-
> pared to grasp the knowledge behind all this. He dwelt pleasurably
> in many-webbed layers of complexity.

So Cummings did not think of "the deep dark urges of man, the
sacrifices on the hilltop [?] . . . ," but thought of "traces of them,
their emotional equivalents, pictures and sensations." But what
might these be? And what, actually, is Cummings' state as he
prepares "to grasp the knowledge behind all this"? What knowledge? Some material force? Some God or devil? Some other
figment of the author's rhetorical imagination? Surely it is a pow-

erful piece of knowledge, since Mailer strains to indicate that even Cummings' fingertips are set to grasp it. But what it is must remain a mystery.

There are countless such passages in *The Naked and the Dead*, each of them coming at moments when, we guess, the author is attempting his highest rhetorical and philosophical flights. Images are stacked so high that we cannot see what is at the bottom of the pile. Chapters, units, and, ultimately, the entire novel grow murky. Is it the author's intention to leave as his final impression the feeling of having survived, just barely, the world of dark and swampy jungles? For that *is* the final impression of *The Naked and the Dead*, stronger than any imprint of the tensions and dangers of modern warfare, or of the souls of these soldiers from their divers backgrounds. The reason is Mailer's sluggish style, with its exasperating accumulation of detailed impressions. It is not as if we are reading a novel by Dreiser or Balzac, where we are able to spot irrelevant detail at a glance and then skip over it. Mailer's descriptions are not mere stage settings for a grander drama; they are the very drama themselves, filled with rhetorical fires which burst forth and spread wildly until finally simmering down, at which point we prepare ourselves for the next such conflagration. Whole scenes are bathed in this white heat, from which the charred characters of Mailer's novel struggle to make themselves known.

Complementary to this bloated narration are the flashbacks in which the author attempts to fill in the backgrounds of his soldiers. Labeled as "Time Machines," these passages adopt a different manner which is not so much brisk as it is laconic. The author is making a necessary but undesired detour from his main-traveled jungle roads. There is something of the Joycean stream-of-consciousness here; something more of the "Camera's Eye" of Dos Passos' *U.S.A.* But Mailer has managed a hodgepodge quite distinct from the methods of the two older writers. He simply cannot shake himself of the habit, to grow worse in future years, of fattening his material up. Sometimes this results in the introduction of non sequiturs; in other cases, it means the use of blunt verbal instruments, with which the reader is beaten over the head. One example here, though dozens are to be found: In the "Time Machine" of General Cummings, in which Mailer is detailing Cummings' progressive revulsion from his wife, a plain sentence stating, "He stares at her with loathing and disgust," is followed by a paragraph-sentence reading, "From Webster's: *hatred*, n. strong aversion or detestation; settled ill will or malevolence." And then a second paragraph-sentence: "A thread in most marriages, growing dominant in Cummings's." Finally, a third paragraph: "The cold form of it. No quarrels. No invective."

All of the "Time Machines" proceed in this manner, to depressing effect: it is like watching the march of clubfooted men, moving forward directly but with great awkwardness and uncertainty. What is most unfortunate about this is that these flashbacks are crucial to the integrity of the novel. Without them, the soldiers are merely the puppets of a prodigious rhetorician, a fairly brutish company of nobodies propelled into strange circumstances by a disinterested narrator; with these passages, Mailer would convince us they are All America. Yet, even the adoring Professor Solotaroff is forced to say that these portions of *The Naked and the Dead* do not come off. He writes, "A close reader of the Time Machines can see that, on the whole, Mailer has quite simply not been there, either in actuality . . . or with full imagination . . . Often he borrowed stereotypes—the bleak life of a Montana miner, the easy-going Southerner with his love of women and liquor . . . And he often tried to cover up his imaginative shortcomings with an inflated, vaguely grand yet over-obvious style."[2] Clearly Professor Solotaroff, who thinks *The Naked and the Dead* to be a great work of art, does not think sloppy character-drawing to be a literary defect of the first magnitude. But then, I do not know, would he also proclaim the greatness of the Sistine Madonna if the face were lightly sketched in pencil, so long as the neckline were mastered in oil?

It is among the fictions of English departments across the Republic that *The Naked and the Dead* represents Mailer's single effort at the composition of a "naturalistic novel"; and that, thereafter, for whatever reason, he abandoned naturalism for the more rarefied air of symbolism. This notion is particularly strong among the anti-Mailer crowd, to whom I referred earlier as those who wholeheartedly approve of *The Naked and the Dead*, but find nothing to please them in Mailer's succeeding work. It is, they say, a simple case of a writer having peaked too soon, and thereby

2 Ibid., p. 18.

feeling forced to abandon his original mode in order to explore new byways—in order, as they say, not to repeat himself. This is nonsense. The primary stylistic difference between *The Naked and the Dead* and its successors is length. The first novel is what used to be called a double-decker—a book long enough to engage the attention of those readers who consume one volume a season, the people who have made James Michener a wealthy man. This public has long since ceased to consider whether a book is naturalistic or symbolistic. Perhaps it realizes, sensibly enough, that the two traditions merged a long time ago. Naturalism historically identified itself through its detailed concern with life's unpleasant aspects. Symbolism involved the suggestion of more than a single layer of meaning, capable of identification by the discerning critic. No contemporary novel is taken seriously unless it traffics in unpleasantness and insists on its profundity. *The Naked and the Dead* is, thus, in the mainstream.

Surely no true naturalistic novel would be susceptible to the kind of analysis which Professor Solotaroff, for example, performs upon *The Naked and the Dead*—finding a little fascism here, a bit of liberalism there, a tittle of Marx in this line, a tattle of Melville in that one, and so on. What are all those vain strivings after Americana in the "Time Machines" if they are not intended to symbolize? What are those fetching tone poems on Mount Anaka? What are the stilted conversations between Cummings and Hearn? What, finally, is the book's conclusion, in which the labor of seven hundred pages is revealed to have been all for naught? As we read *The Naked and the Dead*, we come to feel that all those portentous declarations crowding the book's pages are more than idle and often foolish remarks. When Cummings suggests to Hearn, "You know, if there is a God, Robert, he's just like me," the statement is intended to nourish us through the upcoming pages of fatty narrative. The same applies to Hearn's thoughts on his generation, untimely ripped from the "raucous stricken bosom of America . . ." Here, we are supposed to think, are the keys to this novel full of vague hints and grimy details. Here is the meat of the thing, the heart of the matter . . .

And yet, *The Naked and the Dead* rambles on into what seems an eternity, full of false starts and abrupt halts, like a platoon without a commander, lost in a jungle of its own creation. It is not All America, for its America is too contrived. It is not All Life, for life is not so harsh. It is not even All War, or All Modern War, for war, in our own day as in others, is fought by as many decent men as by the perverse mammals in Mailer's command. No: here is a book filled with abnormal stresses and strains, ripped from the "raucous stricken bosom" of its author. It is too long by half and careless beyond measure. Had Mailer managed better in succeeding works, the inferiority of *The Naked and the Dead* would pass for dictum in the salons of Manhattan. As the works of the following years failed, and Mailer's scheming for publicity succeeded, the literati reached for whatever anchor would hold them. And *The Naked and the Dead* has proved sufficiently heavy to hold down tons of critical bilge.

IV

With *Barbary Shore* we have vacated the physical jungle for an artificial one: a boardinghouse in Brooklyn in which everyone meddles in everyone else's business. Here the author's symbolical pretensions are more overt, and Mailer labels his pretensions "existentialist." The book was published in 1951, three years after *The Naked and the Dead*. During this period, Mailer first conceived his ambition to become "the first philosopher of Hip," the results of which I shall defer from relating until further along in this monody. It is enough for now to mention that Mailer, looking back over the distance of a decade, felt that *Barbary Shore* marked his literary entrance into "the mysteries of murder, suicide, incest, orgy, orgasm, and Time." This is odd, since *Barbary Shore* does not trade in any of these matters with more than passing interest. Though the book can boast of a full Mailerian complement of loose ends, it is in fact a rather sour-tasting allegory of American Communism. Like all bad allegory, it leaves no impression save that of having made a wrong turn someplace, causing it to end up in no man's land. There are, to be sure, heavy dollops of vulgarity in it, as the early reviewers felt duty-bound to remark; but those who have followed Mailer's entire career will agree that *Barbary Shore* is fairly mild in this regard. To readers of *The Naked and the Dead*, it would not seem that Mailer has beat out any path along unfamiliar terrain. The style probes murky new depths, but this is due to the author's incompetence rather than his ingenuity. The characters are even less comprehensible than those of the first book, but only because we are not led through time tunnels. The story, allegory or not, lacks the rough plausibility of *The Naked and the Dead*. But all this merely represents the goose step of an artist marching firmly into the fifth rank.

Of all Mailer's works, *Barbary Shore* requires the least debunking. There are five primary characters in this book: Mikey Lovett, the narrator, lamentably suffering from amnesia and unable to tell us much about himself; Guinevere, the buxom landlady of the informal boardinghouse; McLeod, husband of Guinevere, an old partisan of Trotsky's in the Communist wars; Hollingsworth, Mikey Lovett's fellow boarder, a man of unclear purpose until it is revealed that he is an intelligence agent (for whom it is not clear) whose business is to do away with McLeod; and Lannie, a hysterical young woman who might, with a little stretching, be described as a predecessor of the Beats of the late fifties and the hippies of the late sixties. The plot is little more than a rough tissue of lies and deceptions, and a recapitulation of the book's conclusion is sufficient here.

McLeod, having disgorged thousands of words of revolutionary wisdom, is murdered by Hollingsworth, who flees with Guinevere and her young daughter. Lannie remains behind and greets the police. She informs them, "I love you even if you torment me, for you suffer," and is promptly booked. Mikey Lovett escapes down the alleyways of Brooklyn, a single envelope in hand. It is McLeod's will. When he is safe, Mikey opens it and reads, "To Michael Lovett to whom, at the end of my life and for the first time within it, I find myself capable of the rudiments of selfless friendship, I bequeath in heritage the remnants of my socialist culture." "Almost as an afterthought," Lovett informs us that McLeod has added, "And may he be alive to see the rising of the Phoenix."

To Mailer, *Barbary Shore* "has an air which for me is the air of our time, authority and nihilism stalking one another in the orgiastic hollow of our century." He does not realize that he has created such a neurotic cast of characters that one cannot perceive who is what and what is where. Whatever the "air" of our time is, our pulse is poorly measured by windy doctors of Trotskyism like McLeod. What is to be made of Hollingsworth, the seductive in- telligence agent? What can be gleaned from Lannie, who is, after all, insane? Even the lusty Guinevere is interesting only as a gro- tesque. To expect readers to be patient with such a lot, when the connecting thread is an amnesiac narrator, requires arrogance be- yond any acceptable level, even for authors.

Certain tendencies do begin to emerge in this novel, however. As in *The Naked and the Dead*, an air of conspiracy hovers over the proceedings. No one trusts anybody else, and we wait only to find out who is the worst of a dishonest bunch. No one seems able to tell the truth: Mailer is incapable of portraying people of straightforward decency; at best, there is a heavy price to be paid for honesty. Indeed, nearly all the twists in Mailer's plots proceed from some character having lied at some point along the way. Furthermore, the backgrounds of the characters are kept as shad- owy as possible. In *The Naked and the Dead* we are treated to those neatly packaged "Time Machines," in which each character molds into a stereotyped past, remote from life in the jungles of Anopopei Island. In *Barbary Shore*, narrator Mikey Lovett tips us off in the first sentence: "Probably I was in the war," he says, commencing the confusion. In *The Deer Park* we have barely reached the second paragraph before narrator Sergius O'Shaughnessy informs us, "I grew up in a home for orphans." In *An American Dream* the method is slightly different, but the effect is the same: Stephen Rojack has been a war hero and a con- gressman, has fluttered among the notables of his time, and, at the time his tale begins, has achieved celebrity as a television per- sonality and professor of existential psychology: a compendium of disjointed parts. None of Mailer's important characters are prod- ucts of any normal society of human beings, save those artificially manufactured by the "Time Machines" of *The Naked and the Dead*. Nor are the settings of his books those of normal society: the jungles of Anopopei, a boardinghouse filled with deranged conspirators, the New York underworld (*An American Dream*), the Alaskan forest (*Why Are We in Vietnam?*), a Hollywood resort (*The Deer Park*). All are meant as symbols of civilization, but none are themselves civilized. Man does not face Nature in Mailer's books; nor does Man face Man, in the classic sense; nor does Man face Society, in the modern manner; but, instead of all these, opposing forms of savagery square off against each other, propelled by urges they dare not restrain, suspicious of each other's similarities, and playing to the grandstand behind a smoke screen inflated by bombast.

Of these chronicles of the primitive life, *Barbary Shore* is no baser than, say, *An American Dream* or *Why Are We in Vietnam?*, but it is the most dependent on an ideological framework and, hence, the silliest of them all. How can any work so populated with rootless and unprincipled characters expect to stand up when these characters' most important activity is to deliver ponderous speeches? How can such flutterheads so indulge in the rhetoric of revolution and counterrevolution and still expect us to take them seriously? How can any novel rest its laurels upon these people's heads and expect to succeed on any level, save that of cheap contrivance?

V

Four years later, in 1955, the best of Mailer's novels appeared. *The Deer Park* is by no means first-rate. All of his defects, by now familiar, are there: a gaggle of characters whose origins are unclear and whose destinies are inconceivable; a heavy, laborious style, which fights the progress of the narrative every inch of the way; empty, meaningless rhetoric, passing itself off with haughty airs and threatening us with announcements of its own importance; and a rather eccentric indulgence in commentary on the current political scene. But there are virtues in *The Deer Park*—one central virtue, I should say. The book is a remarkable document on the oversexed imagination of the American male. In *The Deer Park*, the subject of sexuality has moved to the center of Mailer's stage. It has remained there ever since, unfortunately, and long ago chilled into wax in Mailer's unsteady hands. But at the time of *The Deer Park* Mailer was hot with his discovery of the modern variations on this ancient activity. So here, in full flower, is Sex as Transcendence, impersonated by film director Charles Francis Eitel: "For that minute and for another minute he loved her as he had never loved anyone, loved her and knew that the life of such a love was but a minute, because all the while he loved her he knew that he dare not love her." Here is Sex as Evil, with a call girl departing after a performance of fellatio on movie tycoon Herman Teppis: " 'There's a monster in the human heart,' he said aloud to the empty room." Here is Sex as Opportunity, confessed by narrator Sergius O'Shaughnessy:

> Women who have come to know me well have always accused me sooner or later of being very cold at heart, and while that is a woman's view of it, and a woman can rarely know the things that go on inside a man, I suppose there is a sort of truth to what they say.

The Deer Park is primarily set in a Southern California resort cutely named Desert D'or. There is no formal story, except in the sense that orphan Sergius O'Shaughnessy arrives after a stint in the Air Force, plays around a bit, and leaves in order to gain fresh experiences for a writing career. As the book ends, O'Shaughnessy is living in lower Manhattan, operating a bullfighting school, reading and writing feverishly on the side. The bulk of *The Deer Park* describes the sex lives of the resort's inhabitants. Other matters briefly intrude, such as the working concerns of the movie industry, but the reader senses that these intrusions are merely incidental, and not of great importance to the tale. When Charles Eitel is quarreling with members of an obnoxious congressional committee (these were the days of Joe McCarthy) or debating in his mind the advantages of doing cheap commercial work against remaining true to his artistic instincts, we take notice and move along. But when Eitel notices dimples in his mistress' legs, we know that the movie director's deepest anxieties are to be exposed. From cover to cover, sexual experience is succeeded by agonized reflection over the "truths" that such experience has revealed. The gravest conflicts in *The Deer Park* are settled, more or less, in the bedroom.

It is fairly obvious that all this sex among this glittering crowd is meant to symbolize something. But the metaphor lies too close to its master's heart. In the end, the most interesting aspect of the book—the unremitting focus on sexuality—brings the whole show down. *The Deer Park* is simply not a book which can be taken seriously. The old-fashioned, and still useful, word for this sort of book is melodrama. There hangs over its pages that murky, portentous, stilted quality which spoiled the two earlier novels and finally makes this one almost as exasperating. For all their intensity, these characters are too shallow and pitiable to stimulate concern after the first hundred or so pages. Even if it were Mailer's purpose in this book to expose the shallowness, the exposure itself is nothing original and could have been managed at considerably less cost of ink and paper.

Worst of all is the solemn manner in which so many trivial events are related. Mailer's characters enter a bedroom as hired Hessians of old would enter battle—filled with grave forebodings of the consequences, but impelled by an implacable, inner sense of duty. Yet the material of *The Deer Park* is essentially the stuff of comedy. Lord Chesterfield's reminder to his son, "The position is ridiculous," comes to mind; the novelist does well to proceed from there. Instead, Mailer has contrived to display our primal engagements as the source of all weeping, and our pillows as the main receptacles of the world's tears. Of course, he is a novelist, and may treat his material in any manner he pleases; but I believe him to be barking up the wrong tree. The genuinely original artist will take our modern sexual preoccupations and show them off as the absurd and amusing diversions they truly are; he will not moan and mythologize, in the manner of adolescents.

VI

Before assaying the collected confusion of *Advertisements for Myself* and *The Presidential Papers of Normon Mailer*, it is worthwhile to tie a few knots from the loose threads dangling out of the first three novels. As mentioned earlier, the first phase of Mailer's career ended with *The Deer Park*, a shifting of gears occurred, and Mailer began cultivating the literary personality which has marked his middle years. This has involved a rather prolonged series of distractions, during which Mailer has been at pains to identify himself as a "novelist" who merely dabbles in other fields; in short, a novelist who has stopped publishing novels. (Actually, he disgorged *An American Dream* and *Why Are We in Vietnam?*

during this phase, but these occupied him for approximately two of the past twenty years.) Moreover, it has involved an effort on Mailer's part to invest his fiction with extra-artistic values. We are informed, for example, that the last part of *The Deer Park* was written under the influence of mescaline. The only usefulness of such information is to distract the reader from honest and straightforward appraisal. Likewise with the following passage, a climactic moment in Mailer's lengthy and dreary narrative of the composition, publication, and reception of *The Deer Park*:

> Having reshaped my words with an intensity of feeling I had not known before, I could not understand why others were not over-come with my sense of life, of sex, and of sadness. Like a starved revolutionary in a garret, I had compounded out of my need and fever and vision and fear nothing less than a madman's faith in the identity of my being and the wants of all others, and it was a new dull load to lift and to bear, this knowledge that I had no magic to hasten the time of the apocalypse, but that instead I would be open like all the others to the attritions of half-success and small failures. Something God-like in my confidence began to leave, and I was reduced in dimension if now less a boy. I knew I had failed to bid on the biggest hand I ever held.

"Like a starved revolutionary in a garret"; "this knowledge that I had no magic to hasten the time of the apocalypse"; "something God-like in my confidence began to leave": such grandiose pro-nouncements surrounding the publication of *The Deer Park* call up the image of a desperate woodsman trying to inspire the em-bers of a tiny campfire into a great and roaring blaze. If it is the author's intention to cajole his way into immortality, then he is wasting, even as he is buying, time. But this tactic in itself comes as part and parcel of the New Mailer, arising out of the indifferent reception of *The Deer Park* and the slippage of his rep-utation.

If he revised his strategy for fame, he did not change his artistic preoccupations. Only his emphasis has shifted from one book to another. Fundamentally, there are three major concerns in all his writings: God (or some metaphysical variation on the idea of God), sex, and power. Around these three poles Mailer starts his rhetoric dancing at dizzying speeds, until fairly clear concepts are diluted, laundered, mixed, and spiced. Whole new forms emerge, huffing, puffing, and squirming their way out of Mailer's paragraphs. Beneath the locomotion we can trace the skeletal ideas behind Mailer's books.

These ideas have not sprung from the stratosphere full-blown; nor do they follow any traditional pattern, save a fairly systematic irrationalism. But in every novel we find the same characters, or combinations of characters, appearing under different titles. There is the "fascist," whose power drives are rooted in some degree of sexual perversity, and whose ideas about God and the universe are deranged accordingly: in *The Naked and the Dead*, there is General Cummings among the officers and Sergeant Croft among the rank and file; in *Barbary Shore*, Hollingsworth; in *The Deer Park*, Herman Teppis; in *An American Dream*, Barney Oswald Kelly; and in *Why Are We in Vietnam?*, Rutherford David Jethroe Jellicoe Jethroe. Each book has a character against whom this "fascist" faces off. It would be inaccurate to describe such characters as "liberals," for their particular political inclinations are usually irrelevant. Let us instead refer to them as "progressive forces" or "agents of change." These characters also have their sexual difficulties, but they are somehow of a purer, more heroic sort. These also seek power—often as savagely as the "fascists"—but, in Mailer's eyes, they form a separate group, more sympathetic than the "fascists" because their pursuit of power is "existential," they manage to break new ground, admit perished thoughts, shatter old precedents, and not rely on fascist repression. In *The Naked and the Dead*, the primary example of this kind of character is Lieutenant Hearn, though there are others who qualify in a less significant way; in *Barbary Shore*, McLeod, and, in the end, his inheritor Mikey Lovett; in *The Deer Park*, the character shifts from one scene to the next, and sometimes is Eitel, sometimes O'Shaughnessy, and sometimes Marion Faye—a hydra of hipsterism; in *An American Dream*, Stephen Rojack; in *Why Are We in Vietnam?*, D.J. Finally, each novel makes use of some grandiose symbol, existing above and beyond the lives of the individual characters. We may ascribe all kinds of hidden meanings to the symbol, calling it "God's agent" or "the force of the universe" or whatever, but it is enough to say that Mailer's rhetoric ties itself around this symbol before winding its way out into the lives of the individual characters. The characters, in their turn, are forced to identify themselves against the symbol. In *The Naked and the Dead* the symbol is Mount Anaka; in *Barbary Shore*, the "socialist ideal"; in *The Deer Park* there is Hollywood, darkly referred to as "the capital"; in *An American Dream* we have "the moon"; and in *Why Are We in Vietnam?*, a thousand-pound grizzly bear.

When Mailer turned to the writing of what is loosely called "non-fiction," he required very little change of method. Indeed, Mailer's method of novel-writing has never been as well suited to fiction as it has been to his rather eccentric journalism. The professors call his practice "dialectics." I call it the stuffing of straw men. A character, or idea, is introduced, pumped full with hot air, and left to catch the cross winds which Mailer manufactures to keep it aloft. The myth-and-symbol boys are great suckers for this sort of game, and give unrelenting chase. But the character-idea remains sufficiently out of reach, and the hunters for the "existential core" are kept at bay. Permit a quotation, once more, from the choking text of Professor Solotaroff:

> Since he evades most of the vocabulary, problems, categorizations, and thoroughness which we naturally associate with that branch of metaphysics, most serious students of philosophy would probably call him the illiterate half-brother of an ontologist. Yet he is a spinner of hundreds of ideas, most of which have ethical implications and all of which can be traced to the hypothesis that all being is in a Heraclitian flux—either expanding or contracting, growing into something better or deteriorating into something worse.[3]

"The illiterate half-brother of an ontologist"! Here is criticism which prophesies the introduction of the tarot card into the critic's tool chest! Farewell to the classical unities of Aristotle! Sam Johnson's reputation, gone! Announcing Professor Solotaroff's "illiterate half-brother of an ontologist," the first philosopher of Hip, the existential politician, the left-conservative prisoner of sex, the advertiser for himself!

[3] Ibid., pp. 82–83.

VII

Advertisements for Myself resulted from the author's starvation for celebrity. Unable to complete any sustained literary effort, Mailer collected short pieces published in periodicals, strung them alongside the unpublished and unpublishable stuff of two decades, added a verbose and alarming commentary, and called it a book.

He began by writing, "Like many another vain, empty, and bullying body of our time, I have been running for President these last ten years in the privacy of my mind, and it occurs to me that I am less close now than when I began." Nevertheless, his "present and future work" was bound to have "the deepest influence of any work being done by an American novelist in these years." The force behind this opinion welled up from within: "The sour truth is that I am imprisoned with a perception which will settle for nothing less than making a revolution in the consciousness of our time." (Something God-like in his confidence began to return.)

Advertisements for Myself continued with the reprint of mediocre short stories about the Second World War and its aftermath, banal Socialist critiques of world politics, and columns from *The Village Voice* whose unintelligibility recalls the unhappy spirit of Lannie from *Barbary Shore*. As a connecting thread, there is the autobiographical narrative/commentary, which consists mostly of three things: 1) complaints about the author's condition at the time the upcoming excerpt was composed; 2) complaints about the critical and/or popular reception of his books, and the concomitant turmoil this imposed on his life; 3) complaints about the works themselves. Mailer described the truth about himself as "sour" in the first paragraph of *Advertisements for Myself* and drove home his point by moaning on for five hundred pages.

Recognizing the need to help along busy readers lacking time enough to await an improvement in the author's mood, Mailer took what he termed "the dangerous step" of listing "the best pieces in the book." These are: "The Man Who Studied Yoga," "The White Negro," "The Time of Her Time," "Dead Ends," and "Advertisements for Myself on the Way Out." With the exception of "Dead Ends," this list includes those pieces which have received the highest praise from critics, as well as from the prophet himself. This allows for a measure of convenience in the forthcoming analysis.

"The Man Who Studied Yoga" is a long story in which the main event is the viewing of a pornographic movie by three married couples. In characteristic fashion, the story opens with a narrator of uncertain identity: "I would introduce myself if it were not useless. The name I had last night will not be the same as the name I have tonight. For the moment, then, let me say that I am thinking of Sam Slovoda." Sam is thereby identified as a "mild pleasant-looking man" who, in equally characteristic fashion, is not what he seems to be; in other words, he has deep and powerful yearnings and is "pleased to find that others are as unhappy as he . . . How often he tells himself with contempt that he has the cruelty of a kind weak man." This twitch notwithstanding, this is a modest portrait of a modest man. Sam aspires to write a novel. Although we never learn whether or not he gets around to writing it, it is a safe bet to assume that it will be a modest novel. In the meantime, Sam, his wife, Eleanor, and the two other couples are busy watching a pornographic movie on a Sunday afternoon, eating food from a kosher delicatessen, and interlacing all of this with modest conversation. Sam wonders if the movie will prompt the couples to throw off their inhibitions (and clothes) and have an orgy. It does not. Sam concludes that "the movie has made him extraordinarily alive to the limits of them all." It is all so modest as to be practically pointless. But at least one critic (Alfred Kazin) has called "The Man Who Studied Yoga" "extraordinary." He must have been referring to the modesty, so unwonted with this author.

"The Time of Her Time" is a fragment from a "long novel" which has never been completed and probably never will be. I think this improbability fortunate. "The Time of Her Time" signals the coming hilarity of Mailer's sexual scenes in *An American Dream*. I offer one sample, culled from three paragraphs:

> . . . A first wave kissed, a second spilled, and a third and a fourth and a fifth came breaking over, and finally she was away, she was loose in the water for the first time in her life, and I would have

liked to go with her, but I was blood throated and numb, and as she had the first big moment in her life, I was nothing but a set of aching balls and a congested cock, and I rode with her wistfully, looking at the contortion of her face and listening to her sobbing sound of "Oh Jesus, I made it, oh Jesus, I did."

"Compliments of T. S. Eliot," I whispered to myself, and my head was aching, my body was shot. She curled against me, she kissed my sweat, and then she was slipping away into the nicest of weary sweet sleep.

"Was it good for you, too?" she whispered half-awake, for having likewise read the works of The Hemingway, and I said, "Yeah, fine," and after she was asleep I disengaged myself carefully, and prowled the loft, accepting the hours it would take for my roiled sack to clean its fatigues and know a little sleep.

Thus, "The Time of Her Time." "Dead Ends" is another extract from the novel. It is a verse written by a "rich poet," who, according to Mailer, "is obsessed with the thesis that men become homosexual in order to save themselves from cancer." He offers a silly sermon in chopped-up prose, which makes neither sense nor music. To quote: "Narcissism, I say, yes, narcissism/is the cause of cancer/Cancer comes to those who/do not love their mate/ so much as they are loved/when they look at themselves/in the mirror." Then, a few lines later: "Or, better, smiled the host, why not say:/Our weary Father cannot sleep/for fear/that our first act/upon achieving Him/would be/to cut/His throat./So he bribed the devil with cancer/the queer of the diseases." Finally, there is Mailer's personal answer to the regulatory bodies of the U.S. government: "Cancer comes from/television/filter cigarettes/air conditioning/foam rubber/the smell of plastic/deodorant/wit that fails/antibiotics/the mirror, yes,/and all other attempts/of the sucker esprit/to get something/for no."

"Advertisements for Myself on the Way Out" is the final piece in the book. It is identified as the prologue to the unfinished novel. The third-to-last paragraph summarizes the questions which have been raised in the course of the prologue and concludes in a manner so incredible that I find it necessary to record it here, lest I be accused of distortion:

Or worst of all am I?—and the cry which is without sounds shrieks
in my ears—am I already on the way out? a fetor of God's brown
sausage in His time of diarrhea, oozing and sucking and bleating
like a fecal puppy about to pass away past the last pinch of the
divine sphincter with only the toilet of Time, oldest hag of them
all, to spin me away into the spiral of star-lit empty waters.

I turn finally to "The White Negro" as the centerpiece of the
volume. I do so with considerable trepidation, for the pedagogues
have found grounds for the highest praise in this strange essay,
whereas I could muster no more than a feeling of deep bewilderment. Run-on sentences predominate. Fairly simple ideas are announced at such length that even United States senators would be
astonished. We are assaulted by a barrage of threading needles
being shot from cannons.

"The White Negro" offers itself as a paean to conscientious
barbarism. This barbarism goes under the title of "Hip," and its
practitioners are "hipsters," or "American existentialists." Mailer
defines the hipster's role as follows:

> One is Hip or one is Square (the alternative which each genera-
> tion coming into American life is beginning to feel), one is a rebel
> or one conforms, one is a frontiersman in the Wild West of Amer-
> ican night life, or else a Square cell, trapped in the totalitarian
> tissues of American society, doomed willy-nilly to conform if one
> is to succeed.

Having said this, Mailer proceeds to describe the manner in
which one conforms to the standards of Hip. Two elements appear inviolate: 1) develop an obsessive enjoyment of jazz; 2) feel
the "inner experience of the possibilities within death"; this is to
serve as your "logic." These are the formative moments in the life
of the hipster. Resulting from their occurrence, we have a character who is to be regarded as a "philosophical psychopath, a man
interested not only in the dangerous imperatives of his own psy-
chopathy but in codifying, at least for himself, the suppositions
on which his inner universe is constructed." This seems very complicated, and bound to induce difficulties, even for Mailer's "wise
primitive." The difficulties, however, are to be solved in a rather

unique manner. "Orgasm is his therapy—he knows at the seed of
his being that good orgasm opens his possibilities and bad orgasm
imprisons him." There is much heavy balderdash set down in support of this thesis; finally we have come full circle and are back at
Point A: "The only Hip morality (but of course it is an ever-
present morality) is to do what one feels whenever and wherever
it is possible, and—this is how the war of the Hip and the Square
begins—to be engaged in one primal battle: to open the limits of
the possible for oneself, for oneself alone, because that is one's
need." Stranger still, "The White Negro" concludes with a misty-
eyed hosanna for *Das Kapital*, whose implied prescription for
human society would mean death for all hipsters, their prophet
first of all.

No reader with much knowledge of the world could take
seriously this encouragement of selfishness for its own sake. If
there is any more to the message of "The White Negro," I have
not found it, and I have reviewed the piece several times in order
to drive out my initial bewilderment. "To open the limits of the
possible for oneself, for oneself alone, because that is one's need"
really means, What can I do to break free of the torment which is
my life? Heaven only knows, but within three years Mailer was in-
carcerated in New York's Bellevue prison hospital for the seem-
ingly pointless stabbing of his second wife. Later it would be
noted that the stabbing represented only one of many efforts to
apply a philosophy to everyday life.

VIII

The excerpts from the unfinished novel and "The White Negro"
were the first samples of that "present and future work" which
Mailer forecasted would have such shattering impact on our
times. It is possible that he deserves some credit for our contemporary turmoil; it is more likely that he has served merely to illu-
minate it with his own example. The interested reception of "The
White Negro" and the excerpts from the unfinished novel had
something to do with his pursuit of the direction in which these
pieces led. "Advertisements for Myself on the Way Out," for example, revealed an aptitude for scatology which Mailer had fairly

well buried after describing the emptying of a soldier's bowels in the opening pages of *The Naked and the Dead*. "The White Negro" was his first essayistic step into the dizzying heights of metaphysics, though he had licked his chops through the early novels for some chance to enter that arid realm. The combination of scatology and metaphysics would make for some strange moments, and would strain the tri-polar axis of God, sex, and power to incredible lengths, but it seemed to Mailer and his acolytes that this was something new under the sun, and therefore deserving of every intelligent man's notice. As he wrote in a preface to his *Presidential Papers*, "In America few people will trust you unless you are irreverent; there was a message returned to us by our frontier that the outlaw is worth more than the sheriff." Writers of book jackets referred to him as "the badboy of American letters." He cultivated the label, and set out to see what he could get away with.

All those who would follow Mailer's career from the time of *Advertisements for Myself* forward are advised to keep their senses of humor standing guard. In the opening number of *The Presidential Papers*, the following five pieces of "Existential Legislation" are proposed: 1) Abolish all capital punishment, "except in those states which insisted on keeping it." The hitch: the insistent states should be required to engage an executioner in corporeal struggle to the death with the condemned criminal, thus permitting the possibility that the executioner might be the one to die. This, says Mailer, "might return us to moral responsibility." 2) "Cancer is going to become the first political problem of America in twenty years." Therefore, all cancer researchers should be forced to make "progress in their department" within two years or face a meeting with one of Mailer's executioners. 3) Make the sale of "drugs" legal, a good reason for this being, "It is possible that many people take heroin because they sense unconsciously that if they did not, they would be likely to commit murder, get cancer, or turn homosexual." 4) Loan the Russians, on a long-term basis, "countless committees of the best minds we have on Madison Ave." Why? "If our hucksters have been able in fifteen years to leech from us the best blood of the American spirit, they should be able to debilitate the Russians equally in an equivalent period." 5) Abolish censorship, legalize pornography:

this might mean "the salvation of the Republic, for America would then become so wicked a land that Russia would never dare to occupy us, nor even to exterminate us by the atom bomb, their scientists having by then discovered that people who are atomized disseminate their spirit into the conqueror." How sad that this lightheadedness should be supported by leaden feet. Dare we mark this as a sample of Mailer's cancer-causing "wit that fails," and shall we then consign the author to a slow and painful death, a victim of his own verbosity?

Elsewhere in *The Presidential Papers* he turns to the subject of "Totalitarianism":

Totalitarianism came to birth at the moment man turned incapable of facing back into the accumulated wrath and horror of his historic past. We sink into cancer after we have cheated all the diseases we have fled in our life, we sink into cancer when the organs, deadened by chemical rescues manufactured outside the body, become too biologically muddled to dominate their cells. Departing from the function of the separate organs, cancer cells grow to look like one another. So, to, as society bogs into hypocrisies so elaborate they can no longer be traced, then do our buildings, those palpable artifacts of social cells, come to look like one another and cease to function with the art, beauty, and sometimes mysterious proportion of the past.

What lucid nonsense! Totalitarianism has nothing to do with some failure to face "the accumulated wrath and horror of [man's] historic past"; it is, if anything, the most natural and primitive method of government, and is achieved by the triumphant application of brute strength. To no one's knowledge is cancer caused by taking penicillin shots. And does Mailer really protect the cultural seal by stomping into modern buildings and pronouncing them "totalitarian" on the spot?

So saith the illiterate half-brother of an ontologist. The perspectives on totalitarianism, cancer, society, and architecture are hallowed specimens of the Mailer philosophy, spewed forth as if they were major contributions to world thought. How many really accept this stuff at its author's valuation? How many, if called to answer, will hoot at the insensitivity of the rest of us and laugh at our innocence of the existential truths? How many will swallow "The Metaphysics of the Belly" and insist that Mailer has reordered the Kantian categories in the "Political Economy of Time"? This last piece is but three lines old before its first report is heard: "Feces, after all, are first cousin to gold." Stumble on a few pages more, and then retire. "Nobody writing in America," wrote Kenneth Tynan in review, "cares so deeply about so many things, personal and political, vital and various." I reflected upon reading this that he must have intended an ironic reference to the bowels as the source of Mailer's thought. I have since recovered from my hallucination.

IX

He attempted to touch yet another base by mounting a dramatic version of *The Deer Park*. "There were too many years," he later wrote in his coy, third-person style, "when he dreamed of *The Deer Park* on Broadway and the greatest first night of the decade, too many hours of rage when he declaimed to himself that his play was as good as *Death of a Salesman*, or even, and here he gulped hard, *A Streetcar Named Desire*."

But his play was a bore. He turned to politics, where there is always room for another actor. Early in the sixties, he geared up for a run at the mayoralty of New York City. The wife-stabbing brought his candidacy to a prompt conclusion. In 1969 he took another shot at the same office, won the hearts of many New Yorkers with his eccentric views, and finished fourth among five candidates in a primary election.

It was as a writer, however, that Mailer most fervently sought to direct the politics of the day. In 1960 he was assigned by *Esquire* to issue a personal report on the Democratic convention of that year. John Kennedy was the nominee; Mailer watched a star rise and called his article "Superman Comes to the Supermarket." The author thought that "this piece had more effect than any other single work of mine, and I think this is due as much to its meretriciousness as to its merits." Mailer felt that his dubbing of Kennedy as "the Existential Hero" was a matter of great historical moment. "My piece . . . added the one ingredient Kennedy had not been able to find for the stew—it made him seem exciting, it made the election appear important. Around New York there was a turn in sentiment; one could feel it; Kennedy now had glamour."

As Mailer laments his meretriciousness, he tacitly confesses his innocence. He knew very little about his subject, and bounded into political affairs with all of the enthusiasm, but none of the knowledge, that he carried into affairs of the bedroom. Surely this first convention must have seemed wondrous to Mailer, formerly a mere participant in Socialist peace conferences held in musty quarters. So his report was filled with run-on catalogues:

> A political convention is after all not a meeting of a corporation's board of directors; it is a fiesta, a carnival, a pig-rooting, horse-snorting, band-playing, voice-screaming medieval get-together of greed, practical lust, compromised idealism, career advancement, meeting, feud, vendetta, conciliation, of rabble-rousers, fist-fights (as it used to be) and collective rivers of animal sweat.

His admirers will argue that 1960 was his first time out, that each convention improved his political savvy. Alas, it is not so. The witness to a political convention is like the witness to an orgy; an act performed in the extreme masks its rudimentary aspects; only the trained eye can perceive the hidden meanings. Twelve years after "Superman Comes to the Supermarket," in a volume on the 1972 conventions entitled *St. George and the Godfather*, Mailer is still resorting to this sort of thing:

> The war in Vietnam had done much to take away one's faith that lawn tennis, proper posting, and a nose for the shift of the wind had any value in the training of leaders when the most powerful nation in the world had squandered its moral substance in a war of massive bombardments, near to meaningless, a wholly cancerous war of the technological age. (Of course it is possible that the cancer cell, if possessed of a voice, would argue that it is trying to redesign a way out of the insoluble contradictions of the body.)

The country does not fight a war it should not have fought; it "squander[s] its moral substance." Cancer cells arise to argue their case, and lawn tennis, etc., are devalued because of a cancerous war. Mailer does not see the human comedy of politics and political conventions, but concocts instead the transformation of politicians into biological forms, biological matters into moral substances, and morality into the politics of warring biologies. "Were the armies of the final Armageddon," concludes one chapter in *St. George and the Godfather*, "forming in the seed of men not yet born, or would even this calm summer end in blood?" This is the rhetoric of one who feels he must say something, but can cough up nothing intelligent. The metaphysician cannot stay away, and whereas such meddling with the facts makes all of Mailer's journalism somewhat peculiar, it renders his political pieces downright clownish. This is highly ironic, because Mailer does not intend to jest. He ends by joining the large party of intellectuals, past and present, who have determined to discover solemn meanings in American politics. All have made fools of themselves.

Mailer sprouted from the cadre of homespun Marxists. In his early days he was gung ho for Henry Wallace, and all his life he has suffered from noctural visitations in which the FBI and CIA assume the roles of Demon Fascist and Lord Totalitarian. One entire novel, *Barbary Shore*, was sustained by this gory nightmare, and whole batches of Mailer's essays have not a leg to stand on if you pull this prop out from under them. As the years passed, this airtight perspective lost much of its charm, not least because it offered so little explanation for those briny currents beneath the surface of things, the "existential truths." So the novelist-metaphysician came up with a new scheme: "existential politics" or, in plainer if not clearer language, "left-conservatism." This new arrangement enabled Mailer to consolidate his personal fashion of selfishness in the traditional manner of the Left—by socializing it.

If I state the matter a trifle too simply, I still avoid indulging Mailer in his tenacious obfuscation. Conservatives looked long and hard to find the "conservatism" in Mailer's left-conservatism, but most conceded that all they could discover was a certain concern for the individual, and one individual in particular. No less a leader of the Conservative College of Cardinals than William F. Buckley, Jr., wondered aloud if his creed had enough neuroses in it to keep Mailer happy. Certainly there was nothing there of conservatism as it is known to contemporary America. Hear him on the hero of the 1964 Republican convention:

Goldwater was a demagogue—he permitted his supporters to sell
a drink called Gold Water, twenty-five cents a can for orange concentrate and warm soda—let no one say it went down like piss—
he was a demagogue. He was also sincere. That was the damnable
difficulty. Half-Jew and blue-eyed—if you belonged in the breed,
you knew it was manic-depressive for sure: a man who designed
his own electronic flagpole to raise Old Glory at dawn, pull her
down at dusk—he had an instinct for the heart of the disease—
he knew how to bring balm to the mad, or at least to half the
mad. Goldwater would have much to learn about Negroes.

His conclusion about such a man as Goldwater having been nomi-
nated? "The wars are coming and deep revolutions of the soul."
Fr. Buckley aside, the conservatives were not endeared. Were they
even more enchanted by Mailer's confession, in *St. George and
the Godfather*, that he had come to admire the mind of Richard
Nixon? Not when they read on to discover that the source of
Mailer's admiration was his conviction that Nixon's sense of
American vulgarity was even greater than his own. In other words,
Nixon might call them the silent majority and Mailer call them
"wads," but they were talking about the same thing. Nixon's vision was more comprehensive than Mailer's, in Mailer's view, because Nixon held greater power in the Republic. Little matter
that four years before, in *Miami and the Siege of Chicago*, Mailer
had spoken of Nixon as the apotheosis of the mediocre. The glorious years of the first Nixon administration had inspired Mailer's
revised opinion of the President whose abject corruption had not
yet been exposed. His final verdict has not been rendered. Is
Nixon to be inscribed in the history books as the "existential
wad"?

So much for the conservative half of the left-conservative. The
Left, of course, is Mailer's true home. The history of the Left is
all the history he seems to know, and the future of the Left
figures prominently in his concerns, somewhere between the future of the novel and the future of the genital orgasm. "The night
Kennedy was elected," he wrote in a postscript to "Superman
Comes to the Supermarket," "I felt a sense of woe, as if I had
made a terrible error, as if somehow I had betrayed the Left and
myself." Like any fanatic, he feared "the compromises and

hypocrisies of the new Democratic administration." So he hungrily joined other dunces on the Fair Play for Cuba Committee, and drew up the preposterous "Existential Legislation" cited earlier. As things turned out, the first half of the sixties was a good time for the Left, but Mailer's sour temper ruled out any hosannas and hallelujahs on his part.

The second half of the decade, however, was the time of the late, lamented crusade to save South Vietnam for democracy. This was the war in which Mailer believes the United States "lost its moral substance," though it did a great deal to enhance Mailer's fame. He went so far as to dedicate his *Cannibals and Christians* "to Lyndon B. Johnson, whose name inspired young men to cheer for me in public." The American Academy of Arts and Letters cheered too. The novel *Why Are We in Vietnam?* was nominated for a National Book Award in 1967. The following year the Academy was joined by the Pulitzer committee in offering its blessings and prizes to the central volume of Mailer's middle period, *The Armies of the Night*.

Ostensibly the book is an account of the October 1967 anti-war march on the Pentagon. Many others who were there have discounted the book as hopelessly inaccurate, and have, accordingly, dismissed it from further consideration. On this charge I stand with Mailer's defenders, who insist that the book cannot be pigeonholed as a simple journal. For whatever reason, Mailer poured his whole self into this one, as he did not do with his reports of political conventions or boxing matches or the moon shot. The ridiculous metaphysics of the dialogues are here, but so is the lugubrious egotism of *Advertisements for Myself*; the creator of Stephen Rojack and *An American Dream* lets us in to watch as protagonist "Mailer" vomits until his stomach is empty; so does the preacher of "The Psychology of the Orgy" rise in his pulpit to declaim on other matters in a different time. *The Armies of the Night* is only 10 per cent fact and 90 per cent stretchers; it is, thus 100 per cent Mailer.

What was it about a protest march against the Vietnam war which engaged these various energies? Mailer, as usual, answered all questions before they were asked:

Mailer had been going on for years about the diseases of America, its oncoming totalitarianism, its oppressiveness, its smog—he had

written so much about the disease he had grown bored with his
own voice, weary of his own petulance; the war in Vietnam
offered therefore the grim pleasure of confirming his ideas. The
disease he had written about existed now in the open air: so he
pushed further in his thoughts—the paradox of this obscene
unjust war is that it provided him with new energy—even as it
provided new energy to the American soldiers who were fighting
it.

Besides, the "big novel" was stalled again, and the march provided an opportunity to let loose. The self-confessed ham actor
and amateur politician peppers his story by getting drunk, ram-
bling on incoherently, and successfully seeking out arrest. (Eventually, all appeals exhausted, he served a five-day jail sentence.)
He whoops up minor controversies by assessing the literary and
personal qualities of the "competition" which happens to be
along for the march. He doubts his sincerity by complaining that
the arrest will keep him from a fancy party back in New York. He
sketches U.S. marshals and Virginia troopers, finding room
enough to hang them in his portrait gallery of American fascists.
He composes a quick history of the American Left since the Great
Depression, and of the growth of the New Left. And he ends it all
with a full page of heavy breathing on the subject of American
destiny, without which any opus from Mailer would seem incomplete. No wonder the givers of prizes were so pleased! Anyone
who had taken a Mailer volume to heart in the past found something in this potpourri to recall his fondest memories. All those
who had clamored for Mailer to burst into full flower now had
some signal that the great moment was near at hand. Each may
have had a different notion of what form the flowering would
take, but no one could set down *The Armies of the Night* without
plucking from it a single petal to be treasured.

To naysayers, *The Armies of the Night* only magnifies its author's professional flaws: verbosity, pretentiousness, intellectual la-
ziness, and paltry moralizing. Its pessimism is wordy and forced;
even bored with his own voice, Mailer does not fail to repeat himself. We are once more entertained with tirades on the disease of
technological America, the battle lines being drawn, the coming
of Armageddon. But the terms are never clear, the thinking is

foolish, the author throws in a few bad jokes, starts ranting wildly, and the thing goes up in smoke. "Whole crisis of Christianity in America," begins the final page of *The Armies of the Night*, "that the military heroes were on one side, and the unnamed saints on the other!" Stuff and nonsense, as they used to say. The saints are unnamed because they are not saints, and the military heroes of Vietnam were never heroes at all.

A year later, inside the Chicago amphitheater, Mailer once more looked for saints and heroes. He saw the children of the Revolution, sprawled out over the streets and parks of the city. Listening to their music, he heard

> the roar of the beast in all nihilism, electric bass and drum driving behind out of their own non-stop to the end of the mind. And the reporter, caught in the din—had the horns of the Huns ever had noise to compare? knew this was some variety of true song for the Hippies and adolescents in the house, in this enclave of glass and open air . . . crescendos of sound as harsh on his ear . . . as to drive him completely out of the sound, these painted dirty under-twenties were monsters, and yet . . .

The sentence runs on hysterically for a full page, concluding that there was a saintly aspect to the kids. As rich and famous as he had become, he retained his youthful affinity for revolutionaries. Never mind that the kids had one eye on heaven and the other on the television cameras.

The essence of these political reports is their gasping incoherence. Of course Mailer is capable of occasional insights; what prolific babbler isn't? But how worthy is the writer of the description of Hubert Humphrey in *Miami and the Siege of Chicago*? At first, he is seen as having a face "which was as dependent upon cosmetics as the protagonist of a coffin." Two lines later, he has "the shaky put-together look of a sales manager who takes a drink to get up in the morning." Accordingly, he is an actor who tonight has assumed the role of "the bachelor uncle who would take over a family (left him by great-Uncle Baines)," and his oratory converts him into "a holy Harry Truman." When he speaks of peace in Vietnam, according to Mailer, Humphrey feels "like a virgin," and he speaks "with the innocent satisfaction of a drop of oil sliding down a scallion." His calls for national unity signify that, "Back of that drop of oil, he was an emollifacient, a fifty-gallon drum of lanolin." Finally, when he turns around to greet people, he has "the look of a squat little Mafioso of middle rank, a guy who might run a bookie shop and be scared of many things, but big with his barber, and the manicurist would have the Miami hots for him." Like so much else in Mailer, this passage is mere self-indulgence. Scattershot phrasemaking does not constitute description. Hubert Humphrey bears no relation to this wild picture of him; Mailer has no idea of what to do with him. As in his novels, where ordinary patterns of behavior are not represented, in his journalism Mailer cannot get hold of any outward reality. He jumps and hops and skips; he vacillates and contrives what he does not know; he bears armloads of words but mere thimblefuls of wisdom; he improvises for the moment and barks about eternity, but he cannot see steadily through to the morrow and returns the spotlight to face himself.

Rising from these forays into politics, I recall a particular report, in a similar vein, from another year: H. L. Mencken on "The Wallace Paranoia" of 1948. Mencken wrote of the Wallace boosters, cursed with "believing minds," that, "Such types persist, and they do not improve as year chases year." He noted the "many quite honest, and even reasonably intelligent folk, who served as raisins in the cake. Some of them I recalled seeing years ago at other gatherings of those born to hope." Mailer, of course, began in their ranks, hoisting the banners of the mystic Wallace among Mencken's "grocery-store economists, moony professors in one-building 'universities,' editors of papers with no visible circulation, preachers of lost evangels, customers of a hundred schemes to cure all the sorrows of the world." In a sense, I suspect, Mailer has never left them. He has gone on to other things, of course, but the believing mind, once set in its mechanics, cannot revert to the laughing heresies of the skeptic. So Mailer has never been satisfied to step on society's toes; he must lead armies in great crusades of the night, yelling wildly of revolutions that will never come and of enemies who simply stare at him and smile. His reporting amuses civilized men as astrologers and temperance unions do. It offers the pathetic picture of a reporter who is little more than a furious sifter of stardust.

X

"Journalism is chores," opens "The Faith of Graffiti," Mailer's celebration of the defacement of New York's subways. "Journalism is bondage unless you can see yourself as a private eye inquiring into the mysteries of some new phenomenon." The fauna and flora of life do not amuse him so much as they project dark images before his mind's eye. Mailer moves himself front and center, letting his conscience contrive the drama. Whether he writes about a political convention, a moon shot, or a sex goddess, his subject is always himself. Genuine historical figures are mere straw men before the person of "Mailer." A riot of metaphor is unleashed. Strange gods arise to cast their glow. In searching for "the mysteries of some new phenomenon," he seeks to express the inexpressible and assert the truth of what is obviously untrue.

Because God, sex, and power are his themes, Mailer never strays far from his arguments over the warring biologies of politics. I have already termed *Of a Fire on the Moon* Mailer's dullest book, and have stated my reason for saying so. It begins with Mailer's recollection of the death of Hemingway, moves on to recall his experiences as a mayoral candidate, and gradually eases into a discussion of NASA and the space program. Eventually there is an accounting made of the first manned space flight to the moon, replete with descriptions of the astronauts' houses and the author's metaphysical extrapolations from the astronauts' vague mumblings, both in flight and on the moon. The final section of the book reverts back to the author's life at Provincetown, on Cape Cod, detailing the burial of an old car and the ruination of a dinner caused by the drunkenness of one of Mailer's friends. Finally, Mailer curses his "generation" (of writers? Leftists? Hipsters?):

> They had roared at the blind imbecility of the Square, and his insulation from life, his furious petulant ignorance of the true tremor of kicks, but now it was as if the moon had flattened all of his people at once, for what was the product of their history but the bombed-out brains, bellowings of obscenity like the turmoil

of cattle, a vicious ingrowth of informers, police agents, militants, angel hippies, New Left totalists, entropies of vocabulary where they would all do their thing—but "thing" was the first English word for anomaly—an unholy stew of fanatics, far-outs, and fucked-outs where even the few one loved were intolerable at their worst, an army of outrageously spoiled children who cooked with piss and vomit while the Wasps were quickly moving from command of the world to command of the moon, Wasps presenting the world with the fact after prodigies of discipline, while the army he was in, treacherous, silly, overconfident and vain, haters and debunkers of everything tyrannical, phony, plastic and overbearing in American life had dropped out, goofed and left the goose to their enemies.

It could serve as an epitaph, if we might fit this prodigious sentence on a tombstone. Many an evening's exercise was required before I reached it. After fifty pages of *Of a Fire on the Moon* I found myself scratching; after one hundred, snoozing. I do not admit to having read every word. The style, particularly when Mailer reviews the ABCs of space flight, induces daydreams of Prussian academies: of absent-minded professors droning on through lazy afternoons while students plot their escape to the nearest beer hall. There are digressions on every imaginable subject, from Cézanne to the phallic symbolism of the rocket shape. To assure the utmost in soporific effect, there is a piling on of technological data—lest we forget that Mailer took his Harvard degree in engineering. All of this leads him, not only to pronounce the curse on his generation, but also to proclaim the end of the twentieth century: "it had ended in the summer of 1969."

Give Mailer technology, and his mind swirls in stratospheric fantasy; give him biology, and he crawls back into the womb. This is the story of *The Prisoner of Sex*, a belching sermon on the varieties of sexual experience. Vaginal orgasm is morally correct, other sexual positions and practices carry connotations of evil; abortions are all right, because they involve the exercise of conscience and the recognition of evil; birth control pills are symptomatic of technological totalitarianism. "As the male and female blurred into a form which was not yet clearly one, so the center for preoccupation in sex passed from procreation to the 'soft, warm, wet' of the polymorphous-perverse, from conception to contraception, from the vagina to the anus, as if the mark of a civilization dying should be a mountainous sense of excitement for the hole which presides over waste." "For the fuck either had a meaning which went to the root of existence, or it did not; sex, finally, could not possess reasonable funds of meaning the way food does."

And his response to the feminists?

Finally, he would agree with everything they asked but to quit the womb, for finally a day had to come when women shattered the pearl of their love for pristine and feminine will and found the man, yes that man in the million who would become the point of the seed which would given an egg back to nature, and let the woman return with a babe who came from the root of God's desire to go all the way, wherever was that way. And who was there to know that God was not the greatest lover of them all?

This biological chivalry was resumed in *Marilyn*, a biography of actress/sex goddess Marilyn Monroe. As would be expected, the narrative spins off into several directions, and often gives the impression of being deranged. Irrelevant comments on Richard Nixon creep in, until we are offered this historical synthesis: "So the decade that began with Hemingway as the monarch of American arts ended with Andy Warhol as its regent, and the ghost of Marilyn's death gave a lavender edge to that dramatic American design of the Sixties which seemed in retrospect to have done nothing so much as to bring Richard Nixon to the threshold of Imperial power." (What ever happened to the moon shot as the climax of the century?) *Marilyn* is also a lecture in sociology. Here is a sample: "If a void in one's sense of identity is equal to a mental swamp where insane growths begin, then America is an insane swamp more than other lands." Unfortunately, no identification of sane swamps is made.

When relating the subject of sex to Marilyn Monroe, Mailer observes, "She was our angel, the sweet angel of sex, and the sugar of sex came up from her like the resonance of sound in the clearest strain of a violin." Accordingly, she may be seen as "a very Stradivarius of sex." As far as the subject concerned Monroe, "Sex was, yes, ice cream to her." This ice cream had a most unusual flavor and consistency, as elsewhere Mailer writes, "Sex was not unlike an advance of little infantrymen of libido sent up to the surface of her skin." The lover of sex-as-ice-cream thus became "a general of sex before she knew anything of sexual war." And no ordinary general either: she was comparable to Napoleon. "Indeed, if occult histories of the future wish to look for Karma that leads from Napoleon to Monroe, let us recognize that she will die in a house on Fifth Helena Drive." One karmic relation will not do; Mailer wants his piece of the action as well. "If he wished to play anagrams, she was also Marlon Y. Normie, and an unlimited use of the letters in *el amor* gave Marolem Mamroe a forthright Latin sound (considerably better than Morman Maeler)." And yet another: "It was possible that she was the last of the myths to thrive in the long evening of the American dream—she had been born, after all, in the year Valentino died, and his footprints in the forecourt at Grauman's Chinese Theater were the only ones that fit her feet." All in all, thinks Mailer, her power over us is not yet done: "It is the devil of her humor and the curse of our land that she will come back speaking Chinese."

In *Marilyn* it was heroine worship which moved him; in *Genius and Lust*, his edition of the writings of Henry Miller, it was hero worship. In both cases, sexuality was the unifying theme. Elsewhere, Mailer's journalism has confined him to his depiction of life as a tempest-tossed war of competitive barbarisms. Faithful to the Hemingway tradition, he has glorified boxers and bullfighters; faithful to his own, he has honored troublemakers and taken them under his wing. In his long essay on "The Faith of Graffiti," his own logic forced him to conclude of all those blotches on subway walls, "A new civilization may be stirring in [graffiti's] roots." And Mailer asked, "Was it that one could never understand graffiti until there was a clue to that opposite fashion to look upon monotony and call it health?" Consider the reverse: that Mailer has looked upon health and called it monotony—totalitarian and ultimately cancerous; that he has looked upon chaos and called it the beginning of a new civilization. It is his code, and doubtless he will stay true to it until the end.

XI

It is as a novelist that Mailer wishes to be known; we return to his novels of the sixties to see where this "big novel," this crowning glory, is likely to land. We happen upon two awful books, both wildly controversial in their day, and now deserving of our forgiveness and our forgetfulness.

An American Dream and *Why Are We in Vietnam?* are intellectual potboilers. A novelist's weird ideas need not necessarily spoil his fiction: after *My Religion* and *What Is Art?* Tolstoy still managed *Resurrection* and *The Kreutzer Sonata*; Dickens survived a strong injection of Carlyle's hero worship and kept one eye open to humanity's foibles; and Dreiser, after discovering some similarities between squids and men, did not confuse the two. But these were novelists of the first rank. In the case of a Mailer, the problem is more complicated. His symbol-ridden imagination proves embarrassing when the symbols cap stupid ideas. Readers of the novels are not spared the odd notions of cancer and sexuality which inform the essays. They are now more loudly asserted than in the first three novels, and are combined with the dubious characters, awkward plots, and unreasonable demands on the reader's suspension of disbelief.

An American Dream was Mailer's first novel in nearly ten years, and the author had endured much in the interim which had not undergone the transition to fictional form. He had grown intimate with "mind-expanding" drugs, explored "the psychology of the orgy," been married to three different women, and had somehow, out of all this, emerged as a national celebrity. His ideas had hardened into form, and his symbols had been molded with them. But what ideas! And what symbols! It is no wonder that *An American Dream* is such a mess.

I have access to a superb plot summary by Stanley Edgar Hyman, and so shall emulate those wise judges who know a good precedent when they see one:

The novel concerns several days in the life of Stephen Richards Rojack, a New Yorker in his early forties. He was briefly a congressman, and now makes his living as a professor of existentialist psychology at a city university, where he offers a seminar in voodoo, and as a master of ceremonies on a far-out television program; he is the author of one popular book, *The Psychology of the Hangman*. Rojack was a hero in the Second World War, and is in fact "the one intellectual in America's history" with a Distinguished Service Cross. He is separated from his wife, a beautiful rich Roman Catholic of Hapsburg ancestry, Deborah Caughlin Managaravidi Kelly.

Rojack begins his novel's action by a wrestling match with his wife, occasioned by her boasting of perversities with her lovers, in the course of which he strangles her. He leaves the corpse on the carpet, goes downstairs and buggers the maid, who in her enthusiasm admits to being a Nazi, and tells him that he is absolutely a sexual genius. Then he goes back upstairs, cleans up his wife's corpse a bit, and pitches it out the window.

This piles up traffic on the East River Drive, and one of the cars involved contains Eddie Ganucci, a statesman of the Mafia, and a beautiful blond nightclub singer named Cherry Melanie, who looks "like a child who has been anointed by the wing of a magical bird," and with whom Rojack promptly falls in love. As soon as the detectives release him, Rojack goes to the club where Cherry sings, outfaces a burly prizefighter, and takes Cherry home to bed.

The next day there is another interview with the detectives, in the course of which Rojack defends himself so skillfully that he is told: "You missed a promising legal career." Then he learns that his wife's murder has been declared a suicide as a result of his father-in-law's influence. He returns to Cherry, who confesses to being a fan of his television program, and expresses her feeling for him by biting pieces of skin out of his ear. She tells him she was raised by an incestuous half-brother and half-sister, after which he succeeds in bringing her to the first orgasm she has ever experienced in genital intercourse.

While they are engaged in mutual congratulations, Cherry's former lover, a gifted Negro singer and "stud" named Shago Martin, walks in on them. He pulls a switchblade on Rojack, but

Rojack, unarmed, overcomes him, beats him up, and throws him down the stairs. Rojack then goes on to visit his father-in-law, the mysterious tycoon Barney Oswald Kelly, another former lover of Cherry's. While Rojack is at Kelly's, President Kennedy (called "Jack") telephones to express his condolences. The Nazi maid is now working for Kelly and simultaneously blackmailing him, and she tells Rojack that at the time of her death Deborah was involved with lovers high in American, Soviet, and British espionage circles. "Last night there must have been electricity burning in government offices all over the world," she adds.

Kelly compels Rojack to listen to his life story, spiced with father-daughter incest, and Rojack then demonstrates his courage (he intends "to blow up poor old Freud" by showing that cowardice is the root of neurosis) by walking a dangerous parapet near Kelly's terrace. Kelly tries to push him off the parapet with an umbrella, but Rojack smashes Kelly in the face with the umbrella and departs. He goes back downtown and learns that Cherry has been beaten to death by a confused friend of Shago's. Rojack arrives just in time to hear her last words. He then drives to Las Vegas, where he is highly successful at the dice tables. The book ends with his telephoning Cherry in Heaven; we know it is Heaven because "Marilyn says to say hello."[4]

Earlier I identified the grand symbol of this boozy book as "the moon." But Mailer carries his symbolism further here than ever before; he holds it over our heads and effectively demands the sacrifice of our reason in deference to this object of cult worship. Stephen Rojack opens by telling us that he first met and seduced his wife on a double date with then-Congressman John Kennedy. Rojack adds, "Of course Jack has gone on a bit since those days, and I have gone up and down, but I remember a full moon the night we had our double date, and to be phenomenologically precise, there was also a full moon on the night I led my patrol to the top of a particular hill in Italy, and a full moon the night I met another girl, and a full moon . . ." Rojack comments on the deep significance of these moons. "The real difference between the President and myself," he notes, "may be that I ended with too large an appreciation of the moon, for I looked down the abyss on the first night I killed: four men, four very separate Germans, dead under a full moon—whereas Jack, for all I know, never saw the abyss."

We are barely begun, and already Rojack is babbling in this fashion. It all seems rather rude to the reader. To continue, we must absorb this notion that a moon curse has infected Rojack which has somehow escaped President Kennedy, who "never saw the abyss," and who surely would have regretted any association with a jerk like Rojack. The necessity of this absorption becomes clear a page later:

Years later I read *Zen in the Art of Archery* and understood the book. Because I did not throw the grenades on that night on the hill under the moon, *it* threw them, and *it* did a near-perfect job. The grenades went off somewhere between five and ten yards over each machine gun, *blast, blast,* like a boxer's tattoo, one-two, and I was exploded in the butt from a piece of my own shrapnel, whacked with a delicious pain clean as a mistress' sharp teeth going 'Yummy' in your rump, and then the barrel of my carbine swung around like a long fine antenna and pointed itself at the machine-gun hole on my right where a great bloody sweet German face, a healthy spoiled over-spoiled young beauty of a face, mother-love all over its making, possessor of that overcurved mouth which only great fat sweet young faggots can have when their rectum is tuned and entertained from adolescence on, came crying, sliding, smiling up over the edge of the hold, "Hello, death!" blood and mud like the herald of sodomy upon his chest, and I pulled the trigger as if I were squeezing the softest breast of the softest pigeon which ever flew, still a woman's breast takes me now and then to the pigeon on that trigger, and the shot cracked like a birch twig across my palm, *whop!* and the round went in at the base of his nose and spread and I saw his face sucked in backward upon the gouge of the bullet, he looked suddenly like an old man, toothless, sly, reminiscent of lechery.

This passage occurs on the third page of my copy of *An American Dream;* if the reader cannot bear the notion of "it" forcing

Rojack, he is best advised to close the volume and move along. Certainly this is what I would have done had I not pledged myself to a detailed examination of Mailer's career. Did "it," besides making Rojack pull the trigger, also incite the obscene imagery, the verbosity, the dubious inferences? This we must guess for ourselves. Need we analyze this pace-setting passage? Its essence is that moon-brooding has led Rojack to recall one of the events of his life to occur under a full moon: the killing of four German soldiers. In the space of a sentence, one of the Germans, blessed with a "healthy spoiled over-spoiled young beauty of a face . . ." changes upon being shot into an image "like an old man, toothless, sly, reminiscent of lechery." I find it strange that in death he does not look like an old lecher, which would be odd enough, but is "reminiscent of lechery." And the poor fellow has been shot by someone for whom the squeezing of the trigger recalled the squeezing of pigeon's breasts. I am unfamiliar with the sensation. And Rojack thinks about "the pigeon on that trigger" when he squeezes women's breasts! Imagine being Rojack's analyst, and having to note these fantasies with some coherence.

Such a man would feel no pangs after murdering his wife. "Besides," as Rojack says, "murder offers the promise of vast relief. It is never unsexual." Nor is much else for Professor Rojack, allowing for the stew of moons, cancers, vomit, immoral orgasms, and assorted mumbo jumbo. When Rojack murders his wife, who has expressed the fear that she has cancer, he feels that he has inherited that cancer. He says, "Never have I known such a sickening—the retaliation of the moon was complete." When wife Deborah boasts of her perversities, Rojack detects an odor coming from her which has "the breath of burning rubber." But when Deborah is dead, she smells "like a bank." A few minutes later, when he has finished the job on the Nazi maid, Rojack feels as if he "were gliding in the clear air above Luther's jakes" but there is no indication of the atmospheric relation of these jakes to the moon. When he vomits for the second time that evening, Rojack feels like "some gathering wind which drew sickness from the lungs and livers of others and passed them through me and up and out into the water," but this only leads to thoughts on the metaphysics of shirts. The moon fades in and out, depending on the availability of other, more preposterous images and symbols to

gild the narration. In the end, the matter is resolved by the phone
call to Cherry in Heaven. The voice of Cherry, "a lovely voice,"
answers "in the moonlight" (the original sound and light show, I
presume) and offers some advice for Rojack in playing the Las
Vegas gaming tables: "But toodle-oo, old baby-boy, and keep the
dice for free, the moon is out and she's a mother to me." Rojack
does not say what use he makes of Cherry's advice, but we know
that he had good luck. When we take our leave of him, he is
starting "on the long trip to Guatemala and Yucatán." Reading
all this, the late, ponderous Philip Rahv gravely noted, "On the
technical side what the novel obviously lacks is verisimilitude,
even in the most literal sense."

Why Are We in Vietnam? Rahv thought "an even worse performance." He found naught but "more play-acting, more gim-
mickry," and asserted that "in the literary world [Mailer] has become the hero of a claque whose outrageous puffery cannot but
abort his creative career in the long run."[5] In *The New York Review of Books,* however, the shouting continued. "It is a book of
great integrity," wrote the critic there. Dr. Eliot Fremont-Smith
thought it "original, courageous and provocative," while *News-
week* magazine's reviewer was roused to the excitement of a
sportswriter who cannot remember his beat, crying, "Touchdown!
Knockout!"

Published in 1967, this book carries some of the trends of
Mailer's middle period to their extreme development. Scatological
metaphors are so pervasive as to become practically the central
substance of the novel. Sentences bump and crash into each
other; the book's narrator, D.J., is so named because he is a self-
proclaimed "disc jockey to the world," but we hear nothing but
haywire.

The book begins with "Intro Beep 1," which is succeeded by
"Chap 1"; it is not known why the conventional "Chapter" will
not do. The opening announcement goes like this:

Hip hole and hupmobile, Braunschweiger, you didn't invite
Geiger and his counter for nothing, here is D.J., the friend-
Lee voice at your service—hold tight young America—introduc-
tions come. Let go of my dong, Shakespeare, I have gone too

[5] Philip Rahv, *Literature and the Sixth Sense,* Boston: Houghton Mifflin, pp.
415–16.

long, it is too late to tell my tale, may Batman tell it, let him declare there's blood on my dick and D.J. Dicktor Doc Dick and Jek has got the bloods, and has done animal murder, out out damn fart, and murder of the soldierest sort, cold was my hand and hot.

The book involves some two hundred pages of this sort of thing, much of it even more unintelligible than the opening paragraph. "Intro Beep 4," for instance, begins in this manner:

Think of something black-ass and terrible, black as a tumor in your brain, black as the black-ass consciousness of that crippled Harlem genius which D.J. shoves up for gambit as one possible embodiment for his remarkable brain. Shit, shit, and shinola, death in your breath gives a hump to the lung like the silent sound of a pocket turning inside out in the black-ass black-ball closet. Bishop Berkeley, goes the mad comptometer in old D.J.'s head . . .

Make of this what you will: it is still nonsense. The entire book maintains this air of outrageous improvisation, as if the author had taken to defecating on blank sheets of paper in order to see what unusual forms might result. As is well known, the title of the book is irrelevant to the story, except in the most oblique sense. (Extensive American involvement in Vietnam began under Lyndon Johnson, a Texan. The characters in *Why Are We in Vietnam?* are Texans, and the book offers some vague commentary on the nature of Texans, or, at least, on the supposed Texan element in us all.) Vietnam itself is not mentioned until the book's final page: "We're off to see the wizard in Vietnam . . . Vietnam, hot damn." With that single reference, D.J. awaits his induction into the Army and, we must assume, to the Vietnamese war itself.

The main event in the book is the Alaskan hunting exhibition which D.J. takes with his father and others. A thousand-pound grizzly bear becomes the grand symbol; there is hemming and hawing over the nature of masculinity, though one of the book's central problems is the feminine condition of delayed periods. All of this is very familiar to readers of the earlier novels. But this is one instance where style overwhelms all other considerations. The

enthusiastic notices quoted above were hailing the new literature
of illiteracy. Or, to quote our friend, D.J., "A weed thrives on a
cesspool, piss is its nectar, shit all ambrosia."

XII

Now the professorial pundits sit back and await the "big novel"—
long postponed, but now signed for and apparently on the way.
What do they expect to find there? Some confirmation of their
predictions from the past quarter century? Mailer has led them
along as a man would lead his dog, teasing them, throwing them
crumbs, scratching their backs, and encouraging their speculative
essays. A professor is nothing if not vain about his speculations:
the more he makes, the merrier. Mailer has been their Walter
Mitty, playing out their fantasies, plunging in where they dare not
tread. His talent for publicity and the professors' talent for
pedantry have made this writer into something like his book-
jacket label as "the most spectacular intellectual of his time."

Fortunately, this sort of madness will not go on forever. Mailer
will not always be around to advertise for himself, and the present
generation of professors will die out, too, leaving a world which
has not been subject to this author's cajolery. Presently the glare
of the bright lights is too harsh, and all who have sought to see
the work of Mailer clearly have been blinded—beyond repair, I
fear. Those who protest can only squeak, while those who praise
drone on. The fame of Mailer is a by-product of an age of economic inflation and political braggadocio. These things tend to
run in cycles, and Mailer, all his complaints to the contrary, has
been lucky enough to catch the cresting of a wave. Science gave us
the so-called "sexual revolution"; it was incidental that Mailer
shouted from the rooftops about God and the devil's parts in the
matter. Bad judgment created the American role in Vietnam, and
the nerve-wracked common sense of kids who didn't want to fight
helped to end it. Mailer's pronunciamentos on American totalitarianism did little to sway anyone; he was no more than one raucous voice in a wild chorus. The politics of the Cold War combined with scientific and technological ability to send men to the
moon; Mailer's blubbery treatise on the subject pleaded confusion

toward a scientific spirit which has been commonplace for five centuries now. Etc., etc.

There is consolation in the thought that, while the smugness and snootiness of English professors persist from generation to generation, their articles of faith tend to change. Mailer is the sort of writer whose reputation tends to suffer badly from this process. Like D'Annunzio or Oscar Wilde, he is a writer who is as controversial for his behavior as for his books. These separate considerations have been jumbled until Mailer has become a blob of publicity, leaving serious criticism of his work to fall to another age. The present generation of professors has contributed so little of value that the next crop will have to wipe the slate clean and start over. Despite my lack of respect for English professors, I trust that they will find little of Mailer's stuff to be of much worth. This is not because they will be better critics than their predecessors—they will be no better and no worse—but because the foundations of Mailer's reputation are so flimsy to start with: *The Naked and the Dead* and a quarter century of outrage. That first novel will be recognized as the gawky bore that it is, and the outrage will cease to shock, as it always does. Mailer will be relegated to a footnote in the Oxford Companion—which is as it should be. He is a dreadful writer, and deserves oblivion.

Robert Lowell

At the start of the nineteenth century, wrote Will Durant of poets, "Obscurity became a fashion in the ancient order of web weavers." As Goethe, who resisted the trend, noted, "On the whole, philosophical speculation is an injury to the Germans, as it tends to make their style vague, difficult, and obscure. The stronger their attachment to certain philosophical schools, the worse they write."

The problem, of course, did not end with the Germans a century and a half ago. It is very much with us in America today. Ever since T. S. Eliot, fresh from lectures delivered by British Hegelians, joined Ezra Pound, strengthened from having "signed" a "pact" with Walt Whitman ("It was you that broke the new wood/Now is a time for carving."), American verse has been dominated by a passion for the obscure. This driving force has been so intense that an entire generation of English professors has proved its mettle by informing students of the "permanence of modernism," and by outlawing the thought that such writers as Eliot, Pound, and William Butler Yeats may deserve something less than the doctoral Rushmores erected in their honor thus far.

But such is fashion, and such is pedagogy. The bards of the twenty-first century may well amuse themselves by poring over our present anthologies, even as we chuckle over the simperings of the eighteenth-century New England ladies. A relative handful of sturdy old-timers may be left holding the bag for the once glorious "modernist revolution," now given way to upstarts who deplore the modernists' devotion to chasing down footnotes from critiques of the Westminster Confession. I see a time when the young shall ask, "Who gives a damn about what Yeats thought of Druids and Byzantium? Why does Eliot have to quote Dante and mimic Shakespeare to express his feelings? Why couldn't Pound decide on either Greek gods or Hindu saints to symbolize these things? Why do these 'modernists,' for all their talk about 'form,' seem so random and eclectic—so sloppy, if the truth must be told?" The English professors, as I say, have banished such questions, and concentrated their energies on defining movements within sub-movements of schools. Leave them to it: they are harmless, and their day shall pass.

In the meantime, "modernism" is all about us—not only in the comparatively minor art of verse, but in all the other literary and non-literary arts as well. It is not without its virtues, and, in its early days, at least, accomplished a great deal of good by exploding much hollow Victorian deadwood. Whether or not it has served its purpose, and, if so, what is to replace it?—these questions I set aside for another day. That it remains the ruling aesthetic doctrine of our time does not seem to me at all questionable. To be sure, there are professors who have their doubts, but they are not to be taken seriously. Such doubts are the stuff that tenured positions are made on. The single, most identifiable aspect of modernism is its will to obscurity. And its most worthy representative in the poetic arts has been Robert Lowell, descendant of the old Bostonian line best noted for speaking only to the Cabots, and thence to God.

Young Lowell signaled his rebellion from familial tradition by quitting Harvard after two years, in order to study poetry, criticism, and the classics under John Crowe Ransom at Kenyon College in Ohio. The revolt was carried further in 1940 when, at the age of twenty-three, Lowell rejected the God of his fathers and entered the Roman Catholic Church. In the same year he began the first of three marriages—all of them to writers. In 1943, the budding poet again shocked his parents—and particularly his father, a navy man—by refusing to obey a draft call, and choosing instead to serve a jail sentence. Out of prison by 1944, he published his first book—a small volume of elaborate verses entitled

Land of Unlikeness. Several critics raised their eyebrows and asked for more. Two years later Lowell obliged by revising some of the verses in *Land of Unlikeness,* added several new pieces, and issued *Lord Weary's Castle.* The same critics in whom *Land of Unlikeness* had aroused interest now confessed enthrallment. A Pulitzer Prize was awarded in 1947. A new star had risen.

Many of Lowell's admirers hold this first book as their favorite among his works. Along with the embryonic *Land of Unlikeness* and *The Mills of the Kavanaughs* (1951), it marks a distinct period in the poet's career—a time in which his Catholicism was ripe, his fascination with New England history pre-eminent, his private agonies still private, and his gloominess well cloaked in a quasi-grandiose style. "My title," the author explained, "comes from an old ballad":

> It's Lambkin was a mason good
> As ever built wi' stane:
> He built Lord Wearie's castle
> But payment gat he nane . . .

From this cryptic beginning, the book proceeds, often with archaic usage, startling modifiers, and odd points of view. Catholic theology is served up with a heavy sauce of Puritanical indignation. Forgotten Graeco-Roman gods walk the cobbled streets of Boston. Gripped by the Sigourney Syndrome, the poet spends much of his time in graveyards, and a great deal of *Lord Weary's Castle* concerns itself with dead Puritans—the most unattractive subject imaginable. It is both the poet's and the reader's misfortune that a large number of these dead happen to be relations of the poet's. Herewith a partial calling of the roll, with excerpts from Lowell's eulogies:

> Warren Winslow (Cousin, "Dead at Sea")
> > The winds' wings beat upon the stones,
> > Cousin, and scream for you and the claws rush
> > At the sea's throat and wring it in the slush
> > Of this old Quaker graveyard where the bones
> > Cry out in the long night for the hurt beast
> > Bobbing by Ahab's whaleboats in the East.

Arthur Winslow (Grandfather, Dead from Cancer)
Grandfather Winslow, look, the swanboats coast
That island in the Public Gardens, where
The bread-stuffed ducks are brooding, where with tub
And strainer the mid-Sunday Irish scare
The sun-struck shallows for the dusky chub
This Easter, and the ghost
Of risen Jesus walks the waves to run
Arthur upon a trumpeting black swan
Beyond Charles River to the Acheron
Where the wide waters and their voyager are one.

Mary Winslow
Mary Winslow is dead. Out on the Charles
The shells hold water and their oarblades drag,
Littered with captivated ducks, and now
The bell-rope in King's Chapel Tower unsnarls
And bells the bestial cow
From Boston Common; she is dead.

And there are others, less clearly identified, gathered under such titles as: "At the Indian Killer's Grave," "The Death of the Sheriff," "The Dead in Europe," "The Crucifix," "The North Sea Undertaker's Complaint"—all joined through the unifying theme of death. When death grows tiresome as a subject, the twenty-nine-year-old poet turns to the next best thing—old age—with Yeatsian fury. "The Drunken Fisherman" proclaims, "Here tantrums thrash to a whale's rage./This is the pot-hole of old age." Besides graveyards, there are "gray, sorry ancestral" houses to brood about, not to mention all the "water . . . the deep where the high tide/Mutters to its hurt self, mutters and ebbs."

Enter a cross index of historical and mythological figures who float in and out of contemporary scenes with all the immunity that poetic license allows. We have already noted, in the eulogy to Warren Winslow, the picture of bones in the "old Quaker graveyard" crying out for Moby Dick ("the hurt beast/Bobbing by Ahab's whaleboats"), and that of Jesus escorting Arthur Winslow "upon a trumpeting black swan/Beyond Charles River to the Acheron." So, too, does "Charon's raft" come floating up

to Salem, Massachusetts, and some tourists visiting the shrines of
Concord drive the poet to recall "the death-dance of King Philip
and his scream/Whose echo girdled this imperfect globe."
Thoughts of the Napoleonic age and "Blücher's caissons" are not
complete without reference to "Scylla" and "Abel." A verse enti-
tled "The Crucifix" requires mention of "Leviathan," "Greece,"
"Sodom," "Adam," "Ninth Street," "Hallowe'en," and "Via et
Vita et Veritas." In a verse about prison life, entitled "In the
Cage," we learn that, "Here/The Bible-twisting Israelite/Fasts for
his Harlem. It is night./And it is vanity, and age/Blackens the
heart of Adam." "The Death of the Sheriff" is a hash of Greek,
Roman, and Christian mythologies, and the final piece in *Lord
Weary's Castle,* "Where the Rainbow Ends," stands in defiance
of all known ecology, geography, and meteorology:

> *I saw the sky descending, black and white,*
> *Not blue, on Boston where the winters wore*
> *The skulls to jack-o'-lanterns on the slates,*
> *And Hunger's skin-and-bone retrievers tore*
> *The chickadee and shrike. The thorn tree waits*
> *Its victim and tonight*
> *The worms will eat the deadwood to the foot*
> *Of Ararat: the scythers, Time and Death,*
> *Helmed locusts, move upon the tree of breath;*

"Ah, well!" you say. "He is a poet, and may rearrange things as he
pleases. If you don't like it, you needn't read his poetry." Fair
enough, I concede, in which case the question becomes: How
does he go about his rearranging? How does he use the language?

In these early works, Lowell covers all the spilled blood with a
gauze of formality—most often an unrhymed iambic pentameter.
When he wants to be sardonic, he turns to painful punning, as in
the verse "The Dead in Europe":

> *Our Mother, shall we rise on Mary's day*
> *In Maryland, wherever corpses married*
> *Under the rubble, bundled together? . . .*
> > *Mary, hear,*
> *O Mary, marry earth, sea, air and fire;*

wherein puns are transformed into Gongorisms. The mythological and historical intrusions are crucial to these verses, as are the revival of dusty expressions ("to leaguer," "bells the bestial cow") and the use of phrases from foreign languages. All of this seems intended to produce a timeless and universal air, but manages little more than a strain upon our eyes, ears, and thoughts. There are few verses in *Lord Weary's Castle* which are coherent, elegant, or poignant. I think of "Katherine's Dream" as one exception. The two verses concerning Jonathan Edwards, "After the Surprising Conversions" and "Mr. Edwards and the Spider," are forceful and fairly clear, once their frame of reference is understood. These verses are free of the extravagant conceits and historical jumpiness which otherwise pervade the book. For the most part, Lowell is a weak prophet, crying of doom in a trembling voice, lacking the stinging certitude required to bring these gloomy visions of past and present to life.

It was another five years, however, before he realized his problem and made any effort to change his course. For years he had immersed himself in the poetic theories of such men as Ransom and Allen Tate, and had grown to share their enthusiasm for language as a mere ornament of life. He had not learned to write his thoughts in blood, or even water. Instead, he kept busy at snatching phrases out of thin air. In *The Mills of the Kavanaughs*, published in 1951, this turbid flow continued in a depressing little book bearing the mark of too much technique and too little inspiration. Reading this volume, with its vague echoes of the great English poets of the seventeenth century, makes me think of those sentimental Italian painters of the late eighteenth and nineteenth centuries, conscious of their noble inheritance but unsure of what to do with it.

The title poem is a narrative running on for twenty pages. Its "story" is told mostly in the form of a reverie addressed by Anne Kavanaugh to her recently deceased husband, Harry, as she sits in her Maine garden playing solitaire. In a low drone, faithful to a complicated rhyming structure, she tells of a lifetime in New England, peppering her tale with classical and biblical references suggested by the statuary in her garden. There are some interminable descriptions of trivial scenes, the pace is sluggish, and the tone alternately bland and pompous. As we should expect from

Lowell, the reverie eventually hits upon the subject of death (capital D, of course), and the result is frightful:

> *Why must we mistrust*
> *Ourselves with Death who takes the world on trust?*
> *Although God's brother, and himself a god,*
> *Death whipped his horses through the startled sod;*
> *For neither conscience nor omniscience warned*
> *Him from his folly, when the virgin scorned*
> *His courtship, and the quaking earth revealed*
> *Death's desperation to the Thracian field.*

Those who managed to keep from snoring could join "an old man in Concord" in "Falling Asleep over the Aeneid," the subject of the second verse in *The Mills of the Kavanaughs*. The old man, according to Lowell, "dreams that he is Aeneas at the funeral of Pallas, an Italian prince." Again, Lowell is at the same time formal and eccentric:

> *I hold*
> *The sword that Dido used. It tries to speak*
> *A bird with Dido's sworded breast. Its beak*
> *Clangs and ejaculates the Punic word*
> *I hear the bird-priest chirping like a bird.*

The next three verses follow the pattern of *Lord Weary's Castle* in calling up all history and mythology to speak of the recent dead. As in "The Mills of the Kavanaughs," statuary is often discussed as if it had the breath of life. "The Fat Man in the Mirror" is an "imitation" of Franz Werfel, and a part of Lowell's work which we shall examine further along.

Finally, in "Thanksgiving's Over," Lowell tells a dreary tale of suicide. But there is a difference between this verse and the others in *The Mills of the Kavanaughs*. The meter is less strict, the language more colloquial. The reliance on the classics is still present, but the grip is letting up. The subject remains morbid, but its treatment has become less doctrinaire. What is fading is the Roman Catholicism, formerly imposed with all the tactless fury of the convert. The poet was preparing to loosen his garters, shed his cloak, and reveal himself in the naked splendor of Puritanical misery.

II

Thus was born that strange admixture of autobiographical verse and prose, *Life Studies*, which is generally regarded as the central book of Lowell's career. "By the time I came to *Life Studies* I'd been writing my autobiography and also writing poems that broke meter," Lowell later recalled. "I'd been doing a lot of reading aloud. I went on a trip to the West Coast and read at least once a day and sometimes twice for fourteen days, and more and more I found that I was simplifying my poems."[1] By "simplifying," he surely meant "relaxing," and was referring only to the structure of his verses, and not their subject matter or word usage. So, the opening verse in *Life Studies* begins with Lowell writing that the Swiss "had thrown the sponge in once again," and then proceeds to describe a train "lunge mooning across the fallow Alpine snow." The "lunge mooning" is a retention from the early years; the "thrown the sponge in" is something new. The result is somewhat happier than the theological slush of *Lord Weary's Castle*, but still wide of the bull's-eye. Often, obscurity is more briskly achieved. Occasionally, Lowell approaches a simple sort of eloquence; for example, in this opening verse, "Beyond the Alps":

> *Life changed to landscape. Much against my will*
> *I left the City of God where it belongs.*
> *There the skirt-mad Mussolini unfurled*
> *the eagle of Caesar. He was one of us*
> *only, pure prose.*

But, from this interesting reflection, Lowell performs one of his familiar leaps in time. The language is simpler, the reference more temporal than the mythological gods of *Lord Weary's Castle*, but the result is no less jarring:

[1] Quoted in *Robert Lowell; a collection of critical essays*, ed. by Thomas Francis Parkinson, Englewood Cliffs, N.J., Prentice-Hall, 1968, p. 18.

> *I envy the conspicuous*
> *Waste of our grandparents on their grand tours—*
> *Long-haired Victorian sages accepted the universe,*
> *While breezing on their trust funds through the world.*

Next, the Pope declares the validity of the dogma of the Assumption of the Virgin, and references are made to the Pope's "electric razor" and "pet canary." By this time, we have begun to sense that Lowell is not quite sure of where he's headed, and we observe, somewhat sadly, as his verse slides downhill. Our doubts are confirmed in the third stanza, as obscurity settles in, signaled by the arrival of those old stand-bys "Apollo," "Cyclops," "Hellas," and "Minerva." Finally, the verse concludes in total darkness with a couplet that might mean any of a dozen things:

> *Now Paris, our black classic, breaking up*
> *like killer kings on an Etruscan cup.*

So, too, with the oddly rhymed "The Banker's Daughter" and the impossible "A Mad Negro Soldier Confined at Munich." The former contains such things as this:

> *Now seasons cycle to the laughing ring*
> *of scything children; king must follow king*
> *and walk the plank to his immortal leap.*

The latter contains the line "Cat-houses talk cold-turkey to my guards." I do not know whether this is good or bad because I do not know the author's intentions. Sandwiched between these two verses is one entitled "Inauguration Day: January 1953":

> *The snow had buried Stuyvesant.*
> *The subways drummed the vaults. I heard*
> *the El's green girders charge on Third,*
> *Manhattan's truss of adamant,*
> *that groaned in ermine, slummed on want . . .*
> *Cyclonic zero of the word,*
> *God of our armies, who interred*
> *Gold Harbor's blue immortals, Grant!*
> *Horseman, your sword is in the groove!*

> *Ice, ice. Our wheels no longer move.*
> *Look, the fixed stars, all just alike*
> *as lack-land atoms, split apart,*
> *and the Republic summons Ike,*
> *the mausoleum in her heart.*

I find this incomprehensible. I do not understand what is meant by "the snow had buried Stuyvesant." I do not understand "Manhattan's truss of adamant." I do not understand "Cyclonic zero of the word." I do not understand "Horseman, your sword is in the groove!" except that it sounds like one of Yeats's mad dashes from his Irish tower. I do not understand "lack-land atoms." I do not understand "the mausoleum in her heart." Above all, I do not understand why this jumble is presented as a statement of the author's sentiments on the occasion of President Eisenhower's inauguration. I find myself asking, not only what this or that line means, but what this line is doing alongside that one, and what all of this is doing under the heading of "Inauguration Day."

Also curious are the four tributes in the third section of *Life Studies* to writers Ford Madox Ford, George Santayana, Delmore Schwartz, and Hart Crane. As with the other verses in this book, the tone is more colloquial than in the New England eulogies of *Lord Weary's Castle*; yet restlessness and strain are no less prevalent here. The effect is jaggedness and sketchiness. The Ford verse contains a description like, "Sandman! Your face a childish O.," pretends to criticism:

> *Ah Ford!*
> *Was it war, the sport of kings, that your Good Soldier,*
> *the best French novel in the language, taught those*
> *Georgian Whig magnificoes at Oxford, at Oxford decimated*
> *on the Somme?*

and adds a personal sentiment in closing: "Ford, you were a kind man and you died in want." All of this leaves us asking, "Yes, and what of it?" by the time we have finished. The Santayana piece succumbs to that alluring siren of modernism—the run-on sentence; "To Delmore Schwartz" gives way to punctuative bric-a-brac; "Words for Hart Crane" imagines a statement of Crane's and is stronger than its three predecessors, but still fragmentary.

What Lowell had concocted in these peripheral verses from *Life Studies* was a new style without a new substance. The remainder of the book involves the subjects closest to his heart—his childhood, growth, immediate family, and personal anxieties. It is his most painful work, and his most powerful.

III

What has given this work its fame is its supposed "confessional" tone, so unusual (and, some would say, unbecoming) in a proper Bostonian. But anyone looking for lurid revelations will be disappointed. The rather undistinguished prose of the book's second section, "91 Revere Street," tells of the poet's unexciting boyhood, at home and at boarding school. Amid a surfeit of trivia, Lowell informs us that the future pacifist had a love of toy soldiers; that he often got on awkwardly with his parents; that he found his parents' dinners dull and school not much better; that some of his relatives were more interesting than others; that he did not know of his poetic ancestors except for his fat cousin Amy, who was considered a wee bit scandalous; and that such an introverted youth, surrounded by many hints of historical associations, was a likely enough background for a poet. Those who read *Lord Weary's Castle* before opening *Life Studies* may wish that young Lowell had not developed so many crotchets at so early an age; but those who know something of old Boston and old Bostonian families are aware that they have no right to expect any such thing.

Lowell is no master of prose style, and "91 Revere Street" no masterpiece, but part four of *Life Studies*, sharing its title with the book as a whole, is excellent. Here, finally, Lowell's best qualities are harmonized. The reflective, yet informal, tone; the fascination with New England and America as they have been reflected in his family; the yearning for domestic tranquillity which so dominates his own mind: all are brought, in the space of eight verses —from "My Last Afternoon with Uncle Devereux Winslow" to "Sailing Home from Rapallo"—to a summit which stiffness had prevented him from achieving before, and franticness has kept him from reaching since.

Part of their interest, of course, is historical: America likes to know how the Brahmins keep up with the times. We have always, it seems, had to have one "New England" poet. Discounting Frost as a farmer, we can trace Lowell's lineage through T. S. Eliot's *Four Quartets* to Amy Lowell and back into the nineteenth century. The poets never speak *for* their generation of New Englanders (God forbid that any proper public official should share the poet's agonies), but they do speak *of* it, and that is enough to satisfy *hoi polloi*. Robert Lowell is of the generation of the younger Henry Cabot Lodge and Elliot L. Richardson, and his words are gilded with the glaze of history.

But a poet could be intimate with a President and still write bad verse. Lowell's "Life Studies" are first-rate genre paintings. This does not place Lowell alongside Whitman, as some would have it, any more than Vermeer is comparable to Michelangelo or Rameau to Beethoven. It simply means that he has done some fine work on a small scale. Stephen Spender's comment, "And does not Lowell often seem to be writing the poems of Pierre Bezukhov?" should not be taken to mean that Lowell has written another *War and Peace*. Better to compare him, if compare you must, to lonesome Emily Dickinson.

"Nowhere was anywhere after a summer/At my Grandfather's farm," he writes, as innocence dies and is reborn again. Occasionally, he lapses into the tired antique references, though his eye remains so steadily on his subject that we do not feel as much tread upon as before. Watching Uncle Devereux Winslow, dying of Hodgkin's disease, "I wasn't a child at all—/unseen and all-seeing, I was Agrippina/in the Golden House of Nero . . ." Once, we hear of "shockless coffee," but the disturbance is only minor. Searching for his past, Lowell recalls those times when his father, away at sea, was the distant "Daddy," and his grandfather was his "Father." The poet's estimation of the comparative values of life and death has not changed; only his ability to put them into concrete terms has changed. The world of death remains "the world of light":

> Then the dry road dust rises to whiten
> the fatigued elm trees—
> the nineteenth century, tired of children is gone.
> They're all gone into a world of light; the farm's my own.

He offers no chronicle of idle joys and sorrows, but of an old family carving out life and death for itself in an ever changing world:

> *With seamanlike celerity,*
> *Father left the Navy,*
> *and deeded Mother his property.*

> *He was soon fired. Year after year,*
> *he still hummed "Anchors aweigh" in the tub—*
> *whenever he left a job,*
> *he bought a smarter car . . .*

> *Father's death was abrupt and unprotesting.*
> *His vision was still twenty-twenty.*
> *After a morning of anxious, repetitive smiling,*
> *his last words to Mother were:*
> *"I feel awful" . . .*

> *In the grandiloquent lettering on Mother's coffin,*
> Lowell *had been misspelled* LOVEL.
> *The corpse*
> *was wrapped like* panetone *in Italian tinfoil.*

Recalling times once experienced but now forever gone, Lowell's distinction is his objectivity. It is, of course, only a surface objectivity, but a surface so well polished that it becomes transparent. For once Lowell permits us to see the bottom of things as he sees them. No symbols dangle in mid-air to obstruct our view. What is strange, and unfortunate, is that Lowell has so rarely achieved this clarity. He has either been too caught up in theology, as in the early works, or in himself, as in the later. There have been times when he has approached the first eight verses of part four of *Life Studies* (I think, offhand, of the verse entitled "For Aunt Sarah" in *Notebook*), but they are few in number and scattered in a sea of mere scribblings. Even these exceptions show signs of hastiness and coarseness. It has been Lowell's misfortune, as it has been that of others before him, to have gone on working after he has lost his touch.

IV

Where does he begin to slip? I believe it is when he genuinely begins to confess—when he becomes the focus of his "life studies," and starts talking about his immediate concerns. Lowell, like most artists, requires distance from his subject; what is so odd is that he rarely grants it to himself. Instead, his habit is to rush us reports of his current mental condition. Most of the time, the condition is dubious and the reports are crabbed. If Lowell wants to tell us about what it feels like to spend time in a mental hospital, that is his business; I have a hunch, though, that it would be better for him and for his work if he laid off. Then there are his "studies" of marital life, replete with quotations from his wife's letters. These are virtually unintelligible to someone unfamiliar with Lowell's personal circumstances; yet, they dominate two entire books— *The Dolphin* and *For Lizzie and Harriet*—and involve increasingly large portions of other volumes. In addition, note the perpetual revision of already published work, the constant fussing about things that are over and done with.

Something is wrong here—both with the poet and with his technique. Something, also, is wrong with the critics who take this sort of thing in stride. I make no presumptions to judge Lowell's mental health; he has doctors enough for that. But I do demand to know of the poet—and his admirers in the faculty quarters— why they persist in listening to static and calling it music.

Once Lowell stopped writing of himself as one piper in a familial concert and decided to play solo, once the aunts and uncles and parents and grandparents began to fade away to the far corners of memory, all harmony vanished with them. In the first eight verses of "Life Studies," Lowell confessed his confusion toward an ordered world. He did it with elegance and clarity. The vestiges of old New England gone, he started thinking about all of human history, including the history being lived in his midst. He became as convinced of the cosmic importance of daily humdrum as a television journalist—with a difference. The journalist lives by his jargon, and must make that jargon comprehensible to the common man. The poet, too, lives by his jargon, which he must make comprehensible to his audience—in the case of modernists, to the symbol lovers of academe. For a brief moment, Lowell had dumped the trappings of academic poetry— tedious classicism, useless formality, outlandish modifiers, pretentious prophesying—and had shaped his subject and his technique into one euphonious whole. Both the gospel of the modernists: "A poem should not mean, but *be*," and the rejoinder of the traditionalists: "But it must *be* comprehensible," had been satisfied. Perhaps it is too much to expect such a high level of rather delicate work to be sustained. The great artists of domesticity, from Vermeer to Jane Austen, have never been known for their fecundity. A poet who chooses to write impulsively, like Lowell, is bound to pay a price in quality. And our age, in the arts as elsewhere, honors high productivity above solid workmanship. So a poet must either keep churning out volumes or commit suicide in order to draw attention to himself. Lowell seems to have considered the latter and chosen the former. Academic critics are forced to respond by either keeping a reputation afloat, or by letting it sink and thereby having to revise their theories. The former is much less painful, and easier, too. Thus we witness Lowell's work as it declines into paltry abstractions of himself and of human affairs—all to a cheering critical chorus.

V

First, of himself. Decadence can be traced from the summits of "Life Studies" to the low growls of *The Dolphin*. It begins in the verse which follows the "great eight," still in the same section of the book, entitled "During Fever." Lowell shifts from description of the dead to analysis of the living—his daughter, ill, in her crib —and then turns back for one final look over his shoulder at the old days at home with Mother and Father. Indicative of the changing character of Lowell's work, and unlike the verses immediately preceding it, "During Fever" concludes with a judgment:

> *Terrible that old life of decency*
> *without unseemly intimacy*
> *or quarrels, when the unemancipated woman*
> *still had her Freudian papa and maids!*

In the next verse, "Waking in the Blue," the rhetoric begins to bulge, with lines like "These victorious figures of bravado ossified young." Lowell's own circumstances have abruptly changed: "We are all old timers,/each of us holds a locked razor." "Home After Three Months Away" tells of time which has passed while the poet languished in the hospital: "I keep no rank nor station./Cured, I am frizzled, stale and small." It is not so bad yet, but it is getting worse. Language and memory are tangled in "Memories of West Street and Lepke" as Lowell recalls his days of draft resistance:

> *These are the tranquillized Fifties*
> *and I am forty. Ought I to regret my seedtime?*
> *I was a fire-breathing Catholic C.O.,*
> *and made my manic statement,*
> *telling off the state and president,*
> *and then sat waiting sentence in the bull pen*
> *beside a Negro boy with curlicues*
> *of marijuana in his hair.*

"Manic statement"? "Curlicues of marijuana in his hair"? This may be the same poet who remembered his parents in simple language, but without the same perspective on his subject, or that measure of repose. It is no surprise to find, further along, that Lowell has begun to pile up trivial details; this is another symptom of poorly digested experience. Life is being swallowed before it has been chewed. His wife's "old-fashioned tirade," in "Man and Wife," "breaks like the Atlantic Ocean on my head"—a slight exaggeration, even for an anxious poet. "My mind's not right," he pleads in "Skunk Hour," but must he prove it by adding:

> *A car radio bleats,*
> *"Love, O careless Love . . ." I hear*
> *my ill-spirit sob in each blood cell,*
> *as if my hand were at its throat . . .*

A hand at the throat of a blood cell? Of an ill-spirit? A sob?

Five years later, in 1964, Lowell published his next book of non-imitative verses, *For the Union Dead.* The celebrated title poem I leave for my discussion of Lowell's "public" poetry. Here I note that the "personal" or "Confessional" poetry begun in *Life Studies* continued to deteriorate. The first verse in the book, "Water," speaks of two people who are vaguely defined, and seems to strive for some symbolic impression:

> *We wished our two souls*
> *might return like gulls*
> *to the rock. In the end,*
> *the water was too cold for us.*

In "The Old Flame" Lowell struggles with the descriptive process, and ends up with a line like "The Clapboard was old-red schoolhouse red"; and, again, the straining for symbolic effect:

> *In one bed and apart,*
>
> *we heard the plow*
> *groaning up hill—*
> *a red light, then a blue,*
> *as it tossed off the snow*
> *to the side of the road.*

"Middle Age" asks,

> *At forty-five,*
> *What next, what next?*
> *At every corner,*
> *I meet my father,*
> *my age, still alive . . .*

and relies on the ominous capitalization of "father." In "Fall 1961," Lowell informs us, "I swim like a minnow/behind my studio window," which strikes me as unlikely. I know neither New York nor New Jersey well, but I am puzzled when I read, in "The Mouth of the Hudson," that, "Chemical air/sweeps in from New Jersey,/and smells of coffee." "Florence" offers curious notions about apples and tyrannicides such as that Florentine apples are more "Roman" than American, and that Florence patronized "the lovely tyrannicides." "I am tired," he writes in "Eye and Tooth," "Everyone's tired of my turmoil," but he pushes on. There is a dreadful piece about a late gentleman named Alfred Corning Clark, featuring the line, "You were alive. You are dead." An "Epigram" labeled "for Hannah Arendt" was doubtless meant for Miss Arendt's eyes alone, as it lights no fire in mine. A verse entitled "Law" has nothing to do with its title. "Going to and fro" goes nowhere; "Myopia: A Night" is no clearer by daylight. "Returning" returns to images of death, more tiresome than ever. "Soft Wood" is dedicated to "Harriet Winslow" and must have sent that lady hopping to her taxidermist:

> This is the season
> when our friends may and will die daily.
> Surely the lives of the old
> are briefer than the young.

"The Flaw" lives up to its billing and "Night Sweat," I hope, was written in a temporary burst of brain fever. Before we reach "I dabble in the dapple of the day," we learn that:

> . . . the downward glide
> and bias of existing wrings us dry—
> always inside me is the child who died,
> always inside me is his will to die—
> one universe, one body . . . in this urn
> the animal night sweats of the spirit burn.

In *Notebook*, the problem was further aggravated; the time lapses of old reappear. Lowell governed his pen by limiting individual verses to fourteen lines apiece. But one edition gave way to another and still another; *Notebook 1967–68* became *Notebook*, and much of *Notebook* became *History*, while other parts became *For Lizzie and Harriet*. Each time Lowell revised, though he seldom made any real improvements. The matter was made even more complicated by Lowell's insistence that *Notebook* and *History* were each complete and individual works which ought to be read whole. Despite his injunction, there is little perceptible order to *Notebook*, and *History* is weakly chronologized. After *Notebook 1967–68* became *Notebook*, Lowell apologized, "I am sorry to ask anyone to buy this poem twice. I couldn't stop writing, and have handled my published book as if it were manuscript." When *Notebook* became *History*, Lowell offered, "My old title, *Notebook*, was more accurate than I wished, i.e. the composition was jumbled. I hope this jumble or jungle is cleared—that I have cut the waste marble from the figure." I don't know what will turn up next, and I don't care.

The personal-confessional verses in these books are even worse than those in *For the Union Dead*. They seem to be as casually thrown together as the books themselves. The most obvious symptom of their weak condition is the frequent appearance of . . . and —, giving the poet his license to skip back and forth from the timely to the unreal to the absurd. And skip he does, recalling all of those winged messengers we had assumed to be ground into dust in "The Mills of the Kavanaughs." "Half a year," opens *Notebook*,

> . . . then a year and a half, then
> ten and a half—the pathos of a child's fractions, turn-
> ing up each summer. God a seaslug, God a queen
> with forty servants, God . . . she gave up—things whirl
> in the chainsaw bite of whatever squares
> the universe by name and number.

The second stanza speaks of "a repeating fly" in his home, "so gross, it seems apocalyptic in our house." But this is not enough; the fly "is like a plane gunning potato bugs or Arabs on the screen." We have come a long way down the road from Grandfather's house. "I think of all the ill I do and will;/love hits like the polio of better days." "The fall warms vine and wire,/the ant's cool, amber, hyperthyroid eye,/grapes tanning on these tried entanglements." "Death bears us. Life/keeps our respect by keeping at a distance—/death we've never outdistanced as the Apostle boasted . . ."

There are occasional shocks of recognition, as when he writes in a piece "for Mary McCarthy," "I slip from wonder into bluster," but, for the most part, we are left unraveling lines like, "The New York streets drink changes like a landscape," or wondering why something as simple as onionskin paper works Lowell into a frenzy of italic letters. The religious gurglings of *Lord Weary's Castle* are humble prayers beside this eclecticism:

> *Many a youth will turn from student to tiger,*
> *revolutionaries will sleep in the grave,*
> *blasphemous, unavoidable—the Mother,*
> *known in our slow, cold debaucheries,*
> *the bitter, dry pelt of feline undulation,*
> *weeps by her door of colored beads, and holds*
> *youth old as Michelangelo to her bosom.*

What an odd way he has of discussing things!

> *. . . I have been thirty years*
> *deciphering themes in Schubert's Death and the Maiden:*
> *a person dying is death's own impersonation,*
> *Schubert dying is audible; yet Death,*
> *if anything, is melodrama; Death quickly*
> *drops his actors for the living . . .*

When he writes "for John Berryman," "John, we used the language as if we made it," I have my own idea of what he means. Dots, dashes, logic-chopping, thunderous declamation, dry pelts of feline undulation—he doesn't *use* the language so much as he makes it up while he proceeds. It is as if a composer, aware of all the music written before his own, decided to sit down at the piano and pound away wildly at the keys, no plan in mind, letting the chords emerge as they please. So he comes up with the strange combinations recorded above. He makes triumphant declarations, like the one which closes "Plotted" in *The Dolphin*, that "Death's not an event in life, it's not lived through," until an impatient reader is bound to snap, "Of course not, you dummy! And you don't have to be so long in saying it!" When he tries to paint himself as a naughty unbeliever, the onetime Catholic boomer sounds like a jerk:

After a day indoors I sometimes see
my face in the shaving mirror looks as old,
frail and distinguished as my photographs—
as established. But it doesn't make one feel
the temptation to try to be a Christian.

"Big deal!" you say, as do I, but this is the sort of thing which has
brought on the ogling of the oracles at Buncombe U. Despite
their praise, this is feeble stuff. By the time we have reached the
verse on "Freud" in *The Dolphin*, we are no longer impressed by
opening questions like, "Is it honorable for a Jew to die as a Jew?"
succeeded by closing questions like "Must we die,/living in places
we have learned to live in,/completing the only work we're
trained to do?" We have recognized, long before this, that Lowell
has a habit of writing beyond his means—that he hasn't the philosopher's strength of organization, nor the saint's power gained
through the survival of a season in Hell. He is but a man, and a
rather frail one at that; too frail, we conclude, for the ultimate
questions he likes to stab at. Lowell does not stagger us with his
brilliance; to the contrary, he seems to be something of a plugger
—with life and language equally. After a point, he is a bore, and
that point is reached somewhere early in *Notebook* (choose
whichever edition you like). He has told us too much of himself,
and with too great a degree of doubt and hesitation, for us to take
him seriously when he gives his books grand titles like *History*.
We sense that he is happiest contemplating himself in his mirror,
thinking up new ways to be rebellious. We listen to him on the
great issues of the day without much interest.

VI

We have seen Charon lead his ferry up the Charles River, and
seen the same Charles flow, as a tributary, into the Acheron. We
have noticed a parade of mythological figures come marching into
Boston. We have seen a family, evolving out of its puritanical
past, merge into the tumult of our age. And we have watched that
family's youngest son struggle for his sanity amid the confusion,
relying on old myths and personal history to strengthen him in his

trials. Now we observe as he gathers up bits and pieces of human experience, past and present, in order to place them properly in the scheme of all things.

As with his private agonies, so with his public concerns: the further he gets from his original sources, the more inclined to render judgments he becomes; the more he judges, the worse he writes. The signs of decadence are the same: awkward perception, a straining for symbolism, an accumulation of trivia, and a reliance on the classics and the Bible to clear away brambles of thought. One minute he tries to open our eyes to mystery with strange symbols; the next minute he wants to convince us through argument. An "Afterthought" to *Notebook* attempts an explanation of this curious aesthetic:

> I lean heavily to the rational, but am devoted to unrealism. An unrealist must not say, "The man entered a house," but, "The man entered a police-whistle," or "Seasick with marital happiness, the wife plunges her eyes in her husband swimming like vagueness on the grass." Or make some bent generalization: "Weak wills command the gods." Or more subtly, words that seem right, though loosely in touch with reason: "Saved by my anger from cruelty." Unrealism can degenerate into meaningless clinical hallucinations or rhetorical machinery, but the true unreal is about something, and eats from the abundance of reality.

I think this is as complete an explanation as Lowell has ever given of his will to obscurity. It is an unsatisfactory doctrine, leading to more questions than it answers: for instance, how is one to guess that "police-whistle" and "house" have any relation, and how can this sort of thing prevent the degeneration into "clinical hallucination" and "rhetorical machinery" when "reality" is so unclear?

Anyway, Lowell's "unrealism" applies primarily to those things which are either too close or too distant to be properly understood. When he wrote of his deceased parents and grandparents, his memories had crystallized; but when he writes of yesterday's peace march or a war fought a thousand years ago, he is fanciful because he need not be anything else. When he writes of cities such as New York, London, Washington, or Buenos Aires, he sounds like a well-read tourist or a national poetical correspondent

—a visitor trying to make sense of things, and thereby forced into
hasty judgments.

Much of *Lord Weary's Castle* aimed at poetic oratory. After
The Mills of the Kavanaughs, the manner becomes less rigid, the
language often plainer. The problems, too, are similar. "Fall
1961" records, "All autumn, the chafe and jar/of nuclear war; we
have talked our extinction to death," and then slips into the ob-
scuration quoted earlier: "I swim like a minnow/behind my studio
window." Through his cultivation of "unrealism," Lowell con-
tinually casts doubt on his ability to speak about public matters.
Again, the problem is one of perspective—of Lowell's standing
too close to his subject. He strikes some comparison with the ancient Romans and walks away. Or he starts whimpering, and mutters unintelligibly for fourteen lines. Sometimes an Auntie What-
sername dies, and evokes sentiments on the youth of the
Republic. A day of lobstering in Maine brings back memories of
the Depression days; and Lowell, in the symbols of his adulthood,
recalls the time when, as a boy, he dreamed of being an elfin king.
Or he leafs through some history book, quickly versifies an inci-
dent, and comes up with an instant moral. There are never any
prolonged reveries; Lowell is not Anne Kavanaugh beside her husband's grave. Often he stops himself by writing things like, "Almost, almost . . ." or engaging in the hop-skip-jump of dots and
dashes. The impressions he has gained from reading are diluted in
his writing; a notebook by any other name is just as sketchy.

There have been times, however, when his thoughts on public
matters have caught the public eye. I do not speak of his celebrated refusal, in 1965, to join other artists and writers on the
lawn of Lyndon Johnson's White House. At that date, he was
outraged by Vietnam. Nor, of course, do I refer back to his conscientious objection to joining the Allied Forces for the finale of
World War II. These and similar acts have doubtless nourished
his feelings of poetic isolation, and have made his readers study
his verses diligently in the hope of finding battle cries for their
revolutions. Their researches, I trust, have been greatly in vain.
Lowell presents a baffling paradox: for all his self-absorption, he
maintains a basic reserve. Despite his mental and verbal gropings,
he never succumbs to the urge to shout. His anger is that of a
timid man in a harsh world. His complaints are those of a bat-

tered and bewildered gentleman. You will find many a tentative epigram in Lowell's verses, but nary a slogan or campaign song. His problems are technical: misplaced symbols, phrases out of tune, characters out of place, judgments lacking force, doctrines lacking sense. He writes, as I said earlier, beyond his means—too much, too fast, too poorly planned; hence, his need for perpetual revision and tired symbols. He seeks to travel through the history of the world on the currency of old New England; no wonder he often sounds foolish and repetitive!

But this old currency does have its value, even if it has been debased by too great immersion in the classics and the rococo aesthetics of John Crowe Ransom and Allen Tate. Lowell has made his fellow citizens take notice by staying at home and dealing in the hard dollars and sense of his Yankee heritage. His most celebrated public poem offers thoughts on the changing face of Boston, Massachusetts. Marching toward the Pentagon beside Lowell in October 1967, Norman Mailer felt "as if the ghosts of the Union Dead accompanied them now to the Bastille." One cannot ever account adequately for Mailer's sentiments or mixed metaphors: the point is that Lowell's "For the Union Dead" has often been read as something of a patriotic verse!

If so, it has little in common with patriotic verses of the past. There are no floral offerings to Boston's tidy colonial architecture; instead, we learn, "Parking spaces luxuriate like civic/sandpiles in the heart of Boston." The opening line mentions, "The old South Boston Aquarium stands/in a Sahara of snow. Its broken windows are boarded." Attention turns to a Civil War relief in Boston Common featuring Colonel Shaw and his regiment of black soldiers, many of whom died in the service of the Union Army. Looking back at their lives from the vantage point of the Civil Rights movement a century later, Lowell wrote, "Their monument sticks like a fishbone/in the city's throat." Shaw himself "is out of bounds now. He rejoices in man's loyalty,/peculiar power to choose life and die."

> *Shaw's father wanted no monument*
> *except the ditch,*
> *where his son's body was thrown*
> *and lost with his "niggers."*

The ditch is nearer . . .

> *Space is nearer.*
> *When I crouch to my television set,*
> *the drained faces of Negro school-children rise like balloons.*

And Colonel Shaw "is riding on his bubble,/he waits/for the blessed break." The cars around the Common "nose forward like fish;/a savage servility/slides by on grease."

This plea for racial justice is not without its power. Its evocation of wintry Boston, with boarded-up historic buildings and reliefs in the Common and automobiles rolling around oblivious to the monuments of a historic town, is rather interesting. Yet, I dislike "For the Union Dead." It strikes me, finally, as a haughty thing, stuffed full with artifice. I don't ask that poetry be reasonable; if it were that, it would cease to be poetry. But I do wish that Lowell would remove his head from the sand and meet the world on less ideal terms. Instead of looking at his television set and seeing "the drained faces of Negro school-children rise like balloons," I wish that he would walk their streets and catch the banter and babble of their voices; let him, at least, walk like Yeats "through the long schoolroom questioning." Colonel Shaw, he says, "waits for the blessed break." But what is that "break" to be? Glory? Honor? Justice? Or understanding—of his own mind and of the minds of black children growing up a century after him? And what of those automobiles? Is it not hyperbolic, and a little ridiculous, to say of them that they represent a "savage servility"—to the glory of Mammon or whatever—symbolizing the obstacle to Colonel Shaw's "blessed break," as the verse implies?

"For the Union Dead," then, bears the musty odor of the academy. It is the contrivance of an insular mind attempting to act worldly. It has, as I said earlier, its value—old New England currency being set to work in Boston. Lowell's is a point of view which doubtless has its place, but it is narrow and sharply limited. Just as those who would make the writer of *Life Studies* into an all-American boy are mistaken, so are those who proclaim the absolute and universal nobility of "For the Union Dead." It is no more profound than a stern rebuke by a puritan headmaster.

"Waking Early Sunday Morning," written a few years later,

and published in the 1967 volume *Near the Ocean,* marks a further descent into the poetry of raised eyebrows. Beginning with
the thought, "O to break loose" from life's confining requirements, the verse ends up by pronouncing on the state of the world
in dog-eared rhyme:

> *No weekends for the Gods now. Wars*
> *flicker, earth licks its open sores,*
> *fresh breakage, fresh promotions, chance*
> *assassinations, no advance.*
> *Only man thinning out his kind*
> *sounds through the Sabbath noon, the blind*
> *swipe of the pruner and his knife*
> *busy about the tree of life . . .*
>
> *Pity the planet, all joy gone*
> *From this sweet volcanic cone;*
> *peace to our children when they fall*
> *in small war on the heels of small war—*
> *until the end of time*
> *to police the earth, a ghost*
> *orbiting forever lost*
> *in our monotonous sublime.*

Had Lowell's career begun with something other than *Land of
Unlikeness* and *Lord Weary's Castle,* I might feel differently
about "Waking Early Sunday Morning"; however, this strikes me
as little better than assembly-line pessimism, self-mocking and
badly worn. The fourteen-line verses of *Notebook* and *History* dissolve into anonymous mumbles; their author bows to mere word-
slinging. Typical enough is "Election Night," the conclusion of
which begins with a ringing pronouncement, slips into self-
deprecation, and concludes with the author's retirement into a
shell of useless verbiage:

> We must rouse our broken forces and save the country:
> *I even said this in public. The beaten player*
> *opens his wounds and hungers for the blood-feud*
> *hidden like contraband and loved like whisky.*

VII

The beaten poet turns to other poets for help; Lowell has produced some of his best work in those "imitations" which permit escape from the tangled experience of his own life, and the life of "history." From the start of his career he has excelled at this sort of thing: partially original verses, partially translations, they have given him the perspective he requires. Leaving inspirational experience to his forebears, he concentrates on technique. All those years of scholarship prepared him to rise to occasional mastery. His book *Imitations* is my favorite among his collections of verses. His "imitations" of pre-twentieth-century European verse are among his clearest works, and, in the cases of Baudelaire and Villon, his most powerful. With the twentieth-century poets, Lowell apparently draws too close to himself, and his renditions of the Italians Montale and Ungaretti are as puzzling as his unimitative material; we read such things as "the chaos of implacable embraces," "the rock's lockjaw above the sand's detonating dazzle," and "an odor of bruised melons oozes from the floor."

These "imitations" often reflect the stylistic tendencies of the rest of his work; the "imitations" of *Lord Weary's Castle* are windier than those of *Imitations,* which was written around the same time as *Life Studies;* those of *Imitations* are less pompous than those which share a binding with "Waking Early Sunday Morning" in *Near the Ocean.* But there is no question of their being distinct from his "original" verses. In his Introduction to *Imitations,* Lowell says, "I have been reckless with literal meaning, and labored hard to get the tone . . . I have tried to write alive English and to do what my authors might have done if they were writing their poems now and in America." The value of *Imitations* to its author is rather unclear. "This book was written from time to time when I was unable to do anything of my own," he writes in the Introduction, thereby raising the question of what these pieces *are* if they are not his own. And, only a few lines later, he declares, "All my originals are important poems," leaving us to ask *whose* important poems they are. Clearly, the cult of "unrealism" has spread from the quatrain to the paragraph. We are left to sort things out among ourselves. So, too, with the substantive question: why these particular verses? "The dark and against the grain stand out," says Lowell without acknowledging that this is nothing new for him, "but there are other modifying strands." They are well hidden.

But nowhere else in Lowell's work is darkness less mysterious than here. Lowell's Villon can write of poverty as Lowell himself could never do:

> *I descend from no name—*
> *poor from my mother's womb,*
> *poverty claws me down.*
> *My father was poor; Horace,*
> *his father, was the same—*
> *on my ancestors' tomb,*
> *God rest their souls! there*
> *is neither scepter nor crown.*

Lowell's Baudelaire says plainly what Lowell alone cannot:

> *How sour the knowledge travelers bring away!*
> *The world's monotonous and small; we see*
> *ourselves today, tomorrow, yesterday,*
> *an oasis of horror in sands of ennui!*

Boredom! It is something that Lowell never voluntarily admits, despite its apparent influence on those verses which whimper pointlessly for fourteen lines. Lowell's Baudelaire repeats:

> *It's BOREDOM, Tears have glued its eyes together.*
> *You know it well, my Reader. This obscene*
> *beast chain-smokes yawning for the guillotine—*
> *you—hypocrite Reader—my double—my brother!*

Lowell's Juvenal, in *Near the Ocean*, drives his sword into public figures where Lowell alone would recoil and borrow Juvenal's symbols:

War's souvenirs and trophies nailed to trees,
a cheek strap dangling from a clobbered helmet,
a breastplate, or a trireme's figurehead,
or captives weeping on the victor's arch:
these are considered more than human prizes.
For these Greek, Roman, and barbarian
commanders march; for these they pledge their lives
and freedom—such their thirst for fame, and such
their scorn of virtue, for who wants a life
of virtue without praise? Whole nations die
to serve the glory of the few; all lust
for honors and inscriptions on their tombs—
those tombs a twisting fig tree can uproot,
for tombs too have their downfall and their doom.

Here is a grandeur to which Lowell has aspired in his "own" verse —in vain. If he has set the standard of making the old masters sound "as if they were writing their poems now and in America," why has *he,* actually writing "now and in America," not matched his versions of them?

I think it is because he is one of those artists who is at his best when limits are imposed; that is, a basically conservative mind forced into rebellion by an orthodoxy of absolute freedom. It is a conservatism unrelated to politics, and concerned primarily with a respect for the past. Left to wander alone through the world, Lowell goes astray. He becomes worried and depressed, and aches for symbols to express what he sees. Or he withdraws into himself, and writes of the pain he feels in facing the world. Or he stands under the grand banner of "History," and plunders the fruits of his reading willy-nilly in weak capsules of verse. In short, Lowell is one of those unsteady men who craves a faith but cannot accept any of those available. In his youth, he discarded the family religion in favor of Roman Catholicism. As he grew older, he dropped the Catholicism and decided to push on alone. Many in our secular age have managed well enough with agnosticism, but it is harder for puritans, among whose ranks Lowell must be listed. His verses give the impression of perpetual agony over mortal questions—and an inability to solve them with the tools at hand.

So he has turned to history in an effort to understand things. But not even all history is comprehensible; hence, those gnarled, unseemly books, *Notebook* and *History*, which try to sum up the universe on every other page. Even less can Lowell's daily life be ordered in tidy arrangements; so we get the quotation of letters between estranged husband and wife, and love notes from father to daughter—many expressing confusion, most exuding dismay, and all something of an embarrassment to read. Nor can the daily "history" in our midst be apprehended; Lowell at a peace march is dependent upon the clichés of the demonstrators and the reassurances of the classics. To understand the plight of black schoolchildren, he turns on the television, or he looks up the relief of Colonel Shaw on snowy Boston Common.

Lowell's insular mind finds strength in those things which have insulated him—his family and his scholarship. It is for this reason that those excellent genre pieces in *Life Studies* and many of the "imitations" stand above the rest of his work: they are truer to himself. Lowell-Baudelaire despairs of the world more eloquently than Lowell alone, and Lowell-Juvenal on Rome is harsher and more direct than Lowell solo on Washington. He can remember what it was like to be a boy on Grandfather's farm, but he has trouble telling you what it is like to be a man alive today, unless we are to accept his constant agonizing as either normal or useful. "In truth," reads the Afterword to *Notebook*, "I seem to have felt mostly the joys of living; in remembering, in recording, thanks to the gift of the Muse, it is the pain." Thanks to the gift of the Muse, indeed! Perhaps a Maecenas to assure him of his comfort, and an Augustus to reassure him of his welcome in society, would have enabled him to become the American Horace!

VIII

One final aspect of Lowell's work deserves passing recognition—his plays, all of them "imitations" in dramatic form. With the help of the distinguished scholar Jacques Barzun, he translated *Phaedra* and *The Marriage of Figaro* and published them in the same year as *Imitations*, 1961. Three years later he issued a trilogy of dramas based on stories by Hawthorne and Melville under the general title of *The Old Glory*. And in 1967 the School of Drama at Yale University produced his version of Aeschylus' *Prometheus Bound*. In the first and last of these efforts, the line between translation and innovation is very thin; in the case of *Prometheus Bound*, Lowell worked from an English prose translation, "one of the dullest I could find. Seldom was there any temptation to steal a whole phrase." But, he adds, "I kept the structure, either roughly rendering or improvising on each speech. Half my lines are not in the original. But nothing is modernized . . . My idea was for some marriage between the old play and a new one." His plea for acceptance of the work: "I hope I will not be accused of concocting my own anarchic miasma," may be fairly echoed by anyone who seeks to criticize the play in the context of the rest of Lowell's work, especially without having seen it performed. On paper it often seems stiff and quirkish, like most of Lowell's prose writings. On the whole it is probably decent enough, though it lacks the soaring rhetoric generally associated with Aeschylus, or even that of Lowell's Juvenal. After the original performance, Mr. Walter Kerr wrote in the New York *Times*, "The lungs fill, the heart lifts, the head shakes itself free of months of accumulated debris"—so perhaps it has a power on stage that it lacks on paper, or Mr. Kerr viewed it upon recovering from a nasty virus. The pompous Dr. George Steiner protested the "unsteady and capricious bearing on the matter of Racine" of Lowell's *Phaedra*, but it is generally interesting, and some passages rise to the level of Lowell's finest lyric "imitations."

The Old Glory is the most ambitious of Lowell's dramatic efforts. Each of its three plays attempts to evoke a particular period in American history. "Endecott and the Red Cross," based on a story by Hawthorne, concerns the early Puritans, and their conflicts with the Indians and the Anglican Church. "My Kinsman, Major Molineux," also taken from Hawthorne, deals with the period of the Revolutionary War and the clash of loyalties it involved. The third play, "Benito Cereno," originally a short novel by Melville, is set around the turn of the eighteenth into the nineteenth century, when the United States was beginning to expand its interests across the continent and around the world. The trilogy is written in verse which is cloddish and pointless, much like that of T. S. Eliot's *The Cocktail Party*. This style is

rooted in the conviction that genuine poetic drama can be revived
by an author's simple decision to arrange his words into linear and
stanzaic forms instead of sentences and paragraphs. Perhaps it is a
reassuring reminder that the legalistic bias of Anglo-American
thinking does not escape even poets. Of course, it is a mere striving after the wind.

Lowell's decision to write versified drama results in his plays
reading like opera libretti; their language provides no more than a
skeleton of action. It is common to refer to this condition as
"stylized"; I prefer to call it boring. Murders occur; heads roll;
cannons roar; the reader is unmoved. I cannot speak for the
playgoer, as I have not seen these plays produced. Mr. Jonathan
Miller, who first directed the trilogy, wrote that "My Kinsman,
Major Molineux," "needs to be put across with scintillating
artificiality," which says enough. Miller added that "Benito
Cereno" is "an opera without music," which meets my definition
of a libretto nicely, and that "Endecott and the Red Cross" "presents the most awkward puzzles for a director," which I do not
doubt. The point is that by reading the director's testimony, I am
disinclined to think that Lowell's trilogy should be much better
on stage than it is in print, and I feel free to pick at it.

"Death has brought me back to you," Assawamset, chief of the
Narraganset Indians, says to his friend Thomas Morton, Master
of Merry Mount. "Endecott and the Red Cross" thus opens the
trilogy in typically Lowellsian fashion. There is trouble in the settlement; a rebellion is brewing. Mr. Blackstone, representing
Archbishop Laud in Merry Mount, proclaims:

> *I suppose we'll have to work together.*
> *I wonder why Archbishop Laud chose me.*
> *I am a specialist in Church of England ritual.*
> *This is my first taste of exile and authority.*

Connect the undotted lines.

Governor Endecott stews over the impertinence of the Merry
Mounters, particularly their good relations with the Indians. The
young Puritan minister Palfrey is trying to flatter Endecott into
action with verse such as, "There is no man like you. When you
march,/you set the earth on fire." Eventually the problem is re-

solved by killing some Indians and burning down the houses of
Merry Mount, leaving Endecott to offer a flat and undistinguished
reverie over his own behavior:

> I should ask for a day of mourning in the colony,
> or better my own day of mourning,
> for the people we have sent into misery, desperation—
> that I have sent out of life:
> my own soldiers, the turncoat Indians who served our turn,
> and for the other Indians, all those who are fighting
> with unequalled ferocity, and probably hopeless courage,
> because they prefer annihilation to the despair of our
> conquest.

"It's strange I was in such an unmanly terror about a flag. It's a
childish thing," he adds, and the play ends with Endecott kicking
the red cross of England.

"My Kinsman, Major Molineux" picks up in Boston, on the eve
of the American Revolution. The young man Robin and his
brother are ferried across a marsh by a ferryman whose "dress, although eighteenth century, half suggests that he is Charon,"
which should half assure readers of Lowell's other works that they
are in familiar territory. The story stiffly proceeds, with the two
boys going about Boston asking for the whereabouts of "my kinsman, Major Molineux." They get all sorts of strange answers,
until they learn that the major is regarded as a traitor by these
Bostonians. They observe his execution; the major looks at Robin,
asks, "Et tu, Brute?", and dies. The boys are momentarily sad, but
Robin decides that he and his brother will remain in Boston. He
expresses the excitement he feels at becoming part of the young
Republic:

> Yes, brother, we are staying here.
> Look, the lights are going out,
> the red sun's moving on the river.
> Where will it take us to? . . . It's strange
> to be here on our own—and free.

The younger brother says, "Major Molineux is dead." And Robin
says, "Yes, Major Molineux is dead." Curtain.

"Benito Cereno" takes place "about the year 1800 . . . in an island harbor off the coast of Trinidad." The story departs a great deal from the Melville original, but there is little to be gained by spelling out the details of Lowell's revised version. The play concerns an American captain whose ship is docked in the same harbor as a Spanish slave-carrying vessel, and the story involves themes of racism, treachery, and betrayal. The American captain, Amasa Delano, is a laconic Yankee. One dialogue with the fawning slave, Babu, goes like this:

BABU: You say such beautiful things, the United States must be a paradise for people like Babu.

DELANO: I don't know. We have our faults. We have many states, some of them could stand improvement.

BABU: The United States must be heaven.

DELANO: I suppose we have fewer faults than other countries.

A slave uprising climaxes the play. Delano saves Benito Cereno, who thanks him for his life. "A man can only do what he can," answers Delano. "We have saved American lives." Babu, leader of the uprising, pleads for mercy from Delano, saying, "Yankee Master understand me. The future is with us." Delano responds, "This is your future," and shoots him in the head to conclude the trilogy.

Throughout the three plays, there are suggestions of the various moral problems which affect the United States to this day: puritanism vs. nature, loyalty vs. sentiment, black vs. white, authority vs. obedience, and so on. I do not relate these themes to individual sections of *The Old Glory* because Lowell's treatment of them is too spare and superficial to merit debate. I sense that he is shooting at these things with ping-pong balls; ordinarily given to heavy overstatement, he treads too lightly here. Where is the bluster that shook *Lord Weary's Castle?* Where is the merciless honesty which gave life to *Life Studies? The Old Glory* is not a disaster; it is just ridiculously modest.

We might declare him to be out of his ball park, but then, what is his ball park? The classics? Old New England? New New England? New York? His own back yard?

IX

It is fitting that we take our leave of Lowell with *The Old Glory*, in which a struggling man attempts to vent his feelings in a form which is strange to him, and to which he is ill-suited. The stage is the medium of intellectual extroverts, of writers who are willing to let men and ideas crash and slide with minimal regard for right and wrong. The best playwrights are able to see seven sides to an issue, and many layers beneath man's visible skin. Lowell, excellent though his thoughts may be, must pinch himself to see another man's side of the story; like the Lowells of legend, he does not like to be seated at table too far from God. He speaks of "I," and then condescends to let the heavens speak. So, when he writes a play, each of the characters gets pinched, and those halting phrases emerge.

The man often endowed with the label of "our greatest living American poet" is said to be a fellow of great generosity in helping those younger souls who hear the beckoning of the Muse. I do not doubt these reports for a minute, though I gather that the spiritual kinship between teacher and student goes unspoken, while the concentration is on improving technique; for when all these bards return to their desks, their thoughts are of loneliness and despair, and not of the joyous community of poets. At least Lowell is that way. He seems willing to try anything to drive away the darkness: classic gods, family albums, history, poetic dramas, antique forms, "unrealism," phantasms of every stripe. But the darkness remains; a pall hangs over all his work, excepting those bits and pieces we have noted in our survey. The world seems ready to drop on his shoulders any moment; he must make his peace with it, but this he cannot do without judgment. And so he judges, a basically conservative man appalled by what he sees but seduced by much of it. His ideas have become mushy with adverbs. His verse is swollen beyond its natural limits. His passions lay buried beneath a bed of verbal fat. If he is "the best American poet of our time," then these are not good times for verse.

Gore Vidal

We are, as a people, eager for sophistication and uncomfortable with skepticism. Subscriptions to formal ideologies remain low, but the will to believe survives. This is probably not bad: as Socrates failed to say, the life too much examined may not seem worth living. People enjoy the feeling that they have a grip on matters, in order that they may proceed to make a commitment to something or other. The skeptic, in contrast, seeks understanding without commitment. So, in our day, we find the Buckleys, Galbraiths, and Schlesingers snuggling up close to their ideologies when the night grows cold; we watch the pathetic Mailer as he bellows wildly on account of some silly concept that has worked him into a fever; and we witness sadly the anguished Lowell as he wrings his hands in contemplation of the ghosts of the Puritans.

Out from the crowd steps Gore Vidal, mocking the peers and prelates, sneering at the commoners who lend them their support. He confounds by proclaiming himself a democrat and railing against the mob, by parading his learning while denouncing the professors, by trumpeting the virtues of sexual variety while debunking the idea of romance. All this is accomplished in a style

Two university scholars have written critical studies of Vidal which made it unnecessary for me to engage in the more primitive forms of research. They are Roy Lewis White and Bernard F. Dick and their books are, respectively, *Gore Vidal* and *The Apostate Angel: A Critical Study of Gore Vidal*. I am indebted to both.

which shames the jargoneers with its classic force. Here is the closest thing to a true skeptic among contemporary American literary politicians: a perpetual leader of the opposition.

II

Eugene Luther Gore Vidal, Jr., was born at West Point, New York, in 1925. His father was an aeronautical engineer, his mother the daughter of the blind, populist senator from Oklahoma, Thomas Gore. The family moved to Washington, D.C., and lived in the senator's house at Rock Creek Park. The boy enjoyed his elevated status as he accompanied his grandfather around town. According to Bernard Dick, "at seven, he was leading his grandfather onto the floor of the Senate. He guided the Senator through museums, passing his fingers over the faces of the statues and reading off their titles and the sculptors' names. In turn, Senator Gore encouraged his grandson to roam freely through the attic library and call its northeast corner, with its vast collection of fairy tales, his own."[1] The parents' marriage failed; in 1935 they were divorced. The boy preferred his father ("I was very, very fond of him"[2]) but was assigned to his mother's care. She married Hugh Auchincloss and became hostess of a political salon in Virginia. "We were brought up quite removed from real life. By that I mean the Depression and what the family would have termed 'disagreeable people.' "[3] Not yet fourteen, he took a European tour with two schoolmasters and five classmates. The youth was much impressed by Mussolini, and warmed himself by thinking of an ancestral relationship with the medieval troubadour Vidal. A year's schooling in New Mexico followed, then entry into Phillips Exeter. Freed from Washington and family pressures, he blossomed and was happy. He celebrated his emancipation by composing gloomy verses on the loss of religious faith. The following year the poet Gene Vidal disappeared from the pages of the *Phillips Exeter Review* and a storyteller named Gore Vidal emerged. He had chosen his profession and clipped on his badge.

1 Bernard F. Dick, *The Apostate Angel: A Critical Study of Gore Vidal*, New York: Random House, 1974, p. 42.
2 *Time* magazine, March 1, 1976, p. 62.
3 Roy Lewis White, *Gore Vidal*, New York: Twayne Publishers, 1968, p. 21.

In 1943 he graduated and enlisted in the Army Reserve. He discovered an opening for maritime officers in the Army Transportation Corps; taking a lesson from Bernard Shaw's Captain Shotover, he learned navigation and found himelf in Alaska. Before long he developed rheumatoid arthritis and removed himself to a warmer clime. The experience gave him the subject for his first book; by the time he was nineteen he had finished it. A year later the war was over and Vidal was being hailed as the first of the postwar prodigies.

"Williwaw," explains the author, "is the Indian word for a big wind peculiar to the Aleutian islands and the Alaskan coast. It is a strong wind that sweeps suddenly down from the mountains toward the sea. The word williwaw, however, is now generally used to describe any big and sudden wind." *Williwaw* employed the time-honored convention of men at sea. It also assumed the pseudo-naïve style which Vidal later termed "the national manner." So the seamen, facing a williwaw, talk like this:

"That's what I like." Bervick looked at the black unchanging storm center. "Maybe we'll miss the whole thing."

Evans smiled. "No chance, Bucko, we'll get all of it. Right in the teeth, that's where we're going to get it."

"I wish I never left the Merchant Marine."

"You got a hard life."

"That's what I think."

"Don't we all." Evans made his mouth smile again. He tried to be casual.

The main conflict of the book involves the rivalry of the second mate, Bervick, and the chief engineer, Duval, for the attention of Olga the whore. It is resolved when Duval falls overboard and drowns. Although accidental, the drowning was precipitated by an act of Bervick's. The facts are not vigorously pursued. No one on board seems to care that Duval is dead, and the matter is covered up in the official report.

Its author, proud of his first-born, insists that *Williwaw* "still works." It is, in fact, not a preposterous book, and its restraint is admirable in a nineteen-year-old author. But in no respect is *Williwaw* first-rate. Its laconic style is decadent Hemingway; its characters seem not to have red blood flowing in their veins; the thing does not breathe. With this work, Vidal recalled, "my life as a writer began." Indeed, the seed of Vidalian irony is planted in *Williwaw*: the disinterested attitude, exemplified by the death that gets papered over, the violence related in whispered tone. And if the young Vidal was shamming, he was doing so in the most elegant way—by understatement.

A year later came his second novel, *In a Yellow Wood*, which departed from an epigraph taken from Robert Frost: "Two roads diverged in a yellow wood,/And sorry I could not travel both/And be one traveler . . ." It tells the story of one day in the life of a young war veteran, now working as a stockbroker in lower Manhattan. Robert Holton is self-centered and stuffy. Like most of Vidal's early protagonists, he is obsessed with himself in a rather dimwitted way. The author's strained naturalistic style makes Holton an indifferent figure, and *In a Yellow Wood* a tedious book. "Robert Holton," he writes, "though he had never been much of an athlete, had a good build. Sitting at desks, however, would ruin it sooner or later and the thought made him sad. There was little he could do, of course, for he would always sit at desks." The people around him are not much better. A secretary's cough "had a consumptive sound which rather appealed to her." Another member of the firm likes to sit on the toilet and read short stories in magazines. An executive is obsessed with his ulcer, which he has convinced himself is cancerous. The waitress who gets Holton his breakfast hates all the other people who seem close to Holton.

The book's slight drama is provided by the appearance, at a cocktail party, of a woman Holton had loved while in Italy during the war. Carla's husband is homosexual, which leaves her free to tempt Holton. This she does with Latin arrogance, reminding him of their earlier affair: "You Anglo-Saxon! . . . You say it's pretty. You say it's nice. It was beautiful and you know it. That was a beautiful time." After visiting a gay nightclub in Greenwich village, "They decided to walk uptown, to walk to Times Square." Once arrived, she continues to taunt him:

"I think," said Carla, laughing, "this is the peak of your civilization."

"Probably; it's the sign of the century."

"But there will be other centuries." And they thought of other centuries when they would not be alive and they tried to see the square in future years—if the square survived with the dream.

Holton is not quite prepared for all this; he reminds Carla that Italy and the war are in the past. "The only way I could get by," he pleads, "was to do what I'm doing: become a broker . . . I have to be a conventional person and I don't mind." They make love and he enjoys it, but by morning it is clear: "Robert Holton would become a successful broker working in an office. The decision was made and he felt secure at last . . . With great effort he resumed an identity and freed himself from doubt."

Not surprisingly, after this concatenation of banalities, Vidal felt "bored with playing it safe. I wanted to take risks, to try something that no American had done before." At twenty-one, he wrote *The City and the Pillar* and achieved instant notoriety. His subject, once more, is a rather dull lad engaged in a quest for self-fulfillment. What separates Jim Willard from Robert Holton is his homosexuality; what sets off *The City and the Pillar* from *In a Yellow Wood* is the intensity which sexual variation brings to the tale. The book was mysteriously inscribed "for the memory of J.T." Bernard Dick, a clever detective at times, reveals that at St. Albans school in Washington, which Vidal attended from 1936–39, one of Vidal's classmates was a Jim Trimble, who later died at Iwo Jima.[4] References to the boyhood lover who died in battle occur in *The Season of Comfort* ("Jimmy Wesson"), in "Pages from an Abandoned Journal" ("Jimmy"), in *Washington, D.C.* ("Scotty"), and in *Two Sisters* ("Jimmy").

Not even the annoyance of Vidal's early style could suffocate the emotion with which *The City and the Pillar* is infused. "In the interest of verisimilitude," Vidal recalled, "I decided to tell the story in a flat gray prose reminiscent of one of James T. Farrell's social documents. There was to be nothing fancy in the writing." Trouble is that Farrell could not write any other way, and his style was his own. Vidal could, and in time he would, but he had not yet hit his pitch. There is irony in the early books, but of a double-edged sort, not always pleasant: the author knows more

[4] Dick, op. cit., p. 37.

than he tells, the reader knows more than the author. And there is
no sharpening wit.

Even so, *The City and the Pillar* is a powerfully direct work. It
begins with an unhappy scene in which a young man sits alone in
a bar, drinking his way into a miserable intoxication. He brushes
off a woman who tries to pick him up, and slides into a reverie,
wanting "to be alone, a creature without memory, sitting in a
booth." The scene shifts back several years, to the closing days of
Jim Willard's junior year in high school. His best friend, Bob
Ford, is preparing to graduate and ship out to sea. They decide to
spend a final weekend together at an isolated cabin where they
have gone before. This time they wind up in each other's arms.
The following Monday, Bob departs, and Jim's search for him begins. Upon his own graduation a year later, he becomes a cabin
boy, hoping to cross paths with his friend. It is years before they
are reunited, by which time Jim's memory of the weekend at the
cabin has achieved mythic proportions.

In the meantime, Jim sustains his dream by making his way in
the world—first as a cabin boy, then as a ball boy and tennis instructor in Los Angeles, later, consecutively, as the kept boy of a
famous actor, the companion of a novelist, a soldier in the U. S.
Army during the Second World War, and finally a tennis instructor in New York City. In each instance he behaves as a selfish
fellow in a selfish world. Here was his life in Los Angeles at a
great resort hotel:

> According to the newspapers there was a war in Europe, but Jim
> was not quite sure what it was all about. Apparently there was a
> man named Hitler who was a German. He had a moustache and
> comedians were always imitating him. At every party someone
> was bound to give an imitation of Hitler making a speech. Then
> there was an Englishman with a somewhat larger moustache and
> of course there was Mussolini but he didn't seem to be in the
> war. For a while it was very exciting, and there were daily head-
> lines. But toward the end of September Jim lost interest in the
> war because there had been no battles. Also, his days were now
> occupied teaching tennis to rich men and women who were not
> very interested in the war either.

So his story is the *Bildungsroman* of a physical young man, peculiarly American in this sense. The sexuality of the protagonist allowed Vidal to extend the boundaries of realism, as Dreiser had done nearly half a century before. Not since Clyde Griffiths had such a vacuous creature proven so captivating. His progress is sluggish because his mind is slow:

> Jim went through several stages after his discovery that there were indeed many men who liked other men. His first reaction was disgust and alarm. He scrutinized everyone carefully. Was he one? After a while, he could identify the obvious ones by their tight, self-conscious manner, particularly when they moved, neck and shoulders rigid. After a time, as the young men grew used to Jim, they would talk frankly about themselves. Finally, one tried to seduce him. Jim was quite unnerved, and violent in his refusal. Yet afterward he continued to go to their parties, if only to be able to experience again the pleasure of saying no.

But he does not say no forever, and in time he must measure his experience against his dream—no need to say which comes out ahead. He moves from one association to the next without much care for the sentiments of his partners, aware only that each is not Bob. He endures parties where the host confides that he has found "the most wonderful swami" and intends to take up Vedanta. Those who would accuse Vidal of proselytizing on behalf of his sexual preferences have not read *The City and the Pillar* well: it is a document and not an argument, and it does not portray a very decent world. Its characters are united in their estrangement from one another; the author leaves them stranded and alone. Their environment has been poisoned by hostility from the outside, breeding distrust within. So Jim Willard clings ever more desperately to his memory of Bob Ford.

When they meet again, Bob is married to the girl who had, in effect, been Jim's rival in high school. They share a pleasant dinner and Jim invites Bob to call him when he is next in New York. They drink together and return to Bob's room. Jim all the while is trying to seduce this "conscious dream," first with words, to which Bob, recalling the first time, remarks, "Kids always do that, I guess," and then in deed. But Bob is not only uninterested, he is downright affronted by this challenge to his masculinity. He responds with a violent slap, and Jim, his dreams shattered, brutally rapes his old friend and walks out on him.[5]

All this is quite honestly told; the bland style almost justifies itself in this closing section. No subject in the world suffers from so much mystification, romanticization, and general flapdoodle in its treatment as homosexuality. To make matters worse, as someone has remarked, it has in recent years shed its image as the love that dare not speak its name in favor of becoming the love that cannot shut up. This had not happened in the day of *The City and the Pillar*, which might in turn be blamed for the new loquacity were it not for the book's fundamental reserve.

Once started on the business of getting things off one's chest, it is hard to stop. Vidal is no exception to the rule, and so after *The City and the Pillar* he wrote *The Season of Comfort*. This was his revenge on his mother. Although his fourth book, it reads like a first novel, flawed by its inability to come to terms with its material. Vidal was only twenty-three, and still too close to his painful adolescence to treat it properly. The Giraud family, like the Vidals, is a political clan. The maternal grandfather is a United States senator and former Vice-President of the United States. His daughter worships him and imagines a rivalry between herself and her mother. In earlier days she had fallen incestuously in love with her brother, who died in the First World War. In contrast, her husband appears ineffectual and the marriage is unhappy. Her passion and ambition are, accordingly, transferred to her son, Bill. The undercurrent of hostility between mother and son is the connecting thread of *The Season of Comfort*; at the end of the book, it bursts into the open.

The style opens up a bit in this book, with long internal monologues in which adjectives are welcomed. Flashbacks lighten the weight of chronology. Finally, in the climactic exchange between mother and son, the words and thoughts of each are set on opposing pages. This is a most unhappy innovation, subjecting the reader to unnecessary strain. *The Season of Comfort* is cast in the "portrait of an artist as a young man" mold. By the time we take our leave of Bill Giraud, he is a young painter, living in France,

[5] In the original, 1948 version, he murders him. I refer to the revised version of 1965, which is superior to the early piece but essentially the same book.

with an uncertain future. The seasons play their themes like leit-motifs: the descent of autumn, the despair of winter, the promise of spring, the release of summer. Bill's challenge is to break free from his mother and find peace for himself. His handicap is a bad heredity. His grandfather had been "confident of nothing, of Nothing." "His father was an artist who had become a man of affairs." His mother, like his grandfather, was a "pious pagan."

His father delivers the graduation speech at Bill's school, but this only increases the young man's sense of isolation: "All men were islands, separate from one another, and the days, the clear days, when one could see another island, were, unhappily, few. But, of course, his father was speaking politically. His father knew better." Young Bill "wanted only to be left alone, to find, if possi-ble, one other stranger, to be known only to one other." He first loves Jimmy Wesson; later there is a girl he likes "more than any-one else he could think of, his family, naturally, excepted . . . Yet he couldn't love her." It is his mother who overwhelms him, to the point where avoiding thoughts of her becomes "the one defiant act of his life, the one gesture he'd made toward freeing himself completely from her." When with her, he felt "weak." Fi-nally, he concludes that "spring, like the other seasons, was bit-ter."

Bill Giraud, Jim Willard, Robert Holton, and the seamen of *Williwaw* all suffer from the social disease of estrangement. Whatever their worldly gifts, they lack a sound sense of place in the order of things. It is surprising, after reading these four books, to come upon the troubadour Blondel, the hero of *A Search for the King*, the most charming of the first half-dozen novels and, along with *The City and the Pillar*, the most likely to endure. The "search" in the title indicates that this book, too, involves a quest, but the removal to medieval times brings an unwonted sta-bility to the proceedings.

The inspiration for *A Search for the King* came from reading *The Book of Knowledge* when a child in Senator Gore's library. "I reread it often, pondered it and, finally, in the fall of 1947 I de-cided to make a book of it." It became a poetic anecdote, told in prose. Richard the Lionhearted, returning to Europe after the Crusades, is taken captive by Duke Leopold of Vienna, and held for political ransom. Blondel, his troubadour, escapes, seeks help, and survives a series of fantastic adventures. No longer a youth, he looks at war like a philosopher and thinks of the Crusades as a good thing, given the nature of young men: "It was better that they be united here and kill the Saracen than remain at home in Europe and, for want of other diversion, kill one another there." He exemplifies Vidalian tolerance of bisexuality when meeting a giant who reveals a lively interest in shepherd boys, until he learns that his host likes to eat them. All this is told whimsically and with a proper dash of melancholy.

> And so he moved across the land in winter, moved toward a city and, moving, thought of his past in irrelevant fragments; a past that existed only as memory in the single reality of the present: a vague world of deeds performed in a place where castles, land- scapes and even faces were often obscure, confused; where a room might be complete but for its ceiling, say, or the face of a child- hood friend complete except for a nose and eyes: so much forgot- ten, so much that never was.

He dislikes priests for their "false righteousness" and air of "sacer- dotal infallibility" but admires them because they "saved old books and taught people to read and that was, certainly, good." Finally he takes as his companion a youth who dreams of martial glory. At the battle of Sherwood Forest, in which King Richard regains his supremacy, young Karl dies. Blondel reflects, "It has ended; his own youth lay dead in the rain and he would be old now, unprotected, centered in himself and never young again,"— and walks off to the victory feast with the king whose crown he has helped to restore. He has sought and found "the center" of his life in King Richard and medieval ways, yet there are mo- ments when Vidal seems ambitious to nudge him into the quat- trocento.

In order to write *Dark Green, Bright Red,* Vidal moved to Guatemala and studied banana republicanism at close range. This was supposed to be a satire of revolution, but Vidal was not yet out of his solemn phase. J. K. Galbraith wrote the same story in *The Triumph* twenty years later, and beat the novelist at his own game. Satire need not be written by a storyteller. It is more impor- tant to maintain clear, cranky views.

The protagonist is the American Peter Nelson, an uninteresting mercenary who has been court-martialed out of the U. S. Army, wants to make money, and so seeks gainful employment in a revolution. He is, despite his faults, capable of self-understanding, as one patch of dialogue makes clear:

"You're an idiot," said Jose amiably.
"No. Young." De Cluny opened one eye. "The characteristics are of course much the same."
"We're all idiots," Peter agreed. "All young."

All except the general who leads the revolution. A mellow man who seems not to have found exile in America unbearable, he announces at one point, "I've been craving Oysters Rockefeller all day . . . I must say I miss the cooking in New Orleans . . . Why am I doing all this when I'm not young anymore, when I could be living comfortably in New Orleans?" This question is never really answered, and the reader must sit back and watch the revolution fail, as he knows all along that it will. One thing nice about this book: it is short. Having failed to bring it to life, Vidal does not use an artificial respirator à la Mailer. Of all contemporary novelists, he is the easiest to take on his off days. We are best advised to adopt Peter Nelson's unconcern for failure, and close our survey of the six novels in five years amiably. It is smugly satisfying to see that, at twenty-five, he had not yet learned how to create ludicrous characters without writing a foolish book.

At heart Vidal is an ironist, and the first six books represent an extended effort to exert himself as such. He portrays the alienation of the privileged. His protagonists require nothing more than peace within. Jim Willard seems a decent young fellow who ruins himself through overindulgence in fantasy; it is even possible that, having shattered the myth of union with Bob, he will arrive at some co-operative arrangement with the world. Robert Holton, likewise, has had finally to put behind him the passionate wartime romance in Italy. Vidal portrayed him accepting his lot but not very happy about it. Quite possibly he will marry some rich wench, and enjoy an abundant life. Bill Giraud, having made the break with his mother, should become his own man and may even turn out well as a painter. Blondel, reunited with his king, will receive the laurels of eminence and be celebrated among the glories of his time. But Vidal was not prepared to say these things; at this early stage, the irony was that these characters were not doing as well as would be expected. Quietly now, loudly later, Vidal was waging war on the facile.

He presents the perverse in terms of the obvious. That a death should occur, and no one should care, as happens in *Williwaw*, is made to seem the most natural thing in the world. Jim Willard's progress has an air of inevitability about it. In *A Search for the King* the werewolves of legend are shown to be common thieves, and Robin Hood puts in an appearance as a hard-bargaining local boss, ready to deliver Nottingham to King Richard on certain terms.

Above all, Vidal is a careful student of human selfishness. His characters seek gratification, and think themselves righteous in their pursuit. Only Blondel, removed from the modern world, is capable of selfless dedication. All the others have some vague idea of what they want, and cannot understand why they are not getting it. It is sometimes unclear whether their affliction is naïveté or solipsism. Did Vidal similarly suffer? As the years passed, his characters would crawl from their shells into the great world of public affairs, and Vidal would take the same cure.

III

Of the first half-dozen novels, *The City and the Pillar* was distinctly the most important. It infuriated the right-thinkers and announced Vidal as a force to be reckoned with. There emerged the legend of the corrupt young author who cruised with the incorrigible Truman Capote. More important, the book caught the attention of the lions of literary Europe. E. M. Forster received Vidal at Cambridge; in Paris, André Gide presented him a copy of *Corydon*, "as one prophet to another."

Vidal acquired a jeep and toured Italy with Tennessee Williams. Settling for a while in Rome, he made regular pilgrimages to the hospital room of George Santayana at the Convent of the Blue Nuns. The old philosopher was as shrewd as ever. A decade and a half later, Vidal recalled their meetings:

We got on well; he was tolerant; he would answer my questions, but he never asked me a personal question and I'm not sure if he ever bothered to learn my name. But this was as it should be: he was eighty-five and I was twenty-three. He was the master and I was the pupil. When it came time for me to leave Rome, I said good-by to him. He walked with me down the corridor to the main door. He was small and fragile with glittering black eyes; he wore a dressing gown, a Byronic shirt open at the collar and a faded waistcoat of the 1890's. At the door to the hospital we shook hands. Then, as I was halfway through the door, he said, "I think you will have a happy life." I stopped and turned, not knowing what to say. He gave me a smile and added: "Because you lack superstition." We parted and I never saw him again. But I have often thought of what he said. I took it as a benediction laid on with the left hand, but secretly I have hoped it was a prophecy. So far it has proved true.

He returned to the United States and, in 1950, purchased an old house in upstate New York called Edgewater for its proximity to the Hudson River. In this baronial setting he sought communion with the past masters of English literature, rejoicing in the cosmopolitan irony of Henry James and disdaining the provincial embalmers at American universities. And he started work on the two books which would bring to eight his list of published novels before the age of thirty.

In 1952 came *The Judgment of Paris,* an amusing variation on his original theme. Philip Warren, a traditional young man, seeks himself, but is more worldly than his confreres and more humorous. At twenty-eight, a graduate of Harvard Law School, he has come to Europe for a year's sabbatical, ready to be tempted. His overseer, the narrator, is much amused by his situation and takes great delight in presenting it to the "dear reader," as we are quaintly addressed. "What sort of man or boy or youth is Philip Warren? Well, it is much too early to draw any conclusions about his character since he is hardly yet revealed." Revelation must come through encounters with a motley corps of secondary characters. Lord Glenellen and his friends offer boys and exotic political intrigue, but Philip confesses an addiction to girls and old-fashioned American power-seeking. He meets Regina Durham, wife of a powerful congressman, and is promised the presidency in exchange for his subservience. Regina and Philip have an affair which is pleasant but loveless—"That grand nineteenth century passion . . . had never, at this moment in his life at least, touched him with its burnished wing." Philip also attends a party given by the widow of a Greek fig merchant whose vulgarity "was one of the few really perfect, unruined things in Europe."

All this takes place in Rome, which Philip leaves for Egypt. Here he meets a "handsome" female archaeologist, who lectures him on ancient history, remonstrates with him for submitting to Regina Durham's wiles, and offers her asceticism in contrast. They do not become lovers, and Philip shies away from scholarship. He also makes the acquaintance of a man who is extremely obese and longs for death, and a dowdy lady author of detective stories who takes up this challenge and tries to kill him without his knowledge. She fails and fatso dies on his own.

In Cairo Philip meets Anna Morris, wife of an American businessman. In Paris, the third and final stop of his tour, she becomes his mistress. They do not demand too much of each other, and prove admirable companions. Philip satisfies himself that he has known love, and may build his life from there. Hera, Athena, and Aphrodite have dangled power, knowledge, and love before him, and he has chosen love. Older and wiser in the mid-sixties, Vidal acknowledged, "I am not at all sure a decade later that I would still give Aphrodite the prize, but my younger self did so without hesitation, and I still honor that commitment."

He may have realized that *The Judgment of Paris* closed his literary youth. Although one novel remained to be written at Edgewater before he would sell his pen to Hollywood and abandon fiction for a decade, the new work looked toward future preoccupations. As if by way of a farewell, Vidal reintroduced, in the final section of *The Judgment of Paris*, a few of the early heroes: Robert Holton is getting on nicely as a member of the State Department; Jim Willard is not doing so well as a drug addict and kept boy. Lest readers be tempted to moralize, there is also a pair of young American males who live as Jim and Bob Ford would have lived, if subjected to a kinder fate. All the early passions are given an ironic twist; the seekers after love are met halfway, with partners who do not drench them but supply safer passage through life's storms. Philip Warren chooses Aphrodite, but does not delude himself that he has reached his life's goal.

Despite the evident approach of the age of reason, Vidal did not write a very wise book in *The Judgment of Paris*. Its potentially grand themes are squandered in frivolity; the eccentric side show is fun but not too edifying. The high praise often accorded this book is unmerited. The tale lacks bite. It squeaks and giggles and taunts, but vacuity holds the center. "What sort of man or boy or youth is Philip Warren?" Apparently one who handles social relations easily, and would like to satisfy himself with a woman before starting his climb up the greasy pole. *The Judgment of Paris* offers a detailed description of the dispensation of this problem, but not much more.

Messiah was born to the thunder of one hand clapping. The world remains unaware to this day that it is Vidal's most powerful novel, deserving of a long life. It has met with critical stupidity which is genuinely amazing; orginality is now celebrated only if it appears in the form of unpunctuated sentences.

Vidal borrows from his own extended name and calls his narrator Eugene Luther. He addresses us from the turn of the next century, an old man plagued with atherosclerosis who is concluding his days in the Egyptian city of Luxor. His serenity is disturbed by the arrival at his hotel of an American, Butler, who has come to propagate the teachings of one John Cave, which are known as Cavesword. It transpires that Luther had been one of Cave's original coterie when the prophet had arisen out of the west in the middle of the century. His theme had been the goodness of death, and America had responded in a fever of excitement, casting off old faiths as if they were mere garments for a season.

At the time, Luther had been a young man of desultory interests, like his creator living on the banks of the Hudson and writing a book about the apostate emperor Julian. His neighbor, Clarissa Lessing, invites him one day to lunch, where he meets and becomes bewitched by Iris Mortimer, a young woman from Grosse Pointe who is seeking some direction for her life. Later he is reunited with her in California, where they do not become lovers, due to some unexplained infirmity of his. Instead, she introduces him to Cave, an ex-embalmer from Seattle. Cave speaks to a small meeting of the faithful at a funeral chapel, where Luther is impressed by "the purest artifice of his performance." His philosophy is simple: "Death is nothing; literally no thing; and since, demonstrably, absence of things is a good, death which is no thing is good." Cave's mellifluous presentation of this useless idea converts it into a glorious proposition; properly marketed, it becomes the rage of the land.

The job is accomplished by Paul Himmell, the evil genius of the tale and the most perfectly drawn of Vidal's creations. Himmell, a Hollywood publicist by trade, has no respect for Cave and his idea except in the sense that they may be made profitable. Allied with the Jungian Dr. Stokharin, he invests Cavesword with the requisite gaudiness. He enlists Luther as the movement's Matthew, Mark, Luke, and John. "Death is neither hard nor bad," reads the gospel in the prophet's name. "Only the dying hurts." Iris Mortimer becomes Cave's chaste consort. As happens in America, the mass movement is soon transformed into a religion. Paul Himmell declares to Luther, "People don't take the supernatural junk seriously these days but they do go for the social idea of the church, the uplift kind of thing. That's where we'll have to meet them, to lick them at their own game." Stokharin proposes that the feeling of guilt be countered with Cave's benign tolerance; taboos will be abolished by smiles. So Cave arises as Antichrist, and the old churches are swept away. Cavite centers decode Cavesword around the country. Even Presidents embrace the new creed, wanting always to stay on the side of the majority. Suicides, known as the taking of Cavesway, increase. Luther, having retained the intellectual's skepticism toward the movement which he has helped make successful, rises at a meeting of the board of directors to admonish the prophet:

> "You have removed the fear of death, for which future generations will thank you, as I do. But you have gone too far . . . all of you." I looked about me at the pale faces; a faint wisp of new moon curled in the pale sky above. "Life is to be lived until the flesh no longer supports the life within. The meaning of life, Cave, is more life, not death. The enemy of life is death, an enemy not to be feared but no less hostile for all that, no less dangerous, no less wrong when the living choose it instead of life, either for themselves or for others. You've been able to dispel our

fear of the common adversary; that was your great work in the world. Now you want to go further, to make love to this enemy we no longer fear, to mate with death, and it is here that you, all of you, become enemies of life."

But it is too late: Paul Himmell has determined that the gullible Cave should be forced to take Cavesway, in order that the legend may grow and the movement flourish. When Cave starts doubting death's loveliness, Paul Himmell murders him. A power struggle ensues in which Iris Mortimer wins control; Paul Himmell himself takes Cavesway; and Eugene Luther goes into exile, under the name of Richard Hudson. His name is expunged from Cavite records, except for dark references to skeptics, who are known as lutherists among true Cavites. Cavesword triumphs, and in his dying days, Eugene Luther is left alone in Egypt, fearing assassination upon the arrival of the new Resident of Luxor. But this young Cavite, although at first suspicious of "Richard Hudson," checks into his background with the Cavite Establishment and learns that "there was no such person as I thought existed. It was all a legend, a perfectly natural one for gossip to invent." Luther is able to die as an official non-person.

Messiah's superiority is due to its style, which enriches the irony and darkens the satire. It is in a league with Mark Twain's *The Mysterious Stranger*, haunting us with its force, buzzing its searchlight in the face of a society crazed by its own comfort. "To behold the inexplicable was perhaps the most unpleasant experience a human being of that age could know, and during that gaudy decade many wild phenomena were sighted and recorded." Intellectuals "constituted at this time a small, militantly undistinguished minority, directly descended in spirit if not in fact from that rhetorical eighteenth-century Swiss whose romantic and mystical love for humanity was magically achieved through a somewhat obsessive preoccupation with himself." Rousseauian introspection was particularly popular among those "who, in time, like their great ancestor, chose the ear of the world for their confessional."

These evocative descriptions set the scene for the arrival of Cave, who personifies Vidal's nightmare about the native land. In the fabled *Esquire* essay of April 1967 on "The Holy Family," the prognosis was similar: "The rise of the *signori* is about to begin, and we may soon find ourselves enjoying a strange new era in which all our lives and dreams are presided over by smiling, interchangeable, initialed gods." Vidal is no critic of ideas; he does not quarrel with Cave's doctrine of death. What entrances him is the lunacy of public behavior: of demagogues trying to remember what they bellowed yesterday, of sharpies laboring to keep the demagogue in line, of disciples who deny the will to power while contorting themselves obscenely in order to grab a piece of the action. He is, moreover, bemused by the idiots who believe. All this sweeps up his story in a wild collision of competitive selves, a confluence in individuals who declare a variety of aims but share a common denominator of personal desire. John Cave in all his magnificence is never more than an embalmer who seeks the glorification of his trade. Paul Himmell and Dr. Stokharin want only to stretch the bounds of publicity and psychology as far as they can go. Iris Mortimer is the classic rich girl in need of "meaning" for her life, amounting to a passion for self-justification. Clarissa Lessing, "ageless" hostess and matchmaker, is throwing her most ambitious party and, along with Luther, has the sense to see when the guests are getting rowdy. Luther himself is the impotent intellectual, forced to lend his talent to charlatanry when snagged by the revelation of his limited power. All succumb to the personalization of principle. Happily they bathe themselves in dumb Cave's reflected grandeur: narcissists all, they gaze at the prophet and see themselves. Ingeniously the book closes with Luther, having told his story and that of the early Cavite movement, fading into babble, but not before the final irony of mass movements is exposed:

Though my memory is going from me rapidly, the meaning is clear and unmistakable and I see the pattern whole at last, marked in giant strokes upon the air: I was he whom the world awaited. I was that figure, that messiah whose work might have been the world's delight and liberation. But the villain death once more undid me, and to *him* belongs the moment's truimph. Yet life continues, though I do not. Time bends upon itself. The morning breaks. Now I will stop, for it is day.

It is personal ambition which causes people to enlist in such movements; ambition meaning, in a land of puritans, the pursuit of enhanced self-righteousness.

From this pedestal Vidal stepped down gently; the majestic *Messiah* lacked enough of the common touch to keep the lord of Edgewater in his cups. Already in the early fifties, he had written three detective stories under the pseudonym of Edgar Box. In 1956 he collected seven short stories in *A Thirsty Evil*, the final issue of "serious" fiction from his pen until 1964. Three of the tales concern homosexuality; of these, "Pages of an Abandoned Journal" is the best, chronicling the progress of a young man who adopts a career and mode to suit his sexuality. Among the other four, "Erlinda and Mr. Coffin" is an amusing piece about a great lady among the vulgarians.

IV

More important to Vidal was his discovery of television, and his placement of one foot inside the theater door. In three years he churned out thirty plays for the tube, all of them ephemeral stuff. "All things considered," he wrote in 1956, "I suspect that the Golden Age for the dramatist is at hand." He decided, after a succession of his novels had fallen flat, that the novel was dead as a popular form of serious art. Curiously, he continued to sing this song after he resumed writing novels which became best sellers. "I am not at heart a playwright," he wrote in a preface to one of his plays. "I am a novelist turned temporary adventurer; and I chose to write television, movies, and plays for much the same reason that Henry Morgan selected the Spanish Main for his peculiar—and not dissimilar—sphere of operations." He wanted to make more money.

The most notable of the television pieces was *Visit to a Small Planet*, subtitled "A Comedy Akin to a Vaudeville." Vidal rewrote it for Broadway, where it had a successful run. The protagonist is a creature from outer space named Kreton, who sounds something like Vidal. "Frankly," he is informed by a bristling general, "I think you are a spy sent here by an alien race to study us, preparatory to invasion." Kreton responds, "Delicious! Would you say that again? I loved it." It turns out that Kreton has come to start a war. "After all, that's what I came here to see! I mean it's the only thing they do really well." He informs the general he has some great news for him. "What news is that, sir?" Says Kreton: "War! I have arranged a sneak attack for tonight. The good ones always start with a sneak attack."

In contrast, the American earthlings are very bad at making love. "How ravishing! These primitive taboos. You revel in public slaughter: you pay to watch two men hit one another repeatedly, yet you make love secretly, guiltily, and with remorse . . . too delicious!" In contrast, Kreton's people have wiped out "the ultimate disease—passion!" "Now, we feel nothing. We do nothing. We are perfect." They have given up "tangling." Like an anthropologist, Kreton begs a girl to let him watch the next time she makes love; because he is a true Vidalian, he "should particularly want to watch you with some big strapping boy."

He is elegant and totally irresponsible; in his "suburbs of time," he has learned to speak French and banter like an English public school graduate. Reminded by the general that he is a "discovery of the United States" and is "worth more than all the H-bombs in the world combined," Kreton retorts, "Ah, but I make so much less noise." Vidal requires the use of deus ex machina to extricate Kreton from the situation; like the old satirists who dealt with censors prepared to claim their heads, he has Kreton rebuked sternly by a superior, who arrives to reclaim him. Kreton retires with a smile and a wink, while the Americans are reassured that Kreton is regarded as "morally retarded" by his own kind. "Make love, not war" has been accorded few more humorous applications.

In 1960, The Best Man landed on Broadway without a tryout at the television studios. It was far and away Vidal's greatest triumph on the stage. This was more light-hearted melodrama than comedy. Two candidates square off against each other for the presidential nomination. One takes the high road and the other takes the low; neither makes it to Scotland. William Russell is the sort who cites Bertrand Russell at press conferences. He reflects on the politician's presumptive duty to smile, "Is there anything more indecent than the human face when it smiles?" He is a man of Stevensonian uplift who says, "I believe in us. In man," not in

God. Former President Hockstader arrives to dangle the prospect of his endorsement before his former Secretary of State. He also discloses that he is dying of cancer, which proves easier to accomplish than the endorsement. Russell's rival is Senator Cantwell, a folksy Southerner who says, "I don't know why I don't appeal to those would-be intellectuals," such as Walter Lippmann; he seems deeply to admire J. Edgar Hoover. Cantwell lures Hockstader with a file on Russell's sexual promiscuity. The old lion's response startles him: "I couldn't care less. I was brought up on a farm and the lesson of the rooster was not entirely lost on me." Russell, in turn, is handed information on Cantwell's homosexuality in the Army, which he does not want to use. The two antagonists confront each other and the accusations fly. Russell ends by throwing his support to the obscure Governor Merwin: "Neither the angel of darkness nor the angel of light . . . if I may exaggerate my own goodness . . . has carried the day. We canceled each other out." It is also Russell who delivers the moral of the story. He says of Merwin, "Don't underestimate him. Men without faces tend to get elected President, and power or responsibility or honor fill in the features, usually pretty well." Politicians, including John Kennedy, thought *The Best Man* sound work. Its utter lack of ennobling features must have struck a sympathetic chord. The irony points straight at the persiflage, and not a soul comes away unscathed. The best men are degraded insofar as they practice politics.

Vidal's three succeeding dramas fell flat. *Romulus* (1962) sets its table in the days preceding the dissolution of the Roman Empire. I found the Emperor Romulus to be Vidal's finest stage creation, a Kreton with a sense of responsibility. Apparently an effete production distracted critics from the jaunty rhythm of the thing, which comes through in print. Informed by his chief of staff, "No soldier can sleep when he knows his country is in danger," Romulus Augustus snorts, "Ridiculous! If that were so, we would be a nation of insomniacs and quite useless in battle." The problem of the play is the question of justice for Rome. Romulus may save his empire by marrying his daughter to the wealthy businessman Rupf (who is portrayed as introducing pants to the Western world), or he can let it go. The Emperor proclaims:

I did not betray Rome. Rome betrayed herself. Long ago. Rome
knew truth, but chose power. Rome knew humaneness, but
chose tyranny. Rome debased herself, as well as those she governed . . . that is a double curse. You stand, Aemilian, before the
throne of the Roman Emperors. That throne is not visible to you,
is it? To any of you. But it is most visible to its occupant, to me,
its *last* occupant. This throne is set upon a mountain of empty
grinning skulls, streams of blood gush upon the steps to this high
place where Caesar sits, where I sit, presiding over those cataracts
of blood which are the source of power. And now you demand an
answer from this high place where I sit upon the bodies of my
sons and the hecatombs of my enemies. Very well, you shall have
your answer. Rome is old and weak and staggering, but her debt
is not yet paid, nor her crimes forgotten. But the hour of judgment is near. The old tree is dying. The ax is ready. The Goths
have come. We who have bled others must now ourselves be
bled. You have asked for justice. I shall give it! I sentence Rome
to death!

The speech is better than Dürrenmatt's, on whose *Romulus the
Great* Vidal's play is based. The curious elements of Vidal himself, the valetudinarian spirit imposed upon the desire for justice,
are here, as they are in lesser measure throughout the play.
Romulus deserves a kinder fate than is apparently marked out for
it.

Weekend and *An Evening with Richard Nixon and* . . . were
election-year specials, produced in 1968 and 1972, respectively.
Weekend is a melodrama on the lines of *The Best Man*. It tells of
a presidential candidate whose son brings home a black fiancée. It
is not so mean as its predecessor, and never really takes hold.
Nixon is a failed experiment. Presidents Washington, Eisenhower,
and Kennedy discuss the events in Nixon's life, sometimes quoting him unfairly and inserting little side comments on the national behavior. The play bumbles from the start, with Washington announcing, "Good evening, ladies and gentlemen. My name
is George Washington. Your first President. *General* G.W.? You
know . . . 'First in war, first in peace.'" A voice-over asks, "Who
cut down that cherry tree?" and Washington responds, "Later,
Father. I cannot tell a lie. Remember?" Vidal is supposed to be

making fun of America's forgetfulness about history; he manages, pointlessly, to mock history itself. He is even reduced to sight gags, such as having the infant Nixon appear in a blue suit. And he puts idiotic speeches into the mouths of his characters. Thus Kennedy: "The United States has six percent of the world's population. Yet Americans use forty percent of the world's raw resources. That is why we are in Vietnam."

Setting this blunder aside, Vidal has been a civilizing influence in his stage and television writing. He risked wit in Solemnity's preserve, and I must confess that I would rather view his *jeux d'esprit* than listen to Tennessee Williams' violins, Arthur Miller's throaty catcalls, or David Rabe's moaning in the barracks. Again, as in the novels, we have the clash of conflicting desires, parsed out by an elegant and bemused overseer. Yet even at their best, the plays and novels propel us to seek the man himself, for we sense that he is more interesting than any of his creations. We come to the essays, where he is dressed to the nines, standing out front and meeting all comers.

V

Only Buckley and Galbraith can rival him here, and they do not often meet on common ground. Vidal has the literary essay all to himself; behind him the professors do their creepy crawl, never catching him. Wilfrid Sheed bobs his head up now and then, but he has not been visible for as many years as Vidal, and seems reluctant to give chase. Vidal insists otherwise, but he is a natural critic and peaks in his essays. The novels are a notch down, the plays two notches. Like a doctor with a large investment portfolio his office hours are infrequent. But when open for consultation, he is the best general practitioner in America.

Besides literature, sex and politics are his primary subjects. Sometimes the three get tangled and the thunderbolts are heard from Caribou, Maine, to the Ciudad Juárez. He has landed a few blows below the belt, and his adversaries have not hesitated to respond in kind. On most such occasions, Vidal is at fault: people are inclined to go along when they see such a superior fellow playing dirty. It is to Vidal's advantage that I separate the three basic themes, in order that the loutish not obscure the proud.

He is, to begin, an awful prophet, not so bad as Mailer but all the more disappointing because otherwise he is so clearly of a higher grade. As I have already indicated, he predicted with superb confidence that the serious novel was dead as popular art form, and that the golden age of American drama was being inaugurated on television. (He has recanted the second contention: "I certainly got that all wrong," he wrote in a footnote to his collected essays; he is unrepentant on the first, and apparently regards his own huge successes as less than serious works.) But all this is not important. I would rather hear a stupid sermon by a pastor with a lovely voice than endure the learned homilies of a bore. The salient fact about the critic Vidal is that he has led the charge against the entombment of literature in academic vaults. I salute him, and present his record.

He first removed gun from holster in 1953, in an essay on "Novelists and Critics of the 1940's," and he has been shooting at selected targets ever since. In this very first piece the lines of conflict are drawn, and there are moments when the style achieves a mature brilliance:

> Today's quarterlies are largely house organs for the academic world. They seldom publish imaginative work and one of their most distinguished editors has declared himself more interested in commentaries on writing than in the writing itself. Their quarrels and schisms and heresies do not in the least resemble the Alexandrians whom they occasionally mention, with involuted pride, as spiritual ancestors. Rather, one is reminded of the semantic and doctrinal quarrels of the church fathers in the fourth century, when a diphthong was able to break the civilized world in half and spin civilization into nearly a millennium of darkness. One could invent a most agreeable game of drawing analogies between the fourth century and today. F. R. Leavis and Saint Jerome are perfectly matched, while John Chrysostom and John Crowe Ransom suggest a possibility. The analogy works amusingly on all levels save one: the church fathers had a Christ to provide them with a primary source of revelation, while our own dogmatists must depend either upon private systems or else upon those pro-

posed by such slender reeds as Matthew Arnold and T. S. Eliot, each, despite his genius, a ritual victim as well as a hero of literary fashion.

The reaction of the "new critics" has gone unrecorded; like the professors who succeeded them, they pretended that Vidal was of insufficient critical stature to require rebuttal. The whooping leftists seemed equally dubious to Vidal. "It is a poor period indeed which must assess its men of letters in terms of their opposition to their society. Opposition to life's essential conditions, perhaps, or to death's implacable tyranny, is something else again, and universal; but novels, no matter how clever, which attempt to change statutes or moral attitudes are, though useful at the moment, not literature at all." The essay gets rather ponderous at this point, and begins to warble about salvation and the like. But the naysayer was launched. When Malcolm Muggeridge argued that satire tended to flourish in comfortable times, he countered, "I suspect it takes a far more homogenous, more settled, yet more uneasy society to produce satirists." "This age," he concluded, "could be a marvelous one for satirists. Look at the targets: Christianity, Psychiatry, Marxism, Romantic Love, Xenophobia, Science (all capitalized and all regarded with reverence if not admiration)."

What are the aesthetics of the man? He has never laid out any formal critical credo, yet no one's views are more plainly stated. He is inclined to embrace the classic virtues: clarity, order, coherence. He slashes through current obsessions with a knife dipped in acid. Assigned theater reviews, he confronts the heroines of the stage: "Moon-guided, triple crowned, inscrutable, the American Woman in our theater is never so wise as when she's not thinking at all, just being, and listening with a tiny smile to the third act speech of the man, who has had to learn Tenderness the hard way." That capital T is crucial. Vidal knows America to be a land sworn to its Great Truths, most of them self-evident, many of them fraudulent; a land addicted to moralizing but unwilling to admit it; an unruly cast committed to playing out its Passion, with wavering signs of Salvation and Justice up ahead; in short, the home of the self-righteous. Turn left and you see the placards of the People. Turn right and you hear the wails for Free Enterprise. Our slogans represent our myths. Vidal's practice is to cut them until they start oozing. Only he among today's critics could rise to say, "Love in our theater is not really sex though sex is part of it. Love is a warm druggedness, a surrender of the will and the mind to inchoate feelings of Togetherness."

He stands upright without swaggering. His "I" is above the battle, casting fishy glances at the swarm below, composing his vision as he shapes the vermin into capitalized globules. "The human mind," he writes, "is in continual flux, and personality is simply a sum of those attitudes which most often repeat themselves in recognizable actions. It is naïve and dangerous to try to impose on the human mind any system of thought which lays claim to finality." He sees that, "Serious literature has become religion, as Matthew Arnold foresaw that it would. Those who once would have been fulfilled in Talmudic debate or suffered finely between the pull of Rome and the Church of England have turned to the writing of novels and, worse, to the criticism of novels." And he rides the compartmentalizers until they should be ready to shout:

> Surveying the literary output for 1965, Miss Sontag found it "hard to think of any one book (in English) that exemplifies in a *central* way the possibilities for enlarging and complicating the forms of prose literature." This desire to "enlarge" and "complicate" has an air of madness to it. Why not minimize and simplify? . . . There is something old-fashioned and touching in her assumption (shared with the New Novelists) that if only we all try hard enough in a "really serious" way, we can come up with the better novel. This attitude reflects not so much the spirit of art as it does that of Detroit.

Does he come forward with any learned Theory of Literature? Does a sailor state his theory of the sea? Does a duck come forward with a theory of webbed feet? Exegesis is of another world to such creatures. Vidal puts it well, noting that "the unlearned learned professors of English are the new barbarians, serenely restoring the Dark Ages." He says this in the great *New York Review of Books* essay of July 15, 1976, on "Plastic Fiction," wherein the fiction of such luminaries as John Barth, Donald Barthelme, and Thomas Pynchon is awarded a succession of clean uppercuts.

The essay represents the response of the artist to the pedant. "What is art?" Vidal stops for a moment to ask. "Art is energy shaped by intelligence." He will offer nothing more detailed than that. He sees the public novel, written to be read, in the midst of being overthrown by the University novel, written to be taught. "Academics tell me that I am wrong. They assure me that if it were not for them, the young would never read the Public novels of even the recent past (Faulkner, Fitzgerald). If this is true, then I would prefer for these works decently to die rather than to become teaching-tools, artifacts stinking of formaldehyde in a classroom (original annotated text with six essays by the author and eight critical articles examining the parameters of the author's vision)."

This happy intransigence combines with a delight in the detection of deception. Told by Truman Capote, in the late forties, that he had received a gold and amethyst ring from André Gide, Vidal investigated. " 'How,' I asked in my best Phillips Exeter French, 'did you find Truman Capote?' 'Who?' Gide asked. I suspected it was then, in the fabulous summer of '48, that the nonfiction novel was born." The Pecksniffs will claim, of course, that this is not criticism at all, but is mere anecdotal joking, but they miss the flash of insight into another writer's habits which is the core of criticism.

The professorial temperament is repelled because you describe the buttocks instead of the soul. It is, to them, secondary that you *see* buttocks instead of souls; it is tertiary that you describe the buttocks well. Vidalian criticism contrasts with this by employing all five senses, applying rationality to break down sensations, and then setting them to paper as simply and amusingly as possible. He has the aristocratic allergy to highfalutin theory. He also breaks into hives when confronted by native verbosity, preferring the refinements of Henry James or George Meredith. If he occasionally runs on about literature's approaching doom or sneezes at American literature as "a strange list of minor provincial writers," we may recommend an antihistamine but we need not flee from him as from a man drunken or diseased. No healthier or more sober American mind currently applies itself to literature. *Matters of Fact and of Fiction* is the title of his most recent collection of essays; it is more to the point than his earlier titles, *Rocking the Boat* or *Reflections upon a Sinking Ship*, which reflect too little of his detachment. Vidal maintains a stance of hectoring neutrality, like an irritable neighbor who calls down a plague on both houses next to his own.

There are exceptions to this rule, but only when he leaves the field of beautiful and proper letters. When he takes up politics, the hectoring becomes so loud that the neutrality is dropped and war is declared.

VI

The grandson of Senator Gore is a Democrat; for a while he was a fairly conventional one. His political career peaked early. In 1960 he campaigned from Edgewater for the congressional seat in the 29th District of New York State. The district was safely Republican and Vidal lost by 25,000 votes, but this was the best showing by a Democrat in half a century. His slogan was, "You'll get more with Gore," which turned out to be true, even if he did not again run for public office.

By way of Hugh Auchincloss, Jacqueline Kennedy was his stepsister. Vidal basked in the early glory of Camelot. On November 14, 1961, we find him at a White House party. J. K. Galbraith recalled, "It lasted until 4 A.M. I drank a great deal of champagne and remember telling Gore Vidal on the home that Shakespeare was almost certainly better than he. Gore was mortally insulted but took it well."[6] Vidal found "fragile signs (the warm response to the Peace Corps) and favorable omens (popular approbation reflected in polls) that a torpid society has at last been stirred by its youthful leader." But more with Gore did not mean too much of this fawning. At another White House party Vidal took the liberty of touching his stepsister; Bobby Kennedy sternly intervened; Vidal broke with the family. He started writing articles blasting Kennedys, and became an unconventional Democrat.

His liberalism has never sat too comfortably with his disdain for

[6] John Kenneth Galbraith, *Ambassador's Journal*, Boston: Houghton Mifflin, 1969, p. 225.

the mob. The grandson of the prairie populist inherited his elder's misanthropy.[7] He is consistently the most illiberal of liberal spokesmen, denouncing the people for their barbarism and the leaders for their incompetence. "I realize I am not easily placed, politically or critically," he wrote in his preface to *Rocking the Boat* in 1962. "I once found myself staring with empty mind into a television camera as, presumably, millions of bored strangers stared back. I had been asked what my political philosophy was. Was I liberal or conservative? Or what? After a moment of panic, I heard myself say in that grave, somewhat ponderous voice television seminars summon from one's viscera: 'I am a correctionist. If something is wrong in society, it must be fixed. At least someone should try to fix it.'" Admirable, but hardly the stuff that treaties are made on. So Vidal's history as a public debater has been a sad one. Left with defending Democratic Party precepts which were not all that dear to him, he has pounced like a starved panther on opponents. In a series of exchanges with William F. Buckley, Jr., throughout the 1960s, he rocked back on his hind legs and brayed like a jackass.

A fierce animal jumps out at us when the discussion turns to politics, the studio lights flash on, and Buckley is sitting opposite. On the old "Jack Paar Show," Vidal worked up a lather of indignation over Buckley's criticisms of the Pope, the Jesuits, and Harry Truman, all of them highly unlikely candidates for Vidal's protection. Later came the Democratic Convention at Chicago in 1968, where the two antagonists met on ABC-TV, supposedly for purposes of high commentary. They proceeded along these lines:

BUCKLEY: Do you think that Minnesota is such a heavy oil state?

VIDAL: If Minnesota—what has that got to do with anything?

BUCKLEY: What was the advantage in [McCarthy's] yielding to the oil interests?

VIDAL: I dread to think but I—

BUCKLEY: I know you dread to think. That's obvious . . .

[7] Vidal quotes his grandfather as saying regularly, "When the Republicans are in, I'm a Democrat. When the Democrats are in, I'm out of step."

Finally, with a startled Howard K. Smith moderating, the kettle whistled:

VIDAL: As far as I am concerned, the only crypto Nazi I can think of is yourself, failing that, I would only say that we can't have—

SMITH: Now let's not call names.

BUCKLEY: Now listen, you queer. Stop calling me a crypto Nazi or I'll sock you in your goddamn face and you'll stay plastered—

SMITH: Gentlemen! Gentlemen!

The nation was delighted by this brawl; scores of hausfraus and coal miners smirked with satisfaction as these two sterling intellectuals made fools of themselves. Buckley publicly apologized to Vidal a year later, for the "imputation of ['faggotry'] in anger." When *Esquire* published Vidal's account of the affair, Buckley thought it libelous, and sued. Vidal countersued, and lost. Buckley dropped his case letting Vidal stew in his legal expenses. "I have demonstrated," wrote Buckley to J. K. Galbraith, "that, at least in his dealings with me Vidal has proved himself contemptible, a dogged liar, a foul human being."[8] "Tell me," Buckley had asked of his friend earlier, "why do you people put up with V.?" Galbraith avoided defense and responded that "my few encounters with him have been interesting."[9]

This is more than Vidal's encounters with political thought have been. He is an absolutist in favor of civil liberties, a rather boring liberal on social issues, and an ironic isolationist in matters of foreign policy. On the one hand, he will write, "For myself, should the war continue after the 1968 election, a change in nationality will be the only moral response." (Obedience to moral codes is not his strong suit; he retained his green passport.) On the other hand, he rejoices in the national bumbling, which enhances his satiric and critical reputation. He enjoys nothing more than a bloodletting, with his countrymen laid before his surgical hands:

[8] William F. Buckley, Jr., *Execution Eve*, New York: G. P. Putnam's Sons, 1975, p. 326.
[9] Ibid., pp. 323–24.

Historians often look to the Roman Empire to find analogies with the United States. They flatter us. We live not under the Pax Americana, but the Pax Frigida. I should not look to Rome for comparison but rather to the Most Serene Venetian Republic, a pedestrian state devoted to wealth, comfort, trade, and keeping the peace, especially after inheriting the wreck of the Byzantine Empire, as we have inherited the wreck of the British Empire. Venice was not inspiring but it worked. Ultimately, our danger comes not from the idea of Communism, which (as an Archbishop of Canterbury remarked) is a "Christian heresy" whose materialistic aims (as opposed to means) vary little from our own; rather, it will come from the increasing wealth and skill of other Serene Republics which, taking advantage of our own increasing moral and intellectual fatness, will try to seize our markets in the world. If we are to end, it will not be with a Bomb but with a bigger Buck. Fortunately, under that sanctimoniousness so characteristic of the American selling something, our governors know that we are fighting not for "the free world" but to hold onto an economic empire not safe or pleasant to let go.

This presumption of Imperial America and its follies is the only aspect of Vidal's politics to have been tainted by originality. Otherwise, he may be right: without having written certain "adventurous" books, he has argued, he could have been elected President. His dullness is reassuring in so clever a man. He seems to know no more than anyone else who has read *The Population Bomb* and *The Other America*. The carping no doubt does him good, and makes him feel like a first-rate citizen. He is, of course, not taken seriously as political pundit, and this is fine. He has so misbehaved on public occasions that his buffoonery approaches Mailer's in scale. Contemplating the two of them, along with Lowell, I am reminded of Mencken's counsel to James T. Farrell that the three traps for a writer were booze, women, and politics. Vidal has skirted the first two, but the third has almost got him. He survives by imposing a personal theory of American history on his novels. This is politics once removed, and it works for Vidal. I refer to his notions of empire and then withdraw, pledged to return after I have heard Vidal on sex.

VII

At last we have a saber-rattler. Vidal would deny it, pointing to
the exasperation which marks these pieces as much as the political
and literary stuff. Wilfrid Sheed, too, checks in with a demurral:
"Is being a homosexual really on the same level as being a
democrat or a Dodger fan?"[10] But the disavowal comes in the
bulk of references to the subject, in the coherent theory which
Vidal has developed, in his integration of it into his literary and
political criticism. This is something Vidal really cares about; having put himself on the line by publishing *The City and the Pillar*
almost three decades ago, he has determined to see the matter
through until the world ceases to persist in the application of its
prejudices.

He asserts the innate bisexuality of all people. It is by choice
and temperament that one becomes a "heterosexualist," "homosexualist," or moves back and forth between the two. The arguments of psychiatrists are fraudulent; accepting Freud's dubious
categories, they argue that bisexuality and homosexuality are un-
natural. Clergymen are almost as bad, but not quite, since their
argument rests on moral rather than scientific grounds. Better to
read Suetonius, says Vidal, and study the sex habits of the
Caesars: "They were, after all, a fairly representative lot. They
differed from us—and their contemporaries—only in the fact of
power, which made it possible for each to act out his most recon-
dite sexual fantasies." The "simple fact of so many lives (certainly
my own)" is "that it is possible to have a mature sexual relationship with a woman on Monday, and a mature sexual relationship with a man on Tuesday, and perhaps on Wednesday
have both together (admittedly you have to be in good condition
for this)."

Of course, it was Tuesday and Wednesday that alarmed the
public. And Wednesday, in this scheme, is not likely to come
every week. Vidal's own Jim Willard stands in refutation of his
creator's argument for bisexuality; he seems exclusively interested

[10] Wilfrid Sheed, *The Morning After*, New York: Warner Books, 1972, p.
66.

in men. He also contradicts the argument that Vidal wrote any semblance of autobiography in *The City and the Pillar:* Jim Willard detests his father and is indifferent to his mother; Vidal battled with his mother and adored his father. It is the point of his succeeding essays that common perceptions of homosexuality are not only wrong; they are ridiculous. Now the war on the facile rages, with Vidal thrusting brutally at one of the few moral barriers still standing. He reduces the guilt complexes of others to foolish inconveniences. The difference between Tennessee Williams and himself, he writes, is that "I never had the slightest guilt or anxiety about what I took to be a normal human appetite. He was and is guilt-ridden, and although he tells us that he believes in no after-life, he is still too much the puritan not to believe in sin." He sends the psychologists and philosophers of virility reeling:

A beautiful irony never to be understood by United Statesmen given to the joys of the sexual majority is that a homosexualist like Isherwood cannot with any ease enjoy a satisfactory sexual relationship with a woman because he himself is so entirely masculine that the woman presents no challenge, no masculine hardness, no exciting *agon*. It is the heterosexual Don Juan (intellectual division) who is the fragile, easily wounded figure, given to tears.

One example of this is "our own paralyzingly butch Ernest Hemingway." In contrast Vidal poses himself, the paragon of cool reason. Like the protagonists of his novels, Vidal's deepest commitment is to self. He is the poet of rationalistic narcissism. He does not dip into his past for lurid anecdotes to tickle a jaded public; he is too much the politician for that. And as a politician, he knows how to play on people's fears and desires with a rhetoric which avoids inconvenient facts. Homosexuality was not totally acceptable to the classic world; practiced by Alexander and Plato, it was ridiculed by Aristophanes. Enjoyed by the Caesars, it was jeered at by Juvenal.

But it is not Vidal's purpose to present all sides of the case. He is here the advocate of an unpopular cause, serving himself as a rationalistic narcissist must, but staying tuned to political reality at the same time. If he could not be President, he could still get hold of an issue which would fix him in the public eye. Homosexuality filled the requirement admirably (bisexuality is merely a political dilution) and allowed him to speak his mind on a score of other topics about which he had nothing interesting to say. His triumph as a literary politician was predictable, given his willingness to pursue the homosexual theme. Like Senators Morse and Gruening, who earned passing fame by opposing the Gulf of Tonkin resolution, Vidal assured himself of stardom by employing his talents to oppose the prevailing sexual mores. He accepted the lesson of his grandfather and kept yelling until the established powers were forced to listen. Once he had their ears, he published *Myra Breckinridge*, and the debate threatened to become a riot.

"Is this *Paradise Lost?*" asked the London *Times Literary Supplement*, "or merely a *Golden Ass* penetrated?" It was certainly the strangest book Vidal had written. As *The City and the Pillar* had reflected his boredom with playing it safe in the late forties, *Myra Breckinridge* walked on the wild side of the sixties. It arrived in 1968, at the hour of irreverence when the students marched and chanted, "Hey, hey, LBJ, how many babies did you burn today?" "I am Myra Breckinridge," reads the opening chapter,

> whom no man will ever possess. Clad only in garter belts and one dress shield, I held off the entire elite of the Trobriand Islanders, a race who possess no words for "why" or "because." Wielding a stone axe, I broke the arms, the limbs, the balls of their finest warriors, my beauty blinding them, as it does all men, unmanning them in the way that King Kong was reduced to a mere simian whisper by beauteous Fay Wray whom I resemble left three-quarter profile if the key light is no more than five feet high during the close shot.

The elements of the book are planted in this paragraph/chapter: indeterminate sexuality, narcissism, and a wacky fascination with old movies. "In the decade between 1935 and 1945," writes Myra, "no irrelevant film was made in the United States. During those years, the entire range of human (which is to say, American) legend was put on film, and any profound study of those extraordinary works is bound to make crystal-clear the human condition." She rates them above Shakespeare.

The outrageous opinions are more important than the plot; Vidal makes Myra his mouthpiece in this, his most ironic book. It is for us to decide when she is serious and when she is ludicrous. The plot does not take its revenge on the commentary until the book concludes. In the meantime, Myra has arrived in Los Angeles to claim her inheritance from the estate of her recently deceased husband, Myron. The estate is an Academy of Drama and Modeling, run by Buck Loner, her late husband's uncle. He offers Myra a job as instructor in the arts of posture and empathy. Resenting the virility of the American male, she seeks victims to emasculate and discovers the actor Rusty Goldowsky, a notable stud who wears Jockey shorts. This so excites Myra that she subjects him to a physical examination, during which she rapes him with a dildo. Rusty is less than completely willing, but is too stupid to resist:

> When I plunged deeper, the penis went soft with pain, and he cried out again, begged me to stop, but now I was like a woman possessed, riding, riding, riding my sweating stallion into forbidden country, shouting with joy as I experienced my own sort of orgasm, oblivious to his staccato shrieks as I delved and spanned that innocent flesh. Oh, it was a holy moment! I was one with the Bacchae, with all the priestesses of the dark bloody cults, with the great goddess herself for whom Attis unmanned himself. I was the eternal feminine made flesh, the source of life and its destroyer, dealing with man as incidental toy, whose blood as well as semen is needed to make me whole!

This is pure Caesarism, Vidal style. Rusty turns out to be homosexual. Myra leans to lesbian interests, fondling the breasts of Rusty's beloved Mary-Ann. The girl resists her advances, but all is not lost. Myra is hit by a car, and during her convalescence begins to grow a beard and lose her breasts. It transpires that she is Myron Breckinridge, Myra having resulted from transsexual surgery. Myron marries Mary-Ann, and they settle down as a couple of happy reactionaries in the San Fernando Valley.

All of this was made serious enough to provoke the furor of the season. Vidal recommended a reading of Petronius and Aristophanes to the snipers. This would not, however, help us with Myra's opinions of Alain Robbe-Grillet and the French New Novel, which resemble Vidal's; nor with her belief that the memoir is the only literary form of interest to the current public, which meshes with Vidal's view that people are no longer interested in literature, but in the personalities of writers; nor with her conviction that homosexuality is an antidote to overpopulation, which matches Vidal's; nor in her assertion of the efficacy of bisexuality, whose sponsorship is not in doubt *Myra Breckinridge* is either a rude joke or a shrewd political maneuver; because I respect Vidal, I am fairly certain it is the latter It is not at all a work of art, stewing as it does in a vat of ephemera William Buckley, already brimming with asperity, linked Vidal the novelist to Vidal the politician:

> It attempts heuristic allegory but fails, giving gratification only to sadist-homosexuals, and challenge only to taxonomists of perversion . . . It will surely be said about *Myra Breckinridge*, not that the shrewdest readers of it failed to get the message, but that the responsible community betrayed itself, finally, as indifferent: to so acute, so crazed an assault on traditional, humane sexual morality; on the family as the matrix of society; on the survival of heroism, on the very idea of heroism.[11]

Eliminate the strong language, and Vidal's intentions are exposed. The political success of *Myra Breckinridge* is illustrated by the fact that an arch-rival was properly aroused. The book *is* an assault on traditional sexual morality, on the family as a societal matrix, and on the American myth of masculinity, easily transmuted into heroism. It is not intended to "gratify" anyone, and so Buckley's opening roar has a Learish echo. But it no doubt promotes nervous giggles and knowing smiles, and this was Vidal's point: that sexuality should escape the realm of the categorical. It is his dream that we might create a world where sex and morality exist separate but equal.

11 William F. Buckley, Jr., *The Governor Listeth*, New York: G. P. Putnam's Sons, 1970, pp. 314–15.

There are aspects of fantasy to all this, and in *Two Sisters* (1970) the narcissist brings his vision home. He subtitled the book "A Memoir in the Form of a Novel" and later termed it "a memoir done with mirrors." The most interesting thing about *Two Sisters* is that it followed *Myra Breckinridge*, almost as if Vidal needed to establish his footing on this terrain he was freshly stamping out.

He (identified as V.) has met, in a Rome apartment in 1968, a mistress from the late forties named Marietta Donegal. Marietta resembles in almost all respects the diarist Anaïs Nin, but Vidal wishes to divert us from this conclusion and so compares Donegal's prose to Nin's. Marietta starts discussing the critical reception of V.'s book, *Myra Breckinridge*, and we are left puzzling over the level of reality we are exploring. The conversation shifts to the old days in Paris, to old acquaintances real and imagined, and particularly to a pair of beautiful twins, Eric and Erika Van Damm, whose incestuous (but by no means exclusive) love affair provides the book its primary complication. Eric, a film director, had written a script which involved incest in classic times, and V. reads it, along with Eric's journal, in 1968, to see what he can learn about the Van Damms and the early days. V. is informed by Marietta that Eric had died while filming a student riot in Berkeley in the sixties, although there had been no film in his camera. She also tells him that Erika had given birth to a child, which for a moment V. thinks was his, only to learn later that it was Eric's.

Altogether it is a confusing and irritating performance, more perverse than *Myra Breckinridge* because it is more solemn. V. (when is he Vidal? when is he an invention?) has slept with almost everyone in the book, but not Eric, with whom shyness intervened. There are recurrent discussions of the author's situation which clearly comes from Vidal and not just V. These are similar to Mailer's interludes in *Advertisements for Myself* and succeeding collections, except that they are written in Vidal's superior prose. The persona of the essays reappears here, amused and exasperated, alongside a man looking wistfully back toward youth and the protagonists of the early novels:

Death, summer, youth—this triad contrives to haunt me every day of my life for it was in the summer that my generation left school for war, and several dozen that one knew (but strictly speaking did not love, except perhaps for one) were killed, and so never lived to know what I have known—the Beatles, black power, the Administration of Richard Nixon—all this has taken place in a trivial aftertime and has nothing to do with anything that really mattered, with summer and someone hardly remembered, a youth—not Eric—so abruptly translated from vivid, well-loved (if briefly) flesh to a few scraps of bone and cartilage scattered among the volcanic rocks at Iwo Jima. So much was cruelly lost and one still mourns the past, particularly in darkened movie houses, weeping at bad films, or getting drunk alone while watching the Late Show on television as our summer's war is again refought and one sees sometimes what looks to be a familiar face in the battle scenes—is it Jimmy? But the image is promptly replaced and one will never know whether it was he or only a member of the Screen-Actors Guild, now grown old, too.

But the point of this melancholy pose is never clear. The only comprehensible theme in *Two Sisters* is the naturalness of so many different forms of human mating. The narcissism here severs its association with rationality; this is the most self-indulgent book Vidal has written.

Having personalized androgyny, he resumed laughing. Following *Burr* (1973) he revived his transsexual in *Myron* (1974). The sequel, although billed on the paperback cover as "the most outrageous book of the year," failed to outrage. The reviews reflected the country's changed moral climate, and were studded with epithets like "funky," "kinky," and "campy" without any overtone of moral indignation. Readers were delighted, in the years of Watergate, to find Vidal making fun of the Supreme Court. He did this by naming sensitive body parts after justices who had voted to permit local communities to rule on pornography—testicles became powells, penises became rehnquists, vaginas were named whizzer whites.

It is vulgar, harmless joking. *Myron*, I gather, is the last word from Vidal on his most notorious character—or is *Myra Breckinridge Goes to Washington* in the galleys as I write? It does not come blasting from the back benches like its predecessor. Rather, it carries an air of smug jollity, an awareness that its misadventures will be acceptable to the public at large. This time Myron the good, conservative citizen of Southern California is fighting to keep the genie in the bottle; Myra, it seems, pops out now and then and performs her mischief. There is no climactic scene like the rape of Rusty Goldowsky because there is no point to be proved. Reading *Myron* is like spending the day with a club full of eccentrics. The politics are muted to the point where Vidal at last mocks himself.

Myron, in his first entry, is alarmed to find that he will "sit down with ball-point in hand to write a letter to the Van Nuys local paper on behalf of capital punishment or against smut and find that something very like Myra is trying to get out at the tip of my ball point." Myra, in her first appearance, blames her car accident for Richard Nixon's presidency, the energy and monetary crises, and the films of Sam Peckinpah. "I do not exaggerate: *All these disasters are the direct result of my removal from a scene which I was on the verge of transforming entirely.* Proof? Without me everything has gone haywire." Among the more interesting side characters is one Whittaker Kaiser, a parody of Norman Mailer, who finds Myron/Myra in feminine costume and orders him to "act like a man." His ideas are familiar to us: "To stick that breadknife in a woman's whizzer white and make the blood come gushing out! That's what being a man is, Breckinridge. That's what the orgasm is all about. Murder is sex, sex is murder." "Sex," answers Myra, "is sticking a rehnquist not a knife into a woman's whizzer white." "You're sick. You're a sick fruit," Whittaker retorts. And Myra delivers the quintessential speech of this silly book:

"Shut up!" I smiled at Whittaker, preparing for the knockout. "Sex is the union of two things. *Any* two things whether concave or convex or in any combination or number in order to provide more joy for all or any concerned with the one proviso that no little stranger appear as the result of hetero high jinks. So life not death is the big O. Write that down, Whittaker. Tattoo it on your fat blackmun. Drop the news into that frying pan of a brain of yours sizzling with greasy dreams of murder to be served up like McDonald's French fries with real blood for ketchup. A yummy dish for the typical hard-hat soft rehnquistman like you . . ."

It ends as it began, with Myron sounding off in the best tradition of the John Birch Society. *Myra Breckinridge* at least had a focus; the sequel is as random as the sexuality within. I know no reason why Vidal cannot manage better than this fairly worthless parody. From *Myra Breckinridge* to *Two Sisters* to *Myron* runs a stream of self-indulgence which elevates itself to self-assertion at moments but ends as self-parody. What has Vidal accomplished in these books? He has got a few laughs, forced the press gallery to pay closer attention to him, and hinted that he has serious things to say. But he says them elsewhere.

VIII

Sex is the issue on which Vidal has built his political reputation, but the larger part of his writing has dealt with the political labors of others. The characters of his early novels, withdrawn from any concern with the affairs of men, stand as so many adolescents before the heroes of the books that have marked the last decade. The narcissism of youth, the love of the body, is transformed into the narcissism of maturity and the love of power and reputation. His blade sharpened by personal combat, Vidal cuts into history with sharper irony than any contemporary novelist. The once solitary canvases are now crowded with figures trying to work their will.

The four novels are *Julian* (1964) and the loose American trilogy, *Washington, D.C.* (1967), *Burr* (1973), and *1876* (1976). They were underscored by a handful of essays and together they represent Vidal's reach for a lasting reputation of his own. They display an increasing preoccupation with the needless twists of history, and the lies that have given them substance. After *Julian*, they track native grounds. The American preoccupation coincides with Vidal's physical withdrawal from the United States. In 1963, he moved from Edgewater to Italy, and now spends most of the year in Rome or at his villa in Ravello. He returns to the United States mostly for promotional tours, but claims, "I do nothing but think about my country. The United States is my theme, and all that dwell in it."[12]

12 *Time* magazine, March 1, 1976, p. 61.

Even *Julian,* with its classical setting and its account of the war between Christianity and paganism, is a deeply American book. It has always been necessary for our national artists to come to terms with the religious impulse. This is because religion has been the traditional enemy of art in America, where the Catholic co-operation of Europe never took hold. It is not surprising that the American artist is customarily an agnostic. If he is a Lowell, his creations document the collision between the common sense and the immortal soul. If he is a Mailer, he wails at the inconvenience of people regarding a God more knowing than himself.

Vidal, as Santayana said, is without superstition, and his approach to other people's superstitions is clinical. *Messiah,* his finest statement on the subject, dismisses religion as nothing more than a successful mass movement. *Julian,* on which he worked for five years, portrays the resistance. I found the book cluttered with a scholarship that threatens to overwhelm the skepticism at every turn. For once, Vidal welcomed the praises of academicians, who regarded Julian and his times as accurately portrayed. The story is told in the form of a fictitious memoir by Julian himself, complemented by an exchange of letters between Libanius and Priscus, two old friends of the Emperor and survivors of the Christian age which followed his death. Julian, according to history, was an exceedingly solemn fellow, and so Vidal leaves humor to the epistles, which include much friendly haggling between the two old philosophers. Moreover, Vidal explained, he needed some device to expose Julian's occasional lies.

Growing up with his brother Gallus under the Emperor Constantine, murderer of his father, Julian studied for the priesthood, hated war, and cherished the scholarly life. Early on he began to have visions of himself restoring the pagan rites in an empire gone mad with "the Galilean." In time he became Caesar, then Emperor, and established the right of religious tolerance. The Christians wanted no part of this, and their agents in court, Maximus and Ormisda, flattered him and appealed to his vanity, as a result of which he set out to conquer Persia and died in battle, aged thirty-two. With his passing Christianity triumphed. Libanius converses with the Christian bishop John Chrysostom on matters of history and immortality:

"This is all we have, John Chrysostom. There is nothing else.
Turn your back on this world, and you face the pit!"

There was a silence. Then John said, "Do you see no
significance in our victory? For we have won. You must admit
that."

I shrugged. "The golden age ended. So will the age of iron, so
will all things, including man. But with your new god, the hope
of human happiness has ended."

"Forever?" he taunted me gently.

"Nothing man invents can last forever, including Christ, his
most mischievous invention."

Vidal is nothing if not a tease and his historical novels are,
among other things, teasings on a grand scale. Twirling in his
mind are the endless "what ifs" of history. Priscus offers his opinion, which seems fairly close to Vidal's: "I suspect that had Julian
lived, matters would have been just as they were under Constan-
tius, only instead of being bored by quarrels about the nature of
the Trinity we would have had to listen to disputes about the nature of Zeus's sex life." It is taken for granted that history is the
polemics of the victor. Vidal's achievement is to avoid writing the
polemics of the loser. His hero Julian, like himself, is a natural
critic: "I think that the old Roman tendency to look down on the
Greeks is no more than a natural resentment of Greece's continuing superiority in those things which are important: philosophy
and art." Read Americans for Romans, read Europeans for
Greeks. "Fortunately," notes Julian, "now that I am Emperor *all*
my speeches are considered graceful and to the point. How one's
style improves with greatness!" And Priscus and Libanius perform
as critics of the critic. "Have you ever read such nonsense?"
Priscus will snort when Julian's memoir takes itself too seriously,
which happens with increasing frequency as the end nears. The
Emperor places his faith in omens and auguries; he becomes more
king and less philosopher. "I gather strength from the army," he
writes. "They are my life, the element in which I have my being."
He appreciates the irony: "I who wanted to live at Athens as a
student have been eight years a general." He concludes, "Such is
fate." Julian was a mystery in death as in life. Vidal says that he

likes him, finding Julian "an engaging and a good man."[13] Best of all, he was a pagan, a man of intellect and self-discipline. He was clearly superior to all the Christian usurpers at his throat.

The American novels feature no man so admirable, though Aaron Burr is even more engaging. It was typically perverse of Vidal to choose the least admired early American celebrity and present him as the central figure of the Founding Fathers' world. His story is told through the chronicle of Charles Schermerhorn Schuyler (an invention of Vidal's), a young writer who wants to earn enough money in order to live abroad like Washington Irving. He signs on as Burr's amanuensis, and listens to the master's reminiscences. The times play in counterpoint: the mid eighteen thirties, when Schuyler surveys the scene in New York; and the days when Burr glittered on the national scene. Even those parts which are told in Schuyler's words are reflections of Burr's thoughts, and so the early heroes are forced to respond to Burr's elegant but amoral sensibility. From the start, Schuyler charts the course: "I find Colonel Burr's 'unsavoriness' a nice contrast to the canting tone of our own day . . . He is a man of perfect charm and fascination. A monster, in short." Schuyler is fairly incapable of censure, and proves an able guide through a world of brothers, journalists, and politicians. He is "drawn to the past, to what is secret; and drawn to those dreams of domination that make it possible for the dreamer to subvert with the greatest of ease class, nation, honour. Bonaparte fascinates me. So does Burr."

Burr's recollections appear to him, if not exactly revealed wisdom, then certainly beyond criticism. We learn from the old reprobate that Washington's army was composed of "thieves, ruffians, wild men from the forest, murderers, Negroes run away from their southern owners, European adventurers . . . every sort of scoundrel save one, the soldier"; that "the truth is that except for a handful of ambitious lawyers, there were very few 'patriots' in 1775"; that George Washington did not read books and returned to military life because of repeated failures as a farmer; that the "father of his country" took his posthumous designation seriously in his lifetime:

13 White, op. cit., p. 110.

"What was Washington's most notable trait?" I once asked
Hamilton when we were working together on a law case. The
quick smile flashed in that bright face, the malicious blue eyes
shone. "Oh, Burr, self-love! Self-love! What else makes a god?"

For good measure, Burr deems him an "incompetent general."
Jefferson "was the most charming man I have ever known, as well
as the most deceitful. Were the philosopher's charm less, the politician's deceit might not have been so shocking." His clothing
changed from European elegance to democratic shabbiness when
he assumed the presidency. "Like Napoleon, he was a fascinating
actor but far more subtle than the Corsican and ultimately far
more successful . . . It was Jefferson's conceit that he alone
represented democracy and that all the rest of us from Washington to Adams to Hamilton wanted to wear crowns and tax his cup
of tea." "One always dined royally at the great democrat's table."
"Like Washington, he did nothing but complain of the horrors of
political life and, like Washington, he had no desire to let go of
power."

Alexander Hamilton is another rival in roguishness. He was,
first of all, not a gentleman: he "remained to the end a strange
wild little boy thrust by his bastardy outside society, forced to rely
on his beauty and wit to get himself what he wanted, usually from
older duller men." "Are great souls *ever* moral?" Burr asks him.
" 'They are nothing else!' So spoke the seducer of Mrs. Reynolds."
Not that Burr disapproved, but Hamilton's "use of the word
'moral' was practically theological in its implications." Looking
back on the irreconcilability which forced the duel between the
two of them, Burr is drawn to literary allusion: "When I was
young, if I had read more of Sterne and less of Voltaire I might
have realized that there was room enough on this earth for both
Hamilton and me."

Burr leaves the over-all impression that the Founding Fathers
were no better than a talented pack of actors, ambitious for images to match their fantasies. Thus Jefferson, the most successful
of them, emerges as the villain of the piece. "All in all, I think
rather more highly of Jefferson than Burr does," wrote Vidal in an
afterword, but he still does not think highly of this national saint,
and it is often impossible to sever Burr's opinions from Vidal's.

"*Burr*'s revisionism is aesthetically permissible," commented Arthur M. Schlesinger, Jr., "if historically unsubstantiated and unconvincing."[14] Sounding rather professorial and recalling the "you are there" books of G. A. Henty of an earlier day, Schlesinger calls *Burr* "a boy's book written for an adult audience. In fact, it is a Henty book tricked up for the third quarter of the twentieth century."[15] This seems to me less than fair, although Schlesinger is as entitled as anyone to chew out Vidal. *Burr*, after all, embodies a theory of history; it argues that all men engaged in politics and war on a grand scale are so involved in order to attain the pleasure of power and glory. Furthermore, it argues that the American historical enterprise has been no more than an extension of this personal desire to the national level. Finally, it insists that the pursuit of this aim has never sat comfortably on the American conscience, resulting in a historical record out of touch with reality. "Our people have always preferred legend to reality," writes Burr, "—as I know best of all, having become one of the dark legends of the republic, and hardly real." Burr views himself (Vidal gives every appearance of agreement) as a gentleman in a society without honor. He is a man ill-suited to democracy. "None of us —not even Jefferson—foresaw this democracy," he says. "I suspect it will prove a bad thing."

By the time Charlie Schuyler reappears, democracy has taken hold, and has indeed proved a bad thing. *1876* portrays the political nadir of the Republic; the centennial year was the setting for the one indisputably stolen election in American history. Schuyler had achieved his ambition and set out for Europe; along the way he had learned that his father was none other than Burr himself, but this is no mark of distinction in America and is not widely advertised. Now aging and once more impoverished, having lost his money in the Panic of 1873, he arrives back in America with his daughter, Emma, the widowed Princess d'Agrigente. His long absence permits him to look upon the American scene with eyes popping. "None of the Americans I have met in Europe over the past four decades saw fit to prepare me for the opulence, the grandeur, the vulgarity, the poverty, the elegance, the awful crowded

---

[14] Arthur M. Schlesinger, Jr., "The Historical Mind and the Literary Imagination," *The Atlantic*, June 1974, p. 55.
[15] Ibid., p. 54.

abundance of this city . . ." New York seems "more like a city from the *Arabian Nights* than that small staid English-Dutch town or village of my youth." He hopes to marry his daughter to a rich American, in order to secure the family fortune; and ingratiate himself to the favored Democratic candidate for President, Governor Samuel J. Tilden of New York, and secure the family honor. Emma meets John Apgar, and Charlie signs on with the New York *Herald* as a special election-year correspondent. If all works out as planned, he will return to France as the American Ambassador, his comfort assured. It does not work out that way, of course, as the Republicans steal the election from Tilden and Emma marries not an Apgar, but a Sanford. "I now have exactly the same amount of capital that I had when I arrived here on the *Peirere*, less all the prospects I had then." Schuyler dies the following year, and receives a nice eulogy from his old friend, the indestructible William Cullen Bryant.

There is no brilliant reflection of the times, such as the hero provides in *Burr*. Charlie Schuyler is an ingratiating ne'er-do-well of a literatus, and manages to meet anyone who counts, from Mrs. Astor to Sam Clemens, but he is not capable of any more than amiable sarcasm; his America is "this vigorous, ugly, turbulent realm devoted to moneymaking by any means." His account has a pleasant, journalistic interest to it, never tiresome and never too deep. The country is full of amiable scoundrels, and there seems nothing much to be done about it.

Washington, D.C. carries the nation forward and comes to rest in the years between the mid-thirties and the mid-fifties. These were the days of Vidal's youth, and the book maintains an elegiac tone unknown to the purely historical *Burr* and *1876*. It is more like *The Season of Comfort* revisited in maturity, with the agonized young hero gone from the scene, permitting the author to brood on the psychology of politics which he had not understood or cared about in youth.

The canvas is once again crowded with ambitious creatures who keep their public images at a safe distance from their inner selves. Burden Day is a conservative senator, at odds with Franklin Roosevelt, who serves his constituents faithfully. He is incorruptible until he decides to run for President, at which point he accepts a bribe. His legislative assistant is a young hustler named Clay Overbury, who casts aside Day's daughter, Diana, when a more attractive match appears in the form of Enid Sanford, daughter of Washington's most powerful publisher, Blaise Sanford. (Sanford, the stepson-in-law of Charlie Schuyler, is the only connecting thread between this book and *1876*.) The publisher's son, Peter, is inclined to lazy living, and Blaise Sanford adopts Clay Overbury as his protégé.

Overbury begins his political climb with a stint in the military. With the help of his father-in-law's publicity, he emerges as a war hero. His marriage is a failure, and becomes an embarrassment when Enid takes one lover after another. Father and husband try to manipulate her into a mental institution. She rebels and accuses her father of being in love with Overbury. This has enough truth in it to solidify their resolve and she is committed, only to escape and die in a car accident.

Peter Sanford vows revenge on Overbury for the destruction of Enid. He writes an exposé belittling Overbury's reputation for heroism. Overbury responds by reminding Peter that he and his sister had committed incest, a fact once blurted out by Enid during a drunken bout. Overbury now seeks Burden Day's Senate seat. He opens his campaign ingeniously by stating that it is his firm understanding that Day is retiring. The senator resists, and Overbury confronts him with the evidence of his past bribery. Day retires and dies shortly thereafter. Overbury is elected, and takes his place in the Senate as the book ends. Peter falls in love with Diana Day, and resolves to marry her.

Unlike *Burr*, which gave us Aaron Burr's America, and *1876*, which presented Charlie Schuyler's America, *Washington, D.C.* settles on no point of view. As in the early novels, we are reliant upon an unhappy, omniscient narrator. Whenever Vidal attempts psychology, he finds little to admire; there is not a single lovable person in *Washington, D.C.* Like their predecessors and successors, these characters are moved by ambitions which generate a subservient sense of principle. Even Burden Day, the exemplar of failed integrity, does not know when to quit and is devoted to bad ideas. Politics appears little better than a nasty scandal, perpetrated by people who devote their lives to deception. Diana Day sums up the spirit of the times as she contrasts her father and Clay Overbury: "He really believed that there were some things one ought not to do while Clay realizes that the only thing one ought never to do is lose the game. That's why he'll win. He's exactly what the times require." Given this state of affairs, Peter Sanford is left to close the book with a reverie that places him in the line of Philip Warren, who adopted Aphrodite as his way out of the quagmire:

> Loving her for this constancy, he was often able in her company to forget for long moments what he knew to be the human case: that the generations of man come and go and are in eternity no more than bacteria upon a luminous slide, and the fall of a republic or the rise of an empire—so significant to those involved —are not detectable upon the slide even were there an interested eye to behold that steadily proliferating species which would either end in time or, with luck, become something else, since change is the nature of life, and its hope.

I rank *Burr* as the best of the trilogy, although its profusion of characters and abrupt changes of scene and scandal challenge the patience. Its iconoclasm is irresistible, and its central character is Vidal's most memorable creation. Only in *Messiah* did Vidal manage to plant so many bombs in hallowed halls. *1876* is an amiable sequel, as *Myron* was a good-natured successor to *Myra Breckinridge*. But *1876* substitutes abundance for intensity, and the wicked satire of *Burr* does not survive in Charlie Schuyler's arthritic hands. *Washington, D.C.* most approximates Vidal's own experience and is, predictably, the weakest of the three. Like all rationalists, he is best when removed a step from the hurly-burly before his eyes. The sad note of resignation, the concluding admission that happiness is to be found in love: these are secondary themes which appear when the opening salvos of Vidal's critical sonatas fade. Because he is unable to write deeply emotional books, the love theme is feeble, and Vidal is less at home than when among the vicious. He settles for an unsurpassed fluency, but never really comes to terms with his material. Also, when Vidal writes from memory, his voice grows weary and he seems much put-upon. *Washington, D.C.*, like *Two Sisters*, recalls the struggles of the early books, for liberation from private pain. What is required is the filter of history.

IX

"The Inventors," wrote Vidal in an essay on the Adams family, "understood human greed and self-interest. Combining brutal cynicism with a Puritan sense of virtue, they used those essential drives to power the machinery of the state." There is nothing here about faith in human goodness, in the ability of rational man to govern himself. To the contrary, it appears that the most successful men have been those most appreciative of human meanness. Thomas Jefferson was transformed by "nothing more elevated than greed" from the frugality of his first inaugural address into the purchaser of Louisiana and the warrior of Florida. "The author of the Declaration of Independence was quite able to forget the unalienable rights of anyone whose property he thought should be joined to our empire—a word which crops up frequently and unselfconsciously in his correspondence." There is historical motivation for this sort of behavior, which Burr hints at in his memoirs:

> "Worlds are there to be conquered." I was light but I meant what I said. We were living at a time when for the adventurous and imaginative man anything was possible. Bonaparte had inspired, no doubt in a bad way, an entire generation. Certainly, thanks in large part to his example, I saw myself as the liberator of all Spanish America.

So the nineteenth century struggled under the handicap of a romantic fallacy, a belief in the individual which quickly was usurped by a few who then proceeded to exploit the many. By 1876 the dream had faded and the United States was preoccupied by a trivial materialism. Charlie Schuyler found that "all summer long the country has been entirely preoccupied with the Centennial Exhibition, with sewing machines, Japanese vases, popped corn, typewriters and telephones, not to mention incessant praise

for those paladins who created this perfect nation, this envied
Eden, exactly one century ago."

A people which hates history still cannot survive without
myths. The Founding Fathers' wisdom, the goodness of the common man, the freedom of the individual: all survived as myths
well into the twentieth century, long past the time they had
carried any meaning. Even the slick and cynical Clay Overbury,
gone north for a party, "found the New Yorkers' disdain of the
people somewhat alarming (after all, his own career depended entirely upon the franchise of the simple)." Among the primary purposes of politicians was the exploitation of national mythology.

Another purpose was to keep the machinery of government
rolling, something which is accomplished by artful lying. "The
United States has always been a corrupt society." Bribes have always been given and taken, and periodic cleanups do not change a
thing. Moreover, the laws of the country are written in the service
of corruption. "The writing of legislation is perhaps the highest
art form the United States has yet achieved, even more original
and compelling than the television commercial. In tortured language, legislators rob the people of their tax money in order to en-
rich themselves and their friends." It was not enough that the nation conduct its business in this appalling way; it proved necessary
to expand, and then to lie about the nature of extension. Jefferson, one of the saints by reputation, is again exposed as one of the
villains: "Mixing his metaphors, celebrating the empire electric,
appealing to the god Demos whose agent he thought himself to
be, Jefferson II [the author of the second inaugural—MSR] so
clouded over our innate imperialism that we cannot to this day
recognize the nature of American society, even as our bombs
murder strangers (admittedly leprous) 8,000 miles away."

What is needed is a revival of the Puritan conscience, preferably without the Founding Fathers' brutal cynicism and, if possible, embodied in someone like Eleanor Roosevelt. "After all,
Eleanor Roosevelt was a last (*the* last? the *only?*) flower of that
thorny Puritan American conscience which was, when it was
good, very, very good, and now that it's quite gone things are horrid." Senator Burden Day, having stayed on past his time, decided that "It has all gone wrong," meaning the ideal of republi-

can harmony; but when was it right? Not in 1789; not in 1876; not in 1950. Yet by the early seventies Vidal concluded:

> American innocence? Optimism? From 1950 on, our story has been progressively more and more squalid. Nor can one say it is a lack of the good and the great in high places: they are always there when needed. Rather the corruption of empire has etiolated the words like themselves. Now we live in a society which none of us much likes, all would like to change, but no one knows how. Most ominous of all, there is now a sense that what has gone wrong for us may be irreversible. The empire will not liquidate itself. The lakes and rivers and seas will not become fresh again. The arms race will not stop. Land ruined by insecticides and fertilizers will not be restored. The smashup will come.

Had it ever been "right"? The classic times were just as brutal, and spared Vidal's wrath only because of their bisexuality. The intervening years—medieval, Renaissance, Enlightenment—and other nations of history have not been laid before his knife; we can only guess at what thoughts such studies might prompt. In any event, there is not much to be learned from history, once human character is understood. "Make history?" asks Charlie Schuyler. "But there is no history, only fictions of varying degrees of plausibility."

X

For all the clarity and eloquence of its presentation, Vidal's vision of the past is little but a confused jumble of intuitions, postures, and crotchets. He has, in fact, no ideas about history at all, which is why he feels free to dress history in his plausible fictions. His theory of American empire turns out to be no more than an ill-tuned lament for innocence lost, without any accompanying statement to identify when innocence reigned, and of what it consisted. What was that "thorny Puritan American conscience" that made Eleanor Roosevelt so wonderful to Vidal (to him she was "greater" than Franklin!)? Why has it not appeared elsewhere in his essays, earning rare Vidalian citations? I cannot help but wonder if Vidal has worked out any roster of Americans whose "thorny Puritan American conscience" stands out, or if he invented the distinction for his essay on Eleanor Roosevelt.

He prattles on about the national empire, but, except for the one comparison to Venice cited earlier, he offers no descriptions of this empire. Internally, it seems to be constructed of the stuff of leftist nightmares: rich bankers and industrialists who take from the people and give to themselves, and politicians who are in their pockets. Jefferson, meanwhile, is criticized for displaying "nothing more elevated than greed" when he decides to spend public money on the sorts of projects dear to liberal hearts. Is Vidal saying something, or is he just making schoolboy cracks about all-American Tom? Externally, the empire seems interested in dropping bombs on Asians, but for no better reason, to Vidalian eyes, than to protect the property class back home. Why? In what way? Who composes this class? Astors and Rockefellers? Republican campaign contributors? Clothing salesmen with profit-sharing?

Vidal would like to tear down sex barriers, overrun the barricades of class, and refine the barbarous natives. I suggest that the accomplishment of the first two is unlikely to lead to the third. His liberal fustian is so badly out of key with his high-toned carping that his historical commentary, like his political commentary, is beyond redemption. It is clear that Vidal believes in iconoclasm, and after that it is very fuzzy. His heroes in history, Burr and Julian, were iconoclasts of a very superior sort. Beyond the fact that they were inharmoniously mated with their times, they are not all that alike—Julian, the ascetic philosopher turned general; Burr, the womanizer, the cutter of deals, the lawyer. History to them is a hurricane in whose eye they have landed.

Vidal is less a student of history than a student of human behavior. There is little to be learned, in his view, from the rise and fall of nations and empires, and much to be learned from the adaptation of individuals to life in the great world. In much the same way, Vidal the theater critic found it more interesting to watch audiences than to watch plays. Only by studying human reaction can we learn what are the true forces of a given time.

So Vidal, who emerged as the closest thing to a pure skeptic in contemporary America, has developed into the advocate of the self-conscious. His early novels hinted that this might be the direction he would take. Jim Willard, with his search for Bob Ford and Blondel the troubadour, with his quest for a "center" in his life, represent the stirring of self-conscious feelings. Philip Warren refined them in *The Judgment of Paris* and Eugene Luther dramatized their apotheosis in *Messiah*. By the time he came around to writing the stories of Burr and Julian, Vidal was firmer than ever in his conviction. From describing the homosexual in the land of the heterosexual, he had grown to tell of the proud in the land of the timorous. Iconoclasm is the last refuge of the self-conscious man.

Vidal himself has been the picture of artful self-consciousness. He is, as a politician, so superior to his literary contemporaries that he has disguised his self-consciousness beneath a veneer of objectivity. He has avoided writing about himself, except when he has sensed a public need to know. Then he drops a word about a dose of clap picked up in Guatemala, or chats about daily "mature sexual relationships," or writes a *Two Sisters*. All this is just enough to keep the readers interested in what he has to say. Likewise his appearances on television, which are never well-reasoned discussions of matters of general interest, but Vidalian improvisations intended to incite outrage. Altogether he is one of the coolest customers around, cashing in on the national predilection for preachers who combine entertainment with instruction.

Vidal has provided one of the best shows around, gifted as he is in the art of literary impersonation. It is not surprising that his best novels are written with first-person narrators: *Messiah, Burr, Julian, 1876*; nor that his greatest shockers, *Myra Breckinridge* and the essays, have employed a robust "I." The irony is that the first person has been used for promotional, instead of the usual confessional, purposes. Every one of Vidal's ideas and prejudices has used it as a launch pad. Only in an age whose analytical methods are dominated by psychology would this seem strange. One is supposed to strip naked upon pronouncing the first person pronoun. But psychology is the least rational of sciences, and a criticism based upon it is unprepared to handle a writer who speaks in the first person, but rarely about himself.

Perhaps this is why Vidal has been ignored, for surely he is worthier of critical attention than the various serpents crawling in

the grass today. Vidal the artist is a detoured politician, and this
is upsetting to those who like their art neat. Even so, as politicians
have programs, artists have themes. A literary politician requires a
theme that is somewhat programmatic. Mailer promotes the
unabashed self, but it does not get him very far; I sometimes suspect he will die a forgotten man. Lowell has carved out his niche
as the man of conscience, and there seems to be a rugged
durability to it. But Vidal, the rationalistic narcissist, the advocate
of the self-conscious but never the self, is the purest politician of
the bunch. A Roman consul would understand him; so would an
American senator. They would be inclined to accept him as a bird
whose plumage enhances their breed.

PART THREE

———◆———

It was Joseph P. Kennedy who suggested to his son that a book was a nice thing to have on your record if you were going into politics. It made you respected by the intellectuals, he said. So, along with his friend Henry Luce, the senior Kennedy took his son's college thesis and converted it into a national best seller. A decade and a half later, by then a United States senator, John F. Kennedy wrote another book, *Profiles in Courage*, while convalescing from back surgery. It, too, became a best seller. The intellectuals were not all that impressed, but the country was.

After he was elected President, other politicians took his lead and started writing books of their own. It has now reached the point where a serious contender for the presidency is expected to have published a book of revelations before he starts his campaign. The books by Jimmy Carter and Don Riegle are specimens of this literature.

There are, besides this, books written by politicians who are in power's limbo, which is to say they have held posts of great distinction, have reached for the top and missed, but are not ready to be counted out. Nixon's *Six Crises* and Humphrey's *The Education of a Public Man* are of this breed. The Nixon opus was composed in the midst of a losing streak, before the joyous years of triumph and impeachment had begun. Humphrey's book was begun after his defeat at Nixon's hands and his temporary retirement to private life. Its composition continued fitfully after the author's return to the Senate, and publication approximated the 1976 Democratic National Convention, when, it may be recalled, Humphrey was expected to launch the last of his last hurrahs.

The Nixon and Humphrey books reflect a richer experience than the Carter and Riegle gospels, but their authors are at a decided advantage in having the opportunity to project their personalities into notable events.

Finally, and perhaps sadly, the presidential memoir is not yet dead. Three postwar Presidents have written them, a fourth is on the way with the chronicle of his treachery, and a fifth is expected to supply a national soporific. It would be much better if retired Presidents made no effort to give a full and proper accounting of their days on the mountaintop, but simply contented themselves with an explanation of their official lies. Such a format would provide the Republic much more amusement, and would keep the works at a seemly length. Such is not the current situation, however, and I am left in the position of the coroner who must perform an autopsy on the late gentleman whose four hundred pounds lie before him in complete repose.

In addition to these exertions by confessed politicians, another branch of political literature has emerged in the past several decades. I speak of the writings of ambitious professors. Their ambition is less refined by literary impulses than is the case with, say, Schlesinger and Galbraith; rather they seek power by acquainting politicians with their knowledge. If they are painfully bad stylists, as is often the case, their views are still accepted at full value. Writing in journals like *Foreign Affairs, Daedalus* and the *Political Science Quarterly,* they hope to catch the eyes of committee chairmen, who may invite them to testify at hearings, and of presidential candidates, who may ask them for advice. From the days of Franklin Roosevelt's brain trust, their presence has been accepted as an example of the enlightened quality of American politics.

No man has risen higher out of this tradition than Henry Kissinger. Beginning his career as a writer of dull theses, he became the most powerful Secretary of State in the history of the United States. His personal charm served him well, but it was his writing which prompted Richard Nixon to ask for his service.

Of course the books discussed in this section are unlikely to win places in the official literary histories. But they are no less interesting for that deficiency. Like all the other books examined in this study, they represent the effort to practice politics by acting literary.

Henry Kissinger

We came off the beach after a three-mile walk, climbing up the eroded duneland, and Kissinger began to notice that people were waving at him. They had been waving at him all along as we walked, but he had not seen them. A middle-aged man with gray fuzz on his chest asked if he could shake Kissinger's hand—he wanted to say simply he was grateful for peace. Kissinger became very boyish and shy, not his customary carriage; then said to me, "Where else—where else could it happen but in a country like this? To let a foreigner make peace for them, to accept a man like me—I even have an accent."[1]

No wisecracks from the press gallery allowed; of course Henry Kissinger was aware that he stood beside the most eminent chronicler of American politics. But will no one concede that maybe once, in a wistful interlude between diplomatic journeys, the celebrated juggler of nations happened upon the thought which reduced him to modesty in the presence of Theodore White? Of course, those who believe Kissinger's biography to be written in blood concede nothing of the kind. Nor do those who see the professor-Secretary as a mere balancer of power, an ambitious anachronism, a poor man's Metternich, or a bedizened Bismarck. What place, they ask, does this amoralist hold in the great tradition of American republicanism? Wherefore comes all praise of the bomber of Hanoi,

[1] Theodore H. White, *The Making of the President, 1972*, New York: Atheneum, 1973, p. xiii.

of the promoter of Chilean upheaval, of the servant of Richard Nixon?

I regret that I cannot pass upon these sundry contentions. Many have slapped Kissinger with the Metternich-Bismarck tag, as if the latter two were synonymous and Kissinger, therefore, nefarious. Among these denigrators have been journalists confident that all the history worth knowing has been noted in their reports, and socialites gleefully certain that the basic secrets of the world await revelation in salons and boudoirs. There are those professors who have made themselves experts in various fields, but think it incumbent upon their role as soothsayers of the Republic to issue pronouncements on the professor-Secretary's place in history—all of this while the wheels are still spinning, while one crisis fades as a second arises, and the fellow under discussion continues to dominate the headlines. This hurried world is not the subject of my book.

Lately, another group has begun to appear. It is more reasonable than the above conglomeration. Its members have read Kissinger's books, which the others have not done. They have watched Kissinger in action—if not in person, then through the press—which everyone has done. And, having done both, they announce that they have penetrated to the foundations of the man. Many of them write clever essays which offer copious research as a cloak for their prejudices; but they arrive back where they started. Better that they should do their skinny-dipping elsewhere than in Kissinger's Metternich.

Finally, there has been a small amount of pure scholarship—perhaps as much as can be expected in these turbulent days. There has been Professor Stephen Graubard's book *Kissinger: Portrait of a Mind*, which examines every scrap of the professor-Secretary's writings in chronological order. But Graubard gives us little better than a glorified summary; he writes of his friend Kissinger without regard for what Walter Lippmann called "a longer past and a longer future." In addition, there are those who have offered technical assessments of Kissinger's policies, limiting themselves to such arcana as the throw-weight of MIRVs or the institutional arrangement of the State Department.

All of this has its purpose. Partisan essayists, giddy hostesses, and weapon analysts all help to organize discussion of American foreign policy into comfortable national patterns. They give balm unto the future historian. They humanize the international checkerboard.

But, alas, the citizen's tongue becomes tied. Try to lap up all the milk of the world, and the stomach grows unsettled. The system cannot digest too much at once. "Experts" cannot escape their own jargon any more than journalists can escape their deadlines, or revelers their desire for amusement. In politics, there is rarely a universal perception of anything; all meanings dissolve into their origins, or are regurgitated into a messy pool. So, amid a babble of voices, the works of Henry Kissinger seem more complicated than they really are. I speak at the same time of his policies and of his writings. Both involve the entanglement of simple ideas in complicated techniques. Both are more turbid than turgid, and so we hear of their creator that he has "dared to think the unthinkable," that his is a "Metternichian-Bismarckian-Machiavellian mind," that he practices a "metaphysical politics" which attempts to "impose a reality" on a situation which is "subjectively perceived," and other such drivel. Part of this is his own fault, insofar as a man can be blamed for his own literary inferiority. Alone among the subjects of this book, Kissinger does not merit inclusion because of the effect of his *writings* on the American mind. Not that they have been without effect: *Nuclear Weapons and Foreign Policy* was, after all, a best seller: Kissinger has been a literary politician in a most exact sense. He has used words, and often little else, to influence public policy; though his words, too, dissolve into their muddy origins.

I haven't the slightest interest in finding out what Kissinger said to Le Duc Tho on this day, or to Anwar Sadat on that. I do not care about the number of smiles which have passed between the professor-Secretary and Comrade Brezhnev. I do not wish to know whether or not Chou En-lai has sweaty palms. It is true that when Kissinger negotiates with these men, he is using words— words which shall one day be part of the historical record of mankind. But all of these are no more than the epidermis on the body politic of the world. (In the case of Le Duc Tho, I fear that they are little better than ingrown toenails—but the tale of Vietnam is too sad to bear retelling.) And I have the feeling that should Kissinger someday sit himself down to write his memoirs, he will spend much less time discussing the above protuberances than he will spend in laboring over the themes that have exercised him for a quarter century: the need for order, the primacy of political structures, the struggle for stability, the definition of legitimacy. Kissinger's writings gain in consistency what they lack in expansiveness; they substitute repetition for elegance. Public utterance has only slightly altered his tone, and made him sound more hopeful than in his dry critiques; perhaps his mood has been altered by his having been placed in charge of things. But Kissinger is a man of fundamental ideas, which in turn produce a set of principles. It is characteristic of the faulty public understanding of the man that this has not yet been recognized; thus, essays continue to appear which insist that Kissinger's basic interest is in something abstractly called "power," and not in the solid organization of men and of states; that he is, at heart, a knave, and not even slightly impressed that the people of the United States have "let a foreigner make peace for them."

II

Mr. Garry Wills, a sophist of considerable skill, believes that the most influential experience of Kissinger's life was not his humiliation as a schoolboy under the Nazis, but his role in the restoration of order during the postwar occupation. "Henry's fantasy," writes Wills, "does not come from the springs of equivalent fantasy in most of us. Quite the opposite—his comes from a reality. For Henry *did* ride into town alone, gun strapped to his side, and restored law and order, winning a terrified people's nervous adulation. What is more, he did this at the age of 21. He was, for almost a year, the autocratic ruler of an entire German district (Bergstrasse)."[2] Wills proceeds to argue, quite cleverly, that the wisdom gained in those days of youthful responsibility informed all of Kissinger's subsequent work, providing him with firsthand knowledge of the problems of law and order in the starkest circumstances, permitting a close-up view of a society which had broken down, and, above all, giving the young and recently naturalized American citizen his first taste of genuine power. As a bonus,

2 Garry Wills, "Kissinger," in *Playboy*, December 1974, pp. 122–23.

it gave him a strong sense of the power of his adopted homeland in the postwar world. The application of that power would become the primary subject of his studies; a major role in the process may have struck the young soldier, even then, as his eventual destiny.

So, at least, argues Wills, and he is most persuasive. But his basic argument is a bit shaky; that is, that Kissinger's fundamental interest is in the psychology and use of power, and not in its proper ends. In other words, he accounts for the caginess of the negotiator, for the scholarly appreciation of diplomatic nuance, and for the rise to high office. What he misses is the melancholy conservatism from which these characteristics bloomed. Just as remarkable as the exhilaration of authority which distinguished Kissinger's youth is the pessimism which clouded all his ideals, from that hour of triumph forward.

III

Where do we find the sources of this *Weltschmerz?* In the young Kissinger's education? In his parents? In his humiliation? Or did it develop after his arrival in America, with a young man's longing glances back at the country of his boyhood? One wonders—and is a fool to provide ready answers. Someday, perhaps, the eminent scholar-diplomat will abandon his silence on the Germany of his youth, and tell, like Heine, his "Winter's Tale." But it is too much to expect this, particularly from a man for whom authorship is clearly an agony—a Caesarian section when compared to the pangs of others. Anyway, the story would not be likely to startle us. Kissinger's evolution has not been twisted and grotesque; it has merely been arduous, involving much plodding and sweating and a small measure of scrappiness. His life story is not all that fantastic, not in the United States.

In his first years as an American, he wanted to become an accountant—as his father, a schoolmaster in Germany, had become after emigrating. With this trade in mind, he worked by day and studied by night. But the Army changed many things for him. By the time of his return from Europe in 1947, at the age of twenty-four, he was contemplating the history of the world.

I have not read the honors thesis which climaxed his undergraduate years at Harvard, and rely on Professor Graubard's summary for my knowledge of it. It is called "The Meaning of History: Reflections on Spengler, Toynbee, and Kant," and is
described as "passionate, original, and very idiosyncratic" by
Graubard, who adds, "Much of what he learned at Harvard was
incorporated into a thesis that pretended to deal with selected
philosophies of history since the eighteenth century; it was, in
fact, a kind of personal testament."[3] Now, Graubard is often saying this sort of thing, and he seems to rely on Kissinger's "personal testaments" in order to avoid using a critical microscope
where one is required: announce a "personal testament" and you
imply that everything you need to know is all there, that there is
nothing to be added. But, in this case, Graubard may be on the
mark. Without reading it whole, it is impossible to judge its originality; nor can idiosyncrasies be counted, for we cannot detect the
mannerism when we do not know the manner. But the passion is
unmistakable. Kissinger passed from confusion to conservatism in
orotund style.

"Life is suffering," he wrote, "birth involves death. Transi-
toriness is the fate of existence. No civilization has yet been permanent, no longing completely fulfilled. This is necessity, the fatedness of history, the dilemma of mortality." Hear the echoes of
Spengler on the decline of the West, or of Toynbee, writing in an
England becoming little again:

> Though aging in a culture is not analogous to physical decay, it
> does bear a similarity to another problem of existence, the process
> of disenchantment. Just as the life of every person exhibits a grad-
> ual loss of wonder at the world, so history reveals an increase of
> familiarity with the environment, a tired groping for a certainty
> which will obviate all struggles, a quest for a guarantee of man's
> hopes in nature's mechanism.

Our most prominent symptom of decay is the liberal, with his belief in "infinite material progress." The shift from laissez faire,
nineteenth-century liberalism to the meliorism of twentieth-cen-

[3] Stephen Graubard, *Kissinger: Portrait of a Mind*, New York: W. W. Nor-
ton, 1973, p. 6.

tury liberalism is but an adjustment of emphasis; the "cold materialistic intellect" is still at work, and life still "emerges as but a technical problem." So the liberal (whom Kissinger calls by every name but the exact one) engages in a "frantic search for social solutions, for economic panaceas . . ." All testify to "the emptiness of a soul to which necessity is an objective state, not an inward condition, and which ever believes that just a little more knowledge, just one more formula will solve the increasing bafflement of a materialistic surrounding." Forsaken is the basic truth "that matter can defeat only those who have no spirituality to impart to it." Kissinger retreats, and finds solace in something like Kant's categorical imperative:

> But action derives from an inward necessity, from the personal in the conception of the environment, from the unique in the apprehension of phenomena. Consequently, objective necessity can never guide conduct, and any activity reveals a personality. Reason can help us understand the world in which we live. Rational analysis can assist us in developing institutions which make an inward experience possible. But nothing can relieve man from his ultimate responsibility, from giving his own meaning to life, from elevating himself above necessity . . .

What is the nature of this "ultimate responsibility"? Apparently it may be found in something which Kissinger calls "the experience of freedom, which enables us to rise beyond the suffering of the past and the frustrations of history. In this spirituality resides humanity's essence, the unique which each man imparts to the necessity of his life, the self-transcendence which gives peace."

I find all of this rather mystical, and not terribly clear—German thoughts in English words, or something like that. But we grow used to this style of Kissinger's as we go along; it is as bad as that of the great German philosophers. Man's "spirituality" does not refer to his religious instincts, but to his "experience of freedom." "Objective necessity" is something halfway between "based on the facts" and "because I think so." The "self-transcendence which gives peace" would, we might expect, refer to the religious instinct—the will to believe—except that it is actually meant to refer to that "experience of freedom"—which has always struck me as something more of an encouragement to disbelief. Chock much of this off, then, to undergraduate grandiloquence—even if the undergraduate happened to be twenty-seven years old, and even if we know that Kissinger never shook loose from his taste for Germanic obscurantism. What remains beneath this cumulus?

There is something of a relationship between the young scholar and another survivor of the Nazi slaughter, Albert Speer. At the close of his memoirs of life under Hitler, the former architect and Minister of Armaments set down his interpretation of the monstrosity he had helped to create:

> "The catastrophe of this war," I wrote in my cell in 1947, "has proved the sensitivity of the system of modern civilization evolved in the course of centuries. Now we know that we do not live in an earth-quake-proof structure. The build-up of negative impulses, each reinforcing the other, can inexorably shake to pieces the complicated apparatus of the modern world. There is no halting this process by will alone. The danger is that the automatism of progress will depersonalize man further and withdraw more and more of his self-responsibility."[4]

In other words, the forces of history must be recognized—not in order to be accepted as the basis of life, but in order to be controlled through moral rectitude; as Kissinger wrote of Spengler, it is all very well to acknowledge "the fatedness of historical events," but "inevitability is a poor guide and no inspiration." Like Hegel announcing that the dialectic of history culminated in the Prussian monarchy, the young Kissinger and the humbled Speer agreed that the machine age, and its attendant collectivization, found its ultimate expression in Hitler's Third Reich; or, as Kissinger added, in Stalin's Soviet Union. These states marked the extension of the "cold materialistic intellect" in its most cynical and ruthless form. And the progressivism of the United States, in Kissinger's view, might be much more benign, but still managed a kind of fraudulence by denying the moral sources of life. "The past may rob the present of much joy and much mystery," he wrote. "The generation of Buchenwald and the Siberian labor camps cannot talk with the same optimism as its fathers. The

[4] Albert Speer, *Inside the Third Reich*, New York: Avon Books, 1971, p. 658.

bliss of Dante has been lost in our civilization. But this merely describes a fact of decline and not its necessity. Man's existence is as transcendental a fact as the violence of history." What a curious passage this is! What, after all, was "the bliss of Dante," if not that "transcendence" to which Kissinger implores us—and which he now says we are denied. Did not the *Divine Comedy* arise from the ashes of an age as brutal as our own? And is it not Kissinger's idea of "transcendence" that we should plant our feet firmly in the earth while we keep watch upon the heavens? Is not his notion of "the experience of freedom" one involving respect for history and for all its products? Is it not his wish that we should not so much tinker with the human condition as we should sanctify it? That we should not effect the mechanization of life before we have defined a moral basis? That useful change cannot take place without a harmonious order, which requires the establishment of such a basis?

As he looked around him in those Cold War years, Kissinger heard the hue and cry for more of everything, and to hell with Communists. He saw that the people prospered, but did not "transcend." Even his adopted country's great and generous effort, the Marshall Plan, was essentially a materialistic business, feeding Europe on our own abundance. It all left Kissinger unsatisfied. Whatever his religious convictions as an adult (he was raised as an Orthodox Jew, lapsed into agnosticism, but has written nothing on the subject), the absence of transcendental ideals troubled his highly Germanic mind. At a time when everyone else at Harvard was looking forward to a resumption of the New Deal, for another session of what he considered "the frantic search for social solutions, for economic panaceas," Kissinger started thinking about the aftermath of a different slaughter; of how the men who survived had created an order in which human life could flourish. He noted the introduction into warfare of atomic bombs, and then of hydrogen bombs. Perhaps he blinked, but eventually he decided that these new horrors had not changed the nature of man, whose secrets could just as well be found in last century's documents as in yesterday's headlines. So, almost mockingly, he set out in the early 1950s to write his doctoral dissertation on the restoration of peace after the Napoleonic years. It may seem odd that this seeker after transcendence and stability should devote his scholarly energies to the hurly-burly of international relations; but, according to Graubard, "In the relations between states, he believed, lay the future peace of the world, and the destiny of the human race."[5]

IV

His book was finished in 1954, but required three years to find a publisher. So in 1957 it was issued under a triple-deck title: *A World Restored: Europe After Napoleon: The Politics of Conservatism in a Revolutionary Age.* It has not been widely read; nor does it deserve to be. It is 332 pages long, yet demands the reading time of *War and Peace.* Its narrative moves with all the grace of a diesel truck; its characters are badly drawn, their motives subjected to ponderous and oracular explanations; words like "exaltation" and "erstwhile" are hacked to death (anyone dealing with Czar Alexander must reckon with his "exaltation"; any reference to past conditions must include mention of an "erstwhile ally"); singular acts provoke lengthy reflection on "the nature of statesmanship." "One of the things that make *A World Restored* so hard to read," Garry Wills correctly notes, ". . . is that . . . labored maxims stand out like separate essays from the comparatively perfunctory recounting of historical sequences."[6] And what a recounting! Napoleon rises and falls; great armies march over hill and dale; the Congress of Vienna meets to redraw the map of Europe; Castlereagh, one of the book's heroes, slits his throat— and all Kissinger gives us is an antiseptic account of these things as perceived by a handful of men, especially Metternich. There is almost no effort made to interpret anything *through* the psychology of the characters; instead, we hear, over and over, of the conflict between the "insular" statesman (Castlereagh), and the "Continental" statesman (Metternich), or between the man of "will" (Napoleon) and the man of "prophecy" (Czar Alexander, in his exaltation). Of the bloodshed of soldiers, of the turbulent life below the top, of the reaction of such great contemporaries as Goethe, Hegel, and Beethoven, no mention is made, except for an

[5] Graubard, op. cit., p. 9.
[6] Wills in *Playboy*, December 1974, p. 290.

occasional concession to "domestic factors." Indeed, Kissinger's story is barren of interest in non-political life to the point of ignorance; he even writes that Metternich "introduced the Italian opera into Vienna," which is hilarious.

But *A World Restored* is not devoid of interest, not even from the stylistic standpoint. We need to look elsewhere for fauna and flora; we will not, even in this study of states in conflict and resolution, hear of the spectacular death of Byron. But if we stay tuned in long enough, we will catch the strains of a symphony of diplomacy. As Garry Wills puts it:

> Metternich emerges as the book's hero because Kissinger's schemata demand it, not because the historical evidence is unambiguous. Henry often deals in Hegelian triads, and they run all through *A World Restored*, like a musical principle. The "legitimate" orders could not cope with Napoleon because they could not see that all rules are abrogated by a revolutionary power. Napoleon could not deal with the legitimate powers because he thought he had to obey the rules only when he did not care to use his power. Metternich is the Synthesis of the legitimate Thesis and the revolutionary Antithesis—he uses both with an understanding of them, but he is not contained by either.[7]

—In short, a rather heavy, bloated, Brucknerian symphony, but a symphony all the same. Listen closer, and you find notes becoming chords, chords becoming movements, and an ending which solemnly hymns the glory of statesmanship. But for any understanding of the whole thing, we need to go back and trace our steps: the journey is more interesting than the destination, the process happier than the result.

Essentially this is a collection of essays on the nature of diplomacy, with special attention on the period of 1811–22. Kissinger, however, arranged his work in narrative form, and thereby botched it irreparably. Those who regard the writing of history among the highest of human arts cannot help but be appalled by the tedium of *A World Restored*. Since no one, to my knowledge, has dared to claim Henry Kissinger among the literary giants of our age, I shall waste no time in swatting at him for this or that

[7] Ibid., pp. 290–91.

stylistic blunder; nor shall I attempt to summarize his book, which, by nature of its blubbery character, is remarkably resistant to clear explanation anyhow. Those who love narrative history as an art are advised to avoid it entirely.

At the same time excessive theorizing ruins A *World Restored* as a work of history, it marks an extension of Kissinger's mind. His undergraduate honors thesis addressed history by way of a study of the philosophy of history, and spoke in grand generalities. Here, he is dealing in the relations between states, and defining history as "the memory of states"—rather narrow, but not preposterous. And, in his focus on the various statesmen, Metternich in particular, he offers a more penetrating vision, as well as a critique, of the conservative mind in world affairs.

V

The book begins and ends with definitions. The Introduction invokes our own times, "faced with the threat of thermonuclear extinction," and willing to "look nostalgically to periods when diplomacy carried with it less drastic penalties." Such a period was the post-Napoleonic era, when "the concert of Europe" was resumed. We are reminded that talking about peace is not the same thing as attaining it, that "Not for nothing is history associated with the figure of Nemesis, which defeats man by fulfilling his wishes too completely," and, "Stability . . . has commonly resulted not from a quest for peace but from a generally accepted legitimacy." Legitimacy is defined as "no more than an international agreement about the nature of workable agreements and about the permissible aims and methods of foreign policy." It should not be confused with justice, and "does not make conflicts impossible, but it limits their scope." Powers which regard the legitimate order as oppressive are designated "revolutionary," and bound to revolt, for "*nothing can reassure [them]*" (italics Kissinger's). Where conflict arises between legitimate and revolutionary powers, diplomacy is useless, as diplomats "have ceased to speak the same language." In such a "revolutionary situation" powers become interested in the "subversion of loyalties" instead of the adjustment of differences, and "diplomacy is replaced either by war or by an armaments race." The Napoleonic period and its aftermath exemplified a shift in situations, from the revolutionary to the legitimate. The result, according to Kissinger, was "a period of peace lasting almost a hundred years, a stability so pervasive that it may have contributed to disaster" (World War I).

The statesmen involved in these circumstances were all inseparable from their domestic backgrounds. Napoleon had spoken for revolutionary France. Now Castlereagh came to speak for a Britain interested in extricating itself from European affairs in order to pursue its global empire. Alexander spoke for great, ungainly Russia, its eyes fastened on the Ottoman Empire, its heart set on a world conforming to a personal ideal of justice. And Metternich of Austria spoke from his Continental Empire's vulnerable stance. What resulted was a compromise between domestic necessity and their own abilities as statesmen.

Consider Britain and Castlereagh, we are told. Like most Englishmen, Castlereagh—"the most European of British statesmen," according to Kissinger—believed that, "If the war had been caused by bad faith, goodwill was to provide the remedy"; for "An insular power at the periphery of events finds it difficult to admit that wars may be produced by intrinsic causes." Britain had no fear of European revolution, and the Cabinet, therefore, wanted no part of meddling in European affairs once peace had been concluded. Castlereagh, however, saw the general value of British involvement in Europe, and pursued a course which Kissinger called "the statesmanship which had the courage to refuse the easy solution and tragic isolation of the hero, who, because he cannot communicate, must walk in solitude." In other words, he did the best he could. In the end, the pressures overcame him, his mind became unhinged, and he killed himself. Kissinger closes the narrative portion of his book by describing Castlereagh's last audience with the King, at which he grandly announced to His Majesty, " 'It is necessary to say goodbye to Europe; you and I alone know it and have saved it; no one after me understands the affairs of the Continent.' " After which Kissinger, with consummate reticence, remarks, "Four days later he committed suicide."

Castlereagh's story is told very badly. From Kissinger's account we learn nothing of the psychological tensions involved in Castlereagh's conflict with his own Cabinet, let alone what drove this

stolid and plodding figure to relieve himself of the world's cares
through the drastic action of suicide; after all, most outnumbered
British politicians resign from office, salt their lips, and start
impressing on the public how much more clever they are than the
boobs who drove them out. The weakness of Kissinger's account
of Castlereagh's woes is best accounted for by the author's artistic
inferiority; Kissinger cannot sympathize with Castlereagh's plight,
as a greater historian would do. He may speak of Castlereagh's
theoretical problems (e.g., the "insularity" of Britain), but he
knows nothing of the deeper psychology involved. The same
difficulty hinders the portrait of Czar Alexander. What more obvious symptom exists than Kissinger's willingness to explain all of
the Czar's eccentricities by reference to his "exaltation"? I return
once more to Garry Wills's argument that the outstanding characteristic of A World Restored is the schema which Kissinger im-
poses on it—the Hegelian triads, the balancing of forces within a
story about the balancing of forces. To speak intimately of psychological matters would unbalance the tale he is trying to tell; it
would upset the theoretical padding with which he supports the
diplomats' daily deeds. His intention is to offer a philosophy of diplomacy, using history as bait to lure our attention. No wonder
that Kissinger's assessment of Metternich is more valuable than
his interpretation of Castlereagh; he is temperamentally much
closer to him. The British Foreign Minister dealt in hard matter
and solid positions. His story was of the steady elimination of
power to deal in those things he understood best. Metternich, like
Kissinger, operated within a framework of fluctuating ideals, in
yesterdays and tomorrows; as Kissinger wrote, "Metternich's . . .
became a never-ending quest for a moment of tranquillity, for a
suspension, if only for an instant, of the flux of life, so that what
happened, perhaps inevitably, could be represented as a universal
principle instead of an assertion of will and indeterminacy." Kissinger called it "the Conservative dilemma," and A World Restored may be seen fundamentally as an essay on the subject of
that dilemma. It has the air which he ascribes to Metternich himself—of imagining things that were never quite as imagined, and
of dreaming of things that will never match the dream itself; of
evading those to whom matter is all; of striving, in however calculating a manner, for "the self-transcendence which gives peace"—

in the case of Metternich, for a European order out of step with the times; in the case of Kissinger, for a philosophy of diplomacy whose universal truths can be applied to our own, nuclear age.

VI

Whether or not he agreed with Metternich, Kissinger found his plight highly sympathetic. At great length he attempted to draw the eighteenth-century aristocrat as he dealt with the problems of a revolutionary age. He found a rather wistful temperament in this calculating doctor of revolutions. While Metternich certainly "was but delaying the inevitable day of reckoning" for Austria, his choices were never easy ones; "to be sure, a truly successful policy for a polyglot Empire may have been impossible in a century of nationalism." His repressive policies may have been mistaken, but at least he understood the process in which he was caught. Most of his contemporaries could not manage even that much, "and that he decided to defy the tide may be a reflection on his statesmanship but not on his insight." He was the conscience of an older, dying Europe; his fears were well founded and honorable. Was it his fault that the world he tried to restore had already been shattered beyond repair? Kissinger's appreciation of Metternich has something of the quality of that sentence in his honors thesis where he announced that the bliss of Dante is denied to the generation of Buchenwald and the Siberian labor camps. Its basic assumption is that men must do what they can to promote those qualities of life which they deem best. We must all live in historical times; a generation of revolution and war should not be followed by patchwork on the ruins, but by a return to the principles of better days.

This is all that Metternich was trying to do, pleads Kissinger. "Only a shallow historicism would maintain that successful policies are always possible. There existed no easy solution for Austria's tragic dilemma; that it could adapt itself by giving up its soul or that it could defend its values and in the process bring about their petrifaction." While Napoleon lived and ruled, his elimination (at least as a revolutionary force) was Metternich's primary objective. "Revolution was an assertion of will and of

power, but the essence of existence was proportion, its expression
was law, and its mechanism an equilibrium." This was the basis of
classical diplomacy; thus Metternich, "the conservative statesman,
was the supreme realist and his opponents the 'visionaries' . . .
Force might conquer the world but it could not legitimize itself."
What place, asked Kissinger, did justice truly play in the affairs of
men? "There may be a fitness of things in the universe, but it
does not operate in a finite time and certainly not in a brief one."
What use is thunder on behalf of abstractions? Better to stand in
the midst of conflicting passions—let others decide which of these
is good and which is evil—and attempt to quiet them both. As
Kissinger wrote of Metternich's policy after 1809: "To cooperate,
without losing one's soul, to assist without sacrificing one's identity, to work for deliverance in the guise of bondage and under enforced silence, what harder test of moral toughness exists?" As the
question arose between the allies of how to dispense with Napoleon, "it was clear what Austria's moral position required: a war of
states, not of nations, a coalition legitimized by a doctrine of conservatism and stability, and brought about, if possible, in the
name of existing treaties rather than by their rupture . . . It was
not heroic, but it saved an empire." By the time the final campaign against Napoleon began, Austria had become the "unchal-
lenged spokesman of the Coalition. It had not produced any great
conceptions; nor had it used the noble dreams of an impatient
generation. Its skill did not lie in creativity but in proportion, in
its ability to combine elements it treated as given."

With Napoleon gone, priorities changed. After a quarter century of revolution and war, Metternich sought the elimination of
those ideas which had produced the whole mess, and thus set out
upon his "never-ending quest for a moment of tranquillity." Here
the break occurred, both in Metternich's performance and in Kissinger's assessment of it. When preoccupied with defeating Napoleon, Metternich was dealing from a position of necessity; Napoleon's survival meant the death of the Austrian Empire. Now
Europe was Metternich's to create, engaging what Kissinger later
called "the necessity for choice." Refusing to judge him either
right or wrong, Kissinger found that "in all this obtuseness there
was an element of grandeur." In the post-Napoleonic era, Metter-

nich embodied the central position in Kissinger's world view: the conservative as tragic here.

It may reasonably be asked why Kissinger should be identified as a conservative at all. He has little in common with feisty nationalists like Barry Goldwater; nor has he had much to do with such snappy deacons of the native conservative hierarchy as Russell Kirk, William Buckley, and Milton Friedman. Even those who try to draw close parallels between Kissinger and his patron Richard Nixon are confusing their signals.

It is granted that conservatism's business is to rise in opposition to a society's upsetting elements. Kissinger, though perhaps softened by his term at Harvard, gives sufficient evidence that he distrusts tinkering liberals as much as the *National Review* crowd. But the sources of suspicion diverge. The native Americans have awakened from nightmares of IRS agents spouting the "Critique of the Gotha Programme"; Kissinger is haunted by memories of a society which engendered the storm troopers' midnight rap on the door. All conservatives share the horror of the mob, and, by extension, the brutalization of political opponents. But the basis of fear diverges in contemplation of how the mob was brought under control, the native American thinking of five-year plans and the politicization of daily life, the transplanted European recalling the galvanization of frenzied militarism. Of course, one fear does not necessarily exclude the other; indeed, they are perhaps little more than different symbols for what is ultimately the same occurrence, and different *raisons d'être* for the phenomenon of conservatism. Nonetheless, they *are* different, even as the sources of mighty rivers differ in their surrounding terrain. Then too, there are differences in the schools of thought behind such fears—between the metaphysical and empirical schools of modern philosophy, or between the traditions of Anglo-American politics and those of continental Europe.

Both schools know that their redeemer liveth, but they have been so informed by different messengers. The natives, as is well known, start with the gospel according to Edmund Burke. The tradition of Burke reviles the course of history since the French Revolution; accordingly, it chooses to admire those bedrocks of tradition which it views as having withstood the vicious tide. I call

to witness Russell Kirk's evocation of some contemporary manifestations of "true conservatism":

> . . . a worn farmer who holds fast to the wisdom of his ancestors,
> . . . a truck driver in the very heart of the metropolis, surrounded
> by incessant change, confronted every hour by faces and voices
> brutal enough for the Inferno, but retaining within himself a dig-
> nity of soul and a repose of mind that will not admit envy and
> disorder . . . a landed proprietor of an ancient name, great in ad-
> versity, superior to the evils of a rotting country house, a
> shrunken patrimony, high responsibilities with insufficient means
> . . . a physician, who knows the infirmities of human nature too
> well to talk of social perfectibility . . .[8]

In other words, combating an evil empirical tradition with a good
one, and not bothering too much about tying together those eternally loose ends. This is what anti-Communist conservatism has
been trying to do: it has concentrated on pointing out why its set
of values is superior to the Communist set of values, and has left
for liberals the business of refuting the Marxist dialectic of history.

The metaphysical tradition gave the world both Fascism and
Communism. There is no point in tracing that long story here, except to note that the dialectical method was instrumental in the
development of both political philosophies. Their father was
Hegel, student of the categorical imperative of Kant. From Hegel
came both the idea of the state as an organism and the idea of
the inexorability of history. From the beginning, both were challenged, almost always by empiricists. The dialecticians, such as
Marx, accepted them *a priori*, and proceeded with their own variations. With Communism in the ascendant, its European antithesis became Fascism, however deranged and dialectically weak
it may seem to have been. The fall of Nazism and the nascent
Cold War pre-empted what might have become the last battle of
the Second World War—the theoretical attack on the *idea* of
Fascism, fought with dialectics armed by a fresh interpretation of

[8] Russell Kirk, *The Conservative Mind,* quoted in *Communism, Fascism, and
Democracy: The Theoretical Foundations,* Carl Cohen, ed., New York:
Random House, 1972, pp. 511–12.

recent history, and the memory of the Stalin-Hitler pact of 1939. Instead, both anti-Communism and anti-Fascism reverted to the empiricists. Fascism became so thoroughly disreputable that dialectical-historical anti-Fascism was deemed irrelevant.

Nevertheless, an unconscious anti-Fascism moved much of Europe throughout the Cold War era; Communism was the present danger, but Fascism remained the most prominent "memory of states"—by Henry Kissinger's definition, the most intimidating force on the *mind* of Europe. For the dialectical and metaphysical traditions held fast on a Continent whose leading thinkers were men like Sartre, Camus, and Heidegger. The two most influential leaders of postwar Europe, Adenauer and De Gaulle, were the greatest embodiments of anti-Fascist conservatism; but the empirical American perception of them as soldiers in the Cold War, pure and simple, led to basic misunderstandings, and they were praised or hollered at for the wrong reasons.

The rise of the native American conservatism, with its basis in empirical anti-Communism, all but snuffed out dialectical-historical anti-Fascism in this country. Those few men who embodied it were treated as curiosities, even as anachronisms. They tended to be transplanted Europeans who raised questions foreign to the American mind—for example, Professor Leo Strauss of the University of Chicago. Younger conservatives with the memory of Fascism were very rare; Henry Kissinger was one of them. Thus he continues to be misunderstood, and his "balancing of powers" confused with exercises in cynicism. Rather, like Metternich in *A World Restored*, or Adenauer and De Gaulle in the postwar period, he is a man of memory, troubled by thoughts of what might have been. This is the essence of Kissinger's "European" quality, and the contrast he presents to the lawyers who have dominated American diplomacy. The American compares his democracy with utopia; the European compares his with history. We shall read Kissinger's perceptive assessment of De Gaulle a little further on. He attempted no similar study of Adenauer, of whom Golo Mann noted that "he only wanted to return to what to him seemed natural and God-given, to law and order, to Christian morals and manners, and property." Had he risen to high statesmanship in their era, Kissinger the restless Jew would no doubt have differed with these men, but he would have understood their thoughts, and sympathized more readily with them than with the Bible Belt senators with whom he would eventually establish his domestic alliances.

Like the German sociologist Max Weber, who divided the types of legitimate leadership into tribal, rational (bureaucratic), and charismatic, Kissinger saw the individual merging with his circumstances into an ideal abstraction. He was identified by the choices he made, by whether he elected to await the tide willingly or impose his force to withstand it. The decisions of statesmen dealt with entire cultures and challenged civilizations. In the post-Napoleonic era, this meant a decision between the revolutionary society of Napoleon and the legitimate society of the eighteenth century. There might be liberalization in either case, but the basic choice was between these two orders. In the post-World War II world, the choice for the Western nations was between democracy and Communist dictatorship. So, in Western Europe, the anti-Communist Left assumed the mantle of liberalism; the Right was by its nature anti-Communist, but its anti-Fascism is what gave it its sense of dignity. In America, where Fascism had never presented a serious internal threat, there was little comprehension of this phenomenon, which had given De Gaulle and Adenauer the leadership of their nations. But young Henry Kissinger had endured enough of Fascism to give his political thought its peculiar edge; when he started writing, he adopted the language of the Europeans. If the choice between democracy and Communism narrowed political possibilities, it also clarified them. Kissinger, who is not at his most eloquent as a philosopher of democracy, managed instead to develop a unique vision of the democratic, or at least American, potential in foreign affairs.

As he looked back at Metternich's career, he found a man who was, like himself, not particularly in sympathy with the tendencies of his time, but still was able to come to terms with them and even, in a certain measure, control them. His Metternich "had no illusions about the probable developments; he saw his task in ameliorating their inevitable consequences . . ." It is not beyond the bounds of conservatism to establish new orders; the prerequisite is that they be based on correct perceptions of the factors involved:

This is the epitaph of the conservative statesman: History is greater than the individual, but although it teaches its lessons surely, it does not do so in a single lifetime. And the statement also marks the limits of Metternich's abilities. For statesmen must be judged not only by their actions but by their conception of alternatives. Those statesmen who have achieved final recognition did not do so through resignation, however well founded. It was given to them not only to maintain the perfection of order, but to have the strength to contemplate chaos, there to find material for fresh creation.

How much does this sort of conservatism have in common with that of men who have climbed to the top of the greasy pole from stubby roots in Whittier, California, or in the wildcat oil fields of Mexico? Not a whole lot, on the surface; no more, we should say, than America and Europe have generally shared between them. But how different, truly, are the urges of Faust and those of the cowboy riding into town alone, as Kissinger once described the stock American hero in a celebrated interview? Both have found "the strength to contemplate chaos . . . ," have they not? And each has discovered this strength in a categorical imperative of sorts, has he not?

Metternich's failure lay in his refusal to choose from the best options open to him, but his perception of the era was accurate. Accordingly, his historical position became tragic—a man frustrated and, ultimately, deposed by the forces in his midst. Perhaps it need not have been that way; who can say for sure? Kissinger, for one, seemed rather confused by his own propositions. At one point he attributes Metternich's troubles to his historical period; at another he blames the Austrian for his own shortcomings— again, a problem of style on which I've promised not to dwell. But that style is in many ways the essence of *A World Restored*, and of Kissinger's thought. Rising from the Fascist debacle to contemplate the postwar world, the young scholar sought in balance and stability the basis of human harmony. It is a fundamental conservative position, transcending the hot issues of the day. So, while the Buckleys were backing Joe McCarthy, and Nixon was chasing Alger Hiss, the young European transplant was searching for international ideals. He selected the dialectical method, with all its faults, as his mechanism. The trouble with dialectics is that they tend toward fuzziness and imprecision. So it goes with Kissinger's philosophy of international relations.

He does not carry his dialectic far enough in this case, and we are not given a picture of Metternich's system as it careens along its collision course toward 1848. He fails to illustrate the point where ideals are strained in the extreme, thus becoming what George Orwell called Newspeak. By Kissinger's rules, Metternich carried his reactionary version of "legitimacy" to the border of being "revolutionary" itself. This was what happened with Bismarck, who crossed the border, and of whom Kissinger wrote years later that he "sought his opportunities in the present; he drew his inspiration from the future." He became what Kissinger called "the white revolutionary." As Metternich had drawn on the past for collateral, Bismarck "mortgaged the future." The fortunes of both men's states proved ultimately disastrous. Both chose wrongly by the standard of history, if history is truly "the memory of states," and the desire of states is not humiliation. "Each generation," wrote Kissinger, "is permitted only one effort at abstraction; it can attempt only one interpretation and a single experiment, for it is its own subject. This is the challenge of history and its tragedy; it is the shape 'destiny' assumes on the earth. And its solution, even its recognition, is perhaps the most difficult task of statesmanship." Having studied the conservative mind in an age of aristocratic rule and bourgeois revolution, he now tried to apply the basic rules to an age of bourgeois rule and proletarian and anti-colonial upheaval. He needed to mollify those to whom weapons, in themselves, were the greatest issue, and to remind everyone that weapons, after all, were only weapons, and not men. And all the while he kept his composure, as befitted a descendant of Hegel, who had written: "Each nation as an existing individuality is guided by its particular principles, and only as a particular individuality can each national spirit win objectivity and self-consciousness; but the fortunes and deeds of States in relation to one another reveal the dialectic of the finite nature of these spirits. Out of this dialectic rises the universal Spirit, the unlimited World-Spirit, pronouncing its judgment—and its judgment is the highest—upon the finite nations of the world's history; for the history of the world is the world's court of justice."[9]

[9] From *Communism, Fascism, and Democracy*, op. cit., pp. 284–85.

VII

Nuclear Weapons and Foreign Policy, once referred to by its author as "the most unread bestseller since Toynbee," was published in the same year, 1957, as *A World Restored*. Unlike the first book, this one bore the imprint of the Council on Foreign Relations. Those who did trouble themselves to read it were puzzled by its tone, so calmly did Kissinger invoke the specter of limited nuclear wars at the same time he identified the Soviet Union as a ruthless revolutionary state, yet said that congressmen were fools to give the military everything it asked for. Some commentators leaped at the opportunity to classify Kissinger among the eerie specimens who worked in places called "think tanks." Eventually these "think tankers" would be epitomized in the film *Dr. Strangelove*; my fervent wish is that whoever conceived the term "think tank" be awarded a similar debunking. Again, as with *A World Restored*, *Nuclear Weapons and Foreign Policy* is an exercise in gradation. It is a document of the Cold War, but its author is clearly a man who has known other pleasures in life than are to be found in slaughtering Communists; a conservative estimate of our revolutionary times, written by a man who had studied other revolutionary periods and discovered that they did not end in the destruction of civilization.

In analyses of *A World Restored*, too much has been made of the idea that Kissinger was writing a sort of allegory, with the Soviet Union disguised as "revolutionary" France and the United States masquerading as "insular" Britain. Perhaps it is partially true; I avoided reference to it in my discussion of Kissinger's first book for the reason that dialectics explained in terms of allegories make little more than interesting fictions—at best. *A World Restored* is curious enough without being treated as a jigsaw puzzle (Where does Austria fit? What about Prussia? Etc.). Besides, when we come to *Nuclear Weapons and Foreign Policy*, we find the United States being labeled a status quo power, with a character resembling, yet quite distinct from, both British insularity and Austrian insecurity; for the United States is a country without the experience of extramural wartime catastrophe, but at the same time aware of its vulnerability in the nuclear age. Thus the dialectic of *Nuclear Weapons and Foreign Policy* is set: the United States is the status quo power; the Soviet Union, the revolutionary power—from which point the strategies march, in categorical file.

What sort of status quo does the United States represent? Kissinger is somewhat vague on the subject, because his primary concerns are external and strategic affairs. But there is a presumption in Kissinger's view of America the stabilizer—a sense of an adherent national majesty during that postwar period. The problem with this majesty was that its innocent possessors were somewhat repelled by it. At the heart of *Nuclear Weapons and Foreign Policy* is the feeling that America has incorrectly perceived its new position in the world because the circumstances are so unfamiliar; and that a correct appraisal would result in new foreign policy and strategic doctrines, at once grander and more restrained.

Beneath this perception of national majesty lie qualities fundamental to the character of Kissinger's thought; otherwise, he would write books less reliant on the repetition, from one chapter to the next, of those ponderous epigrams couched in dialectical alternatives: "For the lessons of history, as of all experience, are contingent: they teach the consequences of certain actions, but they leave to each generation the task of determining which situations are comparable"; "To seek safety in numerical superiority or even in superior destructiveness may come close to a Maginot-line mentality—to seek in numbers a substitute for conception"; "A legitimate order does not make conflicts impossible; it limits their scope"; "Absolute security for one side means absolute insecurity for another"; etc. The division of the elements of life into dialectical categories remains the source of Kissinger's reasoning, and the basis of his vision of a harmonious order. America is a status quo power, in this view, because it is the antithesis of revolutionary Russia. Kissinger's question is: must this necessarily result in a synthesis of Cold War stalemate and armaments race? The answer is implicit in his having written a book critical of U.S. foreign policy, and he therefore proposes the revision of strategic doctrine as the next thesis in his dialectic; which should, in turn, produce a new Soviet doctrine in antithesis, and perhaps lead to a more palatable synthesis than the Cold War. Also implicit in this argument is the same point used in the study of Metternich,

Castlereagh, et al.: that policy is not foreordained, that however it may be moved by the forces of history, it remains the work of men, of individual conception, of statesmen great and small. All of which returns us, rather elegantly, to the necessity of a moral basis in life—a seed first planted in the honors thesis, but a bearer of fruit throughout Kissinger's later studies.

What is most debatable is Kissinger's conception of America as a status quo power. Certainly it provides further illustration of the conservative tint of his thought. Unlike the émigrés of 1848, this adopted son of liberty sees something different in his new homeland. The Truman years represented "the strategy of a satisfied power, content with its place in the world, eager to enjoy its benefits undisturbed." Inhibited in the use of force, America's "doctrine of power" was "ambivalent" and subject to a "literalness" which "made it impossible to conceive of an effective relationship between force and diplomacy . . . This attitude was well expressed when General Marshall said that he would be reluctant to risk American lives for purely political objectives."

> This approach to the problem of power and its uses came to full expression in our key postwar policy. The policy of containment was based on the assumption that military strategy and diplomacy represented successive phases of national policy: it was the task of military policy to build strength and thereby contain Soviet aggression. After containment had been achieved, diplomacy would take over.

But was this really an expression of "satisfaction," or was it the first, halting assertion of a mission which would climax in John Kennedy's inaugural pledge to "pay any price, bear any burden, meet any hardship, support any friend, oppose any foe to assure the survival and the success of liberty"? When the Kennedy administration came to power, four years after the publication of this book, one of its first actions was to re-evaluate strategic doctrine, leading to an eventual revision along many of the lines suggested by Kissinger. The notion of limited *nuclear* war was rejected, but the *idea* of fighting limited wars and a move toward greater strategic flexibility—the two basic alternatives offered in *Nuclear Weapons and Foreign Policy*—began to make their way into Defense and State Department doctrine. Yet, Kissinger was not terribly impressed by the Kennedy years; to say that they were an improvement over the Eisenhower years said very little. I venture that his dissatisfaction grew from the realization that he and the Kennedy men had some fundamental differences of opinion over the nature of America's role in the world; and, by inference —foreign policy being an expression of national character—over America itself. Where Kissinger saw the United States as a satisfied power, the New Frontiersmen wanted to seize the moment and uplift the cause of "freedom" in the world through new Alliances for Progress, Peace Corps, and the like. It was a policy of jutting jaws and mailed fists against a policy of mysterious smiles and hidden hands. "Military strength decides the contest" wrote Kissinger, "but political goals determine the price to be paid and the intensity of the struggle"; whereas Kennedy declared himself willing to "pay any price . . ."

From the vantage point of America the stable, all of Kissinger's suggestions are of a piece. Limited war is the natural use of force for a state interested in limited objectives; total war is grotesque. Arms resolve conflicts; they do not cause them. It is better to design programs which will mitigate the horrors of war than to try to outlaw war itself. All strategists should move "to bridge the gap between force and diplomacy." The isolation of the various military departments only tangles what ought to be a concerted effort. It is unwise for Congress to accept blindly the recommendations of the military for its own budget; this is too likely to represent the sum total of the proposals by each branch of the armed services. It is unreasonable to insist that the limitation of warfare implies too high a regard for human rationality, "for history offers no example for the extraordinary destructiveness of modern weapons either. A program which sought to establish some principles of war limitation in advance of hostilities would seem to make fewer demands on rationality than one which attempted to improvise the rules of war in the confusion of battle." All of this requires a coherent doctrine, and the leadership of a statesman who "must bridge the gap between a society's experience and his vision, between its tradition and its future":

In this task his possibilities are limited because there is an inherent tension between the mode of action of a bureaucracy and the pattern of statesmanship. A smoothly working bureaucracy creates the illusion of running by itself; it seeks to reduce all problems to administrative terms. The basic motivation of a bureaucracy is its quest for safety; its preference is in favor of a policy of minimum risk. A bureaucracy, therefore, tends to exaggerate the technical complexities of its problems and to seek to reduce questions of judgment to a minimum. Technical problems are susceptible to "objective" analysis, whereas questions of judgment contain too many uncertain elements. An administrative mechanism has a bias in favor of the *status quo*, however arrived at. Short of an unambiguous catastrophe, the *status quo* has the advantage of familiarity. No "objective" criteria can prove that a change of course will yield superior results. The inclination of a bureaucracy is to deny the possibility of great conception by classifying it as "unsound," "risky," or other terms which testify to a preference for equilibrium over exceptional performance. It is no accident that most great statesmen were opposed by the "experts" in their foreign offices, for the very greatness of the statesman's conception tends to make it inaccessible to those whose primary concern is with safety and minimum risk.

It sounds like a prescription for the role which Kissinger himself would eventually play, though at this point in his career it was but another entry in a lifelong monologue on the nature of statesmanship. In a sense, all of *Nuclear Weapons and Foreign Policy* is of this character, with the technical data and practical criticism serving as filling for the pie crust. The conception of the United States as a status quo power is but one of the three most interesting things about this book. The other two are Kissinger's view of the Soviet Union and his interpretation of American relations with the rest of the world. The argument for limited nuclear war is primarily of technical interest, and flows from Kissinger's fundamental ideas, whereas these three matters mark further extensions of the mind which flexed itself on Kant, Toynbee, and Spengler, and then stayed the course for the first time with Metternich and the post-Napoleonic diplomats.

"What is a revolutionary?" Kissinger asks. He then proceeds to argue that a melancholy lesson of history would be that we *don't* know one when we see one. After recapitulating the familiar homilies on revolution and legitimacy, he says that much of the problem of dealing with the Russians has come from the willingness of Westerners to see the Russians as we view ourselves—the classic error of legitimate orders.

> The free world believes that peace is a condition of static equilibrium and that economic advance is a more rational objective than foreign adventures. Therefore the Communists appear periodically in the guise of domestic reformer eager to spread the fruits of material advancement. For each change of pace or tactic, the U.S.S.R. has found defenders among its victims, who justified its course not on the ground of Communist doctrine, but because it fitted in with the preconceptions of the legitimate order.

Again, we hear the echo sounding from that undergraduate thesis, wherein the idolators of "objective necessity" are contemptuously dismissed. "To the non-Soviet world, peace appears as an end in itself and its manifestation is the *absence* of struggle. To the Soviet leaders, by contrast, peace is a *form* of struggle." Astounded by the obtuseness of those unwilling to accept this elemental truth, Kissinger approaches downright invective in censuring the "infinite arguments over whether the Soviet Union was preparing for a 'showdown' or ushering in a period of peace." Then there are those waifs who speak of negotiation and confrontation as options to be chosen between, rather than as thesis and antithesis, requiring union in a synthetic whole. "To the Soviet way of thinking, a settlement is not something to be achieved by the process of negotiation; rather an 'objective' situation is ratified by the settlement . . . To the Soviet leaders, a settlement reflects a temporary relationship of forces, inherently unstable and to be maintained only until the power balance shifts." The American approach is too "legalistic," too disdainful of the "symbolic aspect of foreign policy." We need to be good dialecticians like the Soviets, to develop a "strategy of ambiguity" in order to defend the status quo, and to stop allowing ourselves to become frustrated by behaving in the international arena as if it were a glorified courtroom.

When he turned to American relations with allied and "uncommitted" nations, Kissinger found this same lack of subtlety, this same absence of appreciation for those fluid forces which worked constantly toward historical syntheses. "Nowhere," he wrote, "are the dilemmas of the nuclear age more apparent than in the attempt to construct a system of alliances against Soviet aggression. It reveals once more the problem of establishing a relationship between a policy of deterrence we are prepared to implement, between the temptation to pose a maximum threat and the tendency to recoil before it." The United States risked establishing its own Maginot line with its tendency to make rigid distinctions—Free World vs. Communist, etc. "To us the Soviet threat overshadows all else; but Pakistan is more concerned with India than with the U.S.S.R. and China . . ." Obviously, all matters are not of equal moment; yet the current doctrine implied that they were. This was done by conceiving every war as an all-out war. American strategy was inconsistent with American beliefs. With allies, "We can co-operate on matters of mutual concern, which in almost every case means mutual co-operation. But our allies must understand that we have an obligation to maintain, not only a regional equilibrium but the world balance of power as well." It struck Kissinger as a matter of dignity, as well as plain good sense.

In the dozen pages on the "uncommitted nations," Kissinger's book achieves a sort of climax. Here was a situation inherently ambiguous, where the former colonies of the Western powers had broken loose in an effort resembling in some ways the American experience of two centuries before. If they were often brutal and crude in going about it, they were also highly vulnerable to the most vulgar Communist propaganda. Their only common experience had been anti-colonialism; now they were being asked to support the wishes of the country which they viewed as the great inheritor of the Western imperial tradition. Here, Kissinger's argument for the United States as the status quo power is based on the realities of modern history. It may be true that Americans like to view themselves as—and may, in fact, be—the inheritors of a greater revolutionary tradition than that of China and the U.S.S.R. Yet, we are also the inheritors of European power, and time has tended to place this more recent development on a higher shelf than the Declaration of Independence. In this ironic fact lies the great tragedy of post-World War II American foreign policy, and from it we walk that trail of tears which culminated in the bloodbath of Vietnam. Would that the Russians and the Chinese had gone through their revolutions and civil wars before America had endured her own! But that is not the way it worked out, and the Third World nations staked out their positions behind the Communist brigade. Thus synthesis commands these young nations, and "in the international field," Kissinger wrote sadly, "the division of the world into two contending camps exalts the role of the uncommitted, and the collapse of the old international system creates a fertile field of manipulation for ambitious men."

When we remember that the great empires of Europe were built by tradesmen and preserved by aristocrats, Kissinger's response to this situation falls into a grandly conservative category. He would not make war on every country which seizes an American copper mine; neither would he rely on vituperative bombast in the United Nations. Instead:

> Condescending as it may seem to say so, the United States has an important educational task to perform in the uncommitted third of the world. By word and deed we must demonstrate that the inexorable element of international relations resides in the necessity to combine principle with power, that an exclusive reliance on moral pronouncements may be as irresponsible as the attempt to conduct policy on the basis of considerations of power alone. To be sure we should, wherever possible, seek to identify ourselves with the aspirations of the newly independent states. But we must also be prepared to preserve the conditions in which these aspirations can be fulfilled. We should never give up our principles nor ask other nations to surrender theirs. But we must also realize that neither we nor our allies nor the uncommitted can realize any principles unless we survive. We cannot permit the balance of power to be overturned for the sake of allied unity or the approbation of the uncommitted.

Finally, "In its relations with the uncommitted, the United States must, therefore, develop not only a greater compassion but a greater majesty."

When we think of the exalted status its author would achieve,

Nuclear Weapons and Foreign Policy seems to provide many of the broad strokes supporting the brushwork of shuttle diplomacy in later years. Of course, it was limited by the period in which it was written; Kissinger, for example, had no knowledge of the coming Sino-Soviet split. But these are technical matters, caught up like mere particles in the sweeping dialectical winds. And I would no more read this book for its literary excellence than I would read Faulkner as an introduction to Southern hospitality. What is remarkable about *Nuclear Weapons and Foreign Policy* is, as with *A World Restored*, its method of analysis. For this is a book about the metaphysics of American foreign policy, and how many such books are there? Kissinger took dialectics for his tool, and set about classifying the forces of the age. In one corner he stood the American status quo; in the other, the Soviet revolution; as referee, he appointed himself. Then he made himself the fixer, too, and hedged his bets, just in case. I am not qualified to judge this as either right or wrong; in any event, it is still too soon to say. His book is both ponderous and intriguing—ponderous, because its method requires that analysis go on eternally; intriguing, for exactly the same reason.

VIII

With the publication of *Nuclear Weapons and Foreign Policy* in 1957, Kissinger's truly original scholarship was behind him. In seven years—from the time of his undergraduate honors thesis to that of his best-selling book on contemporary international relations—he had found himself a philosophy, applied it to the lives of states in history, and then plugged it into the cacophony of our own age. In the next dozen years he would turn out three more books and several articles. On the whole, these involved the restatement of old themes and their application to technical problems. They lacked the sweeping dialectical manner of the first two books; or they borrowed so completely as to resemble an interminable sonata, in which the pattern of A-B-A is interrupted by a fresh theme only to keep both performer and listener awake. These rare, fresh themes are what will concern us in the following pages. But it is useful to remember that they are exceptional, and that all the while those old favorites on legitimacy and revolution, bureaucracy and statesmanship, etc. constituted most of Dr. Kissinger's performance time. Graubard tells us that Kissinger was restless at Harvard, and often longed for the exhilaration of making history. His time would come, but not for a dozen years. Meanwhile, he became the Madame Schumann-Heink of strategic studies, engaging in a ceaseless round of farewell tours.

The Necessity for Choice appeared in late 1960. Much of it is a denunciation of postwar foreign policy, particularly that of the Eisenhower-Dulles years. In this sense it only made explicit what had been implicit in *Nuclear Weapons and Foreign Policy*. The tone of *The Necessity for Choice* is more aggressively moralistic, as if to show that Kissinger had been studying these problems too long for him to mince words. This was the first of his books to exude the air of the classroom—that is, a casual use of familiar terminology to the point where an outsider might gain a false impression of the meaning of that terminology. Thus, we are lectured on the value of preserving "liberal democracy," while Kissinger everywhere else implies a preference for conservative democracies which place a premium on stability and order, rather than on change and progress. Sometimes his mood grows testy, and we are told: "Nothing is more important for America than to give up its illusions." The closing line of the Introduction reads like a commandment from a Prussian textbook: "Our ability to master the seeming paradoxes will test even more than our ability to survive; it will be the measure of our worthiness to survive." Perhaps his elevation to the title of Associate Professor of Government gave Kissinger the idea that he was speaking in accordance with his station. Certainly this imperious tone gives testimony to the author's increased self-confidence, and decreased sensitivity to his readers' feelings. The occasional rudeness, unleavened by wit, makes *The Necessity for Choice* the most unappetizing of his flavorless books.

When he was not telling us what is "responsible" and what is "irresponsible," or informing us that such-and-such an occurrence would illustrate "the bankruptcy of the liberal values of the West" and other such tush, he tended to renew his call for a policy of national majesty by indicating how the United States had behaved ingloriously in the past fifteen years. In only one area did he expatiate and broaden his doctrine. This came in the assertion of the primacy of political structures, a concept inherent in the first two books, but now weighed against the fashionable liberal idea that "economic development" was the key to saving the "uncommitted nations" for democracy. It was emphasized in two places in *The Necessity for Choice*: briefly in a section on "The Problem of Germany" in a chapter on American-European relations; and at greater length in the chapter Spinozaically titled "Of Political Evolution."

He wrote of the division of Germany that it "may be unavoidable, but the cohesion of the West and the future of the North Atlantic Community depends on our ability to demonstrate what makes it so." In other words, the morality of the situation was secondary in importance to the requirement of creating a legitimate explanation for it, should that prove necessary. Berlin, the island in the Communist sea, must have its status preserved, lest the Federal Republic become "demoralized" and "the claims of the West to stand for self-determination and human dignity . . . become a mockery." The picture blurs, but the artist's technique is clear. What is important to Kissinger is not the value of self-determination and human dignity in themselves, but their existence as the legitimizing principles of the Western nations and of the Atlantic Alliance. This contention is augmented by the importance of German stability to the peace of Europe. When either too strong or too weak, Germany's position upset the balance of power. In its vulnerable, post-World War II condition, it had once more become an object of rivalry among the superpowers; it could be securely implanted in the Western order only if that order held to its claims of self-determination and human dignity. When the détente in Germany finally came, it was based on the understanding among the parties involved that the reasons for the two Germanies had been sufficiently demonstrated. The celebrated "economic recovery" was, at best, peripheral to a completely political dispute; the political dispute was, at its categorical heart, a moral dispute.

"Of Political Evolution: The West, Communism, and the New Nations" carries this method into different realms of argument. "Perhaps even more worrisome than specific policy dilemmas," he wrote, ". . . has been our interpretation of the contemporary revolution." It has been too optimistic, too much based on "an evolutionary theory in which the assumed forces of history have replaced purpose and action." This is rather vague, but Kissinger clarifies it when he once more declares his sympathy for the dialectical mode. The major difference between Communism and democratic capitalism is "much less theoretical than psychological. Communism uses its philosophy of history as a *spur* to effort. Faith in evolution provides the conviction for major exertions. Too many in the West rely on history as a substitute for effort. As a result, survival becomes their primary goal." Out of conflict emerges creation; out of single-mindedness, stagnation. It is a curious comparison, and perhaps not very accurate, but it is pure Kissinger, even as much as those undergraduate lines scolding America's fond reliance on "objective necessity."

From this initial attack on "evolutionary theory," Kissinger shifted into historical argument. Industrialization had not moved nations toward democracy—witness Imperial Germany and Imperial Japan. So how could democracy arise as a result of industrial development? "On the contrary, in so far as there is a relationship between industrialization and the emergence of democracy, it is that in the nineteenth century political freedom was considered a means *to bring about* economic advance . . . As a result, the economic justification for democracy was little concerned with the moral significance of freedom. Its emphasis was utilitarian: the greatest good for the greatest number." So the man who puts his faith in economic forces is engaged in the self-deception of the practical-minded. Indeed, "The abuses of nineteenth-century industrialism which spawned Marxism were due above all to the enthronement of efficiency and productivity as the primary goals." In contrast, Communism fuses politics and economics to become "the feudalism of the industrial epoch." This fusion has produced a moral basis for Communism's existence, in contrast to the flabbiness of Western convictions:

> When skepticism becomes an end in itself, it can easily lead to stagnation or resignation. Where nothing is certain, nothing will be strongly maintained. This may make for ease of relations in a stable society. It does not provide the motivation for running risks. And without a willingness to sacrifice no entrenched system

can possibly be altered. The phrase "give me liberty or give me death" may be trite. But liberty may indeed require a readiness to face death on its behalf. The power of despotism can be confirmed as much by its subjects' lack of conviction as by its own inherent dynamism.

Thus he returns to his inadequately defined code of political morality. Perceiving the United States as a nation interested in preserving the status quo for itself, he seeks to charge this conservatism with a sense of responsibility for the young nations lacking America's advantages. With great pomp he announces "that unless we address ourselves to the problem of encouraging institutions which protect human dignity, the future of freedom is dark indeed."

But we never know exactly what he means by "human dignity" and "freedom"; his belief in categorical imperatives is clear enough, but the actual *a priori* assumptions are never spelled out; his method is tried enough and perhaps is as worthy as any other; but we are never quite sure of where it has come from or where it is going. Kissinger is too ambiguous to be truly satisfying, and he creates many of his own worst problems. It is not without a touch of amusement that we observe this modern Hegelian grope toward the expressed ideals of Benjamin Disraeli and Edmund Burke. He is like a dancer of minuets confronted with his first waltz; he cannot keep in step, and suffers the embarrassment of tangled feet. Hear him press the need for democratic restraint by calling up the metaphors of Metternich on the external affairs of states:

A key test of democracy, then, is not the claim to justice—this can be made by any system—but the limits to which this claim is pressed. A free system, whatever its formal institutions, cannot function unless it is based on self-restraint. There must be some mechanism for dealing with dissent other than destroying it. To be meaningful, self-restraint must set limits even to the exercise of righteous power.

From this sluggish passage, one could reflect, Tocqueville might as well have been a provincial winetaster for all that his notion of the "tyranny of the majority" had been absorbed by one Harvard political scientist. But such is the method of Dr. Kissinger: all things must be examined in terms of their contradictions, and at great length. How unfortunate that America must be called to majesty in such waddling prose!

IX

In *The Troubled Partnership: A Re-appraisal of the Atlantic Alliance* (1964–65), the focus is once more on Europe, though hardly that of the post-Napoleonic diplomats. On one level, it is a critique of the foreign policy of the Kennedy years, as *The Necessity for Choice* had presumed to judge the Eisenhower years. Now, the postwar era of American hegemony was drawing to a close; there arose the need for a blast of fresh air. Implicit once more in Kissinger's analysis is the notion that the powers-that-be have not succeeded in doing what needed to be done. On a second level, it offers a look at the second half of the anti-colonial revolution— the revised status of the European colonial powers. "In other words," wrote Kissinger, "we are now the only member of NATO with world-wide interests, and this produces unavoidable differences in perspective." Solutions to the problems confronting the Atlantic Alliance relied, as ever, on a "sense of proportion" among nations, particularly in the case of the United States, which must retain its own stability in the process. Always the pessimist, Kissinger found little to cheer about in the European political situation of the early sixties:

> If one moves from Europe in the abstract to an examination of the individual European countries, it becomes apparent how precarious Europe's stability really is. On the Iberian peninsula, stability may not survive two aged dictators. Italy's center-left coalition is tenuous; its capacity for major policy initiatives is limited. A post-De Gaulle France may be rent by internal schisms. Germany suffers from the absence of traditions and the pressures produced by a divided country. The vigor so noticeable in Europe today is very close in time to nihilism; European self-confidence is still shaky. Little would be gained by replacing a nationalism of insufficient strength by a neutralism which exalts impotence.

The prognosis, even then, seemed overly gloomy; but it was typical of its author. Recalling the pratfall of ancient Greece and the ruination of our century's two world wars, he posed "the perennial problem of the West: Whether [the North Atlantic nations] can generate sufficient purpose to achieve community without first experiencing disaster." Of course, it must be one or the other: in Kissinger's stern cosmology of heroic and degenerate statesmanship, no one ever muddles through.

After this opening statement, *The Troubled Partnership* concerns itself mostly with specific problems, Kissinger all the while reminding us that problems of policy are likely to prove deeper problems of structure, which, in turn, reveal problems of fundamental conception. Disputes over the placement of nuclear weaponry, the size of armed forces, the form of negotiations—all designate a clash of character between the nations of the West. Kissinger counters with the argument that we must all learn to get along better, lest we all die together. I omit the usual subtlety and ambiguity of his method, and mention only that this is more of a moral than a technical matter; the order of importance never changes. Many of the issues have since been settled, and the greatest personalities involved—De Gaulle in particular—are dead and gone, or at least chased from power. American-European relations have settled down somewhat since the days when De Gaulle went ranting about French *gloire*. Kissinger's book, though perhaps the most tightly constructed and well organized of his works, retains as little interest today as *The Necessity for Choice*. With the advance of years, its practical and concrete character is less attractive than the categorical generalities of the first two books.

Today, only the chapter on De Gaulle stands out. Perhaps Kissinger had, in his curious manner, been roused by the willful Frenchman's repellent image in the United States; maybe he had been moved by the rebuke of Washington's rigid Grand Design; or he warmed to the presence of a fellow conservative in the noble, Continental style. The analysis of De Gaulle is more thorough than anything Kissinger had attempted on any statesman, historical or contemporary, since *A World Restored*. We read the second chapter of *The Troubled Partnership*, and suddenly we find ourselves transported—out of our own period of long-range missiles and hydrogen bombs, back into those vanished days when one man could fairly call himself the state, and "people's wars" were called "peasants' wars."

"However arrogant his style," wrote Kissinger, "De Gaulle's approach to history is relatively humble. He is the leader of a country grown cautious by many enthusiasms shattered; turned skeptical from many dreams proved fragile; a country to which the unforeseen is the most elemental fact of history." His version puts De Gaulle somewhere among the great frustrated leaders of modern history, in the line of Bismarck and Czar Alexander—straddled between prophecy and will, burdened by his nation's history, lacking the power to institutionalize his ideals.

A society which has suffered severe shocks cannot find fulfillment in the Grand Design of others without risking its identity. Before it can decide what it wishes to become, it has to rediscover what it is. Far from being based on an excessive estimate of France's strength, De Gaulle's policy reflects, above all, a deep awareness of the suffering of his people over the span of more than a generation.

Having endured the worst possible circumstances, Frenchmen found in De Gaulle a man who shared their fears and conducted his office from a basis of fear. It was shallow for Americans to recognize only the veneer of arrogance in De Gaulle, and ignore the tremor beneath the surface. Kissinger saw De Gaulle's assessment of Communism as "more historical" (more realistic) than the opinions of American politicians and diplomats. He attributes opinions to De Gaulle which we know that Kissinger shares. "Peace to him is not a final settlement but a new, perhaps more stable, balance of forces . . . An equilibrium can never be permanent but must be adjusted in constant struggles. Tension, according to De Gaulle, is not caused so much by the personal attitudes of individual Communist leaders as by the dynamics of the system they represent." De Gaulle's attempt to aggrandize France represented no mere ambition on the part of an old general; rather, it marked the effort of a proud people to achieve international dignity, to help create the rules by which they would be forced to live; instead of obediently accepting the dictation of the superpowers. "He would object to *any* settlement that France did not help to formulate—regardless of his opinion of its substance. The major thrust of De Gaulle's policy is to make it impossible for the United States to deal with the Soviet Union over the heads of France and the rest of Europe." And though his tactics engendered strange side effects, his vision remained clear. If his ideals must someday come crashing down, it was not because they were less than great in themselves. "Great men build truly only if they remember that their achievement must be maintained by the less gifted individuals who follow them." Unlike most of his contemporaries, De Gaulle had the courage of a statesman.

As seems mandatory with Kissinger, his analysis is closed with yet another restatement of his definition of tragedy:

> In the meantime, there is something of a Greek tragedy about the dispute between the United States and France. Each chief actor, following the laws of his nature, is bringing about consequences quite different from those intended . . . Tragedy, to many Americans at least, is to find oneself thwarted in what is ardently desired. But there is another and perhaps more poignant tragedy, that of fulfilling one's desires and then finding them empty.

Once again, he was haunted by a vision of things falling apart because they are badly built; badly built because they are misunderstood; misunderstood because they are improperly perceived; improperly perceived because they are not strained through the filter of either/or, and then resolved. Too bad: "Our idealism and impetuosity would gain depth if leavened by the European sense of tragedy. And the European consciousness of history could recover dynamism if bolstered by our hopefulness."

X

During Lyndon Johnson's presidency, Kissinger's outpourings reduced to a trickle. Graubard contends that the major reason for this was Johnson's abandonment of general foreign policy in favor of fighting the Vietnam war, leaving Kissinger precious little to criticize. Furthermore, it is clear that Kissinger had fairly well exhausted his repertoire; even the patches were starting to fall off his worn garments. How many fresh dialectical constructions could be made out of prophetic and bureaucratic leadership, stable and revolutionary orders? The professor was biding his time, waiting for something to turn up. He busied himself by elaborating a foreign policy for Nelson Rockefeller in 1968; when the Albany Maecenas lost his bid for the presidential nomination, Kissinger returned to Harvard.

If Richard Nixon had not beckoned, what would have happened? Judging from the tendency of Kissinger's scholarship in the 1960s, it is obvious that no historical or strategic masterwork was lost to us by his assumption of high office. Indeed, we may gain from the future memoirs of an eminent statesman what could never have been given us by a mere professor of government —namely, a description of the impact of today's world on the principles of Hegelian conservatism. As it stood, Kissinger's writings of the late sixties bear witness to a man badly in need of recharging his batteries, a man whose work had become altogether too routine.

American Foreign Policy, published at a time coincidental to the start of Kissinger's chairmanship of the National Security Council, contains his most ambitious writing from this period, excepting the "Reflections on Bismarck." There are three essays here: "Domestic Structure and Foreign Policy," "Central Issues of American Foreign Policy," and "The Vietnam Negotiations." The first two amount to a weary coda, bringing Kissinger's academic career to a whimpering climax. The article on Vietnam resembles a declaration of principles for the work he was about to assume.

In "Domestic Structure and Foreign Policy," we are treated to a review of Kissinger's theory of the "types of leadership." We have the "bureaucratic-pragmatic type," the "ideological type," and the "revolutionary-charismatic type." The United States, for example, is said to be in the hands of the bureaucrat-pragmatists, the "American élite," though it is not at all clear what is meant by this. If Kissinger is talking about the average foreign service officer, graduate of all the right schools, etc., then, perhaps. But if he is talking about the average congressman, or even the average

Cabinet member, then at age forty-five he was as ignorant of the nature of power in America as when first he set foot on Ellis Island. Within a few years' time, his own experience in government doubtless corrected any false impressions; or is his undefined "American élite" regularly led by refugees from totalitarian regimes? So "bureaucratic-pragmatic leadership" is what we have in America. "Shaped by a society without fundamental social schisms (at least until the race problem became visible) and the product of an environment in which most recognized problems have proved soluble, its approach to policy is *ad hoc*, pragmatic, and somewhat mechanical." Actually, what he wanted to say in all this is that there are an awful lot of lawyers in positions of power in the United States, and that American foreign policy suffered from the concomitant devotion to "legalisms." This is a very old argument with Kissinger, and his bending of it into strange convolutions requiring American élites and societies without fundamental social schisms (a society with fundamental social schisms would be at least two societies, not one) shows how tired his thinking had become. *American Foreign Policy* is distinguished by its slovenly use of language. The old dialectical machine was rusting. In the earlier books he would, for example, have repeated himself ten times before permitting anyone to print such a sentence as, "No war in a century has aroused the passions of the conflict in Vietnam." In the first place, he means "no war involving the United States"; in the second, even permitting my amendment, it isn't true—the Second World War easily aroused more passion, indicating that he wants to say "passionate opposition"; third, the sentence is ambiguous even as amended—it could easily be taken to mean that the passionate Vietnamese conflict might be aroused by wars *elsewhere*, and that said Vietnamese passions concern us here, which is not so. I do not mean to imply that Kissinger's first four books are models of English usage, only to observe that *American Foreign Policy* is worse than the others because its errors appear in more important places. Then too, the little book is heavily tendentious, whereas in the earlier books those grand generalities would be accompanied by reliable references. In sorting out the categories of *American Foreign Policy*, we are left to our wits—which is not fair. The first four books, at least in part, reflected extensions of Kissinger's philosophy; this one mainly reflects his impatience.

Through the haze, we detect that Kissinger was going through many of the same motions. He worried that the United States might be losing its stability, which he valued above all else about this country. Note, for example, the reference to the "race problem": the rights and wrongs of the thing simply do not concern him so much as the thought that racial tension is upsetting America's balance. In the late sixties, as in time immemorial, dialectical understanding and a reasonable sense of history constituted the basic elements of a harmonious order. In "Central Issues of American Foreign Policy," Kissinger bites his nails over the possible loss of both. "The generation which has come of age after the fifties has had Vietnam as its introduction to world politics. It has no memory of occasions when American-supported structural innovations were successful or of the motivations which prompted these enterprises." And when he contemplated the prospects for an "honorable" exit from Vietnam, it was the same craving for stability which moved him, "for what is involved now is confidence in American promises," the loss of which, he felt, invited chaos throughout the world. We were at the start of a new period of international relations, with the balance of power shifting, the fires of ideology waning, the need for international cooperation growing. The sudden abandonment of an ally could have terribly upsetting effects, and drastically revise the world's perception of American intentions. On top of all this, we must grow much more flexible in all our dealings. The choice was not between belligerence and timidity, hawks and doves, but between those who would construct a cogent policy and then stand by it, and those who would improvise on the basis of the morning newspaper. Above all, he counseled, we must be more patient, more majestic, or, failing that, at least more big-brotherly. "The best and most prideful expressions of American purposes in the world have been those in which we acted in concert with others. Our influence in these situations has depended on achieving a reputation as a member of such a concert." If these qualities could once more be brought into practice, he hinted, there was a chance that a legitimate order might finally be created for the nuclear age.

Following a quarter century of Cold War, this would permit suffering mankind a reprieve—and even Henry Kissinger could cheer up a bit.

XI

Six years after taking a position in the American government, three years after a journey to China established him as the world's most eminent diplomat, one year after becoming the first foreign-born American Secretary of State, Henry Kissinger sat down with James Reston of the New York *Times* and declared:

I think of myself as a historian more than as a statesman. As a historian, you have to be conscious of the fact that every civilization that has ever existed has ultimately collapsed.

History is a tale of efforts that failed, of aspirations that weren't realized, of wishes that were fulfilled and then turned out to be different from what one expected. So, as a historian, one has to live with a sense of the inevitability of tragedy. As a statesman, one has to act on the assumption that problems must be solved.

Each generation lives in time, and even though ultimately perhaps societies have all suffered a decline, that is of no help to any one generation, and the decline is usually traceable to a loss of creativity and inspiration and therefore avoidable. It is probably true that insofar as I think historically I must look at the tragedies that have occurred. Insofar as I act, my motive force, of which I am conscious, is to try to avoid them.[10]

Perhaps he was hedging a bit—but not much. This is the same somber analyst of Metternich speaking, reiterating the necessity for choice, the single allotted experiment of each generation, which now had fallen into his hands. He went on to talk about the increasing interdependence of nations, forgoing the use of the term "legitimacy" because it had got him into trouble with Germanophobic journalists. But the meaning was clear enough. "I think we are now at a point," he said, "where the framework of the structure exists, if we can put it together. We have the raw

[10] New York *Times*, October 13, 1974, p. 34.

material, we have the elements, we've identified them, I hope, correctly. We are at the beginning of building a consciousness of the global community that must come after us."[11] Of course it sounded hopeful: he was a statesman now, and statesmen should never sound too gloomy, especially when discussing their own work. But behind the façade of good cheer would seem to lie an honest thought: that the pieces are falling into place and that structures may be sounder than we think, always providing that the proper parts have been "identified . . . I hope, correctly." In the long run, we may smash each other to bits, but such unpleasantness would not seem to be a present danger.

It is rather odd, though, to find Kissinger prefacing his remarks by saying, "As a historian . . . ," for this is something of a change of linen. Graubard opens his study of Kissinger by writing, "Henry Kissinger was not a professional historian; he did not think of himself as such; others did not so regard him."[12] Perhaps he was providing himself a cushion, knowing that "historian" sounds like a more respectable background than "strategic analyst." In a sense, he has been both; in the larger context of our times, he has been neither. Count him as a philosopher of the lives of states: his academic work constitutes a prolegomenon to any future international relations; his temperament is that of a Hegelian conservative, adjusted to the mode of a great liberal Republic in the second half of the twentieth century. A purer devotion to theory might have made him a superior thinker—but then he could never have become Secretary of State. The natives do not understand his sort of thinking, especially in its imperfect state, though they seem to be impressed by it. A clever Tory like George F. Will can still characterize Kissinger as a "formalist" who came to office believing "in the efficacy of the formal arrangements wrought by 'men of affairs.'" In time, says Will, Kissinger could not help but become "fatalistic": "If he is increasingly fatalistic, that is understandable: Fatalism is the refuge of intelligent, disappointed formalists."[13] Of course, he is no more a formalist than any other foreign minister, or, for that matter, any other civilized politician. And it would be impossible for him to have

[11] Ibid., p. 35.
[12] Graubard, op. cit., p. 1.
[13] George F. Will, Op-Ed page, Detroit *News*, January 14, 1975.

become any more fatalistic than he was before assuming power. Indeed, his faith seems greater in fluidity than formality; he believes nothing more grandiose than that men release strange and contradictory forces into their world: so strange that they have survived both the bloodshed and the golden artifacts of history; so likely to move the future that we are best advised to line them up against the wall, take their numbers, and invite them to join us for the ride—at the end of a leash, preferably.

Of Subliterary Politicians

The ancient and noble form of the memoir has always served its purpose for politicians. It has worked like a mirror, tinted to the author's pleasure. It is the ultimate expression of self-love, the composition of one's reflection in indelible ink. What could be finer than to place one's image before the public, unshackled by the press, undenounced by the opposition? Even the bad reviews pass quickly, leaving the memoir to stand on its own, weighty and magnificent, a generous benefaction for the children of the ages. If Plutarch is no longer read by dreamy youths, his example is unforgotten: a life is shaped by its models. In providing a model for future generations, the memoirist offers himself; his book reveals the man he thinks he was.

This is hardly the same thing as the man he really was, but it is in some ways more interesting. A politician is notable for his deceptions. Like an actor, he is an illusionist. Because so much of what he does can be investigated, it is possible to find him deceiving himself. The result is often low comedy, which is still better than none at all.

Because America is in thrall to the common man, currently collectivized as "the people," the politician seeks to invoke the common spirit. This often means the apotheosis of the banal. The political memoir is therefore likely to be plagued by banalities, although touched by irony. The President of the United States is unlike the corner grocer in his recitation of the simple virtues. He has seen, in his lifetime, how little they apply to the world he knows. His homilies sit uneasily beside his deep appreciation of human duplicity. The politician, like most men, has been raised on virtue and has lived by vice. The chances are his memoir will attempt some reconciliation of education with experience. His challenge is to accomplish this and retain his dignity.

The Latin word *gravitas* is still useful in describing the pose favored by our politicians. This has had one regrettable effect on political memoirs: it has made most of them very fat. Here the Plutarchan lesson of brevity has been lost, and our models are constructed on a Rushmorean scale. The affliction is largely confined to Presidents, who have convinced themselves that a morning's chitchat with the Afghanistani head of government deserves better than burial in the sands of time. Non-Presidents are customarily less generous with accounts of handball games in the congressional gymnasium, where approximately the same amount of important business is dispensed with. Perhaps the ceremonial trappings have duped Presidents into believing that all conversations with foreign leaders are important, while the handball game after which votes are sought in the locker room is of less obvious significance. In any case, their inclusion bloats the memoirs of ex-Presidents, while the absence of their counterparts keeps the books by non-Presidents moderately trim.

A statesman, said Harry Truman, is a dead politician. He was almost but not quite correct, and I can forgive him for not wanting to give the game away. A statesman is a politician who has written his memoirs. There is nothing more dignified than to top off one's administration with a volume too heavy to read in bed or on the beach, something that must be studied with great care and at close range. It is amazing how many dull men have pulled it off.

What is the public value of these works? I set aside the question until I have exhumed my corpses and completed my dissections. All are specimens of our own historical period, though one would not know it from their condition in many cases. Rigor mortis is frequently established before the ink is dry.

II

These have been, as Schlesinger said, the days of the imperial
presidency. The memoirs I note here have been written by men of
different standing in the presidential sniffing order, but all bear
the mark of having caught the scent. The essential division comes
between the Presidents and the non-Presidents. There is a sub-
division in the second category, but I leave it for later. Where the
non-President can address his life and times at reasonable length,
the presidential hubris burrows into the reminiscences of those
who have held the office. Even the phlegmatic Coolidge bloated
to obesity in print. The problem, I daresay, has many sides to it.
There is, to start with, the vanity of the average politician, multi-
plied many times over in those men who are exceptional enough
to rise to the top. It is frequently said that the man grows with
the office, but the adage applies mainly to the man's head. A President emerges from his term of office without the power to work
his will, but with his power to instruct others enhanced. He is un-
burdened by political consequence; he is beyond the reach of his
party, as he is one of its guiding spirits; he is almost beyond the
claws of the press, which is addicted to the rush of current events
for its nourishment. Should the ex-President choose to pronounce
his views on one of them, he risks a one-day beating, but little
more. All of this leaves him free to expose the lessons he has
learned, the proverbs that have held true throughout a lifetime,
and the awful limits and responsibilities of power. He can refer to
these things while in power, but never without a political check.
And never does he have time enough to write them down.

There is another prompter: vindication. By the time he leaves
office, every President has made his share of mistakes and enemies. The purpose of the memoir is never to apologize or punish,
however; this would be undignified. Rather, the point is to overwhelm. The bulkier the book the more forgettable the mistakes
seem and the more ludicrous the enemies appear. There is nothing which requires an ex-President to write about the hacks he
transformed into undersecretaries, and it is much finer to recall a

splendid luncheon with the Indian Ambassador. There is the chance that reviewers may bring these indiscretions up, but it is possible to forestall them by condescending to make brief reference, and hint at their insignificance. It is also wise to concentrate on the sweeping importance of foreign affairs, beside which domestic quarrels appear to be the mean concoctions of petty rivals.

It is common for people to speak of "the verdict of history" as if, at some point in the future, a curtain will rise, a gaggle of debaters will shut their mouths onstage, and History will march forward to proclaim its judgment. Nothing is less true. Historians tend to be political-minded men, who form their views as quickly as any storekeeper. If their minds are changed, it is not by prayer and fasting, but by observation of the flow of succeeding events. It does not take an ex-President long to see how History is beginning to regard him. Eisenhower, for one, learned that a poll of prominent American historians had left him with a low ranking among Presidents. This was not too long after he had left office, and before his memoirs were complete. The result was predictable: in the desire for vindication, the length of the memoirs increased. The political mind respects quantity: it thinks in terms of majorities, which measure success; of landslides, which give birth to mandates. The longer the memoir, the more thorough the vindication.

Finally, there is the presidential craving for dignity. The sentiment is itself common to all politicians; a dignified politician stands a better chance of being re-elected than a palpable jackass. This was not always the case, but these days Americans are proud of their sophistication, and do not like to have their senses knowingly assaulted. The President, as the most exposed politician in the land, has at the same time the greatest need for a dignified public image and the most prodigious difficulties in obtaining it. Conspiring against him are the press and opposition, eager to seize upon every mistake. Even more troublesome is the character of the office, which rarely fits the occupant well. The more dignified he tries to sound, the more ludicrous he appears; what could be worse than his periodic defenses of "the dignity of the office"? Such occasions recall the time Ralph Waldo Emerson entertained a guest who began to talk of honor, whereupon Mr. and Mrs. Emerson started counting up their spoons. The desire for dignity increases in correspondence to its visible absence. In the age of television, the absence is not merely seen, but employed as fodder by gabbing commentators. By the time he leaves office, a President's image is badly bruised. The memoir provides the final opportunity to touch up the portrait before the embalmer has his day. The ex-President requires no fellow politician to tell him that a fat book has more obvious dignity than a slim one. Publishers do not disagree, and only the occasional reviewer questions the need for such a long book.

The freedom to preach, the desire for vindication, and the craving for dignity are, then, the primary causes of overweight presidential memoirs. Given this handicap, the author's challenge is to stuff some of himself inside his book and convince the reader that he is reading the words of a personality, and not merely an eminence.

Truman, Eisenhower, and Johnson have tried, and Truman had the most success. His first volume, *Year of Decisions*, offers a chronological unraveling of the nine months in 1945 when the man from Missouri "discovered that being a President is like riding a tiger. A man has to keep on riding or be swallowed." The second volume, lazily titled *Years of Trial and Hope*, handles the next seven years. *Year of Decisions* is, paradoxically, the most crowded with detail and the best of all the postwar memoirs. It is in fact the finest presidential memoir of the twentieth century. Why? Simply because it handles genuinely significant stuff. We are still trying to settle ourselves after that year of tremors, which saw the end of the Fascist empires and the rise of the Communist and democratic ones. Truman needed only to ride his story as he rode the office, and he would come out all right. He approached his tasks, whether literary or political, without awe and without fuss. He reduced his mass of material to a pile of facts in need of sorting. All the emotion in Truman's account is wrapped up in the conviction that the man was doing his patriotic duty.

His pre-presidential autobiography is included in *Year of Decisions*, packed into eighty-six purposeful pages. "I hope to prevent the spread of further misinformation, and for that reason I digress to write about myself. I do so without any introspective trimmings." No *Angst* for him; no wringing of hands and gnashing of teeth; this is the President of the United States speaking. He does not even call Stalin a son-of-a-bitch here, though it is clear he would like to. Memoir-writing is an extension of the presidency itself; it does not allow for undignified explosions. At the same time, wanting to vindicate himself, he makes clear that there was no deference by him toward Churchill, and his description of the Potsdam conference is nothing if not a recitation of how little Harry S. Truman, from Independence, Mo., upheld the office of the President:

> I felt that I had heard enough of this. I told Churchill and Stalin that I had come to the conference as a representative of the United States to discuss world affairs. I did not come here to hold a police court hearing on something that was already settled or which would eventually be settled by the United Nations. If we started that, I said, we would become involved in trying to settle every political difficulty and would have to hold hearings for a succession of representatives, including De Gaulle, Franco, and others. I told them frankly that I did not wish to waste time listening to grievances but wanted to deal with the problems that the three heads of government had come to settle. I said that if they did not get to the main issues I was going to pack up and go home. I meant just that.

Truman's gift for self-dramatization helps him get through his memoirs in good shape. What this amounts to is the ability to assert himself as a matter of principle. This masks the will to power, even while it is employed. It allows the author to get away with things that would trouble a lesser man. Thus, having been an inconspicuous senator, Truman is free to write, "I soon found that, among ninety-five colleagues, the real business of the Senate was carried on by unassuming and conscientious men, not by those who managed to get the most publicity." An air of superiority prevails. Harry S. Truman the citizen may have been a forthright patriot, a meek husband, and a loving son. But Harry S. Truman the President zestily grabbed the office trumpets to proclaim that all actions were taken in the name of a disembodied presidency, awesome as a mountain and about as friendly. So the atomic bombs are dropped ("I was greatly moved. I telephoned Byrnes aboard ship to give him the news and then said to the group of sailors around me, 'This is the greatest thing in history. It's time for us to get home.'"), Douglas MacArthur is fired ("If I allowed him to defy the civil authorities in this manner, I myself would be violating my oath to uphold and defend the constitution"), and great reputations are debunked (Bernard Baruch "had always seen to it that his suggestions and recommendations, not always requested by the President, would be given publicity. Most Presidents have received more advice than they could possibly use. But Baruch is the only man to my knowledge who has built a reputation for himself on a self-assumed unofficial status as 'adviser.'"). The guard is let down a bit when Truman writes to his sister: "Nearly every crisis seems to be the worst one, but after it's over, it isn't so bad . . ."

Truman's ego was as large as that of any other President, but it was better disguised than most. Credit Truman's sense of history, which helped him to understand that the underdog was the most beloved of all creatures in a democracy. "I . . . never had any respect for the so-called political influence of the press. My opinion has not changed over the years. Any good politician with nerve *and a program that is right* can win in the face of the stiffest opposition." Born in 1884 and raised on Victorian principles, Truman never had much doubt about his righteousness. He regarded himself as the most recent in a line of great liberal Presidents. "With such a heritage handed down to me, I could not reject lightly the opportunity and the responsibility which were mine in 1948. I had to make a fight for its continuation." He blasted the "do-nothing" Congress, proposed himself as the champion of the little man, and beat Dewey and the pollsters. Then he projected himself, in his only full term, as the guardian of the prerogatives of his office, facing reactionaries at home and tyrants around the world. By the time he retired, the country was bogged down in a mean little war which the bombast of Truman and others had inflated into a crusade. After eight years at the top, he contrasted his own mind with his successor's, and hinted that it was the office which had given him his wisdom: "There was something about his attitude during the meeting that I did not understand. It may have been that this meeting made him realize for the first time what the presidency and the responsibilities of the President were." Truman *knew,* and he was never more smug than when insisting that History would know that he knew. Told in the accent of the flatlands, his memoirs brim with the pride of the ordinary man exercising more power than anyone else in the world, and doing so responsibly, without getting fancy. It had been a poker player's presidency. Many bluffs had been called, and Truman managed to turn up a winning hand more often than not. There was nothing more to it than that. Watching Eisenhower sit in "frozen grimness" as he briefed him on the world situation, he concluded that the conqueror of Europe would never surpass the man from Missouri when the stakes were highest. This satisfied him. He was proud of his shrewdness, and the memoirs succeeded, as his presidency had, because he knew how to play his hand:

> The man who occupies the high office of President is always aware that he is there only because more people wanted him than the other fellow. But if he is to judge his situation by the people around him, he will hear a hundred voices telling him that he is the greatest man in the world for every one that tells him he is not. A President, if he is to have clear perspective and never get out of touch, must cut through the voices around him, know his history, and make certain of the reliability of the information he gets.

Eisenhower was more of a gentleman, which made him less suitable to be President. His origins were as humble as Truman's, but his experience had conditioned him to think that dignity was conferred by rank. As an American, he regarded top-ranking businessmen as the constituents of a national aristocracy, and he dwelled among them as comfortably as Blücher among the Junkers. His assumption of the presidency was less an ascension than a side step from one mountaintop to another. He never convinces the reader of his memoirs that he felt more powerful as President and commander in chief than as general and Allied commander; they represented merely different sets of duties. Having enjoyed so much power before reaching the White House, he was less willing to explore the possibilities of the office than any other postwar President. At the same time he was a man of innate dignity, unsurpassed in the performance of presidential ceremony.

But the military had provided glory enough for one lifetime, and
as President he was a little older and a little more weary. "For me
those years were exciting," he wrote in recalling his presidency.
"—even if, at times, the ever-present routine became tiresome." It
is the routine which buoys the average politician, serving to
remind him of his ultimate pre-eminence. The mask on Harry
Truman's face—the patriotic citizen doing his duty as President—
wore very well, but Eisenhower's was never so secure. Behind the
presidential visage was a retiree yearning to get out.

His memoirs are nothing if not leisurely, and practice moderation to excess. *Mandate for Change* and *Waging Peace* are careful, sensible, and boring, rather like the presidency that had
preceded them. Only in a single chapter, on "Twenty Busy Days"
late in 1956, when the Suez crisis climaxed in a Mideast war, the
Soviet Union invaded Hungary, and Eisenhower defeated Stevenson, does the noise level rise above a drone. The reflective omniscience is abandoned here in favor of a daily chronicle brisk
enough to persuade us that Eisenhower awakened all his senses in
the living of those days. Here we find a general forced to perform
as President. " 'I don't give a darn about the election, I guess it
will be all right,' " he says that he told Anthony Eden, then the
British Prime Minister, implying that it is wrong to think about
politics in the midst of world crisis; but of course he knew that he
would win easily.

It was probably dismaying for him to find that he could not be
commander in chief without also leading the Republican Party,
and it should have surprised no one that the party took a dive
under his presidency. His partisan platitudes were worse than
most, possessing all the resonance of musical commercials. "There
were two roads, I said, two extreme philosophies of government
that were widely divergent—the Reactionary Right and the Radical Left. Both led to tyranny. The problem was to achieve a balance which would assure individual liberty in an orderly society."
Less a testament than an evasion, this was typical of Eisenhower
the uplifter, who erected straw men to frame his own banalities.
In this way moderation appeared to be the result of genuine
thought, rather than the timid choice between distasteful alternatives. It was the latter which actually marked his presidency, and
is reflected in his memoirs. Acting responsibly meant not having

to shout, and not allowing the screamers to have their way. It required the avoidance of difficulty. Khrushchev banging his shoe at the United Nations "demonstrated that human institutions involving orderly processes can operate successfully only when participants show self-restraint and a sense of responsibility." Eisenhower did for courtesy what Coolidge did for silence. With the power of his office behind him, he fashioned a political philosophy from the rudiments of his own conduct. Having snubbed Truman at his inauguration, he proceeded to reverse himself and preside over an Era of Good Manners.

Consequently, he was fascinated by procedure, and his presidency substituted order for ambition. This is why the diplomatic trivia packed inside these thirteen hundred pages seemed important to him. They are rolled out at such length to show the triumph of orderly and reasonable processes over the hasty irresponsibility which might have taken hold at any time. An intelligent reader can see plainly enough that the center of the story is hollow. There is no serious thought behind any of this, nothing of real consequence likely to reach beyond it. Eisenhower owed less to scoundrels than most politicians, and was able to practice selfishness with honor. His memoirs were the final offering of a man who had nothing to contribute except himself. They have his dignity, and they lack what he lacked, namely, those lively qualities that make books worth reading.

Lyndon Johnson could not manage even that much. Here was a classic battle between the man and the office. Johnson was a salty fellow, given to cussing and spitting at the "sissies" and "nervous Nellies" who opposed him. But somewhere he reserved a feeling about how Presidents should behave, and this restrained him on public occasions. All formal objections to the contrary, the writing of presidential memoirs is a public occasion, and so the narrator of *The Vantage Point* comes on brooding and solemn. Of the three postwar memoirs, Lyndon Johnson's reads least like the work of a man, and most like the work of an eminence.

Vietnam kept nagging at him, and he never figured out what to do about it. Even in his memoirs he divides it into chapters, and separates them with stories about the less miserable aspects of his presidency. Civil Rights gets its turn, and health care, and Russia. But Vietnam keeps coming back, like an old sore that starts oozing and needs to be dabbed at. Johnson tends to it with great regret, as he did when fighting the thing, which is too bad. If there must be war, it should at least be enjoyed by its participants. Johnson was not only a reluctant gladiator, but an incompetent one. He probably sensed it, which is why he made such a pother over having the consent of Congress for his deeds. "I repeatedly told Secretaries Rusk and McNamara that I never wanted to receive any recommendations for actions we might take unless it was accompanied by a proposal for assuring the backing of Congress." So he won the Tonkin Gulf Resolution, and started pointing his finger at all the co-conspirators on Capitol Hill. There ensued the endless debates over the usefulness of bombing pauses. At first, "One concern I had was that a bombing pause might give North Vietnam's leaders the impression we were so eager for a settlement we would do anything." Later he confesses that this is exactly what happened: "As I look back, I think that we perhaps tried too hard to spell out our honest desire for peace. At one time or another we were in touch with every government or other diplomatic source that might have been able to make contact with the North Vietnamese . . . These numerous appeals through so many channels may well have convinced the North Vietnamese that we wanted peace at any price." It is rather sad to hear him repeat how willing he was to "go the last mile for peace," to see how this wily man got in over his head and proceeded to sink.

Vietnam ruined him, and left him low on the presidential totem pole. His memoirs, with their pathetic groping after dignity, should discourage historians from their expected resurrections. They are, among other faults, intellectually dishonest. Of the three postwar presidential memoirists, Johnson had the least learning. Yet it is in *The Vantage Point* that we find quotations from John Kenneth Galbraith on the affluent society and meditations on the relation of the Vietnam war to the Philippine rebellion, the Korean war, and the Greek civil war. Johnson was not only at war with his office; he was also at war with himself. He was basically a bounder who made the most of his talents, and yet he had sat too long at his mother's knee and come away with something of a conscience. So occasionally he hit upon worthy goals in his everyday dealings. Vietnam, however, was beyond him, and he made the fundamental error of believing that he could handle Ho Chi Minh like some precinct boss. His vulgarity was nothing extraordinary, but it was pumped full with Texas pride, which made it *seem* extraordinary. He had no feel for the arts and amenities, and it is hard to say what really mattered to him aside from the projection of an interesting image of himself. There is nothing to be gained from reading statements like "Space was the platform from which the social revolution of the 1960s was launched." It does not really mean anything. He favors words like "revolution" and "massive" to describe the events which took place beneath his gaze, such as in claiming credit for "a revolutionary change in our thinking about health care." This may be nothing more than the traditional effort to tie reform to the spirit of the Founding Fathers, but Johnson seems to have envisioned himself creating a benign revolution from above, working the people's will and cajoling the fence-sitters onto the side of right. After extolling the Johnsonian achievement in health care, he insists, "This is not just a tribute to my administration's concern for the people's health but a tribute to the people themselves —a salute to what they demand of their government and to the system that makes it possible to meet the demand," in short, for letting the grace of Lyndon Johnson shine down upon them.

Johnson damned himself doubly by hoping the people would "understand" as well as respect him. The quest for presidential dignity took an odd turn in his hands. He ended by denying that he loved power, while revealing that he had simply loved and lost:

A great misconception had been built up by the press that I was a man who was hungry for power, who would not conceivably give up power willingly. Those who believed this estimate did not understand that power can lose its charm when a man has known it as many years as I had. I was consistently amused at being characterized as avid for power on the one hand and soundly criticized for not using power the way it is used ordinarily—in a political way—on the other . . . I used the power of the Presidency proudly, and I used every ounce of it I had . . . Men, myself included, do not lightly give up the opportunity to achieve so much lasting good, but a man who uses power effectively must also be a realist. He must understand that by spending power he dissipates it. Because I had not hesitated to spend the Presidential power in the pursuit of my beliefs or in the interests of my country, I was under no illusion that I had as much power in 1968 as I had had in 1964.

In other words, one needed to be a realist to know the romance would not last. Johnson the bounder was no doubt that much of a realist, but probably the downfall of his presidency began at the undefined moment when Johnson caught the glory-bug, and started trying to do everything at once. Before it was over, events had whirled out of his control, and he felt himself a misunderstood man.

He thought his memoirs would restore understanding; instead, people read them with bewilderment and even bitterness. This is regrettable; the public only sets itself up to be disappointed, and when the inevitable comes to pass, the leader gets the blame. Why should Lyndon Johnson, a bad President who read nothing more than newspapers, be expected to write a good book? There persists a superstition that life at the top is somehow grander and gaudier than life elsewhere. Outside a democracy it is probably so, but in this Republic the concern to keep up democratic appearances is so great that all pleasures are taken with a pinch of guilt. There is always the haunting notion that the pomp and glory are temporary, and that the power behind them is fleeting. Good Presidents and bad are chastened by this awareness, and I suspect it makes their days less pleasant, and the difficulties of office less tolerable.

The language of the memoirs reflects this uneasiness, and Johnson's to a higher degree than most. Here is a man who was profane at his most natural, who loved to spend people the way a Mafioso loves to spend money—all for show, for the display of ability, for the exhibition of what one can do at the pinnacle. And here is a Republic which demands adherence to a set of ideals etched in Declarations, Proclamations, Doctrines, and the Constitution. Do the people ask that their politicians *practice* virtue and self-effacement in their public service? Of course not, for the American is a realistic animal, as conscious of human frailties as any man. But the people ask that the *appearance* of virtue and self-effacement be practiced with rigor, lest the old ideals be exposed as hollow and in contradiction with human nature. Along comes the President, who has scaled the heights and can feel the pain of contradiction. He is gifted in the practice of appearances. He is rich in the wisdom of hypocrisy. Upon leaving office, does he bare his knowledge for all to see? He does not, for he is a democrat to the core, and knows the old ideals must be preserved. So he swallows hard, and bites his tongue, and never writes the book that is in him. He grabs for the official papers, sketches his own image, and starts to work upon his memoirs. He hides the inner man from his fellow citizens, sensing that they would be appalled if they knew it well. He writes "without . . . introspective trimmings," except at odd moments when he reveals himself without knowing it. His composition grows fat, and begins to look damn impressive. He achieves his solemn dignity at the expense of leaving the inner man out. If he is a Truman, lucky enough to have been at the center of great events, he tells everyone he was just a citizen doing his duty; if he is an Eisenhower, honored among the glories of his time, he shrugs off the cheers and says he was just a soldier doing his duty; but if he is a Johnson, brought to power by tragedy and leaving it unhappily, he is lost and knows not what to say. He needs to write about the man within, and the agony he feels. But he is trapped by the old democratic ideals, and the expectations of the Republic for a statement of the record. So he writes something like *The Vantage Point*, and dies a discredited man.

III

The non-President has it easier. Not having known the full glory of the presidency, he is less sure of his responsibility, and can write more freely about himself. Only a President embodies a complete branch of government; only his doings have the aura of History itself. Even a Supreme Court justice is but one of nine, and a Speaker of the House but the leader of one half of Congress. A senator or Vice-President is close enough to the center to sense what is going on, and yet distant enough to have a sense of self apart from History. It should not surprise that he will tend to write a better book than a President, who cannot make this distinction.

Richard Nixon and Hubert Humphrey are in many ways the representative men of their parties in the past quarter century. Each has his peculiarities, and Nixon made it to the top while Humphrey missed. Their careers ran parallel, however, and had not Nixon ended disgracefully he would now be the venerated Republican statesman as Humphrey is now Mr. Democrat. Both men wrote their books to buck themselves up after defeats, Nixon in 1960 and Humphrey in 1968. Let us take the two of them together.

Nixon has a well-deserved reputation for deceit, and it is possible his forthcoming presidential memoirs will serve up lies in the grand manner. I rather doubt it, however, and in fact I believe Nixon is capable of writing one of the finest presidential memoirs on record. I deduce this from a reading of *Six Crises*, which is easily the best of the books under consideration in this essay. In his twisted self-congratulations, justifications, and explanations, Nixon comes closer to a portrait of himself than any modern American politician of note. He is as honest a charlatan as exists; he cannot help but expose himself because he seems really to believe that he is a more profound man than his detractors, and seeks to prove it.

Six Crises is an extended meditation on personal performance. It pretends to be a narrative of six great events in the statesman's life, but is actually nothing of the kind. It is rather a report by Richard Nixon on the demons within him, and on how he tamed them in order to work. John Kennedy, remembering his father's advice and his own experience, was among those who encouraged the effort; according to Nixon, "he expressed the thought that every public man should write a book at some time in his life, both for the mental discipline and because it tends to elevate him in popular esteem to the respected status of an 'intellectual.'" But instead of a *Why England Slept* or *Profiles in Courage*, careful and reserved, we get the portrait of a politician, transformed by his own drum rolls into a hero. Crisis appears to have haunted the man, chasing him down on his vacations, feeding his ambitions, driving him onward against the wind. "A man who has never lost himself in a cause bigger than himself has missed one of life's mountaintop experiences. Only is losing himself does he find himself. Only then does he discover all the latent strengths he never knew he had and which otherwise would have remained dormant."

At the beginning of each chapter is a maxim, against whose wisdom Nixon measures himself. "The ability to be cool, confident, and decisive in crisis is not an inherited characteristic but is the direct result of how well the individual has prepared himself for the battle," reads the note before the chapter on "The Hiss Case." Preceding "The Fund," which culminates with the ode to Checkers, we find, "Going through the necessary soul-searching of deciding whether to fight a battle, or to run away from it, is far more difficult than the battle itself." The lesson gleaned from the chapter on Eisenhower's 1955 heart attack is, "Decisive action relieves the tension which builds up in a crisis. When the situation requires that an individual restrain himself from acting decisively over a long period, this can be the most wearing of all crises." When Nixon had his car stoned in Caracas, he learned, "The classic crisis is one involving physical danger. What is essential in such situations is not so much 'bravery' in the face of danger as the ability to think 'selflessly'—to blank out any thought of personal fear by concentrating completely on how to meet the danger." Finger-wagging with Khrushchev taught him that "Communism creates and uses crisis as a weapon. Khrushchev, Communist man at his most dangerous best, has developed this technique to a highly sophisticated science. Plans designed to meet his moves may prove useless because of the unpredictability of his conduct. But intensive planning is absolutely essential, to avoid being knocked off balance by what he does." And "The Campaign of 1960" left him feeling, "The most dangerous period in a crisis is not in the preparation or in the fighting of a battle, but in its aftermath. This is true even when the battle ends in victory. When it ends in defeat, in a contest where an individual has carried on his shoulders the hopes of millions, he then faces his greatest test."

The tale is couched in the verities of the time. Nixon was never one for philosophy; his gifts lay rather in his ability to twist the beliefs of others to his own purposes. So here, pre-détente, "aggressive international Communism is on the loose in the world," and Communists are capable of every manner of deception. There are three crises ("The Hiss Case," "Khrushchev," and "Caracas") in which Poor Richard sees Red, and each time he comes through nicely. In the other three chapters, Eisenhower is the one who stands literally between Nixon and the office of his dreams. Of course, nothing but praise of the chief falls from his lips, but on every page we are reminded of the ghoulish nature of the vice-presidency, as Nixon fills in the details of his readiness. The tone is always serious, and the prose has life in it, unlike that of the presidential memoirs. The generating force is Nixon's desire to prove himself. Instead of the dedication "To Pat: She Also Ran," we might expect to find the epigraph from Schoolboy Rowe: "How'm I Doin', Edna?" It is the story of a man whose life was lived on a contingency basis. Nixon gives no explanation of why he was a Republican, of what he believes to be the function of government, or of what substance his "enemies" were made. It was enough that he *was* a Republican, that his party deplored big spenders and rattled Communists, and that he had many enemies who were after him. These facts created the crises, which he tried to surmount with the force of his will. When it came time to deliver the Checkers speech, he recalled, "I felt now that it was my battle alone. I had been deserted by so many I had thought were friends but who had panicked in battle." Sparring with Khrushchev at the "Kitchen Debate" in Moscow, he proudly remembers that an old sports reporter in the press entourage had been moved to recall the Dempsey-Firpo fight. "Khrushchev had started the encounter by knocking me out of the ring. At the end, I had climbed back in to fight again." Battle, fight, struggle: these are the elements of Nixon's career, as viewed by the man himself; these are the "mountaintop experiences" in which he lost himself in grander causes. He is completely unaware that he uses "cause" as would an actor in a play. All the grandeur is supplied by the fatness of the part. He cites a handful of incidents in that tug of war with Khrushchev, and he gives himself up to dreams. He exchanges insults with Peruvian Communists and finds, "Everywhere I went that afternoon, I was hailed as a hero in Peru." He talks himself into greatness.

A great deal of Nixon's career seems to have been bound up in the effort to convince himself that life was better than it seemed to be. This is usually regarded as the liberal fallacy, but it is just as much the bugaboo of any man who climbs to great power from humble means. All along the way he sees the miseries of the world, and he cannot shake himself of his uneasiness. So he invents causes suitable for his enlistment, but really is only scheming, sorting things out, marking time. He never composes a vision of the world, because he is unsure of his own place in it. So when Nixon wrote his book, having come so close to the top and missed, he made an honest effort at self-understanding. Hence the emphasis on struggle, battle, crisis. These were the elements of his spiritual life. If he shaded the facts in his favor, he still stripped more nearly naked than any other modern American politician. He was psychologically prepared for the exposure of Watergate.

Humphrey offered another profile of the exposed politician. Here is a man who seems to enjoy being slapped about, even by his inferiors. The rough-and-tumble of politics gets his blood stirring. The orators of Hyde Park corner are his kinfolk. There is ample evidence in *The Education of a Public Man* that Humphrey is one of the most gullible men around. He is something of a small-town druggist to this day, taking satisfaction in all the remedies on his shelves. He comes on like a friendly neighbor, gifted with a terrific set of pipes. He writes his book like someone who has dropped in for tea and stayed to tell his life story.

He is a bore only when he gives lessons, as he does at the end of his tale. Otherwise he is a man of sense, whose background resembled Nixon's but whose temperament differed strongly. Indeed, the only significant difference between the two of them, amid their chronicles of thrift, hard work, and eventual success, was Nixon's early smothering in religion. While Humphrey inherited the populist deism of his father, Nixon endured the Quaker snufflings of his mother. He seems never to have outgrown this, and his lifelong search for "mountaintop experiences" grew out of those early affirmations. How many false hopes are imbibed at the mother's knee! Humphrey took his father's home remedies and absorbed an elegant sufficiency of uplifting ideas. He was too happy to become a Communist, too conscientious to become a conservative. "I never got hooked in those chaotic times," he writes of the Depression, "as so many people did, on Marxism or other radicalism as a way out of the depression. Had I continued at the university uninterrupted, I might have, but I was involved instead in a business whose purpose was to make a profit, and I frankly liked the system even if we weren't particularly successful."

There is a buoyancy here, an ability to stay afloat despite all the temptations to gloominess. His first political decision was *not* to run. The congressional seat in his district had an unbeatable incumbent. "I didn't believe then, as I don't believe now, that political defeat is particularly good for one's character . . ." But it was not very long before he was trying to become mayor of Minneapolis, and establishing his style. "It is only a slight exaggeration to say that wherever a group of people paused, I was there. I enjoyed it (and still do)."

Politics is largely a rhythmic affair, its successes and failures marked by the politician's ability to catch the flow of things and make oneself a part of them. Rhythm always supersedes ideology and incorporates partisanship. Nixon, in his stammering way, reflects this in *Six Crises*, with its emphasis on rising to occasions, acting to meet the moment. Humphrey, more boisterously, does the same. "Politics," he writes, "has an intensity and a rhythm unlike anything else I know. Even the quiescent periods, between elections, are filled with power plays, choices, shifting friendships, new adversaries, constant loyalties." The sense of timing is what separates the successful politicians from the losers. It has been Humphrey's distinction to go further in politics, with a bad sense of timing, than any other modern American politician. He began in 1948 by hectoring the elders of his party on the Civil Rights issue. When he arrived in the Senate the following year, he found the place patrolled by Southerners. It took years before he got anywhere. "I . . . learned that as long as you treated other senators as honest men, sincere in their convictions, that you could usually gain the tolerance, if not affection, of even those who disagreed strongly with you." When he straightened himself out in the Senate, he decided to make a run at the presidency. So he chose West Virginia as the place for his showdown with Kennedy, and got walloped; Joseph P. Kennedy had already bought off the delegate slates. But the next few years brought Humphrey to his apogee as a legislator. The peak was the 1964 Civil Rights Act, which he steered through the Senate partly by keeping his mouth shut at key moments. Discretion was an awful strain on him, however, and as Vice-President he felt compelled to boom out on behalf of Lyndon Johnson's imbecilities in Vietnam. He had raised sensible objections to the whole policy at first, but once it had been established Humphrey's voice played the part of the battle trumpets in nobler times. Sentimentality swayed him. He visited battlefield hospitals, cried, and tried to find meaning in the enterprise. "You wanted to make the war stop that minute, but when you knew you couldn't, you had to accept it. If the war could not be won, if we should not have been there, then there was nothing you could say to a man who no longer had legs, whose sight was gone, who smiled through tubes and bandages as you spoke but might never smile again." So he held to Johnson's line, and lost the election to Nixon. Now viewed as a discredited liberal, he tried four years later to steal the nomination of George McGovern by changing the delegate distribution rules after the California primary. His popularity sank still lower among his old constituents.

Four years after that, he was again beloved, and many of the liberals were saying that, finally, his year had arrived. But 1976 belonged to Jimmy Carter; Humphrey was finally promoted upstairs to elder statesmanship. Why the transformation? Time passes, and a decent man can re-establish his reputation. Humphrey, in particular, has always had about him the air of the raw politician. His bad timing has reflected his lack of polish. His success, such as it has been, has resulted from intelligence burnished by exuberance. His vehicle has been the spoken word. *The Education of a Public Man* is, like *Six Crises*, an honest book, because it displays the qualities of its author. The thing appears to have been dictated rather than written, and this is as it should have been. The Happy Warrior and his sullen counterpart knew themselves well enough to write books which really punctuated their careers—Humphrey plowing ahead joyfully, Nixon brooding, wondering, justifying.

IV

Six Crises and *The Education of a Public Man* are political memoirs of a certain kind. They are written by men who are not quite

THE LITERARY POLITICIANS

finished with politics and yet are distinguished enough not to be on the make all the time. They have names and reputations, and want to put some order into their scattered perceptions. They lack the self-confidence of ex-Presidents, who tend to feel they have been great simply because they have been momentous. Neither Nixon nor Humphrey wrote anything approaching the pomposity of Johnson, Eisenhower, and even Truman. Both managed the separation of Self and State. They needed to fill in their stories with more of themselves than the three Presidents, who dangled their state papers and promises of secrets to be unveiled. The presidential flaw is the merging of Self into State.

Another type of political memoir reverses the process, and merges the State into the Self. This is the book written by the politician in search of an audience. As the respect for privacy diminishes and morals loosen, this kind of total exposure may grow more common. The current President's campaign declaration—that he had lusted after many women in his heart—is illustrative. The point of such statements is to invite public appreciation of personal characteristics.

Donald Riegle's book *O Congress* is the most notable literary application of this practice to date. Now the junior United States senator from Michigan, Riegle gained national attention with the publication of the book in 1972. More important, it set him apart from the other congressmen from Michigan, so that when an opening in the Senate appeared, he was first among equals in running. In 1971, aged thirty-three, Riegle was in his third term as the liberal Republican congressman from Flint. The Nixon Reich had unsettled him, and he was building a reputation for independence. His book, a daily journal from March of 1971 to March of 1972, enhanced this reputation. It did not matter that the book tore the cover off an adolescent mind; it showed his independence. In 1973 Riegle switched parties, something he argued against in *O Congress*, and in 1974 he won re-election easily as a Democrat. Two years later and he was a senator.

O Congress was not responsible for all this, but its success made its author's career easier. His book includes details of his separation and divorce from his first wife, and its connecting thread is the love affair between Riegle and his girlfriend, Meredith, who later became his second wife. Still later, after his election to the Senate, she became his second ex-wife—but that one is saved for

O Senate. Older politicians thought that Riegle had cooked himself, but they did not understand that the public now cared little for the old moral code. Riegle's perception was correct: the country wanted to see a politician who appeared to be an honest man. In view of subsequent developments, the parts on Riegle's love for Meredith and his belief in the Republican principles of Lincoln and Roosevelt have not worn well. But that is not important. The book got its message across: Don Riegle is a sensitive man. Sensitivity is the cornerstone of the new demagoguery.

The public wants its politicians to worry and care like the pastors of yesteryear. Riegle would have us believe that he is in agony over his public duty every day, if not every hour. "I thought to myself that many of the experiences that have made me feel old have happened at Arlington National Cemetery," he writes on the second page, and he is off with a whoop and a wail. He is ambitious and now, sadly, he confesses it, hoping to reach humility by routing himself through Contrition. Moreover, Riegle is in love, which is making him a better man. "We had somehow unlocked each other and I knew for the first time in my life that I was only *half* of something. I knew it because the other half was sitting across the table from me. I realized that I loved the soft, gentle spirit behind the green eyes."

It is evident that the gentleman from Michigan is something like *The Greening of America* incarnate in a member of the U. S. House of Representatives. He views *Mad Dogs and Englishman* twice in one sitting with Meredith. The film, he says, is "better than *Woodstock, Gimme Shelter* or *Let It Be,* and I remember saying how absolutely dumbfounded my mother or her friends would be if they witnessed this. It's easy to see why older people have so much trouble understanding their children's attitudes." Riegle, of course, is sensitive to the young; today's sensitive politician is particularly touched by them, as by blacks, Chicanos, and women. One would think Riegle would approve of the extramarital sex lives of his fellow congressmen, but his statements in *O Congress* imply scorn. Perhaps it is because these gentlemen are often elderly, and neither black nor Chicano. They rate a low frequency on Riegle's sensitivity detector, and often draw his indignation instead. "Why should more young men have to die because Hébert says so? Suddenly I felt an urge to smash Hébert in the face." But Meredith is there to soften his temper. "I feel as if I'm coming out of a long winter, moving toward a newness that I can't fully define yet. But it's a young feeling—of exciting possibilities. It's elusive but it's there." So is Riegle, unfortunately. He is, it appears, one of the more slippery mountebanks around. There will be others to follow: look for the mournful visage. Catch a falling teardrop if you can.

Jimmy Carter has more dignity than Riegle, but he too is a specialist in sensitivity. His autobiography, miserably titled *Why Not the Best?*, appears to have been written by the man himself. It is the written testament of a President of the United States—before his ascension.

When he is finished, he will write a rather different book, much more official. It is, we have seen, something like a President's final duty. Composed in the early days of the campaign, this one was calculated to help him find an audience. It manages to be extremely dull, despite its brevity, and there is very little to be said about it. The style will be familiar to readers of *Scholastic* magazine; obviously he hoped the simple folk would read it. His first marriage proposal, for instance, receives this treatment: "I asked Rosalynn if she would marry me, but she said NO." The man wants to make himself heard, but he is not that eager to be understood. His only venture in critical commentary concerns *War and Peace*, and is quite wrongheaded. Boyhood is described by listing all the insects and crops he dealt with as a lad. Everything rates perfunctory treatment, and no more.

About the only belief that comes through is an apparent passion for catalogues. There are dozens of them, concerning everything from the bugs that swarmed in the land of the red clay to the offices held as a citizen of Plains. Even the American people appear as so many characteristics filed away; they are, he says, "inherently unselfish, open, honest, decent, competent, and compassionate." His own candidacy offers a swell collection of qualities: "I am a farmer . . . Also, I can claim with credentials to be an engineer, a planner, a nuclear physicist, a businessman, and a professional naval officer. So, for those who might have an aversion to farmers, for whatever reason, there are some alternative ways of looking at what my candidacy has to offer." He appears to want us to take this seriously.

His catalogues are supported by childish statements of belief in the goodness of people. Otherwise, there is not much to be found in *Why Not the Best?* Human meanness is not acknowledged, except when it pops up in bureaucrats, racists, and legislators who opposed him during his term as governor. The uplift is by now familiar—the promise to bring us a government as full of love as the people, and other such hilarities. As in Riegle's book, the politician is trying to prove himself here, and there is great care not to say something unsuitable to the image. The purpose is to present the man as decent, reasonable, and fair. Riegle's was something different. Both are sorry specimens of political literature, but they have their places.

V

Have they, though, a public purpose? I contend that they do, for they give the politician a chance to offer the public his most handsome profile. If the reader cannot shake himself of the conviction that the author-politician is a public nuisance, then the reader has only himself to blame when some outrage is committed. This seems to me a public service. It helps rid us of the notion that the people are wise, which is the source of much national unhappiness. Once the people are disabused of the fantasy, they will find the exercise of their democratic duties less fraught with worry.

What of the books of the other men, the Presidents and the near Presidents? They, too, work in the public interest, I believe. Their usefulness has two aspects. The first is fairly obvious: they help us know the man better. No matter how hard a politician tries to project an image which does not match his true character, he cannot help but tell us something about himself. It is the nature of writing a book which deals in matters of fact. Either a good many facts are apprehended realistically, or the book is laughed at. The politician knows this, and behaves accordingly. Also, by telling us about himself, the politician enhances our knowledge of the times. This is because a politician's career is entirely bound up in reacting to public pressures. By exposing these pressures, he reveals the current obsessions. Wisdom proceeds from the appreciation of prejudice. A politician's prejudices are those of the people. By writing a book which puts them on record, he gives intelligent men an opportunity to see what they are dealing with.

Finally, these books remind us of the limitations of politics. We finish reading them, and are not satisfied. We sense that things are being left unsaid, stories being left untold. This opens the door for the literary politicians, for the minds which explore the outer limits of politics. Reading a Johnson or a Humphrey, who would not yearn for a Schlesinger to tell him what all this blathering is about? Reading Eisenhower or Nixon on Republicanism, who would not run to his shelves and grab the nearest Buckley? Who would not demand an antidote to the sorrows of young Riegle, and call upon Vidal for mockery? The subliterary politicians keep the professionals in business, which is, all in all, an excellent thing.